Reading as Writers

Preliminary Edition

Edited by Philip Furia
University of North Carolina - Wilmington

Bassim Hamadeh, CEO and Publisher
Michael Simpson, Vice President of Acquisitions
Jamie Giganti, Senior Managing Editor
Miguel Macias, Graphic Designer
Amy Stone, Field Acquisitions Editor
Mirasol Enriquez, Senior Project Editor
Michael Skinner, Licensing Specialist

Copyright © 2016 by University Readers, Inc. All rights reserved. No part of this publication may be reprinted, reproduced, transmitted, or utilized in any form or by any electronic, mechanical, or other means, now known or hereafter invented, including photocopying, microfilming, and recording, or in any information retrieval system without the written permission of University Readers, Inc.

First published in the United States of America in 2016 by University Readers, Inc.

Trademark Notice: Product or corporate names may be trademarks or registered trademarks, and are used only for identification and explanation without intent to infringe.

Cover image copyright © Depositphotos/ Nomadsoul1.

Printed in the United States of America

ISBN: 978-1-63189-936-2 (pbk) / 978-1-63189-937-9 (br)

Contents

Introduction — *1*

Chapter 1. Language and Writing — **3**

Sophocles — 15

Aesop's Fables — 19

Chapter 2. Medieval English Literature — **25**

Caedmon — 28

Anonymous Medieval Ballads — 39

Anonymous Medieval Lyrics — 44

Chapter 3. Renaissance Literature — **49**

Sir Thomas Wyatt — 55

Sir Philip Sidney — 57

William Shakespeare — 58

Christopher Marlowe — 68

Sir Walter Ralegh — 70

Chapter 4. Seventeenth-Century Literature — 73

- Ben Jonson — 76
- Robert Herrick — 80
- Edmund Waller — 82
- Richard Lovelace — 83
- Sir John Suckling — 84
- John Donne — 86
- Andrew Marvell — 90
- John Milton — 93

Chapter 5. Eighteenth-Century Literature — 99

- Alexander Pope — 105
- Lady Mary Wortley Montagu — 106
- Thomas Gray — 110
- Phyllis Wheatley — 115
- Daniel Defoe — 116
- Henry Fielding — 119
- Jane Austen — 122
- Jonathan Edwards — 130
- Benjamin Franklin — 135

Chapter 6. The Romantic Age (1785–1832) — 145

- Robert Burns — 146
- William Blake — 149
- William Wordsworth — 151
- Samuel Taylor Coleridge — 156
- Percy Bysshe Shelley — 159

John Keats	164
Lord Byron	168
Leigh Hunt	169

Chapter 7. The American Short Story — 171

Washington Irving	172
Edgar Allan Poe	186

Chapter 8. The Victorian Age (1832–1901) — 193

Alfred Lord Tennyson	194
Robert Browning	197
Matthew Arnold	199
Elizabeth Barrett Browning	201
Edward Fitzgerald	202
Thomas Hardy	203
Gerard Manly Hopkins	207
A.E. Housman	210
Oscar Wilde	213

Chapter 9. Nineteenth-Century American Creative Nonfiction — 215

Frederick Douglass	215
Mark Twain	226

Chapter 10. Nineteenth-Century American Poetry — 247

Walt Whitman	247
Emily Dickinson	256

Chapter 11. American Realistic Fiction — 261

- William Dean Howells — 261
- Henry James — 273
- Guy de Maupassant — 274

Chapter 12. American Naturalistic Fiction — 295

- Jack London — 295
- Stephen Crane — 309

Credits — 319

Introduction

This anthology has been created for students in CRW 203: Forms of Creative Writing at the University of North Carolina, Wilmington (UNCW). It provides students with short works of creative writing—poems, stories, and essays—to supplement longer works—novels, plays, and books of nonfiction—that also may be required reading for the course.

The selections have been organized historically. That organization is based on the belief that students can better understand works of creative writing with some sense of how these works developed over time.

In this anthology, there are historical background notes, as well as brief biographical introductions to the writers that provide a context for their works. To help students understand and appreciate works that are historically remote, there are also explanatory notes and interpretive guidelines. Several sections of this anthology deal with language and with the historical development of the English language. You will become better writers if you know more about the nature of your medium—language—and the history of your particular language—English.

The main goal of this anthology—and the course CRW 203: Forms of Creative Writing—is to help students think in the way writers do as they struggle with problems of literary form, craft, and technique. Unlike English courses, where the emphasis is on *interpretation*—"What does this piece of literature *mean*?"—in a Creative Writing forms course, the emphasis is on *analysis*—how does this piece of writing *work*? As you read the works and notes in this anthology, you will learn to think about how writers make decisions about form, craft, and technique in creating a work of literature.

An analogy could be made to what you might learn in a basic course in film studies. If you took a course that involved cinematography, lighting, and editing, you would learn to look at movies in a different way. Instead of just following the story, as most other film viewers would, you would be aware of how the camera shoots from different distances and angles, how lighting creates certain effects in a scene, and how one shot "cuts" to another shot in the process of editing. Filmmakers have many different options to choose from in making each decision about where to place the camera for a shot, how to light the set, and how to edit the film footage. In viewing a film with your new knowledge about cinematography, lighting, and editing, you would be able to see why the filmmakers decided to create a film in the way they did.

By thinking about similar issues of craft, technique, and form as you read the works in this anthology, you will see why writers made the decisions they did. Seeing that will make you better readers and better writers.

I would like to thank the College of Arts and Sciences of UNCW for supporting the preparation of this anthology with a Summer Curriculum Initiative Grant. The Department of Creative Writing also lent its support in numerous ways. The students in the Master of Fine Arts in Creative Writing Program who worked with me as graduate teaching assistants in CRW 203 made many helpful suggestions that have gone into the preparation and revisions of this anthology. My colleague, Raymond Burt, in UNCW's Department of Foreign Languages, polished my rusty German and offered some suggestions to illustrate the differences between the English and German languages. Finally, Professor Laurie Patterson, of UNCW's Department of Computer Science, helped organize and format the text of this anthology in ways that will be helpful to students.

In the course of preparing the historical, biographical, and explanatory material in this anthology, I have relied upon more books than I can name, but the most helpful have been:

The Norton Anthology of English Literature, M. H. Abrams, ed.
Heritage of American Literature,. James E. Miller, Jr., ed.
History of English Literature, Martin S. Day
The Greek Way, Edith Hamilton
A Concise History of the Theatre, Phyllis Hartnoll
Preface to Plato, Eric Havelock
On Literacy: The Politics of the Word from Homer to the Age of Rock, Robert Pattison
The Rise of the Novel, Ian Watt
Shakespeare's Metrical Art, George T. Wright

Chapter 1
Language and Writing

We begin our study of forms of creative writing with *language*, which goes back to the earliest creatures we call humans. The first human-like creatures appeared about four million years ago in East Africa. Then, about three hundred thousand years ago, creatures who walked on two feet (*Homo erectus*) appeared in Europe, Asia, and Africa. These creatures then evolved with larger brains (*Homo sapiens*—"thinking humans") in Europe and Western Asia around 100,000 B.C. Almost all of these species of *Homo sapiens* died out by 30,000 B.C., except for one species, which scientists now call *Homo sapiens sapiens*. These truly human ancestors learned to use tools, traveled in packs, and eventually cultivated crops, raised animals, and settled in specific places, instead of migrating in search of food. From those settlements, primarily in the Middle East but also in China, India, and Central and South America, came the first civilizations.

To give you a sense of how short-lived human civilization is, let me quote this analogy from Thomas H. Greer and Gavin Lewis' *A Brief History of the Western World*:[1]

> Viewed in relation to more ancient life forms (fish, reptiles, insects) and in relation to the age of the planet, humans are latecomers. Though the age of the earth (about four billion years) is beyond comprehension, the human-to-earth time relationship can be grasped through a drastic reduction in the time scale. If we reduce the age of the earth to the period of our familiar twenty-four hour day, the time that elapsed prior to the appearance of humans is twenty-three hours and fifty-eight minutes. And of the two remaining minutes, the period of civilization is less than the last half-second.

In those last two minutes of relative time, the most important feature that marked creatures as "human" was their capacity to use language.

Language is the primary *tool* that sets humans apart from other animals. Your dog may know a few words—*come*, *sit*, *treat*—but knows them only as *signals*; when you say the word "treat," it looks for something to eat. If you ask me if I would like a treat, I can respond to it as a signal, like your dog, and expect you to give me a treat. However, if you ask me what kind of treat I think would be a good dessert for a dinner party, I can think about a treat as an *idea*. Instead of expecting you to provide me with candy, I can advise you about the relative culinary merits of Peach Melba, Bananas Foster, and Baked Alaska.

---

[1] Thomas H. Greer and Gavin Lewis, *A Brief History of the Western World*, Seventh Edition (Fort Worth: Harcourt Brace, 1997), p. 6.

Your dog can't do that.

Helen Keller, who was born deaf and blind, had only a dog's sense of language until a special teacher came to her home to teach her how to use language as a *human*. Years later, when she wrote her autobiography, Helen Keller recounted this momentous lesson:[2]

> The most important day I remember in all my life is the one on which my teacher, Anne Mansfield Sullivan, came to me. I am filled with wonder when I consider the immeasurable contrasts between the two lives which it connects. It was the third of March, 1887, three months before I was seven years old.
>
> On the afternoon of that eventful day, I stood on the porch, dumb, expectant. I guessed vaguely from my mother's signs and from the hurrying to and fro in the house that something unusual was about to happen, so I went to the door and waited on the steps. The afternoon sun penetrated the mass of honeysuckle that covered the porch, and fell on my upturned face. My fingers lingered almost unconsciously on the familiar leaves and blossoms which had just come forth to greet the sweet southern spring. I did not know what the future held of marvel or surprise for me. Anger and bitterness had preyed upon me continually for weeks and a deep languor had succeeded this passionate struggle . . .
>
> I felt approaching footsteps. I stretched out my hand as I supposed to my mother. Some one took it, and I was caught up and held close in the arms of her who had come to reveal all things to me, and, more than all things else, to love me.
>
> The morning after my teacher came she led me into her room and gave me a doll. The little blind children at the Perkins Institution had sent it and Laura Bridgman had dressed it; but I did not know this until afterward. When I had played with it a little while, Miss Sullivan slowly spelled into my hand the word "d-o-l-l." I was at once interested in this finger play and tried to imitate it. When I finally succeeded in making the letters correctly I was flushed with childish pleasure and pride. Running downstairs to my mother I held up my hand and made the letters for doll. I did not know that I was spelling a word or even that words existed; I was simply making my fingers go in monkey-like imitation. In the days that followed I learned to spell in this uncomprehending way a great many words, among them pin, hat, cup and a few verbs like sit, stand and walk. But my teacher had been with me several weeks before I understood that everything has a name.
>
> One day, while I was playing with my new doll, Miss Sullivan put my big rag doll into my lap also, spelled "d-o-l-l" and tried to make me understand that "d-o-l-l" applied to both. Earlier in the day we had had a tussle over the words

---

[2] Helen Keller, *The Story of My Life* (Garden City, NY: Doubleday & Company, Inc., 1954), pp. 35-36.

"m-u-g" and "w-a-t-e-r." Miss Sullivan had tried to impress it upon me that "m-u-g" is mug and that "w-a-t-e-r" is water, but I persisted in confounding the two. In despair she had dropped the subject for the time, only to renew it at the first opportunity. I became impatient at her repeated attempts and, seizing the new doll, I dashed it upon the floor. I was keenly delighted when I felt the fragments of the broken doll at my feet. Neither sorrow nor regret followed my passionate outburst. I had not loved the doll. In the still, dark world in which I lived there was no strong sentiment or tenderness. I felt my teacher sweep the fragments to one side of the hearth, and I had a sense of satisfaction that the cause of my discomfort was removed. She brought me my hat, and I knew I was going out into the warm sunshine. This thought, if a wordless sensation may be called a thought, made me hop and skip with pleasure.

We walked down the path to the well-house, attracted by the fragrance of the honeysuckle with which it was covered. Some one was drawing water and my teacher placed my hand under the spout. As the cool stream gushed over one hand she spelled into the other the word water, first slowly, then rapidly. I stood still, my whole attention fixed upon the motions of her fingers. Suddenly I felt a misty consciousness as of something forgotten—a thrill of returning thought; and somehow the mystery of language was revealed to me. I knew then that "w-a-t-e-r" meant the wonderful cool something that was flowing over my hand. That living word awakened my soul, gave it light, hope, joy, set it free! There were barriers still, it is true, but barriers that could in time be swept away.

Language, as Helen Keller learned to use it and despite being born blind and deaf, allows us to communicate with one another, to express ourselves, and as she implies when she wonders "if a wordless sensation may be called a thought," to *think*.

Language defines us as humans, and a critical step in human evolution was the acquisition of a facial structure that enables us to produce, easily and rapidly, the many sounds needed for language. Try this experiment: put your fingers around your chin and say the various vowels—*a, e, i, o, u*—and feel how little the various parts of your mouth move. Now try making the consonant sounds. Use your lips to say *pea* and *bee*; your tongue to say *la* and *re*; your teeth to say *do* and *to*; then teeth and tongue to say *sit* and *zit*; speak through your nose to say *no*; with your throat say *go*. You have just produced a wide range of sounds with very little effort. By combining those vowel and consonant sounds, you can produce thousands of words. Such *economy* of sound production is essential to language, since we have to be able to produce a great range of sounds that make words in order to converse, words that may sound similar but are distinct from one another so that we can understand if someone is talking about a *cat* or a *rat*.

One of the greatest economies in producing the sounds of words comes from using your vocal cords—or not using them. You can make the exact same sounds with your teeth, tongue, lips, nose, and throat but vary them by vibrating—or not vibrating—your vocal cords. Try another experiment: put your fingers on your vocal cords and say these pairs of words: *pat* and *bat*; *tot* and *dot*; *kill* and *gill*; *sip* and *zip*. When you said the first word in each pair, you should not have felt your vocal cords move; when you said the second you should have felt your vocal cords vibrate. *P* and *B*,

T and *D*, *K* and (hard) *G*, *S* and *Z* are the exact same sounds, except that the first letters are *unvoiced* (your vocal cords don't move) and the second letters are *voiced* (your vocal cords vibrate). With that *economy* of language—where all you have to do to create two distinctly different sounds is vibrate your vocal cords—humans nearly doubled the number of words they could create.

No one knows how humans acquired language, but one theory is that language was part of *festal* (playful) behavior. When a primitive tribe celebrated some accomplishment—defeating an enemy, killing a large animal for food—they expressed their joy in communal rhythmic cries and movements that then developed into song, dance, music, speech—and poetry.

Oral Poetry

In the earliest human cultures, poetry was an important tool for preserving history, tradition, and customs. Before the development of writing, there were no libraries, archives, encyclopedias, or other written records, so the cultural fabric had to be maintained and passed on to later generations through oral transmission. Poetry is an effective means of such oral transmission, for it is *mnemonic*, which means it helps you remember something (like tying a string around your finger). The word comes from the name of the Greek goddess of memory, Mnemosyne, who was the mother of the nine muses. Each muse provided inspiration for one of the various arts—Terpsichore for dance, Thalia for comic drama, Erato for lyric poetry, etc. By conceiving of the arts as daughters of the goddess of memory, the Greeks recognized that, in oral cultures, the arts were a vital means for remembering a culture's past.

For example, we all rely on poetry to help us remember how many days are in each month by this *mnemonic* poem:

Thirty days hath September

April, June, and November

Two devices in this poem that help us remember it are *rhythm* and *rhyme*. Rhythm is created by the pattern of accented syllables, a pattern that is the same for each of the two lines (the accented syllables are in **boldface**):

Thir-ty **days** hath Sep-**tem**-ber,

Ap-ril, **June**, and No-**vem**-ber

Can you see that both lines have the same number of syllables, and in both lines the first, third, and sixth syllables are **accented** to create a parallel rhythm?

Rhyme is the *exact* similarity between terminal vowel and consonant sounds, as in (rhymes in *italics*) Sept*ember* and Nov*ember*. By contrast, *home* does not rhyme with *alone*, because only the vowel sounds are the same; *home does* rhyme with *roam*, *foam*, and *comb*, because even though the words are spelled differently the terminal vowel and consonant sounds are exactly alike. Many contemporary songwriters do not understand the nature of rhyme. Bruno Mars in "Grenade," for example, rhymes "trash" and "asked," "blade," and "train," and "same" and "pain." While some of the vowel and consonant sounds in these pairs of words are similar, they are not *true rhymes*.

Because of the regularity of rhythm and rhyme, most of us can recite poems from memory:

> *'Twas the **night** before **Christ**mas and **all** through the **house***
>
> *Not a **crea**ture was **stir**ring, not **even** a **mouse***

By working with such features of language as rhythm and rhyme, poets in primitive, oral cultures were able to compose and recite poems that passed on the culture's history, customs, legends, and beliefs from generation to generation long before the creation of writing.

Form in Oral Poetry

The oral poets who created and recited the poems that held their cultural fabric together did not simply memorize their poems. Instead, they composed them, on the spot, by using poetic *formulas*. Poetic formulas can be found in all poems that had their origins in oral culture. For centuries, readers of Homer's *Iliad* and *Odyssey* puzzled over what they did not realize were oral poetic formulas. For example, when a character such as Odysseus was described, his name would be preceded by descriptive adjectival *epithets*, but the epithets varied; sometimes he was described as "crafty Odysseus," sometimes "resourceful Odysseus," sometimes as "many-minded Odysseus." Why, readers wondered, were these epithets used over and over to describe Odysseus? There were also similar, repeated phrases that described such events as the breaking of dawn—"When rosy-fingered dawn lit the skies" or "When dawn spread her rosy fingers against the sky." For centuries, readers also wondered about such phrases and why they were used so frequently.

Then, in the 1920s, a scholar doing research in Serbia, came across an illiterate mountain tribe that had a vital oral poetic tradition. He witnessed festivals where oral poets recited long historical poems—similar to *epic narratives*, such as *The Iliad* and *The Odyssey*. What he found was that the poets did not memorize their poems verbatim but used poetic formulas just as the ancient Greek poets must have done. What these poets learned, when they were studying how to become poets, were the poetic formulas—different ways of describing characters and events—how a ship sets sail, how one warrior kills another, how dawn breaks. Each of these formulas had a different number of syllables so that they could fit into different *poetic lines*. Each of those lines had to have the same total number of syllables, so in one line a poet might need a formula that was three syllables long, in another line he might need a formula that was four syllables long, and in another line he might need a formula that was five syllables long.

If the young poet were Greek, for example, he would need to learn various formulas so that each poetic line could be eighteen syllables long. If he were composing a poem about Odysseus (pronounced in three syllables: "O-dys-seus" so that the third syllable rhymes with "Zeus"), for example, he would learn a one-syllable adjective formula for Odysseus ("brave" Odysseus), a two-syllable adjective formula ("crafty" Odysseus), a three-syllable formula ("resourceful" Odysseus), and a four-syllable formula ("many-minded" Odysseus). Depending on where he needed to describe Odysseus in a particular line of 18 syllables, he would use a formulaic epithet of one, two, three, or four syllables.

Think of these different-length formulas as the Lego™ blocks you probably played with as a kid—some Lego pieces had one dot, some two, some three, etc. If you were building a structure with Legos, you used various-sized blocks to create lines of the same length to, say, build the walls of a house. The oral poet worked much the same way with formulas of different syllabic lengths. Imagine yourself as an ancient Greek poet orally composing a poem about Odysseus waking up at dawn aboard his ship. You would have various formulas—like differently-sized Lego blocks—to describe the action so that the poetic line would come out to be eighteen syllables long.

You might start out with a formula of five syllables to describe dawn breaking:

Ro-sy-fing-ered dawn

Then in a formula of eight syllables you might describe Odysseus awaking (using the two-syllable epithet to describe him):

a-wa-kened craf-ty O-dy-sseus

Then finish the line with a formula of five syllables that describes a ship:

on his swift black ship

Thus, you would have composed a line of eighteen syllables out of several formulas you had learned, using them like pieces of Lego blocks. You could also use different formulas to say the same thing in a different line of eighteen syllables:

Dawn's rose fin-gers roused ma-ny-min-ded O-dys-seus from sleep on his dark ship

In neither line of poetry would you have said anything new—just put together several formulas you had learned.

Because each poetic line had a certain number of syllables, poetry differed from ordinary conversation, where there is no set pattern of syllables (or rhythm or rhyme). Such regularity of *line* gave poetry *form* and set the language of poetry apart from everyday language. The use of many poetic formulas, moreover, set poetry even further apart from everyday language. The formulas were contrived, pre-set, and *artificial* (in the best sense of the word, meaning *patterned*, rather than *fake* or *phoney*). Such artificial language was different from the "natural," spontaneous, and unpatterned flow of everyday conversation. When oral poets composed and recited such poems, poetic language seemed quite different from everyday speech—grander, more elevated, more formal. Poetic form, therefore, was initially the result of the way poets composed poems in oral cultures.

Ever since those early times, writers have debated whether poetic language should be different from the language we use in conversation—more elevated and formal—or whether poetic language should try to come as close as possible to the way people talk. At one end of the debate is a poet such as Milton, whose poetic line is so formal that it soars far beyond the realm of ordinary speech. Here is how Milton describes Adam and Eve in the Garden of Eden in *Paradise Lost*:

For contemplation he and valor formed,

For softness she and sweet attractive grace.

This is Milton's contrived, artificial, formal way of saying something as simple as "Adam was created to think and to act bravely; Eve was created to be gentle, sweet, graceful, and attractive." It's very different from the way we talk, but it has a kind of grandeur because of that difference. That's why, when people get married, they prefer saying "With this ring I thee wed" rather than "I'm marrying you with this ring."

By contrast, a poet such as William Wordsworth begins "Tintern Abbey" with language that sounds almost as if he were chatting, off the cuff, about a return visit to a beautiful landscape after a five-year absence:

> *Five years have passed; five summers, with the length*
>
> *Of five long winters! And again I hear*
>
> *These waters, rolling from their mountain springs*

Wordsworth may sound much more "conversational," but his poetic line is every bit as formal, contrived, and, in the best sense of the word, artificial as Milton's.

The Invention of Writing

Spoken language belongs to all, but *writing* initially belonged to only a few—the educated, priestly, and wealthy classes. The earliest writing appeared around 3,000 B.C. in Sumer, roughly the land now called Iraq, between the Tigris and Euphrates Rivers. This writing, called *cuneiform*, used written symbols to depict objects and actions. In Egypt and China, similar written systems, *hieroglyphic* and *ideogrammic* writing, were created around the same time. For many centuries, writing was only used to keep business records of transactions, such as how many heads of cattle landowners bought and sold.

It's hard for us, who live in a culture where writing is absolutely vital, to understand why it played only a minimal role in ancient cultures for so long. But there were problems with these early writing systems. Creating symbols to depict different things and actions required having an enormous number of such symbols—Chinese had nearly 30,000—and it was hard to remember what each symbol referred to. Even a rudimentary reading knowledge of Chinese today requires knowing at least 500 symbolic characters.

Also it was difficult to make each symbol recognizably different from other symbols and, at the same time, make them look something like the thing or action they referred to. Here, for example, is the Chinese symbol for the word *sun*:

It may not look like our idea of the sun, but it depicts the sun as seen through a window.

This next ideogram incorporates the *sun* ideogram but adds more written elements to it to show that the sun is *rising*

This next ideogram combines the first two but adds more written elements to show that the sun is rising *in the east*.

Can you see how cumbersome such a written system would be? Characters are hard to tell apart, they take a long time to write down, and each one has to be memorized. While there is some connection between characters, once we go beyond ideograms that depict specific things and actions to represent abstract ideas such as *courage* or *truth*, it's hard to recognize the concrete images behind such ideas.

A much better writing system was developed around 800 B.C. by the Phoenicians, a Semitic people who lived at the eastern end of the Mediterranean in what is now Lebanon. Their written symbols did not try to depict *things* but, rather, the *sounds* people made when they spoke. This system gradually developed into the *alphabet*, in which each symbol represents a different sound in a spoken language. Thus, written language, which had begun by creating a vast and complex system of symbols to represent things *visually*, became much more simplified by creating a relatively small number of symbols to represent the sounds people make as they speak *orally*.

Although the Phoenician alphabet was a much simpler and more flexible form of writing that used only about two dozen easily drawn and easily recognizable symbols to represent speech sounds, the Phoenicians did not use writing any more creatively than the Sumerians or Egyptians. A culture of seagoing traders, they too used writing primarily to keep business records. It was when their alphabetic system of writing spread to other cultures that writing became truly *creative*.

One of these cultures was that of the Hebrews, another Semitic people of the Near East. The Hebrews used writing to record their history, laws, and, most important, their religious beliefs in written works, such as what Christians call the *Old Testament* of the Bible.

The Greeks and Writing

Another people who adopted the Phoenician alphabet were the Greeks. The legendary Greek hero Cadmus, inventor of the alphabet, was probably a Phoenician trader. The Greeks were a people who enjoyed debating ideas, relished humor, and pondered scientific and philosophic questions about the nature, purpose, and quality of life. When the Greeks acquired writing, their culture developed in a way that has never been equaled. "Writing did not make the Greek mind skeptical, logical, historical or democratic," explains historian Robert Pattison in his book *On Literacy*. "Instead it furnished an opportunity for these dispositions to flourish." [3]

One of the reasons Greeks were disposed to logic, skepticism, and democracy, it has been suggested, is that the geography of Greece is mountainous and rugged, as opposed to the vast, flat, desert civilizations of the Near East. In the Near East, a single ruler could dominate large groups of people across a flat landscape; in Greece, the mountainous culture made such domination difficult, and local, independent, democratic societies developed.

Whether because of its geography or not, Greek culture developed in markedly different ways from the Near Eastern civilizations that preceded it. In Egypt, Mesopotamia, and other Near Eastern cultures, a pharaoh or other ruler was in supreme command, a small group of priests controlled all knowledge and religion, and most people lived in miserable subjugation. Little wonder that in such cultures people turned away from their life in this world and looked longingly beyond death to another, better world.

In Greece, people lived under forms of government much closer to democracy; priests were relegated to the sidelines as all people pursued knowledge and engaged in rational discussion; and their focus was on this world—how to understand the workings of nature, how to achieve goodness in this life, how to exult even in the tragedies life—and death—bring. As Edith Hamilton observes:[4]

To rejoice in life, to find the world beautiful and delightful to live in, was a mark of the Greek spirit which distinguished it from all that had gone before.

The Greeks, in a word, were the first *humanists*. And, they made the most of *writing*.

In writing, as the Greeks found, we can revise our sentences over and over—as I revised many of the sentences you are now reading in order to make them as clear, succinct, and engaging as possible. In reading, we can also reread sentences over and over to make sure that we grasp their meaning, ponder whether we agree with what they say, appreciate or criticize the quality of their style. We can even put a written text aside for hours, days, or even longer, then return to read it again after we have thought extensively about issues raised (as you will return to this book when your final examination approaches), and the written words will be exactly the same as when you first read them.

The Greeks took writing to, as we would say in a cliché today, a whole new level. They saw written language as a way to obtain knowledge of the world, to understand the meaning of life, and to debate ideas. Homer may have been the first oral poet who saw the possibilities writing opened up for literature. Instead of singing his poems to an audience, he could write them down for readers who could reflect, reread, and ponder a passage of poetry before they went forward with the rest of the narrative. He could even, as he does in *The Odyssey*, tell a story in flashbacks and "meanwhile, back at the ranch" segments, instead of the strictly chronological narrative we find in most other oral stories.

---

[3] Robert Pattison, *On Literacy: The Politics of the Word from Homer to the Age of Rock* (New York: Oxford University Press, 1982), 45

[4] Edith Hamilton, *The Greek Way to Western Civilization* (New York: The New American Library, 1960), p. 19.

Writing made Greeks even more resourceful, skeptical, reflective, and witty. During Greece's war with Persia (today called Iran), Greek ships battled with Persian ships at sea. The Greeks knew that there were Greek prisoners of war on the Persian ships who would probably have to fight on the side of the Persians, so they created a huge sign that said, "Greeks, if you must fight, fight poorly." The Persians, of course, could not read the sign. The defeat of the Persans by the Greeks meant that Western culture would develop and spread across Europe in a distinctly different fashion from any culture of the Near East—embracing humanism, democracy, and individualism.

Writing freed Greeks from having to adhere to the formulas of oral poetry. They began writing history, philosophy, and scientific works in *prose*. Prose did not have to use the rhythm, meter, and formulaic phrases of oral poetry, so it could be more precise, refined, and varied. Even Greek written poetry became more flexible and diverse, employing shorter lines, different rhythms and meters, and original images, rather than the formulaic phrases of oral poetry.

At first, reading was more widespread than writing. Many Greeks could read, but only professional scribes learned the art of writing with alphabetical symbols. Those who could read often read aloud to those who could not, so writing reached even those who could neither read nor write. In this way, reading blended oral and written culture, and reading aloud to people who cannot read—such as children—has continued to the present day. But the gradual spread of reading and writing eventually changed literature from a communal, oral art where people gathered together to hear a story, poem, or play, to an individual art form, where the writer thinks of his or her audience as a single individual, silently reading the author's words.

It's been argued that reading and writing helped promote Greek democracy, since people began to identify themselves, through reading, as self-conscious individuals rather than as members of a group. It's also been suggested that, in modern times, reading and writing have alienated people from one another, strengthening individuality but at the price of the sense of community that flourished in ancient, oral cultures. Even the greatest of Greek philosophers grappled with the spread of reading and writing. Socrates, who taught his pupils orally and put nothing in writing, once told them that writing would destroy the power of human memory which had developed so vitally in oral cultures. Plato, Socrates' greatest pupil, was also skeptical of reading and writing. Writing lacked the immediacy of speech, its social context, the give-and-take of conversation; what's more, writing *seemed* to carry authority, objectivity, and permanence. Yet Plato also recognized that writing could be more precise, reflective, and subtle. While Plato wrote down many of his ideas, he wrote them as *dialogues*, in the form of spoken exchanges of conversation. It was Plato's greatest pupil, Aristotle, who wrote down his ideas in straightforward prose.

Some Greeks, however, were openly opposed to reading and writing. Ancient Greece was a loose confederation of small city-states, each with its own character and culture. While Athens, the greatest of these city-states, embraced reading and writing, Sparta, the great rival of Athens, used writing only for business records. Spartans regarded writing as a necessary evil. They feared that writing laws down would make law so complex and convoluted that only professional "lawyers" would grasp the once-simple laws that everyone understood in an oral culture. (They may have had a point.)

Writing helped ancient Greece create the philosophy, literature, science, and political heritage it passed on to the Western world. That heritage might not have been passed on, ironically, had Greece not been conquered. After its great cultural flowering in the fifth century B.C., Greece was conquered by Philip of Macedonia (a country north of Greece). Then, Philip's son, Alexander the Great, who had been tutored by Aristotle, established an empire and spread Greek culture throughout Egypt, the Near East, and even as far as India. At that time, the most important city in the world was Alexandria, named after Alexander, in Egypt, which housed a great library of written works—until it burned (always a danger to the written word). The "Hellenistic"(named after a Greek tribe called the "Hellenes") culture of Greece endured throughout the Mediterranean long after the empire established by Alexander had crumbled.

Greek Drama

In ancient Greece, religious celebrations involved a chorus of fifty men—five from each of Greece's ten city-states—who would chant *dithyrambs*, poems about a god, singing as they danced around the god's altar. According to legend, sometime in the fifth century B.C., one of the members of this chorus, Thespis, enlivened such performances by stepping aside, assuming the character of the god, and engaging in dialogue with the rest of the chorus. This innovation of Thespis was all the more revolutionary, since only a consecrated priest could impersonate a god. In honor of Thespis, actors have since been referred to as *thespians*.

The Greek god whose ritual celebrations primarily led to the development of drama was Dionysus. Dionysus was a relatively late arrival in the Greek *pantheon* (group of gods), which already included such gods as Zeus (the sky god, who was also king of all the other gods), Athena (the goddess of wisdom and patron goddess of the city of Athens), and Aphrodite (the goddess of love, whom the Romans called Venus). While these other gods had been worshipped for centuries, Dionysus was a new, cult god from the Near East, whose worship spread quickly throughout Greece. Dionysus was the god of wine and revelry. He was frequently depicted as half-human and half-goat, and his caricature influenced the way Christian artists later depicted the devil—with horns and cloven feet.

While older gods, such as Athena (goddess of wisdom) and Apollo (god of poetry and song), reflected the Greek love of rationality and order, Dionysus (god of wine and fertility) was worshipped in frenzied, drunken rituals where people lost their sense of reason, decorum, and consciousness. When a chorus of his worshippers sang and danced hymns to Dionysus, the rituals usually turned into drunken orgies. The idea of "acting"—pretending to be someone else—may have its roots in such Dionysian revels, so that Thespis would have assumed the role of the god himself by losing his own sense of self-identity (as actors today "become" the characters they portray on stage and screen).

Following the lead of Thespis, other members of the chorus stepped out to become *characters* in the poems that were being recited. First, such characters may have spoken only with the chorus, but at some point they also exchanged dialogue with one another. With the emergence of more actors, the size of the chorus was reduced from fifty to twelve men. These developments from chanted poetry to acted drama eventually shifted away from religious rituals. Instead of being presented in front of the altar of a god, these performances were presented in outdoor theaters near the temple of a god.

The audience, which could number as many as 30,000 people, sat on concentric stone seats that rose up the side of a hill. At the bottom of the hill stood a stage that jutted out from a *skena* (the source of our word for "scene"), a wall with doors so actors could enter and exit from behind the stage (there was no curtain across the stage). Below and in front of the stage was the *orchestra*, where the chorus sang, danced, and conversed in dialogue with the actors on the stage (in theaters today, there is usually an *orchestra pit* in front of the stage).

Actors wore costumes and large masks that also served as megaphones so that their voices could be heard by everyone in the audience. The actors were all male, but, because of their masks, could play female parts (they could also, with a change of mask and costume behind the *skena*, play several different roles, a practice, called *doubling*, that was common in Shakespeare's theater, where a single actor might play two or three roles). There was no scenery other than an occasional painted backdrop that hung in front of the *skena*.

Early dramas were presented in annual festivals, where many productions competed against one another for prizes. The biggest of these festivals was the "City Dionysia," held in Athens every April. During the day, *tragedies* were performed, whose name derives from the Greek word *tragos* (goat), one of the animals associated with Dionysus. In the evenings, *comedies* (from the Greek word *comos*—a revel or masquerade) were presented, which grew out of antics performed by worshippers of Dionysus dressed as *satyrs*, lecherous creatures who, like the god himself, were half-human, half-goat.

The Form of Greek Drama: The Stage

Dframa emerged from chanted poems that were "acted out," but the crucial formal elements in drama are the *stage*, the place where the drama is performed, and the *scene*, which begins when characters enter the stage and ends when they exit the stage. Therefore, in studying dramatic writing we will concentrate upon the stage and the scene.

The fundamental challenge a playwright faces is to persuade an audience that the stage is a place other than a stage in a theater. In modern theatrical productions, scenery, props, and lighting can make an audience imagine they are witnessing a play set in ancient Egypt, eighteenth-century France, or a modern suburban home. In Greek theatre, however, there was virtually no scenery on the stage. Actors had to indicate, through dialogue, what place the stage represented. One of the *conventions* that characterized Greek drama was that the stage represented the same place for the duration of the play.

The "Unities" of Aristotle

The Greek philosopher Aristotle described this and other formal conventions of Greek drama as *unities*. The first of Aristotle's unities was the Unity of Place, by which he meant that in Greek drama the stage always represented the same place in a play. Aristotle thought that Greek dramatists felt that once an audience had come to believe that the stage was, say, the area outside the King's palace at Thebes, it would strain their credulity if, over the course of the play, they were later asked to imagine the stage was suddenly a different place. In *Antigone*, for example the stage is always the area outside of the palace of Creon. Actions that take place in other locations—such as the death of Antigone and the suicide of Haemon—are not portrayed on the stage but reported by characters who witnessed them off stage. A lot of what happens in Greek drama, in fact, consists of what characters come on stage to report about something that has happened off stage.

Another of Aristotle's unities was the *Unity of Time*. In studying the drama of his era, he noticed another convention: that the action represented on stage took place approximately in the same amount of time it took to present that action in the theater. Again, Aristotle thought it would seem unrealistic to audiences, who had accepted the idea that a play started at a certain time, if the playwright suddenly shifted to action that took place days, weeks, or even years later. In Sophocles' *Antigone*, all of the action portrayed on the stage occurs in about the same amount of time it takes the audience to watch the play. Sophocles even makes this Unity of Time dramatic by having Creon realize—too late—that he should rescue Antigone from her tomb.

The third "unity" that Aristotle discerned in drama was what he called *Unity of Action*. In real life, events occur that usually have little relation to one another, but in Greek drama every action is caused by a preceding action and, in turn, causes a subsequent action. Such a series of causally-related action was what Aristotle called *plot*, as opposed to the unrelated sequence of episodic incidents we might encounter in a contemporary movie or novel. Plot gives a dramatic work *structure*, usually involving a beginning, a middle (with a "turning point" in the conflict), and an end. Plot, in drama as well as fiction, is based on *conflict:* conflict between two characters (a *protagonist* and an *antagonist*) or groups of characters; conflict between a character and some larger entity, such as nature or society; or conflict *within* a character torn between two different impulses, longings, or fears.

Sophocles (ca. 496 B.C.–406 B.C.)

Sophocles wrote during the *Golden Age* of Greek culture when Athens was the dominant military power, democracy flourished under leaders such as Pericles, and artistic and literary life was at its height. The Acropolis was built, which featured the Parthenon; Socrates, Plato, and Aristotle defined the course of Western philosophy; and other playwrights, such as Aeschylus and Euripides, competed with Sophocles in dramatic contests.

Over the course of his long life (he lived to the age of ninety), Sophocles wrote more than one hundred plays, but only seven have survived. In addition to writing plays, Sophocles was a military and political leader during Athens' greatest age.

The Form of Greek Drama: The Scene

Like all plays, *Antigone* consists of a series of scenes. The first scene of the play occurs between Antigone and her sister Ismene. Although the ancient Greek audience would have known the story of *Antigone*, Sophocles still supplied *exposition*, or what in today's movies is called "back-story," bringing the audience up to date on what happened before the beginning of the play. As part of this exposition, Sophocles also has to identify *who* his characters are and *where* they are, since there were no printed programs, as there are in modern productions, to identify the characters by name and indicate the setting of the scene. Therefore, Sophocles has Antigone address Ismene as "Ismene, my dear sister," even though one sister would not normally address another in such a way. Antigone also lets the audience know that she and Ismene are meeting "outside the gates" of the City of Thebes, establishing the setting of the play.

While Sophocles provides exposition, he also introduces *conflict*. Ismene has not heard about Creon's edict prohibiting the burial of their brother Polyneices. So, Antigone has to tell her—and the audience—about it. In doing so, Antigone also brings the audience up to date on the history of their family—the tragic marriage of their father Oedipus to their mother (and grandmother), the rivalry between their brothers Etiocles and Polyneices for the rule of Thebes, and the war between the two brothers and their armies—the Theban army led by Etiocles and the Argive army (from the city-state of Argos) led by Polyneices. In the battle, both brothers were killed, and the rule of Thebes fell to their uncle Creon.

Such extensive exposition presented through dialogue could make for very dull theater if Sophocles did not make it interesting through the conflict that develops between the two sisters. Ismene is shocked by Creon's edict prohibiting the burial of their brother Polyneices, but she is even more horrified that Antigone plans to defy the edict—and wants Ismene to help her. The scene begins with the two sisters talking confidentially with one another, conflict erupts when Antigone tells Ismene that she plans to defy Creon and bury their brother, and the scene reaches a turning point when Antigone urges Ismene to join her—but Ismene refuses to break the law.

This conflict opens between two sisters but, then, develops into a larger conflict of ideas: should an individual obey the laws of the stare or defy them when the state's law violates fundamental human decency. In her horror at what her sister is proposing, Ismene gives us more exposition. Their father Oedipus unwittingly killed his own father. Greeks would have known that, when Oedipus was born, it was prophesied that he would kill his father, Laius, so Laius had the baby given to a soldier to be killed. But, the soldier didn't have the heart to kill the baby and just left him to die on a hillside. The baby was found and raised by shepherds in Corinth, another Greek city-state. When Oedipus, visited Thebes as a grown man, he met a man at a crossroads along the way, quarreled with him, and killed him—not knowing the man was his own father. Oedipus traveled on to Thebes, where he met and married Jocasta, his own mother and widow of the man he killed.

In Sophocles' play *Oedipus Rex*, when this information comes out, Jocasta, hangs herself and Oedipus puts out his eyes. Before the beginning of *Antigone*, the family curse extends to their two sons, Etiocles and Polyneices, who kill each other in battle. Now, in this opening scene from *Antigone*, the two sisters are in conflict over the burial of their brother Polyneices. The scene ends with Antigone stubbornly saying she wouldn't want Ismene's help now even if her sister changed her mind. When Ismene tells her to at least keep what she is going to do quiet, Antigone angrily says she wants everyone to know that she's going to give her brother a proper burial. In just one scene, Sophocles has painted the two sisters as very different characters. Ismene is timid, practical and realistic—a woman very much aware how powerless she is in a male-dominated society. Antigone is idealistic, defiant, and self-destructive.

As both actors leave the stage, the first scene comes to an end. The relationship between the two sisters has changed over the course of the scene. At the beginning, the two sisters sought each other out for comfort and protection. By the end of the scene, the two sisters are estranged. The turning point came in the middle of the scene when Ismene refused to help Antigone bury their brother, Polyneices.

In the orchestra below the stage, the chorus of elder statesman of Thebes—a kind of city council—recount the battle between the Theban and Argive armies and how the two brothers killed each other. Then Creon comes on stage and engages in dialogue with the chorus. As the ruler of the city, Creon has decided that, as a rebel and traitor, Polyneices must be disgraced by not being given burial rites (which involve just covering the corpse with dirt, not placing it in a grave or tomb). In any culture, but especially in ancient Greece, this is a brutal punishment, but Creon believes he has to make a point—that this is what happens to people who try to destroy the city. The chorus doesn't like it—this profaning of proper burial customs—but they are clearly cowed by this powerful ruler and meekly acknowledge his right to make such decisions.

Then another actor comes on stage (though it probably was one of the actors who portrayed Antigone or Ismene, now wearing a different mask and different costume). He adds a slightly comic touch with his fear of bringing bad news to a powerful ruler. In effect, he's saying, "Please don't shoot the messenger" as he tells Creon that someone has violated his edict by partially burying the body of Polyneices. Like much of what happens in Greek drama, this action took place somewhere *off stage*; we only hear about it from an actor who comes *on stage* to provide such exposition. The exposition is more dramatically interesting, because the messenger is afraid to report this news, which he knows will anger Creon. He and the other soldiers drew lots to see who would come and tell Creon. The messenger's trepidation makes his news more dramatically interesting and comical as Creon has to drag the expository information oiut of him.

When the chorus hears the messenger's report, they subtly indicate their disapproval of Creon's edict by saying that maybe the gods did this—trying to get Creon to relent. But, Creon shows he is as wrapped up with being in charge as stubbornly as Antigone is with defying the law. Two such powerful characters make for a dynamic conflict of personalities and values. Creon doesn't listen to the chorus, telling them they are dumb old men. He also accuses the guards of taking bribes to allow the burial of Polyneices. Creon is clearly a ruler who fears he's surrounded by enemies and conspirators who resist his orders. Carried away by his anger, he even threatens to kill the guards unless they find the culprit. Both the messenger and Creon exit, ending this scene.

The chorus then sings and dances an ode about humanity's great achievements but also its evildoings that tear at the unity of the community. We then get another dramatic scene as three actors (probably the total number of actors in the original production)—the guard, Antigone, and Creon—interact on stage. The guard, again, reports something that has happened offstage as he describes how he caught Antigone trying to finish the burial rites for Polyneices. Such an action would be hard to present on stage and, if it were, would violate the "Unity of Place." The guard gives his exposition vividly, describing how Antigone screamed when he and the other guards brushed the dirt from the corpse of Polyneices. Again, he brings a comic touch to his exposition. He's glad Antigone doesn't try to deny what he reports; he's just an ordinary guy who wants to save his own neck (and job).

The play has been moving to this moment of direct conflict between Creon and Antigone. Creon tries to give his niece an out, asking her if she did not know the burial of Polyneices was forbidden. Stubbornly, she refuses to take this chance to save herself, saying "Of course I knew." She defends herself by saying she followed the law of the gods in trying to bury her brother, a law that is above the laws of "mere men" like Creon. Antigone accepts the fact of her own death, almost as if she wants martyrdom. The chorus tells her she's as stubborn as her father Oedipus. Creon hates her as much for doing the deed as "exulting" in it, and he sees her as a challenge to his power and even manhood. He also wants to condemn Ismene, but Antigone insists she acted alone. On the one hand, she is trying to save her sister, but she also wants the glory of what she's done all to herself. She accuses the chorus, who she knows sympathizes with what she has done, of being timid before Creon. Much of the dialogue between Creon and Antigone occurs in *stichomythia*—single short lines that heighten the dramatic conflict.

Over the course of this scene, Ismene provides a critical piece of exposition when she asks Creon if he will kill the woman who is to be the "bride of your own son." Antigone, we thus learn in a piece of very dramatic exposition, is engaged to Creon's son, Haimon. That expository information thickens the plot and prepares the audience for the next scene, in which Haimon enters to try to dissuade his father from carrying out his edict that anyone who tries to give Polyneices burial rites will be put to death. Haimon, clearly, is a son who knows his father, for he does not challenge Creon's authority at first but tells his dad that he is an absolutely obedient little boy. He then tactfully hints that the whole City of Thebes is on Antigone's side, but that information only feeds Creon's suspicions that people are conspiring against him. Haimon urges his father to be like a tree that bends in the wind or a captain who slackens the sail of his ship to adjust to changing winds. Creon, however, is the kind of father who would never take advice from his son or any other young person.

Since Creon is clearly not going to relent, Haimon gradually drops his pose of obedience and openly defies his father. In this scene, Creon's character comes out very much as the ruler who is afraid that he will seem weak if he backs down from the order he has given. He's also very much "the man" who regards women with condescension. He tells Haimon that Antigone would not have known her proper place as an obedient wife but would have rebelled against him, even cheated on him, if they had married. As their exchange grows more heated, Sophocles has his characters speak in *stichomythia* again. Creon digs in his heels, saying he's the boss and that the city can't tell him how to rule. Haimon tries to say he loves his father, but Creon sees only rebellion from a son who is influenced by a woman. Haimon finally calls his father a fool, and Creon calls him the slave of a woman—the lowest thing, in Creon's eyes, that a man can be.

Still, the argument with Haimon has touched Creon, particularly when Haimon hints, as he leaves, that he will commit suicide if Antigone is executed. Creon starts to back off a little. In answer to a question from the chorus, he takes their advice and says he won't kill Ismene. Then he says he won't have Antigone "stoned" to death—a brutal way of executing someone—but just shut her up in a cave with food and water where she can "love the dead"—unlike Creon himself who, as the ruler of Thebes, deals with the living. He even hints that Antigone may not have to die at all.

At this critical moment, Antigone reenters, ready, almost eager, to die. The chorus tells her she will be famous for standing up for the laws of the gods, but when she compares herself to the goddess Niobe, the chorus warns her not to place herself so high. She, in turn, lashes out at them for not confronting Creon. She then gives in to lonely grief for herself. The chorus tells her she was too bold and defiant, but she defends the burial of Polyneices by saying a brother, unlike a husband or child, cannot be replaced.

In the next scene, the blind prophet Tiresias enters. He, too, tries to be tactful with Creon, telling him he's done a good job of ruling Thebes. But then, Tiresias tells Creon that not allowing Polyneices proper burial rites is corrupting the city and angering the gods. Backed into a corner again, Creon condescends to this "old man" and thinks Tiresias has been bribed. But Tiresias prophesies that Creon will lose "one from his loins" because of what he has done to Polyneices and Antigone.d

After Tiresias leaves, Creon, again, begins to waver. For the first time in the play, he asks the chorus what to do. Part of what drives the story is that his character begins to change from an autocratic ruler to a confused, hesitant man. While all other characters remain the same throughout the play, Creon alone undergoes a change that drives the dramatic action. When they tell him to give Polyneices a proper burial and to free Antigone, he rushes offstage to do just that. Once again, a messenger comes on stage to tell the chorus (and audience) what then happened offstage. His exposition is made more dramatic when it is interrupted by the entrance of Eurydice, Creon's wife, who wants to hear the messenger's news. The messenger says Creon first gave burial to the corpse of Polyneices then went to free Antigone from her cave. There, Creon heard the screams of his son when he discovered that Antigone hanged herself. When Haimon sees his father, he first tries to kill him, then stabs himself. Such action would be very difficult for a Greek playwright to present on stage, so Sophocles renders it through exposition, but the exposition is made dramatic by details such as Haimon's blood dripping on Antigone's neck.

As one tragic event follows another—each event in the plot causing the next event to give the drama Unity of Action—Eurydice leaves the stage and kills herself too. Creon enters carrying the body of Haimon and, then, goes off at the end of the play a broken man, so that one of the things that happens in *Antigone* is an internal event—Creon's character changes from a powerful, arrogant ruler to a humbled, bereft man. The chorus reflects on this action, saying that an "over-proud" man needed to learn to act with knowledge and reverence.

The great age of Greek drama was the fifth century B.C. when playwrights such as Sophocles, Aeschylus, and Euripides competed in festivals, such as the *City Dionysia* held in Athens every April. Gradually, the role of the chorus in drama diminished, and plays focused on actors speaking to each other. Comedy became increasingly popular, and actors became more influential than playwrights, both developments contributing to the demise of the great tradition of Greek tragedy.

Greek Narrative: Aesop's Fables

Drama presents a story in a way we would not normally do in real life—solely through dramatic scenes, with dialogue and spectacle, on a stage. The dramatist never speaks in his or her own voice in a play but gives the story over to the dialogue and actions of the characters. We have seen how Sophocles used dialogue to present exposition and let the audience know the names of the characters and where the play is set. Presenting a story through scenes with dialogue and spectacle on a stage is very *artificial* but also very powerful. In fact, we have come to refer to the way a playwright presents a story as *showing* the story through dramatic scenes rather than *telling* it.

Telling a story through a storyteller or *narrator* is a much older form of creative writing than *showing* a story through dramatic scenes. Here, for example, is one of the animal *fables* of Aesop, an ancient Greek storyteller, who probably was a slave on the Island of Samos off the Greek coast:

The Fox and the Grapes

One hot summer's day a Fox was strolling through an orchard till he came to a bunch of Grapes just ripening on a vine which had been trained over a lofty branch. "Just the thing to quench my thirst," quoth he. Drawing back a few paces, he took a run and a jump, and just missed the bunch. Turning round again with a One, Two, Three, he jumped up, but with no greater success. Again and again he tried after the tempting morsel, but at last had to give it up, and walked away with his nose in the air, saying: "I am sure they are sour."

It is easy to despise what you cannot get.

Almost everything that happens in this little story is *told* in *narrative summary* rather than *shown* in *narrative scene*. Although the fox says "Just the thing to quench my thirst" at the beginning of the story and "I am sure they are sour" at the end, there is really no dialogue between the fox and any other character. The voice of the *narrator* tells us what happened, and at the end, the narrator states the *moral* of the story: "It is easy to despise what you cannot get." In saying that, the narrator is talking directly to us as readers (in a way a playwright never could), summing up the *didactic* point of the story he has told (the lesson that the story teaches). A playwright could not narrate his story or comment on its meaning; he or she can only "speak" through the characters of the play.
In other fables, Aesop mixes telling with showing, narrating parts of his story but also presenting some parts of it as a dramatist would—in scenes that occur at a particular time and place and where characters engage in dialogue. Notice how in this fable, Aesop narrates some of the story but, at other points, "shows" it—as it would be presented in a play—in *narrative scenes*:

The Hare and the Tortoise

The Hare was once boasting of his speed before the other animals. "I have never yet been beaten," said he, "when I put forth my full speed. I challenge any one here to race with me."

The Tortoise said quietly, "I accept your challenge."

"That is a good joke," said the Hare; "I could dance round you all the way."

"Keep your boasting till you've beaten," answered the Tortoise. "Shall we race?"

So a course was fixed and a start was made. The Hare darted almost out of sight at once, but soon stopped and, to show his contempt for the Tortoise, lay down to have a nap. The Tortoise plodded on and plodded on, and when the Hare awoke from his nap, he saw the Tortoise just near the winning-post and could not run up in time to save the race. Then said the Tortoise:

Plodding wins the race.

Can you see how Aesop alternates between telling and showing in this story? In the first sentence, he tells how the rabbit was boasting about his speed to other animals. For the rest of the first half of the story, however, Aesop *show* what happens, as a playwright might, in a narrative scene with dialogue between the hare and the tortoise. Only when Aesop describes how the tortoise speaks "quietly" does he intrude upon the narrative scene as a narrator who describes the way the tortoise accepts the challenge.

With the paragraph that begins "So a course was fixed ... ," Aesop returns to telling the story in narrative summary. Only at the end do we go back to dialogue as the tortoise, rather than the narrator (as in "The Fox and the Grapes"), speaks the moral: "Plodding wins the race."

Thus, while dramatic form always involves *showing* (presenting a story through dialogue and spectacle on a stage), fictional form can alternate between *showing* and *telling*. For many years, young writers of fiction were given the advice "show don't tell," meaning that they should *show* everything in their story through narrative scene rather than *tell* what happens in narrative summary. To be a good writer of fiction, however, one has to know when to *show* and when to *tell*—which parts of a story are best presented in *narrative scene* with dialogue and which parts of the story are best told by the narrator in *narrative summary*.

Oral Narratives

While Aesop wrote in prose, many other early writers, such as Homer, created their long, epic narratives, such as *The Iliad* and *The Odyssey*, in poetry. Such epic poems were originally composed in poetic lines based on oral formulas and recited by "bards" or "rhapsods" in public performances. In the many centuries before the widespread use of writing, such oral poems comprised an illiterate culture's history, customs, laws, and other records, passing them on from one generation to another.

The great storyteller we call Homer, in fact, may just be a name we give to a long series of different oral poets who composed, elaborated, and recited such stories as the anger of Achilles during the Trojan War and the return of Odysseus after the wat to his home in Ithaca. Such oral poets told these stories for centuries before the works we know as *The Iliad* and *The Odyssey* were written down in manuscripts (sometime in the eighth century B.C.). Or, Homer may have been one of these oral bards, an especially good one, whose performances of *The Iliad* and *The Odyssey* were so renowned that a scribe who could read and write decided to "take down" some of Homer's performances in writing.

It may even be that "Homer" was an oral poet who learned to read and write himself (again, sometime around 700 B.C.). If so, it may be that some of the innovative ways of telling stories that we find in *The Iliad* and, especially, *The Odyssey* were the result of an oral poet experimenting with narrative form. Instead of telling a story chronologically, as most oral performers must have done so that the audience could follow the order of the events with a simple "and then … and then … and then … " pattern of narration, the writer of *The Odyssey* begins in the very last year of a story that spans twenty years, tells much of that story through "flashbacks," and moves from one part of the story to another in a kind of "meanwhile back at the ranch" departure from chronological narrative.

The Romans

Much of Greek culture was adopted by the Romans, who established an even greater empire, an empire that lasted until the fifth century A.D. One of the things that enabled the Roman Empire to endure for so long was writing. In adopting so much of Greek culture, including its literature, art, science, and even its religion, the Romans recognized the superiority of the Greeks in these areas. But, writing also helped the Romans in fields where they excelled—military power, engineering, and government. By encouraging many of its citizens to learn to read and write their Latin language, Romans created efficient soldiers who could read their orders, bureaucrats who could follow government directives, and citizens throughout a vast empire, which stretched around the whole of the Mediterranean, who felt drawn together, despite their regional differences, by a common language.

Christianity, which was opposed to the Roman Empire, was also initially opposed to writing. Jesus Christ put nothing in writing; he communicated his ideas purely through spoken language. "He that hath ears," Jesus said, "let him hear." The gospels that record his ideas were not put into writing until nearly fifty years after his death. Persecuted by the Romans, early Christians resisted the Latin language. When Christians finally took to writing, they did not put the books of the *New Testament* into Latin but into *Koine*, a form of Greek that was spoken among the common people of the Eastern Mediterranean. Once the Roman Empire adopted Christianity as its official religion, however, the Church found that written Latin was essential for communication, administration, and record-keeping. While the Church used Latin, it restricted the language to its priests and other clergy, much as the ancient Egyptians and other cultures made writing the province of a small, priestly caste.

Roman Drama

The Romans adapted the forms of Greek drama, as they did so much of Greek culture. Roman theaters were built on flat ground rather than on the steep hillsides that surrounded Greek theaters. Roman plays did not include a chorus, so all of the action took place on a high stage rather than, as in Greek drama, between the stage and the orchestra. Behind the stage was a large, elaborately decorated wall that was several storys high and had balconies, doors, and other sections where action could be presented. The Romans also introduced the curtain, which rose and receded into a trough in front of the stage.

To appeal to a Roman audience that loved gladiator fights and chariot races, Roman playwrights made the stage a place of spectacle. In Greek drama, most of the violent and bloody action takes place off stage and is only reported by actors on stage through expository dialogue. In Roman drama, such action was presented directly on the stage. The Romans also dispensed with masks and allowed women to portray female roles.

While the Romans adapted the form of Greek drama, they never attained the quality of Greek dramatic writing. As Phyllis Hartnoll notes:[5]

> Their staple fare was bawdy and obscene mimes and farces dealing mainly with drunkenness, greed, adultery, and horseplay, or lavish acrobatic spectacles featuring scantily clad dancers ... Theatrical performances, once the glory of Greece, and of some importance even in Republican Rome, became under the empire little more than a vulgar form of popular entertainment. The time came when they were forbidden altogether.

With the decline and fall of the Roman Empire in the fifth-century A.D., drama, as the public performance of plays before an audience in a theater, largely disappeared.

The Roman Conquest of Britain

At the beginning of the Christian Era, the British Isles were inhabited by various Celtic tribes. Celtic tribes also lived on the European continent between the Roman Empire to the south and Germanic tribes to the north. These Celtic tribes spoke languages that were part of the vast group of *Indo-European* languages (so named because they include most of the European languages, as well as Sanskrit, which was spoken in ancient India). A few of these languages survive today as Welsh in Wales, Gaelic in Ireland, Erse in Northern Scotland, and Breton in the northern part of France that is called Brittany. The Celts in Britain left no written literature, and only a few of their words have become part of the English language: *Britain*, the names of the cities *London* and *York*, of the rivers *Thames* and *Avon*, and such terms as *brogue, shamrock, galore, flannel, maggot, clan, slogan*, and *whiskey*. The Celts were considered "barbaric" peoples because they were not part of the "civilized" world of the Roman Empire. In the first century, however, Roman legions conquered Celtic tribes in the part of the British Isles we now know as England.

In Joseph Conrad's *The Heart of Darkness*, on which the movie *Apocalypse Now* was based, Marlowe, the narrator, tells a story to sailors sitting on the shore of the Thames River in London about his experience on the Congo River in Africa. As he begins his story, Marlowe notes that the Thames River, too, has been one of the "dark" places of the earth. He conjures up an image of a young Roman centurion sailing up the Thames to confront the fierce Celtic tribes, one of whom was led by Queen Boudicaa, who had a penchant for cutting off the testicles of Roman soldiers and hanging them from her spear.

---

[5] Phyllis Hartnoll, *A Concise History of the Theatre* (London: Thames and Hudson, 1968), p. 29.

The power of the Roman army was relentless, however, and the Celts in England were finally conquered and became Roman citizens. As such, they enjoyed the "civilizing" force of the Roman Empire. The Romans brought laws, administration, and general peace—the *Pax Romana*—throughout the empire. The only danger to these Romanized Celts came from Northern Celtic tribes who lived in Scotland. The Roman emperor Hadrian had a stone wall—some of which is still standing—built in 123 A.D. across England near its border with Scotland to keep out—or at least slow down—these marauding "barbaric" Celts from the north in the area we now call Scotland.

The Romans built houses with glass windows, plumbing, and central heating. They built stone roads along lines that still function as the major highways of England. Cities were created, such as London and Bath, with huge public bath houses. Latin became the official language of England as it was throughout the Roman Empire, and the Celtic languages survived only in outlying parts of the English countryside.

The Romanized Celts in England also became Christians when the Roman Empire embraced Christianity. Although Rome initially persecuted Christians, the emperor Constantine officially adopted Christianity in 313 A.D. after he had a dream that he would win a battle under the banner of the cross (*"In hoc signo vincit"*—"in this sign you will conquer"). He won the battle and adopted Christianity as the empire's religion. Christianity spread to England, and a Romanized Celt from England, St. Patrick, converted the Irish Celts to Christianity in the fifth century (and, according to legend, drove snakes out of Ireland).

Chapter 2
Medieval English Literature

The earliest literature composed in the language we now call English was not created in England or in any of the countries that make up the British Isles (England, Scotland, Wales, and Ireland). It was created, instead, by Germanic tribes, such as the Angles (who gave their name to the English language), the Saxons, and the Jutes (who lived in what is now called Schleswig-Holstein in Jutland--Denmark and Northern Germany). At the height of the Roman Empire (100 A.D.) much of England was part of the Roman Empire. But Northern Europe, where the Angles, Saxons, and Jutes lived, was beyond the boundaries of the empire. These tribes plied a seafaring, warrior culture that, today, we would term piracy, and they would have been referred to by the Romans as "barbarians," because they were not part of the "civilized" Roman Empire.

The Anglo-Saxons (to use a collective term for these Germanic tribes) spoke a language we now call *Anglo-Saxon* or *Old English*, because it is the ancestor of today's modern English. Like so many other tribes, the Anglo-Saxons did not have a written language but created an oral poetry that they passed down from generation to generation. The most famous of these poems is *Beowulf*, which tells the story of a Danish warrior who travels to Sweden to help rid the kingdom of a terrifying, man-eating monster named Grendel.

Their poetry did not use *rhyme* but did employ *rhythm*. As a Germanic language, Anglo-Saxon was an *accentual* language. That means that in words of more than one syllable, some syllables are accented more than others. When we mispronounce a word, for example, it's frequently because we put the em**pha**sis on the wrong syllable (instead of saying **em**phasis and **syl**lable).

Many words in English are spelled the same, but their accents, and, therefore, their meanings, differ:

> **Con**-tract...........................Con-**tract**
> **En**-trance ....En-**trance**
> **In**-va-lid ....In-**val**-id
> **Pro**-ject...........................Pro-**ject**

With words of only one syllable, we give some words more emphasis than others in a sentence: usually main verbs, nouns, adjectives, and adverbs are accented while articles, pronouns, conjunctions, prepositions, and auxiliary or "helping" verbs are not. Most of us, for example, would say this sentence by accenting the words in **bold**:

I want to **take** a **walk** and **see** the **trees** in **bloom**

In some other languages, such as French, all syllables receive pretty much the same emphasis. If you said "Est-ce qu'il y a un livre sur la table?" ("Is there a book on the table?"), you would probably not accent any syllable more than another.

The Anglo-Saxons used the accentual character of their language as one way of creating poetic form. They crafted the *poetic line*—the most fundamental formal unit of poetry—by using a pattern of accents. Each poetic line was divided into two halves. In the first half of the line, there would be two strongly accented words, as in this excerpt of a translation by the American poet Ezra Pound of the Anglo-Saxon poem, "The Seafarer" about an old sailor's who has lost all of his friends and now sails his boat alone on the harsh northern seas:

> *Bosque taketh blossom, cometh beauty of berries, The woods bloom*
>
> *Fields to fairness, land fares brisker,*

They also underscored those accented syllables with *alliteration* (the repetition of the same or similar consonant sounds at the beginnings of words)—in the above lines the "b" sound in the first line and the "f" sound in the second. Germanic languages have a lot of strong consonant sounds, and when the same consonant sounds are repeated, it makes for a poetic effect: "**P**eter **P**iper **p**icked a **p**eck of **p**ickled **p**eppers." Such alliteration makes a line catchy, not just in poetry but in advertising slogans: "When **B**etter Cars are **B**uilt, **B**uick will **B**uild Them."

In addition to using accent and alliteration, the Anglo-Saxon oral poet or *scop* would pause after the first half of the line, perhaps to strum a stringed instrument such as a harp or lyre. That pause remained in English poetry for centuries as a *caesura* that divided lines into halves, usually marked by punctuation such as a comma or period:

The woods decay,	the woods decay and fall
(Tennyson, "Tithonus")	
The woods around it have it.	It is theirs.
(Frost, "Desert Places")	
They fuck you up,	your Mum and Dad
(Larkin, "This Be the Verse")	

After the caesura, the Anglo-Saxon poet created the second half of the poetic line, which had either one or two strongly accented words. This word or words also had to alliterate with the accented syllables in the first half of the line:

> *Bitter breast-cares have I abided,*
>
> *Known on my keel many a care's hold,*   keel *(framework of a ship)*

There could be any number of syllables in an Anglo-Saxon poetic line; what gave the line its formal character were *accent*, *alliteration*, and *caesura*.

The Anglo-Saxon Conquest of Britain

The Roman Empire fell in the fifth century A.D. Historians have long speculated about the reasons for its fall, but the amazing thing is that such a vast and complex empire, stretching across Europe,

Northern Africa, and into the Near East, lasted as long as it did. Rome's fall was first felt at its outermost provinces—including Britain—as troops were withdrawn to protect the City of Rome itself. The withdrawal of Roman legions left the Christianized, Romanized Celts exposed to attacks by Celts from Scotland, as well as other barbaric tribes.

One legend has it that the British Celts appealed to the warrior tribes of the Angles, Saxons, and Jutes for protection. The Germanic tribes, however, responded by conquering England themselves. It's more likely that, as the Roman Empire collapsed, the Angles, Saxons, and Jutes raided and conquered the outermost parts of the empire. The legend of King Arthur, a Christian Celtic leader in the waning days of the Roman Empire, concludes with his valiant but doomed efforts to save England from the onslaught of barbaric armies that were probably the invading Angles, Saxons, and Jutes. Celts fled to Wales, to Ireland, to Scotland, and across the English Channel to Brittany in Northern France. By 600 A.D. the Anglo-Saxons were in control of what, today, is England.

The Jutes settled in the far eastern part of Southern England, today known as Kent; the Saxons made London their base and settled along the southern part of the country; the Angles took over Northern and Central England. Eventually, there were seven Anglo-Saxon kingdoms in England: Kent (Jutes); Essex (East Saxons), Wessex (West Saxons), and Sussex (South Saxons); and East Anglia (Eastern Angles), Mercia (Angles), and Northumbria (Angles). The collective population of these kingdoms was approximately a quarter of a million people.

Christianity Comes to England

Legend has it that an Angle warrior was captured in a battle with Roman troops and paraded in the streets of Rome, where the pope saw him and asked who the blond-haired, blue-eyed captive was. "An Angle," the pope was told, who immediately associated the word with "angel," sent missionaries to convert the Angles, Saxons, and Jutes to Christianity. The first missionary to arrive was St. Augustine (not the same Augustine who wrote his *Confessions*), who in 597 A.D., touched shore at Canterbury, on the east coast of England, which still remains the center of Christianity in Great Britain. He converted the Anglo-Saxon King Ethelbert of Kent, the Anglo-Saxon kingdom at the southeastern tip of England. Within seventy-five years, Christian missionaries had converted most of the other Anglo-Saxon kingdoms in England.

Remnants of the Anglo-Saxon pagan religion endured, however. Their love of warfare was reflected in various warrior gods who have given their names to most of our days of the week: Woden to Wednesday; Thor to Thursday; and Tiw to Tuesday. Frigga, wife of Woden, lent her name to Friday. The pagan view of life was bleak and stoical; even the gods were subject to *Wyrd* (fate—from which we get our modern word *weird*). They regarded nature, particularly in its most powerful manifestations such as storms, with awe. To their tribal leader, the *cyning* (king), all warriors pledged loyalty even to their death, and he, in turn, gave presents to his *thegns* (thanes, followers) of gold rings that symbolized the binding together of the *comitatus* (band or tribe).

Along with Christianity, the missionaries from Rome brought something that would have a profound effect on Anglo-Saxon oral poetry—*writing*. Throughout the Middle Ages ("Middle" because they were between ancient *classical* and our *modern* era that began with the Renaissance in the sixteenth century), Latin remained the standard written language of the Church, as well as the standard language of international political communication, scholarship, and science. At the same time, the spoken languages in various parts of the Roman Empire evolved into the Romance languages we know today as French, Spanish, Italian, Portuguese, and Rumanian. The Germanic languages, such as English and Dutch, and other languages, such as the Slavic languages, which had been spoken beyond the boundaries of the Roman Empire, continued to evolve. In the 8th and 9th centuries, under rulers such as Charlemagne in France and King Alfred in England, priests were urged to translate into writing certain important Latin works so that they could be read in the common languages spoken by the people. Much of what we know about the Anglo-Saxons, for example, comes from a translation into English of a history, written in Latin, of the Anglo-Saxons in England by a monk called the Venerable Bede.

Anglo-Saxon Poetry

The Christian priests who came to England from Rome also wrote down some of the oral poems they heard the Anglo-Saxon *scops* sing in Old English. They wrote these poems using the Latin alphabet, which did not always have letters that corresponded to the sounds of Old English. The five vowels of Latin—*a, e, i, o, u*—cannot represent the more than ten vowel sounds in Old English (hence today, we must resort to *long* and *short* versions of vowels). The most striking instance of this lack of *fit* between written letter and spoken sound was with the sound we now represent with "th" in *the, this,* and *that*. It is a very common sound in Old English, so the priests borrowed symbols from a rudimentary alphabet used by the Anglo-Saxons to mark graves. This alphabet, called the *futhark*, had symbols called *runes*, two of which represented the "th" sound--ð (*eth*), the *voiced* sound of "th" in "the" when it precedes a word starting with a vowel ("the ocean") and þ (*thorn*), the "unvoiced" "th" sound in *the* when it precedes a word starting with a consonant ("the sea"). Priests used these runes when they encountered those "th" sounds in the oral poetry of the Anglo-Saxons. Later, when printing was invented, printers took the letter of the Latin alphabet that most resembled these runes—Y—to represent the "th" sound. Thus, we find references to "Ye Olde Curiosity Shop," where *ye* is really a symbol for ð or þ and simply means *the*.

Most of the oral poems of the Anglo-Saxons have been lost; only those few that were written down by priests in England have survived. The priests also altered some of the Anglo-Saxon poems to make them reflect Christian beliefs. In turn, the Anglo-Saxon poets affirmed their pagan beliefs in such lines as "God is great, but Wyrd is stronger" (*wyrd*, you may recall, was the Anglo-Saxon name for *fate*, from which we derive our word *weird*). Even when the Anglo-Saxons created Christian poems, they threw in pagan touches. In "A Dream of the Rood," a poem about Christ's crucifixion and resurrection (*rood* was the Anglo-Saxon word for *cross*), the poet portrays Christ as heroically mounting the cross himself and emphasizes "the harrowing of Hell," where Christ, after his crucifixion on Good Friday, fights his way through hell with a sword so he can be resurrected on Easter morning.

Caedmon

The first poet we know by name who created poems in the English language was Cædmon. His story is told in *The Anglo-Saxon Chronicle*, a history of the Anglo-Saxons written by the Venerable Bede. In his history, Bede tells of a feast among Anglo-Saxons. As was customary at such feasts, each person was expected to be able to compose and recite a poem, and a harp was passed among them. Cædmon, however, felt he was not talented enough to create poetry, so as he saw the harp being passed his way, he quietly left the castle with the excuse that it was his turn to take care of the cattle. There, he fell asleep and dreamed that a voice told him to sing a poem. In his dream, Cædmon tried to excuse himself, but the voice insisted that he create a poem about how God created the world. Cædmon dreamed that he sang such a hymn about creation. From then on, Bede tells us, Cædmon became the greatest of Anglo-Saxon poets and could compose an oral poem in Old

English on any subject on the spot. Here is Cædmon's poem about the Creation, along with a modern translation. Notice the accents, alliteration, and caesura that characterize the poetic line.

Cædmon's Creation-Hymn

Nu sculon herigean	heofonrices Weard
Now let us praise	*heaven-kingdom's Guardian*
Meotodes meahte	and his modegeþanc
The Creator's might	*and his mental plans*
Weorc Wuldor-Faeder	swa he wundra gehwæs
The work of the Glory-Father	*when He of wonders of all*
Ece Drihten	or onstealde
Eternal Lord	*established the beginning*
He ærest sceop	ielda bearnum
He first created	*for the sons of men*
Heofon to hrofe	halig Scyppend
Heaven's roof,	*holy Creator*
ða middangeard	moncynnes Wea*rd*
then (he created) mid-Earth	*mankind's Guardia*n
ece Drihten	æfter teode
eternal Lord	*afterwards created*
firum foldan	Frea aelmihtig
for men the Earth	*Master almighty* ca. 700

Caedmon's poem is completely in the tradition of oral poetry, consisting of formulaic phrases cobbled together. There are a few innovations, such as taking the formula that describes an Anglo-Saxon king, *"rices weard"* ("keeper of the kingdom") and expanding it to *"heofenrices weard"* ("the keeper of heaven's kingdom"—God).

Caedmon's importance as the first poet we know by name who wrote in English lies not in his originality but in his adaptation of Anglo-Saxon oral poetry to Christianized, written poetry. Even though Caedmon himself probably could neither read nor write, he created his poems in a literate culture of monks and scribes who could write them down and school him in biblical stories that inspired his other poems.

Anglo-Saxon Culture and the Vikings

Anglo-Saxon culture flourished in England from 600 A.D. through 1000 A.D., especially during the reign of England's first powerful king, Alfred the Great (871–899 A.D.), who united most of the Anglo-Saxons kingdoms in Southern England. Alfred created the English navy, ever after England's primary military power. Literature was translated from Latin to Anglo-Saxon, and historical records kept in *The Anglo-Saxon Chronicle*. A man of letters himself, Alfred insisted that his officials and churchmen master Latin, the universal language of religion, scholarship, and political affairs. Buildings, such as Westminster Abbey, and fortified towns, such as Oxford, were erected under his rule.

Alfred the Great also withstood the raids of the Vikings, warriors who, in the 8th and 9th centuries, sailed out of Norway, Denmark, and Sweden and attacked virtually all of Europe—first Ireland, then London and Paris, then across the Mediterranean all the way to Constantinople (known today as Istanbul). Although Scandinavians today are among the most peace-loving people on earth, their Viking ancestors were brutal warriors who would attack in their "dragon ships," burn, loot, pillage, rape, and kill—sometimes tossing babies to one another on the points of their spears. They destroyed precious manuscripts, churches, and other artifacts of Western European Christian culture. After driving the Arabs from the Island of Sicily, off the southern coast of Italy, the Vikings settled there, which explains why Frank Sinatra and so many other Sicilians have blue eyes (a Scandinavian trait) and why the most powerful and brutal modern criminal organization, the Mafia, traces its roots not to Italians but to the ferocious Norwegian, Swedish, and Danish Vikings who settled in Sicily. Perhaps instead of calling the Mafia Italian, we should refer to it as the Norwegian Mafia.

In England, the Vikings overwhelmed one after another of the seven Anglo-Saxon kingdoms until only Wessex remained, under the rule of its young King Alfred. Alfred fought the Vikings, and in the Treaty of Wedmore in 878, he managed to stop their advance. Under the treaty, half of England, roughly the area south and west of London, remained under the rule of Alfred the Great as a united Anglo-Saxon kingdom. The northern and eastern part of England was under the Dane Law control of the Vikings. Alfred even managed to persuade the Vikings to convert to Christianity and to stop destroying churches and monasteries. At times, Viking England and Anglo-Saxon England were united, as under the reign of King Canute from 1017 until 1035, a kingdom that included Denmark and Norway, as well as England.

The Viking language, Old Norse, also a Germanic language, blended with Old English, the first of several other languages that would combine to make English a *hybrid* or "mongrel" language. From Old Norse, Old English took such words as *birth, root, scare, ugly, die, hit, anger, dirt, rotten, egg, law, happy, odd, ill,* and *wrong*. Such simple, strong words are some of the most frequently used terms in modern English.

The Vikings in France

The Vikings also settled in the northern part of France after reaching a truce with the King of France by which they were given control of the northern part of the country in exchange for ceasing their attacks. Their part of France was called Normandy (after the French word for Vikings—the Normans or Northmen), and their leaders were Dukes of Normandy. They spoke French and adopted French customs, including French poetry and other literary traditions. Since these Normans would eventually conquer England and bring their French traditions—including poetry—with them, we need to know something about the *form* of medieval French poetry.

Medieval French poetry differs from Old English poetry in that it does not use accent and alliteration to shape the poetic line. Instead, the French poetic line has a set number of syllables and usually ends in rhyme. Here, for example, is a translation of the opening of a poem by the medieval French poet Jacques Tahureau:[6]

Within the sand of what far river lies

The gold that gleams in tresses of my Love?

What highest circle of the heavens above

Is jeweled with stars such as are her eyes?

Each line is ten syllables long and the first and fourth lines rhyme with one another as do the second and third. Can you see how, even in translation, this kind of poetry differs from Cædmon's "Creation Hymn?"

Courtly Love

The subject matter of French poetry also differs from that of Old English poetry. In the eleventh century, poets in the South of France called *troubadours* created many songs about what we have come to call *courtly* or *romantic love*. While earlier poets writing in Greek, Latin, and other languages wrote about love, the troubadours developed a view of what was then called courtly love that is still with us today in poems, novels, movies, and popular songs: that one falls in love at first sight: "I took one look at you, that's all I meant to do, and then my heart stood still"(Rodgers and Hart, "My Heart Stood Still"); that one is usually captivated by the beloved's eyes: "Jeepers creepers, where'd you get those peepers? Jeepers creepers, where'd you get those eyes?"(Johnny Mercer and Harry Warren, "Jeepers Creepers"); that when one is in love, he or she is sick with fever or chills:"You give me fever, fever when you kiss me, fever when you hold me tight"(Eddie Cooley and Otis Blakwell, writing under the pseudonym "John Davenport," "Fever"); that the more the beloved scorns her lover, the more he adores her:"I get a kick ev'ry time I see you standing there before me—I get a kick though it's clear to see you ob'viously don't adore me" (Cole Porter, "I Get a Kick Out of You"); that even though the beloved rejects the lover, he or she can express heartache in a *planh* or "complaint": "The night is bitter, the stars have lost their glitter, the winds grow colder, and suddenly you're older, and all because of the man that got away"(Ira Gershwin and Harold Arlen, "The Man That Got Away").

If you think about such *conventions* of courtly love, they are pretty silly. Why would anyone love someone who constantly spurned their romantic overtures? Do you really fall in love with someone at first sight? By looking into their eyes? In Anglo-Saxon poetry, for example, such ideas would have been considered absurd. Yet, thanks to the songs of the medieval troubadours of Southern France, these conventions of courtly love have endured to the present.

Some of our most basic associations with romantic love also come from the troubadours. In their language, Provencal, two of the words that rhymed with *amor* (love) were *cor* (heart) and *flor* (flower). To this day, we associate love with our hearts (as opposed to other organs) and flowers (think of the presents we give on Valentine's Day)—simply because those words rhymed in Provencal.

---

[6] Jacques Tahureau, "Shadow of His Lady," http://www.poemhunter.com/jacques-tahureau/poems.

The Norman Conquest

Once the Vikings were established in Northern France as Dukes of Normandy, they were largely independent rulers, subservient in name only to the King of France. In 1066, a date as familiar to English school children as 1492 is to American kids, Duke William of Normandy saw an opportunity to invade England. The opportunity presented itself, because after the reign of Alfred the Great, Anglo-Saxon England had lost its unity and strength, and England had even been ruled by Viking kings, such as Canute. Duke William, who would become known as William the Conqueror, because he led the last successful military invasion of England, sailed across the English Channel with his troops and landed near the town of Hastings. As he disembarked from his ship, Duke William tripped and fell on the shore—an omen, his men feared, that their invasion would be unsuccessful. Duke William, thinking quickly, stood up, clasped two handfuls of dirt and told his troops how easily he had already acquired English turf. In the ensuing battle of Hastings, Duke William's forces defeated the Anglo-Saxon army of King Harold, and he became King William I of England.

Having been conquered by the Romans, then by the Anglo-Saxons, England was once again subjugated by a foreign power, and for several centuries—until the 1300s—it was merely a colony for the Dukes of Normandy, who resided in Northern France and ruled England from across the English Channel. Despite their absentee rule, the dukes of Normandy, who also served as kings of England, such as Richard I ("The Lion-Hearted"), brought profound changes to English life, language, and poetry. French, not English, became the language of government, which was conducted in a building called "Parliament" (from the French "parler"—"to speak"); law (so many legal terms, such as "tort" and "jury" derive from French); and literature (little was written in English for three centuries after the Norman conquest). Those 300 years were peaceful and prosperous ones for England. Learning flourished in monasteries and abbeys, and twenty-seven great Gothic cathedrals were built, as well as many parish churches.

Gothic cathedrals were first built in France, but with the Norman Conquest, many of the most beautiful were built in England under the reigns of the Norman kings. Gothic cathedrals soared heavenward like modern skyscrapers, but inside, they felt light and full of illumination. Architects used stone arches called "flying buttresses" to support the weight of the walls outside the cathedral so that the walls could be filled with huge stained glass windows to let in light. To stand inside such cathedrals is to feel both an upward pull to heaven and the down-pouring of celestial light.

Despite building magnificent cathedrals, the kings of England still thought of themselves as French dukes of Normandy and regarded England merely as their colony. Their involvement in European wars, sometimes with the king and other dukes of France, gradually forced the Normans out of France and made England their home base. With the reign of Henry III (1216–1272), England finally got a Norman king who resided in England, rather than France. Although later kings of England tried to re-establish their French territories until the fifteenth century, by then, the colony of England had become the country of the Norman kings, who no longer had any territory in France.

The English Language after the Norman Conquest

In the three centuries after the Norman Conquest, the English language changed profoundly. Little was written in English. While Old English had been the language of the aristocracy during Anglo-Saxon times, after the Norman Conquest, the aristocracy in England spoke—and wrote in—French. Latin was the language for international communication, and educated English people used *Anglo-Norman*, a dialect of French spoken by the Normans, for their daily communication. With French the official language of government and law, English fell into disuse. Anyone who aspired to government office or a profession spoke Anglo-Norman French, and English was regarded as the language of the common folk. If a social-climbing aspirant suddenly used a "crude" English expression, he excused himself by saying, "Pardon my French." England was not the only country where French was the dominant language. In half of the countries of Europe, French was the official language of the royal court from the thirteenth into the eighteenth century.

By 1200, with the dominance of French, English was dying out as a language. One sign of that decay was that English broke up into dialects. One dialect, Northern English, was spoken in the northern part of England; where it spawned another dialect, Scots, that reached up into lower Scotland. Two other dialects were spoken in the middle part of the country—East Midlands and West Midlands. A fourth dialect, Southern English was spoken in the area along the English Channel. A fifth dialect, Kentish, was spoken in the far southeastern corner of England around Canterbury. The differences among these dialects could sometimes be so marked that a person from one part of England could not easily understand someone from another region—a clear sign that a language is dying.

After the Norman Conquest, English became a much simpler language. Complexity in language is often a way to enforce class distinctions. In America today, people who say, "I ain't" or "he don't" mark themselves as uneducated and lower class. In other languages, there are many more subtle distinctions that mark a person as either educated and middle or upper class or uneducated and lower class. German, for example, the language family to which English belongs, is an *inflected* language, which means that words change their spelling depending on how they are used. In German, every noun has a *gender* designated by its definite (*the*) or indefinite (*a* or *an*) article: it is either masculine (Der Mann, Ein Mann), feminine (Die Frau, Eine Fraue) or neuter (Das Haus, Eines Haus).

As if these gender designations weren't hard enough to remember, the definite or indefinite article changes depending on what *case* the noun takes in a particular sentence. If, for example, the noun is in the *nominative case* as the subject of a sentence, it takes one form: *Der* Mann. If, however, the same noun is in the *objective case* as the direct object of a sentence, its article takes a different form: *Den* Mann. But if the noun is in the *dative* case as the object of a preposition (such as beside the man) it takes still a different form: (*Dem* Mann). Finally, if the noun is in the *genitive* or *possessive* case (such as The man's house) it takes yet a different form: *Des* Mann. In English, by contrast, whether the noun is in the nominative, objective, dative, or possessive case, the definite article is always the same, simple *The* Man.

These distinctions in gender and case are so complicated in German that even such simple words as knife (Das Messer), fork (Der Gabel), and spoon (Die Löffel) are different genders—and, thus, take different case endings depending on how they are used in a sentence. I once lived in Austria and struggled to learn German. After asking a friend at a restaurant "Gib mir der Gabel" ("Give me the fork"), only to have him correct me by saying "Gib mir *den* Gabel"), I exploded: "How the hell do Austrian kids learn such complex distinctions?" He smugly replied, "The lower class children don't. The middle- and upper-class parents make sure their children learn all of that. That way, when kids talk, you can tell if they come from lower- or upper- and middle-class families." Similarly, in France, middle-class parents correct their children when they ask for a small loaf of bread, which is feminine ("*une baguette*"), and when they ask for what we would call a crescent roll, which is masculine ("*un croissant*").

As a Germanic language, Old English was full of similar distinctions in the gender and case of nouns. It also, like many other languages, had extremely complicated verb forms, a few of which still exist today, such as *lie* and *lay*. How many people today know that the proper *conjugation* of the verb "to lie" is "I am going to *lie* down today": "I *lay* down yesterday;" "I have *lain* down every afternoon this week"? Again, how many would know that the proper conjugation of the verb "to lay" is "I *lay* the book down;" "Yesterday I *laid* the book down;" "I have *laid* the book down every day for a week"?

Well, you can imagine what happened to all of these complex grammatical distinctions during the centuries after the Norman Conquest when English became the language of the lower classes. Working-class people don't put up with such niceties of grammar as gender and case discriminations or intricate verb conjugations. In the hands of the poor people, over the course of a couple of centuries, Old English lost its gender distinctions and its different case endings. There remained a single definite article, the, though it was pronounced *the* (rhyming with *ha*) before nouns beginning with a consonant ("the pear") and *the* (rhyming with *sea*) before nouns beginning with a vowel ("the apple"). Similarly, there was a single indefinite article, *a* before a noun beginning with a consonant ("a banana") and *an* before a word beginning with a vowel ("an orange"). These articles remained the same whether the nouns they modified were the subjects of a sentence, the direct object, or the object of a preposition. How much simpler could a language be?

About the only remnants of the *inflections* of Old English, where words change to indicate a shift in their syntactic use in a sentence, are in a few pronouns. When we refer to ourselves as the subject of a sentence, for example, we say *I*, but if we are the object of the sentence or the object of a preposition, we say *me*. And, if we refer to ourselves in the possessive case, we say *my* or *mine*. Even these minor inflections confuse speakers of English today, many of whom do not know when to say *I* or *me*. Notice how often people will say "As for myself" or "between you and I," when they should say, "As for me" and "between you and me." It's as if *me* were a dirty word, rather than a grammatically correct pronoun. Such inflections, however, are far more widespread in other languages, making English one of the easiest languages to learn to speak.

Such simplification of noun gender and case, however, came with a price—a price that would deeply constrain poetry in English. Because *the* and *a* no longer indicated whether a noun was a subject, direct object, or object of a preposition in English, our understanding of a noun's function in a sentence usually depends on word order. Most sentences in English follow the word order of *subject-verb-object* (direct object or object of a preposition). For example, in English we would say,

The dog bit *the* man.

In German, one would say,

Der Hund beisst *den* Mann.

However, in German one could also reverse the order of these words without changing the meaning because "Der Hund" indicates that "The dog" is the subject of the sentence and "Den Mann" indicates that "the man" is the direct object of the sentence:

Den Mann beisst *der* Hund.

The sentence still means "The dog bit the man." However, if we say, in English,

The man bit *the* dog

the word order completely changes the meaning of the sentence, because the same definite article, *the*, describes both "The dog" and "The man." While English is a simpler language than German, it is much less flexible in its *syntax* (the way words are arranged in sentences).

Many English poets have longed for the flexibility of languages, such as German, where words can be moved around more freely and where the normal subject-verb-object word order does not threaten to make sentences boringly repetitive. A German poem by Jakob van Hoddis, "Weltende," for example, begins with this line:

Dem Bürger fliegt vom spitzen Kopf der Hut

The line is so wonderfully complex that it cannot be translated literally into English. Loosely it means, "The bourgeois citizen's hat flies off his pointed head." But literally the line begins with "The bourgeois citizen" in the dative case ("Dem Bürger") as the object of the preposition "vom" (from), but we don't get that preposition until after the verb "fliegt" (flies) and the adjective "spitzen Kopf" (pointed head). The subject of the sentence, "der Hut" (the hat), comes at the very end of the line. By so intricately rearranging the normal word order of the line, the poet imitates the sudden disruption of the orderly world of the bourgeois citizen as the wind blows the hat off his pointed head. Poets writing in English could never hope to achieve such intricacy in a language where the meaning of a word depends so heavily on its position in the sentence.

Not much us words around move allow to will the language English.

Thus, what English gained in becoming simpler grammatically after the Norman Conquest was balanced by a loss in flexibility that poets in particular have lamented. Poets have sometimes tried to recapture some of that flexibility through *poetic diction*. A poet might write a line such as "My mind to me a kingdom is," mixing up what we would say, in more straightforward terms as "My mind is a kingdom to me." Such inversion of normal word order sounds more artificial and "poetic." Poets, such as Milton, use poetic diction to create a sonorous grandeur, but their lines run the risk of confusing the reader, because English is not, like German, a language where words can be moved around within a sentence without changing their meaning.

The same gain in simplicity and loss in flexibility can be seen in what happened to verbs as English changed after the Norman Conquest. Most verbs in Old English were what we now call *strong* verbs, because their form changes as we move from present to past to present perfect tense, as in:

I see	I saw	I have seen
I swim	I swam	I have swum
I take	I took	I have taken

Such distinctions were otiose to the common people who used the English language in the centuries after the Norman Conquest. They threw out most of these strong verbs and substituted them with *weak* verbs; their form simply adds –*ed* as they move from present to past to past perfect tense:

I walk	I walked	I have walked
I borrow	I borrowed	I have borrowed
I rent	I rented	I have rented

In Old English, half of the verbs were strong ones; in modern English only 68 of those have survived, and we even call them *irregular verbs*, because they differ from the normal pattern of conjugating verbs by adding "-ed" to indicate past and present perfect tenses.

To get a sense of how verbs became more simplified in the centuries after the Norman Conquest, compare the *conjugation* of a verb in Spanish to a verb in modern English:

Yo hablo	I talk
Tu hablas	You talk
El/ Ella habla	He/She/It talks
Nosotros hablamos	We talk
Vosotros hablais	You talk
Ellas/Ellos hablan	They (feminine)/ They (masculine) talk

Notice that, in Spanish, every verb has a different ending; in English, every verb is "talk" except for the third-person singular "He/She/It talks."

Thus, English became simpler but, again, less rich and varied a language as it evolved from Old English into Middle English during the Middle Ages. Another simplifying change was the loss of vocabulary. Working-class people do not use a lot of abstract, philosophical terms, and such words largely disappeared from English after the Norman Conquest. So, too, did the *synonyms* of the language, words that express the same idea but with a subtly different nuance, such as *happy*, *blithe*, *gay*, *cheerful*, *jocund*, *merry*, *jolly*, gradually dwindle. By 1200 A.D., such changes threatened to make English disappear as a language in a country where the dominant written and officially spoken idiom was still Norman French, and the universal language of theology and scholarship was Latin. Had that happened, those of you who today are native speakers of English would be speakers of French instead.

The Resurgence of the English Language

Just as English was on the verge of dying out as a language, several things happened that revitalized it. For one, the Norman dukes were driven out of Northern France by the French King, though for several centuries afterward, Norman kings of England continued to try to reassert their claims on French territory. Several of Shakespeare's history plays, such as *Henry V*, depict the many years of warfare between the Norman dukes and the French kings. By the end of the thirteenth century, partly inspired by the leadership of Joan of Arc (whom the English captured and burned at the stake), the French drove the Normans out of France. What had once been the colony of the Norman dukes now became their homeland.

At the same time that the Normans were forced out of France, the bubonic plague, the "Black Death," swept across Europe in the mid-1300s. So many people died from the plague in England—between a third and a half of the population in the space of two years—that there were not enough people left who could speak French fluently enough to conduct legal and government affairs. Gradually, law courts and government business were conducted in English, and soon, English reasserted itself over French as the official language of England.

The Black Death also contributed to social upheaval in the Middle Ages. For centuries, under *feudalism*, there had been only two classes: a small aristocracy that owned most of the land and a large peasantry that worked the land. The Black Death killed a great many workers and, thus, made laborers more prized than they had ever been before. The surviving laborers, realizing their new-found worth, left the lands where they had worked, as *serfs*, and offered their services across countryside. Laborers chanted a poetic couplet that challenged the ancient medieval hierarchy:

When Adam delved and Eve span	*When Adam gardened and Eve spun wool*
Who was then the gentleman?	*Who was then an aristocrat?*

Along with these changes in the peasantry, a middle class of merchants, bankers, and other business people began to emerge that would further transform European life by substituting the manufacture, sale, and trade of goods for money over the medieval pattern of growing, making, and bartering for goods.

The French Influence on English Poetry

Although it ceased to be the official language of England, French left its mark on English poetry. In Anglo-Saxon poetry, the poetic line was formed by *accent*, *alliteration*, and *caesura*; in French poetry, the line was formed by *meter*—each line was measured by having exactly the same number of syllables—and *rhyme*, so that each line ended in a word that rhymed (had the same terminal vowel and consonant sounds) with a word at the end of another poetic line, such as "*round*" and "*found*."

English poetry absorbed this French influence in various ways, but the most enduring was to create a poetic line that combined both English *accentual rhythm* with French *meter* and *rhyme*. On the one hand, the English poetic line now, like French poetry, had a fixed number of syllables. But these syllables were measured in *metrical feet* that involved rhythmically accented and unaccented syllables. The most common rhythm in English poetry was *iambic,* where an unaccented syllable is followed by an accented syllable:

*Is **this** the **face** that **launched** a **thou**-sand **ships**?*

This line is from Renaissance playwright Christopher Marlowe's *The Tragical History of Doctor Faustus* and is uttered by Faust when, having sold his soul to the devil, he gets the love of Helen of Troy, the most beautiful woman who ever lived and whose beauty sparked the Trojan War. Notice that the *iambic rhythm* of alternating unstressed and stressed syllables sounds like perfectly natural English speech. The rhythm is the same as it would be in many everyday English sentences:

I **went** to **town** to **buy** my-**self** a **car**

Yet when this rhythmic pattern continues on throughout a poem, it assumes an elegance and grandeur that lifts poetry above ordinary speech.

This iambic rhythm is *metrical,* because in each line of poetry, there are *five iambic feet*. An *iambic foot* is one pair of unaccented and accented syllables: "Is **this**." Such a *foot* is also called an *iamb*. When a poet writes an iambic line of ten syllables—five iambic *feet*—it is called an *iambic pentameter line*. "Pentameter" is taken from the Greek word for "five" (as is "pentagon") and means that the meter of the line consists of five iambic feet (five *iambs*). We can divide Marlowe's line into five iambic feet by putting slashes after each *iamb*:

iamb/   iamb/   iamb/   iamb/   iamb
*Is **this**/ the **face**/ that **launched**/ a **thou**-/sand **ships***

Poets also write lines of different *metrical lengths*. The lines may be in iambic *monometer* (one iambic foot), iambic *dimeter* (two iambic feet), but the most common metrical lines are iambic *trimeter* (three iambic feet), iambic *tetrameter* (four iambic feet), and of course, *iambic pentameter*. One of the oldest and most popular forms of poetry in English is the **ballad**, which alternates lines of *iambic tetrameter* with lines of *iambic trimeter*:

Should **auld**/ ac-**quain**-/tance **be**/ for-**got**
And ne-/ver **brought**/ to **mind**?

Of course, good poets would never write a poem where every line followed the exact same accentual rhythm. As with everything in life, varying a pattern makes for artfulness. A baseball pitcher would never throw a fastball on every pitch but would vary fastballs with curveballs, sliders, and change-ups.

So, too, poets vary the usual line of iambic feet by *metrical substitution*—substituting an iamb with a different metrical foot, such as a *trochee* (which reverses the iambic pattern by having an accented foot followed by an unaccented foot):

Trochee/trochee
Jen-ny/ **kissed** me

Another way a poet can vary the iambic meter is with a *spondee*, a two-syllable foot where both syllables are accented:

Spondee / spondee
Birds sang/ **road hog**

and a *pyrrhic* foot, where neither syllable is accented:

pyrrhic/ spondee   pyrrhic/spondee
by the/ **sea shore**   if it/ **stops here**

Two other metrical feet poets use to vary the iambic rhythm are *anapestic* and *dactylic* feet. Like *iambs* and *trochees*, *anapests* and *dactyls* are opposites: an anapest consists of two unaccented syllables followed by an accented syllable:

anapest   anapest   anapest   anapest
Not a **crea**-/ture was **stir**-/ing not **ev**-/en a **mouse**

A dactyl consists of an accented syllable followed by two unaccented syllables:

dactyl   dactyl
Wad-ing through/ **Whis**-per-ing

If you learn these six basic metrical feet—iambic, trochaic, pyrrhic, spondaic, anapestic, and dactylic—you will be able to appreciate the way most poets use *metrical variation* to enhance the meaning of a poem.

Let's, for example, take one of Shakespeare's most famous sonnets, sonnet number seventy-three, to see how he starts out with three lines of regular iambic pentameter to talk to someone he loves about growing old, comparing himself to a tree in autumn:

That **time**/ of **year**/ thou **may'st**/ in **me**/ be-**hold**
When **yel**-/low **leaves**,/ or **few**,/ or **none**/ do **hang**
Up-**on**/ those **boughs**/ that **shake**/ a-**gainst**/ the **cold**

In the fourth line, however, Shakespeare varies his meter for emotional emphasis:

Bare, ru-/ined **choirs**,/ where **late/** the **sweet/ birds sang**.

He starts the line with a *spondee* instead of an *iamb* and, after three iambic feet, concludes with another spondee. Can you see how the spondees intensify the poet's feeling that his life is slowing down, like the tree that loses its leaves and where birds no longer perch on branches to sing as choir boys do as they sit on their pews in church?

Anonymous Medieval Ballads

The formal pattern of the *ballad* emerged among the common people in the centuries after the Norman Conquest, primarily in the "borderlands" of Northern England and Southern Scotland. For many centuries, the English and Scottish ballads were not written down but, instead, were passed along, generation after generation, as songs preserved in an oral tradition. Only in the late eighteenth century, when scholars and writers took an interest in these old ballads, were their words and music written down, along with the variations that had developed over the centuries. Many of the ballads migrated with settlers to America, where they continue to be performed today in such regions as Appalachia.

Many of these old ballads were written in the *ballad form*. That is, they consisted of four-line units, *quatrains*, of alternating lines of *iambic tetrameter* (four iambic feet per line) and lines of *iambic trimeter* (three iambic feet per line). Their rhyme scheme was *abxb* (only the second and fourth lines rhymed), and they drew on the Anglo-Saxon formal traditions of alliteration and caesura.

Ballads were *narrative* poems that told stories. Ballads told their stories quickly and dramatically, omitting the kind of detail we are used to in contemporary storytelling. Many ballads are told largely through dialogue, so that they resemble miniature plays. Even when they are told by a narrator, that narrator seldom comments on the meaning of the story but instead presents it objectively.

Some ballads seem to have been based on actual, historical incidents, such as "Sir Patrick Spens," which may have been about a wedding between a Scottish princess and a Scandinavian prince that required Scottish royalty to sail to Norway across the North Sea during the dangerous winter season. The poem uses the ballad quatrain, but as with much folk poetry, the form is not handled elegantly. The first quatrain consists of alternating lines of iambic tetrameter and iambic trimeter, but with some interesting metrical variations, rhyming *abxb*:

> The **king**/ **sits** in/ Dum-**fer**-/line **town**,
>   **Drink**-ing/ the **blude**-/red **wine**: *blood-red wine*
> "O **whar**/ will I **get**/ a **guid**/ **sai**-lor
>   To **sail**/ this **ship**/ of **mine**.

Can you spot the metrical variations in the first three lines (only the fourth line is perfectly iambic)? Can you also hear the alliteration from Anglo-Saxon poetry in the many "d" sounds of the first two lines? No one knows how the ballad quatrain evolved after the Norman Conquest, but one theory is that it took the traditional poetic line of Old English poetry, with its alliterated accentual beats, and split it into tetrameter and trimeter lines. Where an Anglo-Saxon poet might have written:

The king sits in *Dum*ferline *town*,/ *Drink*ing the blu*de* red wine

The Middle English poet, under the influence of French rhyme and meter, divides that Anglo-Saxon line into two separate tetrameter and trimeter lines:

The king sits in Dumferline town
Drinking the blude-red wine

Here is the ballad in full from one of its many oral versions:

Sir Patrick Spens

The king sits in Dumferling toune,
    Drinking the blude-reid wine:
'O whar will I get guid sailor,
    To sail this schip of mine?'

Up and spak an eldern knicht,   *up spoke an elderly knight*   5
    Sat at the kings richt kne:
'Sir Patrick Spence is the best sailor
    That sails upon the se.'

The king has written a braid letter,   *a sweeping, commanding letter*
    And signd it wi his hand,   10
And sent it to Sir Patrick Spence,
    Was walking on the sand.

The first line that Sir Patrick red,
    A loud lauch lauched he;   *a loud laugh laughed he*
The next line that Sir Patrick red,   15
    The teir blinded his ee.   *The tear blinded his eye*

O wha is this has don this deid,   *O who has done this deed*
    This ill deid don to me,
To send me out this time o' the yeir,
    To sail upon the se!   20

'Mak hast, mak haste, my mirry men all,
    Our guid schip sails the morne:'
'O say na sae, my master deir,   *Oh, say not so, my master dear*
    For I feir a deadlie storme.

'Late late yestreen I saw the new moone,   *yesterday evening*   25
    Wi' the auld moone in hir arme,
And I feir, I feir, my deir master,
    That we will cum to harme.'

O our Scots nobles wer richt laith	*right loath (reluctant)*	
To weet their cork-heild schoone;	*To wet their cork-heeled shoes*	30
Bot lang owre a' the play wer playd,	*before things played out*	
Their hats they swam aboone.	*Their hats swam above them*	
O lang, lang may their ladies sit,		
Wi' thair gold kems in their hand,	*combs*	
Waiting for their ain dear lords	*own dear husbands*	35
Cum sailing to the land.		
O lang, lang may the ladies stand,		
Wi' thair gold kems in their hair,		
Waiting for thair ain deir lords,		
For they'll se thame na mair.		40
Haf owre, haf owre to Aberdour,	*Half over (the sea) to Aberdeen*	
It's fiftie fadom deip,	*It's fifty fathoms deep*	
And thair lies guid Sir Patrick Spence,		
Wi' the Scots lords at his feit.		ca. 1300

Notice how deftly the story is told in this ballad. Although Patrick Spens carries the title "Sir," he is clearly subservient to the King of Scotland and must do as the King commands. The "eldern knicht" who suggests to the King that Sir Patrick Spens sail the ship through the stormy winter seas may be someone who respects Sir Patrick's abilities as a sailor, but he may also be someone who wants to send Sir Patrick on a suicide mission. Although he sees how foolhardy the order to sail in winter is, Sir Patrick accepts the King's command as his duty.

The middle part of the poem, quatrains five through seven, is rendered through *dialogue*; this is typical of ballads, which often tell their stories through conversations among characters. Another characteristic of ballads is that they bring in elements of the *supernatural*, such as the sailor who warns Sir Patrick, in the seventh quatrain, of the ominous position of the moon.

In the eighth quatrain, the narrator of the poem provides more commentary about what happens in the poem than we usually get in ballads. The narrator notes, with grim humor, that as the Scottish nobility boarded Sir Patrick's vessel, they were "richt laith" to get their fancy shoes (with heels of wooden cork) wet. But, the narrator tells us, in a foreshadowing of the tragedy, in the end, these nobles drowned, and their hats swam above them.

Then, in quatrain nine, the narrator suddenly cuts away from Sir Patrick's ship, and the nobles who have boarded it. Similar to the way one scene cuts to another in a modern film, we see the wives of the nobles waiting for their husbands to return from the voyage. In a repeated phrase (another characteristic of ballads was just such use of repetition), "O lang, lang," we learn that the husbands are never coming back to their wives, who wait—in another concrete image, "Wi' their gold kembs in their hair"—to entice husbands who never will return.

In the last quatrain, the narrator comes closest to expressing a protest against a society where people in lower classes must obey those in the upper classes. At the bottom of the sea near Aberdeen, where Sir Patrick's ship has sunk, the nobles he was transporting now, in death, lie at his feet in a reversal of the social order. While Sir Patrick has heroically undertaken a mission that he knew would lead to his death, the nobles meet their death as an unexpected accident.

Not all ballads are written in *ballad quatrains*. Here is a ballad that uses *couplets* (two adjacent lines that rhyme) rather than the ballad quatrain. Notice how several of the rhymes are not true but *off-rhymes* or *near-rhymes* ("back" and "lake"). "The Three Ravens" also uses a nonsensical *refrain*—repeated phrases ("*Down a down, hay down, hay down*") after or between the lines of each couplet. Again, remember that these ballads were sung, so such refrains function in the same way the phrase "Fa-la-la-la-la-la-la-la-la" does in the Christmas carol "Deck the Halls." As oral works, the ballads would often be sung to an audience by a wandering minstrel, and the audience would join in on the refrain.

The Three Ravens

There were three ravens sat on a tree,
    Down a down, hey down, hey down,
They were as black as black might be,
With a down, derry, derry, derry down, down

The one of them said to his mate,   5
"Where shall we our breakfast take?
With a down, derry, derry, derry down, down

"Down in yonder green field,
Down, a down, hey down, hey down,
There lies a knight slain 'neath his shield,   10
With a down, derry, derry, derry, down, down.

"His hounds they lie down at his feet,
So well they do their master keep,
With a down, derry, derry, derry down, down.

"His hawks they fly so eagerly,   (fiercely, protectively)   15
    Down a down, hey down, hey down,
No other fowl dare come him nigh."
With a down, derry, derry, derry, down, down.

Down there comes a fallow doe   fallow (reddish brown)
As great with young as might she go   (pregnant woman) walk   20
With a down, derry, derry, derry down, down

She lift up his bloody head,
    Down a down, hey down, hey down,
And kissed his wounds that were so red,
With a down, derry, derry, derry, down, down..   25

She got him up upon her back,
And carried him to earthen lake,   hole in the earth (grave)
With a down, derry, derry, derry down, down

She buried him before the prime   (first hour of the morning)
    Down a down, hey down, hey down,   30

She was dead herself ere e'en-song time, *time for evening prayers*
With a down, derry, derry, derry, down, down..

God send every gentleman,
Such hawks, such hounds, and such a leman. *such a lover*
With a down, derry, derry, derry down, down   ca. 1300

Notice that the early couplets consist of dialogue among the three ravens, who would like to swoop down and eat the dead knight but are afraid to do so, because his body is protected by his hunting dogs and hawks (medieval knights often carried trained hawks or falcons). At line nineteen ("Down there comes a fallow doe"), however, we leave the dialogue of the three ravens and go back to the voice of the narrator who opened the poem by telling us, "There were three ravens sat on a tree." Just as the knight's dogs and hawks remain loyal to him after death, so does what seems to be his "leman" (lady love), portrayed as a deer, who kisses his bloody wounds and carries him off for burial, an effort since she is pregnant ("great with young"), that brings on her own death. Why do you think the poet chose to start the story with a line by the narrator, shift to the dialogue among the three ravens, then return to the narrator for the latter half of the poem?

This next ballad, "The Twa Corbies" (Scottish for "The Two Crows"), follows the form of the ballad quatrain more closely. It is thought to be a song produced not by the common folk (note the absence of a refrain, such as that of "The Three Ravens") but a sophisticated rebuttal to "The Three Ravens." Can you see what makes it more sophisticated in both theme and form? Notice that, like "The Three Ravens," the poem opens with a narrator who says "As I was walking all alane," but after shifting to the dialogue between the two ravens, the ballad never returns to the voice of the narrator. Why do you think the poet decided to leave almost the entire poem to the dialogue between the two ravens?

The Twa Corbies

As I was walking all alane,
I heard twa corbies makin a mane;   *moan (complaint)*
The tane unto the ither say,   *one unto the other*
"Whar sall we gang and dine the-day?"   *go and dine today*

"In ahint yon auld fail dyke,   *Beyond the old turf ditch*   5
I wot there lies a new slain knight;   *I know that*
And nane do ken that he lies there,   *None knows*
But his hawk, his hound an his lady fair."

"His hound is tae the huntin gane,   *has gone hunting on his own*
His hawk tae fetch the wild-fowl hame,   *fetch wild fowl (prey) home*   10
His lady's tain anither mate,   *taken another mate (lover)*
So we may mak oor dinner swate."   *our dinner sweet*

"Ye'll sit on his white hause-bane,   *neck bone*
And I'll pike oot his bonny blue een;   *pick out his pretty blue eyes*
Wi ae lock o his gowden hair   *one lock of his golden hair*   15
We'll theek oor nest when it grows bare."   *thatch (patch) our nest*

"Mony a one for him makes mane,   *Many a one (many people)*
But nane sall ken whar he is gane;   *none shall know*
Oer his white banes, whan they are bare,   *bones*
The wind sall blaw for evermair."   ca. 1300

Some readers find this poem a brutal portrait of how nature violates human ideals of fidelity, selflessness, and charity. But, other readers see it as a grim but admirable depiction of how life goes on after death as the birds feed on the dead knight and use his hair to feather their nests. Which reading seems more reasonable to you, given the tone of the dialogue between the two birds?

Narrative Form in the Medieval Ballads

Thus far, we have concentrated on the *poetic* form of the Medieval ballads. What do you notice about their *narrative and dramatic form*—how are they presented as *stories*? One obvious feature of their narrative form is that the stories they present are very short. What, for example, is left out of the ballads—what kind of details, description, information, etc.? How many of the really gripping events of the stories take place *before* the ballad begins?

The Medieval ballads give us the best sense of how poetry emerged from oral cultures. Many of them seem to have started out as communal songs of the folk, but then individual singers/poets emerged to give the stories and songs a distinctive narrative structure. Within that structure, however, the role of the rural community was retained in the refrains, where the audience joined in with the poet songster. The songster, for example, would sing the first line of "The Three Ravens"—"There were three ravens sat on a tree"—then the communal audience would join in on the refrain—"*Down a down, hey down, hey down.*" The repetitive form of many ballads reflects their origins in oral culture, where formulaic phrases—called *commonplaces*—recur within a ballad and even across several ballads.

Anonymous Medieval Lyrics

While medieval ballads are *narrative* poems that tell a story, medieval *lyrics* are poems that do not narrate a story but simply express the poet's feelings. While the narrator in a narrative ballad is usually an objective storyteller, the poet in a medieval lyrical poem is more openly emotional. Here is one of the most famous of the Medieval lyrics, by a poet who remains anonymous, that uses the *ballad quatrain*:

Western Wind

Westron wind, when wilt thou blow?
The small rain down can rain.
Christ, that my love were in my arms,
And I in my bed again.   ca. 1300

As short and simple as this poem is, it is quite sophisticated in theme and form. If you look back at a map of England, you will see that the southwestern part of the country juts into the Atlantic Ocean. The Gulf Current flows northward and eastward from the Gulf of Mexico, bringing warm water—and warm air—from the tropics so that the southwestern parts of England—and even of Scotland—are warm enough to support palm trees. In a country that is cold and damp during the winter months, the "western wind" from the Gulf Current brings spring zephers (from the Greek name for the god Zephyrus, who was the warm west wind).

Thus, this poet, rather than celebrating the arrival of spring, longs for the western wind to come so that the gentle "small rain" (as opposed to cold, harsh winter rains) can warm the land. After voicing that longing for seasonal renewal in the first two lines, the poet suddenly couples it with an agonized cry—half plea, half curse—for something that probably cannot come again—the return of a lost love and the warm joys of love-making. The first two lines long for a natural renewal that always, eventually comes; the last two lines long for a human renewal that time usually denies us.

The form of the poem is also subtly sophisticated. It is primarily in iambic rhythm, but the first line starts off without an unaccented syllable so that the very first syllable is accented:

West/-ron **wind**,

After the caesura after "wind," the rhythm is regular iambic:

when **wilt**/ thou **blow**?

Can you see that the abrupt opening with the accent on "**West**-ron" gives the poet's appeal an immediacy and anguish that would be lost if the first line was purely—and sing-song-like—iambic:

Oh **West/**-/ron **wind**/ when **wilt**/ thou **blow**?

The metrical variation is even more pronounced in the second line (remember that important words, such as nouns, adjectives, and main verbs usually take an accent):

The **small**/ **rain down**/ can **rain**

Here, the first foot is an iamb, the second a spondee, and the third another iamb. Then the third line starts off with a powerful trochee, followed by an iamb, then a pyrrhic foot, and ends in an iamb:

Christ, that/ my **love**/ were in/ my **arms**

Then, the real metrical razzle-dazzle comes in the fourth line, which starts off with an iamb, followed by—of all things—an anapest, then ends with another iamb:

And **I**/ in my **bed**/ a-**gain.**

Can you see—and, rhythmically, **feel**—the power metrical variation gives to the poet's desperate but futile longing? Compare how weak the line would be if it were simply three iambic feet:

And **I**/ in **bed**/ a-**gain**

"Western Wind" is written in a form that is one of the most enduring in the history of poetry—the *ballad quatrain*. For all of its metrical variation, it is basically written in iambic rhythm. The first and third lines have four iambic feet, making them lines of *iambic tetrameter*. The second and fourth lines have three iambic feet, making them lines of *iambic trimeter*.

The *rhyme scheme* follows this metrically alternating pattern, with the first and third lines ending on words that do not rhyme, while the second and fourth lines end in rhymes. Thus, the rhyme scheme would be:

blow	*a*
rain	*b*
arms	*x* (*x* denotes the absence of a rhyme for *a*)
a-gain	*b*

This form represents a merger of French and English poetic traditions. We have seen how the poem, in the French manner, uses regular metrical rhythm and some rhyme. It also goes back to Anglo-Saxon poetry in its use of alliteration:

Western wind, when wilt thou blow?

Notice that the *ou* sound in "thou" has the same sound as "w," so watch for alliteration in poetry even when the letters are different ("gain" and "cane," for example, start with the same consonant sound, even though their letters are different). *Alliteration* describes words that start with the same consonant sound, but those consonant sounds can recur within and at the end of words. When they do, as in "thou" and "blow," it is called *consonance*.

Like Anglo-Saxon poetry, too, "Western Wind" uses *caesura*. In the first line, the caesura, marked by a comma, comes after the third syllable. In the third line, it comes after the first syllable. Again, think of musical repetition and variation as a way of giving form to a poem.

The French—and Latin—Influence on the English Language

In the three centuries after the Norman Conquest, most writing in England was done in French, the language of the Norman conquerors, or Latin, the international language of religion, politics, and scholarship. Virtually no literature was written in English. Before English could, again, become a vehicle for literature, it would have to overcome the losses it had suffered under the Norman Conquest. While Middle English had become a simpler, more streamlined language than Old English, it had lost a great deal.

For one thing, as we have seen, it had broken up into dialects, so that people living in one part of England might not be able to understand people living in other parts of England. People living in Northern England, near the Scottish border, for example, spoke a dialect called "Northern English," which was different from the dialect of people living in the middle of the country. Even there, people in the Midwest of England spoke in the "West Midlands" dialect, while people in the Mideast of England, near London, spoke "East Midlands." In the southern part of the country, people spoke "Southern" English, while in the far eastern corner, in the county of Kent, they spoke "Kentish." Thus, while in Old English, one would say a person *lufoð* somebody, in the northern dialect of Middle English, one would say he or she *loves*; in the Midland dialect, *loven*; and in the southern dialect *loveth*. In order for English to become a major vehicle for literature, these dialects would have to give way to a single, standard form of English.

The second problem for the English language, which we have also seen, was that, during the centuries after the Norman Conquest, its vocabulary shrank. The common people who spoke English had little need of abstract, philosophical words. If English was to become a literary language, however, it would also need to expand its vocabulary. From where were the new words to come? Given the dominance of French after the Norman Conquest, many French words, more than 10,000, were simply adopted into English. Since French had been the language of government and law, many of these were political and legal terms: (*parliament, assembly, state, tax, treaty, tariff; advocate, jurisprudence, warrant*). But French words were also adapted for literature and the arts (*beauty, color, figure, story*), as well as religion and philosophy (*communion, confession, faith, mystery, virtue*).

French words, to the English ear, sounded more *elegant*, *chic* and had more *cachet*. Thus while English farmers raised *cows*, *calves*, *sheep*, and *pigs*, when they sat down to eat, they preferred to say they dined on *beef*, *veal*, *mutton*, and *pork*—all words derived from French. The influence of French as a more mellifluous language also softened the guttural pronunciations of many English words. While the *ough* sound would have been harsh in Old English, sounding more like "Ugh"), it gradually softened so that the same combination of letters is pronounced differently in such words as *cough*, *though*, *through*, and *ought*.

Latin was the other language that enriched the vocabulary of English with such abstract and scientific words as *astronomy, conspiracy, genius, history, infancy, intellect, mechanical, nervous, picture, private,* and *solitary*. Thus, English, which in its earliest years had borrowed words from the Vikings' Old Norse (*dirt, food, kill*), became even more of a mongrel language with these borrowings from French and Latin. As time went on, it would absorb words from Greek (*orchestra*), Spanish (*galleon*), Dutch (*dock*), Hindo (*ketchup*), and many other languages. Today, as a result of such borrowings, English has the largest vocabulary of any language.

Those borrowings make English a wonderful language for writers, because almost every word has several *synonyms*. A hero, for example, might be described as *bold* (English), *valiant* (French), or *audacious* (Latin). Someone can *ask* (English), *question* (French), or *interrogate* (Latin). If your writing teacher advises you to use fewer words when you write, she can tell you to be *terse, pithy, concise, succinct,* or *laconic*—all words that mean the same general idea but with shades and nuances derived from their French, Latin, Anglo-Saxon, or Old Norse roots. English is also a wonderfully innovative language. When a new invention comes along, such as the *car* (or *automobile*), English can name its various parts by drawing on Latin (*transmission, radiator*), French (*carburetor, chassis*), and Anglo-Saxon and Old Norse (*clutch, brake*).

The Rebirth of Drama in the Middle Ages

While classical drama came to an end with the fall of the Roman Empire, some forms of popular theatrical entertainment continued during the Middle Ages. Acrobats, puppeteers, jugglers, and animal trainers with bears and monkeys traveled across Europe, giving informal performances wherever they could gather a crowd. At first, the Christian church attacked such performances just as it had banned Christians from attending the licentious Roman theaters. Gradually, however, leaders of the church realized that common people would be edified by acting out *liturgical drama*—brief plays that illustrated scenes from the life of Christ or Bible stories from the Old Testament.

Such liturgical dramas initially were presented in church services at Easter. The priest might stand before the church altar in a white robe as the angel before Christ's tomb. He'd ask, in Latin, "Whom seek ye?" of three altar boys pretending to be the three Marys who visited Christ's tomb on the first Easter morning. They would say, in unison, "We seek Jesus of Nazareth, the crucified." Then the priest would say, "He is not here. He has risen again as He foretold. Go, announce that He is risen from the dead." Then, the priest and choirboys would lead the congregation in an Easter hymn.

As simple as such dramas were, they had a profound effect upon the congregation. The Christian church, which had once banned drama, would give this literary form new life, just as in ancient Greece, religious celebrations of the god Dionysus gave rise to tragedy and comedy.

The Form of Medieval Drama

But the form of medieval drama differed sharply from that of Greek drama. Instead of being presented on a stage in a public theater, these liturgical dramas were first presented inside a church and then in the outdoor churchyard area. As the pageants got longer, they portrayed several different events in the life of Christ, such as his trial before Pontius Pilate, his crucifixion, and his resurrection on Easter morning. Plays that depicted stories from the Old Testament might shift from Noah's ark to Daniel in the lion's den to David and Goliath. Such shifts in time and place made the church or churchyard a much more flexible "stage" than the Greek stage, which was always the same place and where action took place in the same time that it took to perform it—adhering to Aristotle's "unities" of place and time.

Just as Greek drama shifted from performances by priests of Dionysus to professional actors, the liturgical drama of the medieval Christian church was taken up by members of the various guilds of medieval craftsmen. These craftsmen would perform brief Biblical dramas in English, rather than Latin, and their plays reflected their craft. Ship builders, for example, would portray the story of Noah's Ark, carpenters would do a pageant about the building of the Tower of Babel, fishermen would act out Jonah and the whale. Each guild would use a cart as its stage and would pull the cart around to perform its little play before one group of people after another. Such performances built up a theatrical convention different from that of ancient Greece—that the stage could represent different places and different times.

At certain religious holidays, there might even be a whole *cycle* of short plays that spanned the whole of time from the Creation through Noah's flood, the life of Christ, and the Second Coming, replete with "devils" throwing the damned into the pit of hell that blacksmiths could make belch fire and brimstone. The craftsmen in these guilds also added bits of comedy not in the Bible, such as Noah, when his wife stubbornly refuses to get into ark, carrying her aboard, kicking and screaming.

The form of such dramas had none of the Aristotelian unities of place, time, or **a**ction. The stage could be various different places; the stories could make huge leaps in time; and the action was not plotted, with one event causing the next, but *episodic*, where one scene had little to do with the scenes that preceded or followed it. It was this form of drama that flourished in the Middle Ages and influenced the drama of William Shakespeare and other playwrights of the Renaissance.

Chapter 3
Renaissance Literature

The Renaissance

The fifteenth century was one of the most tumultuous in English history. The Norman-English kings continued to fight wars to maintain their lands in Normandy, but they were eventually driven out of France. There were also internal wars, The Wars of the Roses, over control of the English throne by the dynastic *houses* (noble families) of Lancaster and York. Shakespeare wrote several plays, such as *Richard II*, *Henry IV*, and *Richard III*, about the military and political upheaval of the era. The mascot of the House of York was the white rose; that of the House of Lancaster the red rose. To this day in England, because of the memory of those wars, one never gives a bouquet of mixed red and white roses. Finally, in 1485, the bloody Wars of the Roses ended with the defeat of Richard III by the man who would become Henry VII and establish a new dynastic line, the House of Tudor, whose descendants would rule England for more than a hundred years.

With the ascension of Tudor monarchs came other changes that mark the gradual shift from the Middle Ages to the period we call the Renaissance. The printing press had been created by Johannes Gutenberg in 1436 and introduced into England in 1476 by William Caxton. The advent of printing would eventually change the form of creative writing. One estimate is that while barely thirty percent of English people could read in the fifteenth century, that number doubled by the early sixteenth century.

When writers came to realize that they were addressing their work to *readers* rather than *listeners*, it would profoundly change the form of their writing. Even though writers, such as Chaucer, wrote down their works and had them copied by hand, those manuscripts were still often read aloud to groups of people rather than read by individual readers. Given the expense and rarity of hand-written manuscripts, there were very few people who had the ability to read them, let alone afford to own them. Literature, therefore, was still largely an *oral* art form, as it had been since primitive times. Writers had to write in such a way that their meaning could be grasped at first hearing; when they began to write for readers, who could pause and reread certain passages, writers could write with more intricacy and subtlety.

Another change that led Europe from the Middle Ages to the Renaissance was the fall of Constantinople to the Turks in 1453. Constantinople (today named Istanbul) was the capital of the eastern half of the Roman Empire (sometimes called the Byzantine Empire). Even after the collapse of Rome and the fall of the western half of the Roman Empire, the Byzantine Empire continued to flourish. With the fall of Constantinople, however, Greek scholars fled to Western Europe. With them, they brought Greek manuscripts by writers such as Plato and Sophocles who had been forgotten in Western Europe since the fall of Rome.

Beginning in Italy, but quickly spreading to the rest of Europe (and helped by the invention of printing), the translation, publication, and circulation of ancient Greek philosophy, literature, and science helped revitalize Europe. Renaissance humanism (or, as it was sometimes called, "The New Learning" and after the introduction of the teachings of the Greek philosopher Plato into Western Europe, "NeoPlatonism") challenged the medieval ideas that the Christian Church had promulgated for centuries. Instead of the medieval emphasis upon preparation for life after death, humanism stressed the Greek celebration of life. In place of the medieval view of humanity as tainted by original sin, humanism, again harking back to ancient Greece, celebrated humanity in mind, body, and spirit. And, where the Middle Ages thought in terms of faith and the authority of the Christian Church, humanism stressed the importance of science, reason, and individual thought.

As the literary historian Martin S. Day has written (albeit at a time when writers used "man" and the pronoun "he" almost exclusively to refer to all people, men and women alike):[7]

> Probably the most "modern" of the Renaissance traits was its spirit of optimism and dynamism. No longer need men give at least lip service to the statement that this life was no more than a "vale of tears." The Renaissance emphasized the goodness and fullness of life. Men of this era were aware that change was rife. Western society had experienced no such vivid sensation since the fall of ancient Rome, a time of dire troubles and apparent retrogression. Now, in the Renaissance, man could feel a vigorous change, and a change for the better. However, because the humanists idolized antiquity and saw themselves as reaching once more upward toward its grandeur, this sense of change did not contain in it the idea of progress, a concept largely instituted by the 18th century and dominant in the 19th century.

Along with the spread of humanism, the world of the Middle Ages was breaking up as the feudal social order of aristocratic landowners and laboring serfs and peasants was giving way to a rising middle class. Cities grew, where commerce, rather than agriculture, drove economic development, and the mayors of London, such as Dick Whittington, were businessmen rather than land-owning aristocrats. The wool produced by English sheep was manufactured into cloth that was exported to other European countries as trade developed between England and the Continent, trade carried out by a growing fleet of merchant ships. The world itself seemed to be changing as Columbus reached America, and the Portuguese navigator Vasco de Gama found a sea route to the Far East by sailing around Africa. From trade with the Far East came such imports as gunpowder, so that soldiers with pistols and rifles replaced medieval knights in armor with swords and lances.

The English Language in the Fifteenth Century

Just as English, after nearly dying out as a language, became the standard spoken language of England during the Renaissance, it also became the standard language for writing in the country. Until then, most scholarly, religious, and scientific writing was in Latin, since that was a language that scholars, clergy, and scientists all across Europe could understand. While Latin would remain the international language of Europe for at least another century (Isaac Newton would publish his

---

[7] Martin S. Day, *History of English Literature to 1660* Garden City, NY: Doubleday & Company, Inc., 1963), p. 147.

scientific findings in Latin as *Principia Mathematica* in the eighteenth century), the spirit of Renaissance humanism inspired the translation of the great classical Latin and Greek writers into English.

Although Latin continued to develop as a language during the Middle Ages, it was no longer a widely-spoken language and, thus, did not maintain its vitality. As a "dead" language—one that did not grow and change through widespread use—it could not develop in response to new discoveries, new ideas, new inventions. With the Protestant Reformation, moreover, Latin was associated with Roman Catholic "popery," and Protestant countries, such as England and Germany, debated religious issues in their own national language rather than in Latin.

As Latin receded in importance, more of its words were absorbed by English, such as *axis*, *climax*, *epitome*, *index*, *major*, *minor*, and *pauper*. Latin words, such as *consultare* and *exoticus*, were anglicized by cutting off their inflections to create *consult* and *exotic*. By a similar process of adaptation, Latin *sanitas* became *sanity* and *susceptibilis* became *susceptible*. Given the Renaissance humanists' adoration of all things Greek, many Greek words were adopted into English, such as *athlete*, *autonomous*, *comedy*, *comma*, *drama*, *dialogue*, *emphasis*, *epic*, *gymnastics*, *hyphen*, *idiom*, *paragraph*, *period*, *poetry*, *rhythm*, *stadium*, *synonym*, and *trophy*.

As it had done throughout the Middle Ages, English continued to absorb words from French during the Renaissance: *alloy*, *duel*, *entrance*, *mustache*, *tomato*, *volunteer*. Through England's ongoing conflicts with Catholic Spain and Portugal, both in Europe and in the New World, English absorbed such words as *alligator*, *banana*, *cannibal*, *hurricane*, *mosquito*, *potato*, and *tobacco*. From Italy, the cultural center of the Renaissance, English took *balcony*, *design*, *granite*, *stanza*, *volcano*, and many other words. Other Italian words, such as *bankrupt*, *gala*, and *infantry*, and other Spanish words, such as *cavalier* and *grenade*, entered the English language through French.

While purists maintained that Latin should remain the official language of intellectual writing, most writers embraced these growing changes in English as exciting and vigorous. All in all, the Renaissance was an exciting, even intoxicating, time to be a writer whose medium, the English language, was bursting at its seams.

English Spelling

Because of the adoption of so many foreign words into English, the spelling of English words has long been illogical. The fact that these changes occurred at the same time printing was developed has preserved all sorts of irregular spellings. Into the 1600s, a writer might spell our modern word *fellow* as *felowe*, *fallow*, or *fallowe*. By the end of the 1600s, the spelling of English words had become standardized, though even today, dictionaries give alternative spellings for such words as *gullible* and *gullable*, and Americans spell the British *colour* as *color*.

As spelling became more regularized, however, it also grew more confusing. The scholars who helped regularize English spelling were great admirers of Latin, and they often tried to spell English words in ways that were similar to the way the same words were spelled in Latin. In Chaucer's time, for example, our modern word *debt* was spelled, more simply, *dette*. Where did the "b" come from? Scholars felt that, because in Latin, the word was *debitum*, in English it should have a "b." While we do not hear the "b" in *debt*, it is pronounced in *debit*. Similarly, because the word for *island* in Latin is *insula*, English scholars thought that there should be an "s" in *island*, even though it has never been pronounced.

For all of these reasons, many words in our language are not spelled the way they are pronounced. While non-native speakers find English an easy language to learn grammatically (largely because, as we have seen, it has fewer *inflections* than other languages), it is a nightmare for them to learn how to spell its words. Even those of us who are native speakers of English found this to be true in grade school. Many of us competed in "spelling bees" because of the quirky nature of English spelling. Even some of the little rules we learned, such *"I before E except after C,"* might help us spell *believe* and *receive*, but they break down when we come to a word such as *foreign*.

Tudor England under Henry VIII

King Henry VII, who established the Tudor dynasty in 1485, was succeeded in 1509 by Henry VIII, probably the most notorious of England's kings. In his reign of nearly forty years, England enjoyed stability, peace, and prosperity. On the continent of Europe, however, deep religious divisions developed. The New Learning had made individuals more independent of the authority of the medieval Catholic church. The invention of printing made the Bible available to anyone who could read. Before the creation of the printing press, the Bible had only been available to priests and other clergy in hand-written manuscripts. With the advent of printed books, anyone could have access to the Bible, first in Latin translations from the original Hebrew Old Testament and Greek New Testament, then in translations into the national languages of German, French, and other European tongues. Along with these developments, there was criticism by many people of corruption in the church; criticism of materialistic priests who sold *indulgences* to people who wanted to avoid the punishments of hell and purgatory; holy relics such as the bones of martyrs; and even papal pardons of sins.

All of these forces combined to prompt Martin Luther, in Germany, and John Calvin, in Switzerland, to protest against the practices and universal authority of the Roman Catholic Church and to set up their own *protestant* churches in defiance of the pope in Rome. To these Protestants, the Reformation was a return to the simplicity of early Christianity, when people worshipped and studied the Bible, as equals, without the authority of priests, bishops, and popes and without the elaborate cathedrals, ceremonies, and trappings of the medieval church. Just as their political allegiance was to their nation, their religious allegiance was to their national protestant church. To the established Roman Catholic Church, these Protestants were heretics who were breaking up the unity of the European Christian world, "Christendom," defying the supreme authority of the pope, and giving their own secular rulers the power to decide religious issues.

The conflict sometimes centered on such intellectual issues of biblical interpretation as whether people were *saved* from eternal damnation in hell by the good deeds they had done in life or whether they were *saved* by a transforming experience of faith in God. That conflict involved a related question of whether, as the Roman Catholic Church taught, people had "free will" and could choose to do good or evil, or whether, as John Calvin and other Protestant leaders taught, people were *predestined* by God to be saved or damned and had no power to control their eternal destiny. Even more arcane were conflicts over whether, in the sacrament of communion, bread and wine became the body and blood Christ or only symbolized his body and blood. Over such issues countries went to war, cities were destroyed, and people were tortured, maimed, and burned.

But back to England—and Henry VIII. Although there had been some Protestant sentiment in England, such as the "Lollard" movement, led in Chaucer's time by John Wycliffe, England remained staunchly Catholic in the early years of Henry's reign. In fact, Henry VIII defended the Catholic Church by writing a book attacking Martin Luther, for which Pope Leo X deemed Henry "Defender of the Faith." However, Henry's marriage to Spain's Catherine of Aragon did not produce the son he needed to succeed him on the English throne—only a daughter, who became known as "Bloody Mary" during her brief reign as Queen of England when she persecuted Protestants. Henry asked the pope to grant him a divorce so that he could marry Anne Boleyn in the hope that she would produce the son he wanted. When the pope refused to grant him the divorce, Henry VIII broke from the Catholic Church, created a national "Church of England" (that we also call the Episcopal Church) and proclaimed himself its supreme head. As such, he dissolved the Catholic Church's considerable landholdings in England, such as vast monasteries, and awarded the properties to nobles, who, in return, supported him and his newly-created "Church of England."

But, Henry's marriage to Anne Boleyn also failed to produce a son—only a daughter named Elizabeth. Henry went through wife after wife—usually disposing of them by execution—until finally he produced a son, who succeeded him as King Edward VI in 1547 at only ten years old. Although Edward VI ruled—through older advisors—for only six years before he died, his reign solidified his father's move to make England a Protestant country. When his older half-sister Mary succeeded him and married her cousin, Philip II of Spain, she tried to re-impose Catholicism on England, persecuting Protestants or forcing them to flee from England. Had she been able to produce an heir, England, and probably America, would be Catholic countries today, but when "Bloody Mary" died, her half-sister Elizabeth became Queen of England in 1558, and she ruled until 1603.

England under Elizabeth I

Queen Elizabeth I proved to be one the greatest monarchs England has ever had. She kept the Catholic and Protestant factions within England from tearing the country apart in the kind of religious civil wars that flared in other European nations. She made the Church of England a *via media* (Latin for "middle way") between Catholicism and Protestantism. She also made England's "middle way" religious position an instrument of foreign policy, sometimes siding with Catholic countries, such as France and Spain, sometimes with Protestant countries, such as Holland. One of her shrewdest policy maneuvers was her manipulation of her own unmarried state; the "Virgin Queen" could dangle the prospect of marriage to royal houses in various countries as a promise of political alliance.

In 1570, the Roman Catholic pope issued a *papal bull* excommunicating Elizabeth and freeing the English people from obeying her rule. Instead of undercutting her monarchy, however, the papal bull only drew the English people together around their queen. Their devotion to Elizabeth and to their country was deepened when a small, agile fleet of English ships defeated the huge Spanish Armada that King Philip II of Spain launched to conquer England in 1588. Elizabeth also challenged Spain's dominion in the New World by countenancing pirate raids by mariners, such as Sir Francis Drake, on Spanish galleons bearing treasure from America back to Spain. Under her rule, too, England began to establish colonies of its own in what is now North Carolina and Virginia.

Renaissance Drama

In many ways, the stage Shakespeare and other Elizabethan playwrights wrote for was similar to the stage used by classical Greek dramatists. It was an outdoor theater where the audience sat on benches or stood in a semicircle around the stage, which "thrust" forward so that actors were surrounded on three sides by the audience. All actors were male, and female roles were played by boys whose voices had not yet changed. Actors entered and exited through doors at the back of the stage. There was a small balcony above the stage where scenes could also be performed, such as the famous scene in *Romeo and Juliet* between Juliet on her bedroom balcony and Romeo in the garden below. As in the Greek stage, too, there was virtually no scenery or furnishings; the stage was essentially bare. Performances, as in ancient Greece, usually took place during the afternoon in full daylight, and there were no programs to let the audience know who the characters were, where the play was set, or when the action took place. Finally, there was no curtain, so the playwright had to find a dramatic reason for each actor to enter and exit the stage (including "dead" characters).

Despite these similarities in stage and theater, the *form* of the plays of Shakespeare and other Renaissance dramatists was very different from classical Greek drama. Shakespeare and his contemporaries paid little heed to the Aristotelian *Unities* of time and place. Drawing on the more flexible conventions of medieval drama, Renaissance playwrights used the stage to portray different times and different places. In the opening scenes of *Othello*, for example, the stage is first a street in Venice near Brabantio's home; then, it is the area outside the hotel where Othello and Desdemona are spending their wedding night; then, the stage becomes the chamber where the Venetian senate holds an emergency session.

By the beginning of the second act of *Othello*, we have made a great leap forward in time and place. At the end of Act One, Othello, Desdemona, and Iago are setting sail from Venice, across the Adriatic Sea, to Cyprus, off the coast of Turkey, to engage the Turkish fleet in battle. In the opening scene of Act II, however, Iago, Desdemona, and Cassio are already in Cyprus, and we learn that the Turkish fleet has sunk in a storm as Othello's ship arrives. The rapid shift in time and place is all the more remarkable when you learn that Shakespeare did not divide his plays into scenes and acts; those divisions were added after he died, when his plays were published. Although no manuscript of a play in Shakespeare's own hand has ever been found, it's clear that he wrote his plays in a much more fluid sequence of action that is closer to a modern movie screenplay.

Shakespeare was a great playwright, because he started out as an actor and learned how to make exposition dramatic, how to build a scene, how to play on audience response. One thing he learned is never bring on your main character at the beginning of the play—always keep the audience in suspense about the main character and have other characters talk about him or her. Like all playwrights, Shakespeare cannot tell us what his characters are thinking (the way a novelist or short story writer can). He has to rely on the convention of the *soliloquy*, in which a character speaks his or her thoughts aloud so that the audience—but no other characters—can hear them.

Tudor and Elizabethan Poetry

Like all monarchs, Henry VIII and Elizabeth had a retinue of courtiers, and the court was a scene of intrigue, preferment, and disappointment—much like Capitol Hill today. A courtier could be rewarded with a well-paid government position or punished by being imprisoned in the Tower of London. Still, the court was a center of political, intellectual, and artistic vitality. Courtiers were expected to be *Renaissance men* who could serve as politicians, diplomats, military officers, business entrepreneurs, and poets, since the writing of poetry was one of a gentleman's many skills. Poems were frequently written by hand, and the manuscripts circulated privately, so the authors did not address a general reading public, but rather a circle of learned and sophisticated fellow-courtiers.

Some poetry was printed in books—either in a book of poems by a single author or a *miscellany* (or as we would say today, an anthology) of poems by various writers. Wealthy patrons supported the publication of books of poetry much as they paid artists to paint portraits or commissioned musical works from composers. Such poetry was created by—and for—aristocrats in court society.

Some of the poetry produced by courtiers during the reigns of Henry VIII and Elizabeth I criticized courtly life as artificial, unpredictable, and dependent upon flattery and what we today would call *networking*—using your contacts with important people to get ahead. Such poetry still worked within the courtly love conventions that were inherited from French poetry. The beautiful woman without mercy is usually a lady of the court who rejects a courtier's love in as fickle a way as the king or queen, who might imprison, exile, or execute a courtier for giving unwelcome advice.

Sir Thomas Wyatt (1503–1542)

Sir Thomas Wyatt was a courtier during the reign of Henry VIII. He served as an administrator, an ambassador, and a diplomat, spending many years in France, Spain, and Italy, where he was deeply influenced by Italian poetry. Just as English poetry had been influenced by the courtly love poetry of the medieval troubadours of Provence in Southern France, Italian poetry also was influenced by the troubadour tradition. Many Italian poets wrote *complaints* about a *merciless* lady whose rejection of their love left them forlorn, anguished, and physically ill with fever and chills. Such poems were probably not based on real-life experience but were a conventional poetic *game* that challenged poets to find new ways of expressing the formulaic sentiments of a distraught courtly lover.

While these poems may seem all too alike today, at the time, courtly love poetry gave poets a chance to talk about their emotions in intricate and nuanced ways. Compared to the simple, stoical sentiments expressed in medieval ballads, the poets who wrote courtly love poetry expressed a subtler range of emotion. Such poetry, as we might say today, let men express their feelings under the convention of courtly love in a way that, in the mid-twentieth century, popular singers, such as Frank Sinatra and Bing Crosby, while idolized by female listeners, also appealed to men as they sang songs that expressed a man's capacity for tenderness, vulnerability, and heartache.

Many of Wyatt's poems were published by the printer Richard Tottel in 1557—fifteen years after Wyatt's death—in an anthology of poems by Wyatt and others that was called *Songs and Sonnets* but now is referred to as *Tottel's Miscellany*. One of Wyatt's most famous poems is a courtly love poem about a mistress who once loved him but now rejects him. Her vacillation of romantic feeling could also be taken as the whimsical vagaries of the Tudor court. Keep in mind that conventional puns in English courtly love poetry equated the beloved *dear* with the shy animal *deer*, plus an additional pun on *hart* (a male deer) and *heart*.

They Flee from Me

They fle from me, that sometyme did me seke   *once used to seek me out*
With naked fote, stalking in my chambre.   *stalking me in my bedroom*
I have seen theirn gentill, tame, and meke,
That nowe are wyld, and do not remember
That sometyme they put theimself in daunger   5
To take bred at my hand; and nowe they raunge
Besely seking with a continuell chaunge.   *Busily seeking(new lovers)*

Thancked be fortune, it hath ben otherwise   *Thank goodness*
Twenty tymes better; but ons, in speciall,   *once, especially*
In thyn arraye, after a pleasaunt gyse,   *pleasant fashion*   10
When her lose gowne from her shoulders did fall,
And she me caught in her armes long and small, *long and slender*
Therewith all swetely did me kysse
And softely saide: "Dere hert, howe like you this?"

It was no dreme: I lay brode waking.   *broad (wide) awake*   15
But all is torned, thorough my gentilnes,   *But all is turned, through my chivalry*

Into a straunge fasshion of forsaking;	*(strange way of rejecting my love)*
And I have leve to goo of her goodness,	*I'm "allowed" to go by her "goodness"*
And she also to use new fangilnes:	*newfangledness (fickleness in love)*
But syns that I so kyndely am served,	*(unkindly) yet "in kind" for a woman* 20
I would fain knowe what she hath deserved.	*like to know how she should be treated*

ca. 1540

In addition to treating the theme of courtly love, Wyatt's poem shows another influence of Italian poetry in its *rhyme scheme*. Each stanza has a rhyme scheme of *ababbcc.* Can you see how that rhyme scheme gives form to the poet's developing thoughts? How do the sentences of the poem develop in relation to the rhyme scheme? How many sentences are there in each stanza, and how do they unfold in relation to the rhyme scheme? Which lines are *end-stopped*, and which are *enjambed*?

On returning to England, Thomas Wyatt was charged with treason (perhaps for having an affair with Henry's second queen, Anne Boleyn). Henry VIII had Wyatt imprisoned in the Tower of London and stripped him of all his possessions—but later pardoned him after Anne Boleyn was executed.

The Sonnet

One of the forms Italian poets adapted from the troubadours of Provence was the *sonet* ("little song" in the language of Provençal), which, in Italian, became the *sonetto*. The Italian sonnetos were usually complaints voiced by a courtly lover about the disdainful lady he adores. Some of the greatest of these poems were written by the poet Petrarch and addressed to his beloved, Laura (pronounced, in Italian, as "La-ooh-rah"). The lines of the *sonetto* were of equal metrical length, and a rhyme scheme divided the poem into two parts: an *octave*, consisting of eight lines, usually rhyming *abbaabba*, followed by a *sestet* of six lines rhyming in one of several patterns, such as *cdecde, cdeedc,* or *ccdccd*. The rhyme scheme gives form to the sonnet by working with or against the pattern of thought created by the sentences of the poem. Sentences, in writing or in speaking, move thoughts forward as we write or converse, but the rhyme scheme inserts a pattern of repetition into that forward movement of the sentences, inviting the writer—and reader—to linger over a thought, expand upon it, or modify it.

Thomas Wyatt was so taken by these Italian sonnetos that he translated and imitated them in English poems called *sonnets*. In his sonnets, Wyatt used the iambic pentameter line, which had been developed in the Middle Ages by the poet Geoffrey Chaucer, and devised a rhyme scheme similar to that in an Italian poem—an octave and a sestet. Another Tudor poet, Henry Howard (1517–1547), crafted a different rhyme scheme for the sonnet. Instead of Wyatt's octave/sestet pattern of what has come to be called the *Petrarchan* or *Italian* sonnet, Howard moved the form of the sonnet toward what would come to be called the *English* or, after the greatest user of this sonnet form, the *Shakespearean* sonnet. Howard's sonnet's rhyme scheme is *abab cdcd ecec ff*— three quatrains followed by a couplet. Soon, poets who wrote English or Shakespearean sonnets often used a rhyme scheme that differed even more from the Petrarchan or Italian sonnet: *abab cdcd efef gg*. Shakespeare's sonnets, as we shall see, follow this rhyme scheme. Poets, such as Sir Philip Sidney, as we shall also see, combined elements of both the English and Italian sonnets.

These Tudor and Elizabethan poets developed the English sonnet largely, because it was difficult, given the nature of the English language, to write sonnets following the Italian pattern. As we have seen, English is not an inflected language, like German, French, Spanish, and Italian. The inflected nature of these languages makes for plentiful rhymes, because many words have the same ending, such as the many words that end in *-ia* or *–io* in Italian, providing five times the numbers of rhyming words than we have in English. In French, too, rhymes are plentiful. There are, for example, fifty-one rhymes for *amour* in French. But in English, how many words rhyme with *love*? Only a handful: *above, dove, glove, shove*, and, with a stretch, *of*. With so few rhymes in English, it is hard to write an Italian sonnet, especially its octave where a poet must find rhymes for only two words over the course of eight lines. In the English sonnet, by contrast, the poet need only find one rhyme for each of seven words.

The differing rhyme schemes give the Italian and English sonnet two very different patterns in which the poet's thought can develop. In the Italian sonnet, the thought develops in two large movements: the first thought develops through the eight lines of the *octave*; then, it shifts to the six lines of the *sestet*. In the English sonnet, the thought usually develops in the smaller steps of the three *quatrains*, then comes to its conclusion in the *couplet*—the two rhymed concluding lines. Remember that a poet's thoughts also develop in *sentences* in the same way a writer of prose develops ideas. The poet, thus, has both a sentence structure and a rhyme structure to develop his or her thoughts. In the sonnets that follow, notice how the rhyme scheme and the pattern of sentences provide a structure for the development of the poet's thought.

Sir Philip Sidney (1554–1586)

Like Thomas Wyatt, Sir Philip Sidney was born into a prominent family and served as a soldier, diplomat, and courtier. He also suffered the whims of Queen Elizabeth's favor and disfavor. Among his many writings was *Astrophel and Stella* (Latin for "Star-lover and Star"), one of the best *sonnet sequences* of the Elizabethan age. A sonnet sequence was a collection of sonnets about the same theme. Although the sonnets do not tell a story, they express the various moods the courtly lover undergoes in his frustrated efforts to woo his disdainful beloved.

For the most part, such sonnets were the conventional "complaints" of the courtly lover who is rejected by his "merciless" lady. In Sidney's case, however, the poet's frustration may reflect his real-life love of one of the ladies of Queen Elizabeth's court. Even if his "complaints" are not autobiographical, Sidney's sonnets register a rich and varied range of emotional expression within the conventional formulas of the courtly love tradition. The sonnet, thus, served as a poetic vehicle for poets to express a wide range of emotions.

Sonnet 31

With how sad steps, O Moone, thou climbst the skies!	
How silently, and with how wanne a face!	*wan (pale, sickly)*
What, may it be that euen in heau'nly place	*even ("u" is used for "v")*
That busie archer his sharpe arrowes tries?	*busy archer (Cupid)*
Sure, if that long-with-loue-acquainted eyes	5
Can iudge of loue, thou feel'st a louers case,	
I reade it in thy lookes: thy languist grace,	*languished (listless)*
To me that feele the like, thy state discries.	*Reveals your (lovesick) state*
Then, eu'n of fellowship, O Moone, tell me,	*Then, since we're fellow lovers,*
Is constant loue deem'd there but want of wit?	10
Are beauties there as proud as here they be?	
Do they aboue loue to be lou'd, and yet	
Those louers scorn whom that loue doth possesse?	

Do they call vertue there vngratefulnesse? *call rejecting love being virtuous*
ca. 1591

    The form of this sonnet is largely cast in the Italian pattern of an octave rhyming *abbaabba* and a sestet rhyming *cdcdee* ("wit" and "yet" would have been pronounced more closely alike in the Renaissance than they are in modern English). Notice, however, that the sonnet ends in a couplet, after the English pattern. It also resembles the English sonnet pattern in that, while the rhyme scheme creates an octave of eight lines, the sentence pattern breaks that octave into 2 four-line units so that the "Sure" in line five marks a new development of the poet's thought as he answers his own question about whether the moon is a heart-broken lover like himself.

    As the sonnet moves from octave to sestet, we get a change in what the poet says. In the octave, he develops the idea that the moon is a distraught lover, like himself. Then, in the sestet, he addresses the moon directly with four questions, but the sentences that form these questions run counter to the rhyme scheme of the sestet. The first question takes up lines nine and ten (which don't rhyme with each other). The second question forms line eleven. The third question straddles lines twelve and thirteen, thus spilling over, in terms of the rhyme scheme, into the first line of the couplet. Sidney further emphasizes that spilling over of the third question by enjambing line twelve into line thirteen. The last question dangles, all by itself, in line fourteen. What other lines in this sonnet are enjambed and how does that enjambment emphasize the emotional tone of what the poet is saying? Which lines have caesuras and where do they fall? How do those caesuras add to the emotional development of the poem?

    Sir Philip Sidney died at the age of thirty-two while fighting against Catholic forces in the Low Countries (Holland and Belgium). As he lay mortally wounded on the battlefield, his servant rushed to him with water, but when Sidney saw another dying soldier, whose thirst was even greater than his own, he instructed his servant to first give the other man a drink—the final chivalric gesture of a Renaissance courtier.

William Shakespeare (1564–1616)

Shakespeare was not born into an aristocratic family; his father was a prominent middle-class citizen of the provincial town of Stratford-upon-Avon in the western part of England. Shakespeare went to the local school, married Anne Hathaway in 1582, and had three children by 1585. In a few years, however, he left his family to go to London to pursue a career as an actor and playwright. He found success with one of London's most prominent dramatic companies and went on to become its major playwright. He also became one of the owners of the company, which built its own theater, the Globe, across the River Thames from London. Shakespeare wrote successfully for the theater for nearly twenty years then, in 1610, retired and moved back to Stratford, a wealthy and respected man.

    Sometime in the 1590s, he wrote his own sonnet sequence, which was published, perhaps without his authorization, in 1609. The sequence is far richer in emotional power and depth than other sonnet sequences of the era. Many of the sonnets are addressed to a young man, admiring his physical and spiritual beauty and urging him to marry and beget children who will sustain that beauty after he himself grows old and dies. Whether writing sonnets to a young man was Shakespeare's shrewd variation on the convention of courtly love "complaints" to a haughty woman, whether such sonnets were an expression of paternal affection, or whether they gave voice to Shakespeare's homoerotic desire have been matters of speculation for centuries. Whatever their inspiration, they render some of the most intimate and intricate emotional expressions in all of poetry.

Other sonnets in Shakespeare's sequence are about or addressed to a "dark woman"—dark in the physical sense of being a brunette with dark skin and eyes (as opposed to the blond-haired, blue-eyed ideal of woman that has long been a staple of beauty in Western culture). These sonnets clearly reflect a sexual relationship that, at times, is tawdry and jaded but, again, gives voice to an extraordinary range of the poet's emotions—from cynical sophistication to abject self-loathing.

What has been called the "love-triangle" that shapes Shakespeare's sonnet sequence may be a Renaissance variation, given its new-found reverence for Greek culture, of a Greek idea of love. For some ancient Greeks, love between a man and woman was "natural" in that it linked them to the "natural" cycle of copulation, birth, and death. As such, it was a necessary fact of life that made us earthly, lustful, and mortal. However, an "unnatural" love between, say, an older and younger man, was "ideal" in that it produced no progeny and, thus, transcended the natural cycle. Such an ideal love was subject only to the ravages of time, and many of Shakespeare's sonnets address the force of time with eloquence. Whether such eloquence stems from Shakespeare's own bi-sexual involvement with a handsome young man and a sensuous "dark" woman or whether it is simply his own intricate variation on the courtly love tradition of a lover's "complaint," we'll probably never know.

The first two of the sonnets below are addressed to the young man; the next two are about Shakespeare's affair with the "dark lady."

Sonnet 73

That time of year thou may'st in me behold
When yellow leaves, or none, or few, do hang
Upon those boughs which shake against the cold,
Bare ruin'd choirs, where late the sweet birds sang.   *branches like church choir stalls*
In me thou see'st the twilight of such day   5
As after sunset fadeth in the west,
Which by and by black night doth take away,
Death's second self, that seals up all in rest.
In me thou see'st the glowing of such fire,
That on the ashes of his youth doth lie,   10
As the death-bed whereon it must expire
Consum'd with that which it was nourish'd by.
This thou perceiv'st, which makes thy love more strong,
To love that well which thou must leave ere long.

Sonnet 116

Let me not to the marriage of true minds
Admit impediments. Love is not love
Which alters when it alteration finds,
Or bends with the remover to remove:
O no! it is an ever-fixed mark   5
That looks on tempests and is never shaken;
It is the star to every wandering bark,   *star that a wandering ship uses to navigate*
Whose worth's unknown, although his height be taken.   *the star's height measured*
Love's not Time's fool, though rosy lips and cheeks
Within his bending sickle's compass come: *Time's scythe is like the Grim Reaper's* 10

Love alters not with his brief hours and weeks,
But bears it out even to the edge of doom.   *to the end of the world*
If this be error and upon me proved,
I never writ, nor no man ever loved.

This next sonnet, the first about Shakespeare's affair with the "dark lady," is a bitter look back at a night of passionate love-making. Shakespeare plays with the Renaissance idea that in sex, a man "wastes" part of his spiritual nature in an orgasm and, thus, comes close to death. Notice how the elision of "The" and "expense" into "Th'expense" starts the poem off with a rapidity that carries through the first quatrain, with its frequent caesuras and enjambed lines. Also notice how in the second and third quatrains, the pace slows down, and Shakespeare uses more balanced caesuras and end-stopped lines to reflect more calmly upon his lustful behavior.

Sonnet 129

Th' expense of spirit in a waste of shame
Is lust in action; and, till action, lust   *Is the fulfillment of lustful longing*
Is perjured, murderous, bloody, full of blame,   *lust will do anything for satisfaction*
Savage, extreme, rude, cruel, not to trust,
Enjoyed no sooner but despisèd straight,   *once our lust is satisfied, we despise it*   5
Past reason hunted, and no sooner had
Past reason hated as a swallowed bait   *like a fish hates the bait it's swallowed*
On purpose laid to make the taker mad.
Mad in pursuit, and in possession so;
Had, having, and in quest to have, extreme;   10
A bliss in proof, and proved, a very woe,   *blissful during sex, but after it disgusting*
Before a joy proposed; behind, a dream.
All this the world well knows, yet none knows well
To shun the heaven that leads men to this hell.

In this next, and much more comically light, sonnet, Shakespeare pokes fun at the many courtly love poems about ladies whose eyes are brighter than the sun, whose lips are as red as coral, whose skin is as white as snow, whose blonde hair is as soft as silk, whose cheeks are like roses, whose breath is like perfume, whose voice is like music, and who seem to walk on air like a goddess.

Sonnet 130

My mistress' eyes are nothing like the sun;
Coral is far more red than her lips' red:
If snow be white, why then her breasts are dun;   *her breasts are dull brown*
If hairs be wires, black wires grow on her head.*
I have seen roses damask'd, red and white,   *roses mingled together*   5
But no such roses see I in her cheeks;
And in some perfumes is there more delight
Than in the breath that from my mistress reeks.**
I love to hear her speak, yet well I know
That music hath a far more pleasing sound.   10
I grant I never saw a goddess go:
My mistress, when she walks, treads on the ground.

And yet, by heaven, I think my love as rare
As any she belied with false compare.

> *any woman described in such
> extravagant metaphors ("compares") as
> we find in much courtly love poetry*

Since what we think of "wires" did not exist in Shakespeare's day, he is probably alluding to the custom of women wearing gold nets on their head to accent their blonde hair

** "reeks" did not in Shakespeare's time mean, as it does today, "stinks" but simply "exhales"*

The English Poetic Line: Iambic Pentameter

The immense popularity of the sonnet at the end of the sixteenth century established the iambic pentameter line as the major vehicle for English poetry for the next three hundred years. Not only did the iambic pentameter line give form to many great poems in English, it was used by dramatists, such as William Shakespeare and Christopher Marlowe, in their plays. As we saw from the outset, poetry is *mnemonic*, and actors found it easier to remember their lines if the lines had metrical regularity. The poetic line that most closely approximated English conversation was *blank verse*, unrhymed iambic pentameter ("blank," because the lines do not rhyme). Thus in Marlowe's *Tragical History of the Life and Death of Doctor Faustus*, when Faustus s given a vision of the beautiful Helen of Troy, his astonishment is expressed in a line of pure iambic pentameter:

Is **this**/ the **face**/ that **launched**/ a **thou**-/sand **ships**?

To keep their lines of dialogue close to everyday speech, dramatists seldom employed rhyme, though Shakespeare made an exception when his most famous young lovers meet at a dance; Romeo and Juliet's initial dialogue forms a sonnet.

The iambic pentameter line has proven to be a rich, flexible, and powerful instrument for poetry. Sometimes an iambic pentameter line can sound as off-handed as everyday conversation, as in the opening line of Robert Frost's sonnet, "Design:"

I **found**/ a **dim**-/pled **spi**-/der, **fat**/ and **white**

At other times, the iambic pentameter line can be as passionate as what we say—and think—at our most ecstatic or agonized moments. Percy Byshhe Shelley laments his suffering in a metrically regular line of iambic pentameter from "Ode to the West Wind"

I **fall**/ up-**on**/ the **thorns**/ of **life**!/ I **bleed**!

Alfred Lord Tennyson, in "Ulysses," his poem about the great Greek hero Odysseus (whom the Romans called "Ulysses") has the aging warrior rouse his old crew of sailors for one last heroic voyage in stirring, resounding iambs:

To **strive**,/ to **seek**,/ to **find**,/ and **not**/ to **yield**

Shakespeare's sonnets give wonderful examples of how supple the iambic pentameter line can be in registering not only the way we speak at our most impassioned moments, but the way the mind thinks at its most intense. Look again at the opening of "Sonnet 129" as Shakespeare looks back in disgust at a night of riotous debauchery:

> Th' ex-**pense**/ of **spi**-/it in/ a **waste**/ of **shame**
> Is **lust**/ in **ac**-/tion; and/ **till ac**-/tion, **lust**
> Is **per**-/jured, **mur**-/d'rous, **bloo**-/dy, **full**/ of **blame**,
> **Sa**-vage,/ ex-**treme**,/ rude, **cru**-/el, **not**/ to **trust**;

Can you see how Shakespeare's use of the iambic pentameter line to register powerful emotion is enhanced by his use of caesura, enjambment, and metrical substitution?

The English Poetic Line: Iambic Tetrameter/Trimeter

Next to the iambic pentameter line, the most widely-used poetic line in English is iambic tetrameter, sometimes in combination with iambic trimeter in what we have seen is the *ballad quatrain*. Even though the pentameter line differs from the tetrameter line only by having one additional iambic foot, the rhythms of the two kinds of lines create strikingly different effects. A line of iambic pentameter, for example, cannot be divided evenly into two equal halves. A poet can place a caesura directly in the middle of a line, as Shakespeare does in the second line of "Sonnet 129:"

> Is **lust**/ in **ac**-/tion; and/ **till ac**-/tion, **lust**

But even though the caesura falls after the fifth syllable of the line, the caesura does not divide the line into two balanced halves, for there are two strong accents in the first half of the line and three strong accents in the second part of the line. Iambic pentameter resists evenness and balance—as does spoken English.

The iambic tetrameter line, however, easily divides into balanced halves:

> **Come live**/ with **me**/   and **be**/ my **love**

If poetic language ranges along a continuum between song and speech, then the tetrameter (sometimes combined with the trimeter line) pushes poetry toward song. Most hymns, for example, are written in the ballad quatrain of alternating iambic tetrameter and trimeter lines:

> A-**maz**-/ing **grace**,/ how **sweet**/ the **sound**,
> That **saved**/ a **wretch**/ like **me**.
> I **once**/ was **lost**/ but **now**/ am **found**,
> T'was **blind**/ but **now**/ can **see**.

Many other songs also uses tetrameter and trimeter lines:

> Should **auld**/ ac-**quain**-/tance **be**/ for-**got**
> And **ne**-/ver **brought**/ to **mind**?
> Should **auld**/ ac-**quain**-/tance **be**/ for-**got**

> And **days**/ of **auld**/ **lang syne**?   *old long ago*

Even when poets do not use the tetrameter line to sound like song, the line often sounds very poised, polished, and elegant, as if the speaker of the poem had thought it up in advance and rehearsed it before speaking. When the contemporary poet Donald Hall became the father of a son, the sight of the baby made him feel his own mortality, and he wrote "My Son, My Executioner," a poem that begins with the tetrameter line,

> My **son**,/ my **ex**-/e-**cu**-/tion-**er**

Poems written in this elegant, urbane rhythm are like listening to debonair film actors, such as Fred Astaire and Cary Grant, speak in well-turned, insouciant phrases. By contrast, iambic pentameter lines seem closer to the "method" acting style of speaking in halting, broken, uneven phrases, like that of Marlon Brando and Dustin Hoffman, who often sound as if they were speaking before their thoughts were really formed.

The sleek, simple tetrameter/trimeter line not only lends itself to poetry that is sophisticated and poised; it can also suggest simplicity and innocence. Iambic tetrameter is often used in pieces written for children ("I **tought**/ I **saw**/ a **pud**-/dy **tat**") and has been used by many poets to express horror or anger beneath its innocent-sounding surface. When the nineteenth-century American poet Sarah Nordcliffe Cleghorn wanted to protest child labor, she used the ballad quatrain in "The Golf Links" to portray children working in a textile mill while nearby wealthy factory owners played golf:

> The **golf**/ **links lie**/ so **near**/ the **mill**   *golf course*
> That **al**-/most **ev**-/ery **day**
> The **la**-/boring **chil**-/dren **can**/ **look up**
> And **see**/ the **men**/ at **play**.

Can you see how the form of this little poem derives from the Middle English ballads, such as Sir Patrick Spens'? The alternating lines of iambic tetrameter and iambic trimester rhyme *abxb* and, just as Sir Patrick Spens drew on the alliterative tradition of Old English poetry ("*Drinking the blude red wine*"), Cleghorn's poem subtly repeats the same consonant sounds ("The go*lf l*inks *l*ie so near the mi*ll*).

Notice, too, how artfully Cleghorn uses metrical substitution to enhance her smoldering outrage at child labor . In the second line, she probably wants us to *elide* the word "every" so that instead of pronouncing it as a three syllable word ("e-ve-ry"), we pronounce it as a two-syllable word ("ev'-ry"). If we do that, the line comes out as perfectly iambic trimeter. In fact, we probably pronounce "every" as a two-syllable word in everyday conversation, so the poet is just asking us to follow our normal habit of speech. Sometimes poets will clearly indicate *elision* by omitting a letter from a word and writing "every" as "ev'ry." Many such elided words have become associated with a poetic effect: "e'er" instead of "ever"; "e'en" for "even"; "o'er" for "over." (Sometimes I think poets elide words not just because they fit the meter, but because they sound so poetic.) Poets also practice elision between words, running one word into the next so that we drop a syllable and, thus, keep the metrical pattern. Instead of saying "It was," for example, poets love to say "'Twas." Frequently they will elide the final vowel of a word so that it runs into the initial vowel of the following word, dropping a syllable to fit the metrical pattern: "th'orient" instead of "the orient."

By eliding "every" in the second line of her poem, Cleghorn makes it metrically regular.

That **al**-/most **ev'**-/ry **day**

Can you feel how the metrical regularity makes the line sound eager, cheerful, childlike? Imagine a child gleefully shouting:

I'd **love**/ to **play**/ **all day**

Can you hear a similar gleefulness in the metrically regular fourth line?

And **see**/ the **men**/ at **play**

The stark contrast between the metrical joyousness of these two lines and the grim injustice of children working in a factory while, outside their window, men play golf underscores Cleghorn's poetic point.

But now, look at the first and third lines of the poem. These tetrameter lines are anything but cheerfully metrical (and, of course, in the tradition of the ballad quatrain, do not rhyme). The heavy spondee—"**links lie**"—emphasizes the brutal irony of having a golf course so close to a factory where children work, an emphasis further underscored by the alliteration between the two words. The third line is even more metrically irregular. After the first iamb ("The la-"), we get three metrical substitutions. First an anapest: "or-ing **chil**-;" some readers might be tempted to elide "laboring" to "lab'ring" to make it fit the iambic meter, but can you see—and hear and *feel*—how that would mar the uneven quality of the anapest? That unevenness underscores how long and hard the children toil (children working in factories frequently worked much longer than eight hours a day in dismal, dirty, dangerous conditions). The anapest also places greater emphasis on the first syllable of "children" by having it preceded by two unaccented feet; on that syllable, we can almost hear Cleghorn's anger beneath the apparent nonchalance of the rest of the poem:

The **la**-/bo-ring **CHIL**-/ dren!!!!!

To keep the line irregular, the poet does not return to the iambic rhythm but extends the uneven feel of the anapest by two more metrical substitutions: first a pyrrhic ("-dren can") then a spondee ("**look up**"). Such unevenness of rhythm underscores the pathos of hard-working children looking up from their toil to see men playing golf outside. Once again, notice, how Cleghorn uses the rhyme scheme of the ballad quatrain: the second and fourth lines are metrically regular and rhyme in ironic cheerfulness; the first and third lines are metrically irregular and do not rhyme, underscoring the unfairness of the situation.

In a similar way, twentieth-century African-American poet Countee Cullen used the ballad quatrain to describe a childhood trip to Baltimore in a poem called "Incident." The poem's simple tetrameter and trimeter lines at first register Cullen's glee as he rides a streetcar in the big city, but they turn ugly when he encounters a white boy:

Now **I**/ was **eight**/ and **ve**-/ry **small**
And **he**/ was **no**/ whit **big**-ger.
And **so**/ I **smiled**,/ but **he**/ **poked out**
His **tongue**/ and **called**/ me **nig**-ger.

Can you see how effectively Cullen uses caesura and enjambment in the third line of this quatrain? The comma after "smiled" at first seems to neatly divide the line in half metrically after two perfectly regular iambic feet:

And **so**/ I **smiled**,

But instead of the second half of the line following with two more regular iambs. Cullen substitutes a pyrrhic ("but he") and a spondee ("**poked out**") so that unevenness in meter underscores the unfairness of racism, particularly among children. To further emphasize that impropriety, Cullen does not make the third line end-stopped, like the first two lines, but enjambs the third line so that, in terms of syntax and sense, it runs into the fourth line. Such enjambment neatly reflects what Cullen is describing—the line "sticking out" poetically like the nasty white boy's tongue.

Cullen also uses rhyme very effectively in this quatrain. The rhymes in lines two and four— "**big**-ger" and "**nig**-ger" are two-syllable words whose accents fall on the first rather than the second syllable. Such rhymes are called *feminine* rhymes, as opposed to *masculine* rhymes where the accent falls on an accented syllable, such as "re-**lieve**" and "de-**cieve**." Masculine rhymes are much more common in poetry. Most monosyllabic words that rhyme are masculine. Look back, for example, at the first quatrain of Shakespeare's "Sonnet 72:"

> That time of year thou may'st in me be-*hold*
> When yellow leaves, or none, or few do *hang*
> Upon those boughs that shake against the *cold*,
> Bare, ruined choirs, where late the sweet birds *sang*.

"Be-*hold*" is a two-syllable word but the accent falls on its second syllable ("Be-**hold**). It, thus, rhymes with the monosyllabic "*cold*." Both "*hang*" and "*sang*" are monosyllabic masculine rhymes that are accented.

Feminine rhymes are used so infrequently in English poetry that, when a poet does use one, it sometimes produces a surprising and comic effect. Lord Byron was a poet who frequently used feminine rhymes for humor, such as his satire on the way Protestants and Catholics have persecuted each other in the belief that the apostles would have approved their cruelty:

> Christians have burnt each other, quite per-*sua*-ded
> That all the Apostles would have done as *they did*,

In this rhyme, the accent is on the next to the last syllable ('per-**sua**-ded") (as **they** did") so that the final syllable is unaccented.

Part of the comic effect of such rhymes is surprise, but the distinction between masculine and feminine rhymes also reflects our culture's long-standing sexism. With their strong final accents, masculine rhymes are—as men were thought to be—bold, decisive, firm. With their unaccented final syllable, feminine rhymes are—as women were once thought to be—weak, tentative, flighty. When Edwin Arlington Robinson wanted to satirize an effeminate character, Miniver Cheevy, who lived in the modern world but longed for the romantic days of the Middle Ages, he alternated masculine with feminine rhymes:

> Miniver loved the days of *old*
>   When swords were bright and steeds were *prancing*;
> The vision of a warrior *bold*

>   Would set him *dancing*.

Notice how the masculine rhymes, **old** and **bold** sound forceful, but that the feminine rhymes, **pranc**ing and **danc**ing, capture the silliness of Miniver who, as he envisions a powerful knight in armor, breaks into a dance.

For the first half of the twentieth century, school children were required to memorize poems and recite them before their classmates and at school assemblies, frequently accompanying their oral performance with spirited gestures. One of the most memorized and recited poems was "The Boy Stood on the Burning Deck." The poem was written in 1826 by the British poet Felicia Dorothea Hemans. It was based on an incident that took place in 1798 during the war between England and Napoleonic France. A young boy named Giocante de Casabianca served on a French ship commanded by his father. After a fierce battle with the English navy, their ship, *The Orient*, was engulfed in flames, and all the sailors on deck, except for Giocante, were dead. The poem, written in ballad quatrains, but rhyming *abab* rather than *abxb*, begins:

> The boy stood on the burning deck
> Whence all but he had fled;
> The flame that lit the battle's wreck
> Shone 'round him o'er the dead.

Rather than try to save himself by fleeing the burning ship, as other sailors had, Giocante keeps calling out to his father, below decks, to ask permission to save himself by deserting his post and jumping overboard. What he does not know is that his father is dead and cannot respond. Rather than do something without his father's permission, Giocante remains at his post until he, too, dies in the fire.

School children who had to memorize and recite this poem grew to hate it—and its moral of always waiting to get your parents' permission before doing anything. Therefore, many parodies of the poem were created to render it comic, rather than tragic. One of these parodies altered the opening quatrain to read:

> The boy stood on the burning deck.
> His feet were full of blisters.
> He climbed aloft, his pants burned off,
> And now he wears his sister's.

Can you see how the feminine rhyme of "**blist**ers" and "**sist**ers" adds to the comedy of the parody?

Along with Byron, another master of the feminine rhyme was W. S. Gilbert, whose witty poems were set to music by Sir Arthur Sullivan for a series of wonderful operettas in the latter part of the nineteenth century. Gilbert frequently pushed feminine rhymes even farther by creating *triple rhymes* of three syllables—the first accented syllable followed by two unaccented syllables. In *The Pirates of Penzance* (1879), a self-important major general brags, in feminine rhymes, about his extensive knowledge:

> I am the very model of a modern Major-**Gen**-er-al
> I've information vegetable, animal, and **min**-er-al
> I know the kings of England, and I quote the fights his-**tor**-i-cal   (*famous battles*)
> From Marathon to Waterloo, in order cate-**gor**-i-cal   (*chronological order*)
> I'm very well acquainted too with matters mathe-**ma**-ti-cal,

I understand equations, both the simple and qua-*dra*-ti-*cal*

Many poets have written poems in iambic tetrameter, rather than use the ballad quatrain of alternating tetrameter and trimeter lines. When the tetrameter line is used by itself, it seems less like song and more like speech (though not nearly so speech-like as iambic pentameter). twentieth-century British poet Philip Larkin began a poem, "This Be the Verse," with this startling tetrameter quatrain:

They **fuck**/ you **up**,/ your **mum**/ and **dad**.
They may/ not **mean**/ to, **but**/ they **do**.
They **fill**/ you with/ the **faults**/ **they had**
And **add**/ some **ex**-/tra, **just**/ for **you**.

Think about this tetrameter quatrain in terms of those formal qualities of meter, rhyme, caesura, and enjambment. Why do you think that the word "they," which Larkin uses frequently is not accented (as pronouns usually aren't) except at the end of the third line ("**they had**"). Why is that line enjambed? What is effective about the caesuras? What does the phrase, marked off by the caesura in the fourth line, "Just for you," suggest about parents and children? (Have your parents ever said that phrase to you—if so, how did they mean it?) Why are the simple, masculine rhymes effective given what Larkin is saying?

Notice that rhyme can come elsewhere in a line of poetry than at the end. A poet can use *internal rhyme* as well by placing rhymes within a line of poetry. Cole Porter, for example, wrote a lyrical line that was packed with internal rhymes:

Fly-ing too *high* with some *guy* in the *sky* is *my i*-dea of nothing to do.

Can you find the internal rhymes in Larkin's quatrain?

Thus, the tetrameter line has proven to be almost as effective and flexible as the iambic pentameter line. By the end of the sixteenth century, therefore, English poetry had its two great lines—iambic pentameter and iambic tetrameter/trimeter—that would produce great poetry for hundreds of years. Yet the lines, even though differing only in the length of one or two iambic feet, are, as we have seen, strikingly different in form. The tetrameter or tetrameter/trimeter line is song-like, poised, elegant, and balanced. It can easily divide neatly into two balanced halves:

They **fuck**/ you **up**,/   your **mum**/ and **dad**,

The iambic pentameter line, however, as we have also seen, cannot be evenly divided. Even if a poet placed a caesura after the fifth syllable of the line, it would leave the first half of the line with only two stressed syllables:

Kill me,/ then **kill**/ me,

And three stressed syllables in the other half of the line:

dash/ me **with**/ thy **chains**.

The iambic pentameter line is, by nature, uneven, asymmetrical, closer to the way we talk. It can, thus, be used as blank verse, without rhyme, to imitate human speech. Iambic tetrameter, along with tetrameter/trimeter, cries out for rhyme. As poet and literary critic George T. Wright observes:[8]

> It is probably because of these numerical oddities and our perceptual response to them that iambic pentameter, except in the hands of its dullest practitioners, keeps the most highly patterned language from sounding trivial. It can lend gravity, dignity, portentousness, even grandeur to statements and utterances; and where rhymed tetrameter couplets often evoke a feeling of easy elegance, of achieved simplicity, iambic pentameter, whether in rhymed stanzas, heroic couplets, or blank verse, usually conveys a sense of complex understanding, as if the speakers of such lines were aware of more than they ever quite say, or as if there were more in their speeches than even they were aware of. If the language of everyday life or even the language of other forms of poetry seems usually to leave untouched, unsounded, certain depths of human experience, iambic pentameter has seemed to centuries of poets and listeners the poetic form most likely to reach those depths and to make their resonances possible. The iambic pentameter line, then, has amplitude and asymmetry to carry significant English speech.

Although the iambic pentameter line of the sonnet was the favorite form of Tudor and Elizabethan poets, they also used the *iambic tetrameter* line.

Christopher Marlowe (1564–1593)

Like William Shakespeare, Christopher Marlowe was born into the middle-class, rather than the aristocracy. His father was a shoemaker, and "Kit" went to Cambridge University on a scholarship designed to train him as a minister. When he graduated, however, Marlowe became a playwright rather than a preacher. He also was suspected of Catholic sympathies and even of conspiring against Queen Elizabeth, but the Queen herself excused him, because he had done the court good service. He had his first great success with the play *Tamburlane* in 1587, when Marlowe was only twenty-three years old. Soon after, more trouble followed; he was jailed for fighting in a brawl in which another poet was killed. His disgruntled homosexual partner, the playwright Thomas Kyd, told the government that Marlowe was an atheist and a traitor. After creating five more successful plays, Marlowe was stabbed to death in a tavern over an argument about the bill. He was not even thirty years old.

In addition to writing plays, Marlowe wrote poetry, and one of his most famous poems is written in the style of courtier poetry. One of the conventions of courtier poetry was the *pastoral*, which went back to ancient Greece. "Pastor," in Greek, means "shepherd," and the sophisticated, urbane Greeks of Athens wrote pastoral verse and prose that extolled the virtues of living in the country, like shepherds, rather than in the hectic, bustling city. The Athenians, who were caught up

---

[8] George T. Wright, *Shakespeare's Metrical Art* (Berkeley: University of California Press, 1988). p. 6.

in politics, business, and war, liked to imagine how much simpler life would be if they lived in the country, did nothing but tend sheep, and sing love songs to their shepherdess "nymphs."

The pastoral ideal has endured for centuries, as city dwellers have sought escape from the pressures of modern life and dreamed of retreating to a simple, rural lifestyle. In eighteenth-century France, Queen Marie Antoinette and her ladies of the court would dress up as peasant girls and tend a flock of sheep on the grounds of the magnificent Palace of Versailles. To this day, harried and overworked businessmen and women often dream of quitting their jobs, moving to the country, and enjoying the life of farmers (little do most of them know how hard and long farmers have to work in their "idyllic," pastoral world).

In the pastoral world city-dwellers from the Greeks to the Renaissance dreamed of, about the only conflict came from poetry contests, where rural poets composed *ecologues* about the joys of rural life, as opposed to the hectic pressures of life in the big city. Even these poetry contests—the forerunners of our contemporary poetry "slams"—were gentle and friendly. One of these contests began when Christopher Marlowe wrote a poem inviting a lady of the court to leave London and move to the country with him. In the poem, the poet assumes the character of a shepherd, and writes this "plea" to his nymph in iambic tetrameter quatrains:

The Passionate Shepherd to His Love

Come live with me and be my love,
And we will all the pleasures prove, *test*
That valleys, groves, hills, and fields,
Woods, or steepy mountain yields.

And we will sit upon the rocks, 5
Seeing the shepherds feed their flocks,
By shallow rivers, to whose falls
Melodious birds sing madrigals. *popular songs*

And I will make thee beds of roses,
And a thousand fragrant posies, 10
A cap of flowers and a kirtle *a skirt worn over a petticoat*
Embroider'd all with leaves of myrtle:

A gown made of the finest wool,
Which from our pretty lambs we pull;
Fair lined slippers for the cold, 15
With buckles of the purest gold:

A belt of straw and ivy buds,
With coral clasps and amber studs;
And if these pleasures may thee move,
Come live with me and be my love. 20

The shepherd swains shall dance and sing
For thy delight each May morning;
If these delights thy mind may move,
Then live with me and be my love. 1599

As you think about the form of this poem, notice that some of the rhymes are not quite right. In the first quatrain, Elizabethan English may have pronounced "love" and "prove" so that they rhymed. In the second quatrain, however, while "rocks" and "flocks" are true masculine rhymes that, thus, form a *tetrameter couplet* of two adjacent rhyming lines, "falls" does not really rhyme with "madrigals," whose accent is on the first syllable, "**mad**-ri-gals," and whose third syllable, "-gals,' is pronounced more like "lulls" and, thus, does not fully rhyme with "falls." Such rhymes are called *slant rhymes* or *near rhymes*, because they do not fully rhyme.

Similarly, in the last two quatrains, Elizabethan English may have made "move" and "love" rhyme, but notice, in the last quatrain, that "**sing**" is a masculine word that takes an accent but "**mor**-ning" is a feminine word whose second syllable is unaccented. In order for the two words to rhyme, we would have to distort the pronunciation of "**mor**-ning" to "mor-**ning**." Do you think these near or slant rhymes are just errors by Marlowe or do they have something to do with the meaning of the poem?

Sir Walter Ralegh (1552–1618)

Probably the most famous courtier of the Age of Elizabeth was Sir Walter Raleigh, who will always be remembered for his gallant gesture of removing his velvet cloak and placing it over a mud puddle so that Queen Elizabeth would not have to dirty her feet. Raleigh was a soldier, an explorer, a scientist, a poet, and an historian. He helped defeat the Spanish Armada in 1588 and founded the colony of Virginia, establishing the English presence in America. A great favorite of Queen Elizabeth, he was imprisoned in the Tower of London after her death in 1603 and, in 1618, was beheaded.

Among his poems, is this "rebuttal" to Marlowe's "The Passionate Shepherd to His Love," in which Raleigh assumes the voice of the "nymph" addressed by Marlowe's "shepherd:"

The Nymph's Reply to the Shepherd

If all the world and love were young,
And truth in every shepherd's tongue,
These pretty pleasures might me move
To live with thee and be thy love.

Time drives the flocks from field to fold 5
When rivers rage and rocks grow cold,
And Philomel* becometh dumb;
The rest complains of cares to come.

The flowers do fade, and wanton fields
To wayward winter reckoning yields;   10
A honey tongue, a heart of gall,
Is fancy's spring, but sorrow's fall,

Thy gowns, thy shoes, thy beds of roses,
Thy cap, thy kirtle, and thy posies   *girdle (outer petticoat)*
Soon break, soon wither, soon forgotten—   15
In folly ripe, in reason rotten.

> Thy belt of straw and ivy buds,
> Thy coral clasps and amber studs,
> All these in me no means can move
> To come to thee and be thy love.   20
>
> But could youth last and love still breed,
> Had joys no date nor age no need,
> Then these delights my mind may move
> To live with thee and be thy love.   1599

Philomel was a character in Greek mythology. She was raped by Tereus, the husband of her sister Procne, who then cut out her tongue so she could not identify him as her rapist. Undaunted, Philomel wove a tapestry in which she portrayed her rape by her brother-in-law. When her sister Procne saw it, she avenged the rape by killing her son, Itys, cutting him up, and baking him in a pie which she fed to her husband. When Tereus realized he had eaten his son, he threatened to kill both Procne and Philomel, but the gods changed them into birds—Philomel into a nightingale and Procne into a swallow—so they could escape.

What do you find are the most effective metrical substitutions, enjambments, and caesuras in this poem? In the line "**Time drives**/ the **flocks**/ from **field**/ to **fold**," how does the initial spondee underscore what Ralegh is saying in the line?

Chapter 4
Seventeenth-Century Literature

England after Elizabeth I

For all of her political acumen, the one thing Elizabeth failed to do was marry and produce an heir to her throne. When the "Virgin Queen" died in 1603, it was the end of the Tudor dynasty and the beginning of troubles that would increase as the seventeenth century rolled on. Elizabeth's successor was her cousin, King James VI of Scotland, who became James I of England and started the Stuart dynasty. In 1605, two years after he was crowned, a Catholic radical, Guy Fawkes, was foiled in his attempt to blow up Parliament in what came to be called the "Gunpowder Plot." Fawkes, along with other conspirators, was put to death in a particularly gruesome manner: he was "drawn and quartered" by having each arm and leg attached to one of four horses who then pulled him in four opposite directions until his body was wrenched asunder. To this day, English children stuff little rag dolls of Guy Fawkes on November fifth, hang him in effigy, set off firecrackers, and chant this quatrain:

> Remember, remember, the fifth of November,
> Gunpowder, treason, and plot.
> I see no reason why gunpowder, treason
> Should ever be forgot.

As they display their effigies to passersby, the children ask, "A penny for the old guy." Can you see how the rhythm of this little poem uses various metrical feet, as well as masculine, feminine, and internal rhymes?

While right-wing Catholics such as Guy Fawkes tried to return England to the Roman Catholic Church, radical left-wing Protestants called *Puritans* tried to purge the Episcopal Church of all traces of Catholicism, such as rituals, sacraments, and statues. The most critical doctrinal disagreement between the Puritans and the Episcopal Church was over free will versus determinism. The Episcopal Church, like the Roman Catholic Church, believed that humans had free will to choose between doing right and wrong and could earn their salvation by doing good deeds and living a pious life. The Puritans, following John Calvin, the Protestant leader of Geneva, Switzerland, believed in predestination—the doctrine that God had determined who would be saved and damned even before people were born. The only way people could know whether they were bound for heaven or hell was to have a deep religious experience of "amazing grace" that promised—but did not assure—that they were among the "elect" whom God had chosen to save rather than damn.

King James and, even more so, his son Charles, who succeeded him in 1625, lacked the flexibility, tolerance, and political savvy of Elizabeth I. They adhered to the autocratic doctrine of the "divine right of kings," which regarded the King as God's emissary on earth whose every command must be unquestioningly obeyed. They frequently collided with the largely middle-class Parliament, which held the power of taxation to raise money and regarded the Stuart kings as far too friendly with Catholic nations, such as France and Spain, rather than Protestant Holland and Germany. James I and Charles I also tried to stamp out Puritanism and other forms of political and religious dissent in England. Rather than challenge the English state and church, however, frustrated Puritans emigrated to other Protestant countries, such as Holland (which had recently fought for its independence from Catholic Spain), or to America, where they set up their own colonies at Plymouth and Massachusetts Bay.

The Puritans who remained in England fought back against the Stuart kings. Along with their political and religious disagreements with King James, Puritans were appalled by the behavior of his court. Diplomats from other countries, too, described the drunkenness, debauchery, and other immoralities of the king and the lords and ladies of his court. Parliament often refused to raise taxes to provide the king with money. By mid-century, these tensions became so exacerbated that King Charles dismissed Parliament and tried to raise the money he needed by reviving old medieval taxes that kings used to levy on the people without the approval of Parliament. In 1642, civil war broke out between supporters of King Charles and the Puritan wing of Parliament under the leadership of Oliver Cromwell.

Supporters of King Charles were dubbed *Cavaliers*—mostly nobles who wore their hair long, dressed in opulent garb, and rode horses ("cavalier" comes from the French "chevalier"—horseman or knight). Parliament's Puritan forces led by Oliver Cromwell were called *Roundheads*, because they wore their hair short—what in America came to be called the "pumpkin cut" as Puritans placed the stem of a pumpkin on their hair and cut around it in a small circle (what today we would call a "bowl cut"). Their army prayed before battle, sang hymns as they marched, and relied on muskets and cannons. Cromwell's army defeated King Charles and his Cavaliers in 1645. Cromwell, after failing to reach an agreement with King Charles, had him beheaded in 1649. Parliament then declared England a "Commonwealth," abolished the monarchy, dismissed the aristocratic House of Lords, and ruled the country as a small group of like-minded men.

Yet as much as they shared common beliefs, these men quarreled endlessly as England was threatened by attack from Catholic countries across the English Channel who were appalled at the execution of King Charles. The country was also threatened by closer neighbors: Ireland, which had always remained Roman Catholic, and Scotland, which, while it was Protestant, remained faithful to the Stuart dynasty that had long ruled it. England even went to war with Holland, another Protestant country, over fierce trade competition between Dutch and English sea merchants. Finally, there were threats from within England by Roman Catholics and Anglicans still sympathetic to the king. Cromwell endured the squabbles in Parliament—even after it had been reduced to an even smaller number of Puritans—then marched his army of Roundheads flourishing their muskets into Parliament and "dismissed" its members in 1653. Refusing to accept the title of King, he ruled England as "Lord Protector"—a euphemistic name for a dictator—for the next five years.

England under Oliver Cromwell

Cromwell was a remarkably effective dictator who protected England from invasion and subversion. He was also remarkably tolerant, lifting England's ban against Jews that had been in effect since the thirteenth century and ensuring freedom for other minorities. Still, he persecuted Catholics and Anglicans and waged such brutal warfare in Catholic Ireland that many Irish hate England to this day for Cromwell's cruelty.

When the Puritans, who had long been persecuted by Anglicans, came to power under Cromwell, they, in turn, imposed their doctrines on the country. Just as Puritan "blue laws" in America still outlaw such things as the sale of liquor on Sundays, the Puritans in England outlawed swearing, gambling, drunkenness, horse racing, cockfighting, and bear baiting (setting a pack of dogs on a chained bear). The Puritans also outlawed all sorts of theatrical entertainment. Theaters were closed, and the great tradition of English plays that had featured the works of Shakespeare and Marlowe came to an end. Performers caught juggling, doing acrobatics, or other circus-like feats were arrested and sometimes had their ears or noses cut off. Even something so innocent as dancing around the maypole, which children now do in grade school, was banned as the remnant of an ancient fertility rite where young maidens danced and wove ribbons around a pole that represented a gigantic phallus.

The Puritans even outlawed Christmas! We now think of Christmas as one of the most sacred of Christian holidays, but in the seventeenth century—and continuing well into the nineteenth—Christmas was largely a pagan celebration. The major Christian holiday was Easter. Because Easter was tied to the Jewish holiday of the Passover, it could be definitely dated, but no one was sure of what day Jesus Christ was born. The Eastern Orthodox Church, in fact, still places Christ's birth well into January. In Western Europe, the date of Christ's birth was set at various earlier times in late December, and that brought it closer to many pagan celebrations of the winter solstice. The winter solstice, which we traditionally set at December 21, is the "shortest" day of the year since there is less sunlight on that day than on any other. After that date, the days gradually start growing longer, and many pagan cultures celebrated the solstice as the "rebirth" of light. In England, they celebrated the solstice by lighting candles, decorating evergreens (trees that stay green throughout the year), exchanging presents, and feasting, drinking, and general merry-making. Such "pagan" celebrations around Christmas, however, were anathema to the Puritans, so they banned them. After the Puritans lost power, such Christmas celebrations resumed, and in the American Revolution, George Washington knew that if his troops crossed the Delaware River in the darkness of Christmas Eve, they would find British troops on the other shore drunk from celebrating Christmas (in the twentieth century, the Japanese employed a similar strategy by attacking Pearl Harbor early on a Sunday morning, because they knew most servicemen would have spent the previous Saturday night drinking).

Despite these mounting conflicts, scientific, economic, and literary life flourished during the seventeenth century. John Napier invented logarithms in 1614 and developed the use of the decimal point. William Harvey discovered circulation of the blood in 1626, and the greatest of the century's scientists, Isaac Newton, discovered laws of gravity and other physical motion. On the Continent, scientists such as Galileo challenged the common belief that the earth was the center of the universe and that all heavenly bodies (including the sun) rotated around it.

Agriculture flourished as more land was opened up for cultivation, and the manufacture of wool, cotton, and even silk made for important export trade. English merchant ships expanded trade around the world, and England established more colonies along the eastern coast of North America, as well as elsewhere around the world.

Great works of prose emerged, most notably the *King James Bible*, probably the most beautiful of all translations of the Bible, with such eloquent passages as the twenty-third Psalm: "The Lord is my shepherd; I shall not want. He maketh me to lie down in green pastures." This translation, also known as "The Authorized Version of the Bible," was commissioned by King James himself and carried out between 1604 and 1611, the same years that Shakespeare was writing his greatest plays. The style of the King James Bible, as well as the style of Shakespeare's plays, have been the two greatest influences on how later writers have used the English language.

The English Language in the Seventeenth Century

In the 1600s, the English language came to resemble our modern English so that we can read the Bible and Shakespeare much more easily than we can read Chaucer. In Chaucer's Middle English, for example, the plural form of nouns took many forms, such as "eyen" for "eyes" and "shoon" for "shoes," but in the seventeenth century, most plurals were formed by simply adding an –s to a noun. In Chaucer's English, possession was shown by following a noun with a possessive pronoun, such as "as red as Mars his heart." In the seventeenth century, people began to abbreviate this practice by replacing the "his" of "Mars his heart" with an apostrophe s ('s): "Mars's heart." Like many other languages, Middle English had various forms of *you* as a pronoun: *thou*, *thy*, and *thee* were singular forms and *ye* and *you* were plural. By the 1600s, *you* was becoming the sole form of the second person pronoun, singular and plural, another step in the ongoing process of simplifying the language.

Similarly, *its* began to appear as a possessive pronoun—but that development would create the confusion many people have today between *its* and *it's*, the first a possessive pronoun ("The dog bit its tail") and the second a contraction of *it is* ("It's time to go"). *Who* also started appearing as a relative pronoun referring to people (though the King James Bible still said, "Our Father, which art in Heaven"). Verbs dropped the *eth* ending ("giveth," "restoreth") for a simple –s or –es ending ("gives," "restores"), though here too the King James Bible uses the older form ("He restoreth my soul"), and Shakespeare and other writers used verbs such as "doth" and "hath" long after most English speakers had switched to "does" and "has."

By the end of the seventeenth century, dictionaries were created to explain unusual words in the English language and to try to make spelling and grammar uniform. Letters such as *u* and *v* or *j* and *i*, which had often been used interchangeably, were regularized and used as we use them today—*i* and *u* as vowels and *j* and *v* as consonants. The letter *e* at the end of a word lengthened the preceding vowel so that "dam" became "dame."

Poetry in the Seventeenth Century

Poetry also continued to thrive in the seventeenth century, largely because of a healthy controversy between two groups of poets who wrote in very different styles and had very different ideas about what poetry should be. One group of poets, calling itself the "Tribe of Ben," followed the poetic style of Ben Jonson, who regarded poetry as elegant, poised, verse that was based on classical Greek and Latin poetry. His poetry was close to *song* and, as such, frequently used the tetrameter or tetrameter/trimeter line.

Ben Jonson (1572–1637)

Shortly after Ben Jonson was born, his father died, and the boy was adopted by a bricklayer's family. Although he never went to college, Jonson received an excellent grammar-school education, especially in the classics, and learned much more on his own. He worked for a while as a bricklayer before joining the army and fighting in Flanders on behalf of the Protestant Dutch who were battling Spain for their independence. Returning to England, he became an actor and playwright, much like his friend William Shakespeare. His comedies, such as *Volpone* (1606), have been as enduring as Shakespeare's plays. He also wrote elaborate musical plays, called *masques*, for King James and his court and, in 1616, was appointed *Poet Laureate*, the official poet of England. In that position, he received a *pension*, a modest salary, and was called upon to write poems for various state occasions.

As a poet, Jonson followed the example of classical Greek and Latin poets by writing in clear, simple language instead of the florid and extravagant idiom of many of his Elizabethan contemporaries (including Shakespeare). His poems earned Jonson the admiration of a group of young poets—Robert Herrick, Richard Lovelace, Sir John Suckling—we now call the "Cavalier Poets." Like Jonson, these poets thought poetry should be as direct and immediately clear as song, and many of their poems were set to music, as was this one by Jonson himself:

To Celia

Drink to me only with thine eyes,	*Toast me with a only a look*
And I will pledge with mine;	*I'll return it with my look*
Or leave a kiss within the cup	*kiss the wine glass*
And I'll not ask for wine.	
The thirst that from the soul doth rise	5
Doth ask a drink divine;	
But might I of Jove's nectar sup,	*king of the gods, who drank nectar*
I would not change for thine.	*not exchange it for your kiss*
I sent thee late a rosy wreath,	*wreath of roses*
Not so much honouring thee	*Not so much to flatter you* 10
As giving it a hope that there	*But hoping that with you*
It could not withered be;	*The wreath's roses would not die*
But thou thereon didst only breathe,	*All you did was breathe on it*
And sent'st it back to me;	
Since when it grows, and smells, I swear,	15
Not of itself but thee!	1606

Can you see how debonair, polished, and "rehearsed" this poem is—a characteristic of poems written in the tetrameter and trimeter line of the ballad stanza. (Notice that each of Jonson's eight-line stanzas consists of two ballad quatrains, each rhyming *abxb*). Jonson is so, as we used to say, "cool" and "smooth" as he drinks a toast to his beloved. It's as polished as a toast you might give at a wedding or other formal occasion where you try to come up with something clever and elegant. That's the quality of so much of Jonson's poetry, as well as those of the Cavalier poets, so if you feel the debonair, urbane quality of Jonson, you will find the same insouciance in Herrick, Suckling, and other poets who write in this style.

Part of this limpid quality of Jonson's style comes from the fact that he varies his meter considerably. He starts the poem with a trochee, "**Drink** to," then an iamb, "me **on-**," then slips in a pyrrhic foot, ""ly with," then ends on a spondee, "**thine eyes**."

Drink to/ me **on-**/ly with/ **thine eyes**

The line thus has a lightness, a rapidity to it.

The 2nd line moves much more regularly in iambic trimeter:

And **I**/ will **pledge**/ with **mine**

Pronouns don't usually take accents, but, in Jonson's intimate love toast, by putting the unaccented "And" before "I," it places more stress on the pronoun and gives the line a solemn touch as he vows to return her look of love.

And I/ will pledge/ with mine

The 3rd line has a little lightness to it, like the first, for after two iambs ("Or **leave** / a **kiss**") he skips along on a pyrrhic, "but in," before landing on a solid iamb ("for **wine**").

Or leave/ a kiss/ but in/ the cup

Again, it's not an exact science, so it's okay to place an accent on "**in**" (a preposition, which is usually not accented), if you feel you want to read it that way, but then, you lose the lightness that makes line three similar to line one—in contrast to the regular meter of lines two and four:

And I'll/ not ask/ for wine.

Such metrical regularity in lines two and four and metrical irregularity in lines one and three give more form—pattern—to these lines, in which the poet is paying a witty compliment to his beloved: her eyes are so lovely that all she has to do is look at him, and it's like drinking a toast with wine; then, all she has to do is put her lips to an empty cup, and he'd rather "drink" the kiss from the empty cup than drink a cup of wine. (Her kisses, are, as the old song goes, "sweeter than wine.")

We get a similar pattern in the next four lines. The first line starts with an iamb, but then, we get what I'd read as a pyrrhic—"that from"—then two iambs to give this line, too, a little "lift."

The thirst/ that from/ the soul/ doth rise

The sixth line, like the second and forth lines, is perfectly regular iambic trimeter:

Doth ask/ a drink/ di-vine;

But the seventh line (like the first, third, and fifth, gets lighter with, after an initial iamb, another pyrrhic, followed by a heavy spondee, then a final iamb:

But might/ I of/ Jove's nec-/tar sup

The rhythmic heaviness at the latter part of the line underscores Jonson's boast that even if he could drink the nectar (Greek and Roman gods drink nectar and eat ambrosia—the most deliciously delicate food and drink in the universe, unavailable to mere mortals) that is served to Jove, the ruler of earth and sky and all the other gods (the Romans also called him Jupiter; the Greeks called him Zeus) refuse to exchange it for the glass that has only his beloved's kiss in it.

I would/ not change/ for thine

(By the way, do you think Celia is falling for all this hyperbole? Or has she heard Ben go on like this before?)

The next four lines open with a straightforward line of iambic tetrameter—

> I **sent**/ thee **late**/ a **ro**-/sy **wreath**

—but then, he goes light again. You could keep things regular by accenting "so"—"Not **so**"—and by pronouncing "honoring" in two syllables—as if he'd written "hon'ring"—to make it come out "Not **so**/ much **hon**-/'ring **thee**," but can you see that the more irregular way of scanning the line makes it have more of a lilt with an opening pyrrhic and then concluding with an anapest:

> Not so/ much **hon**-/or-ing **thee**

This reads more like real conversation rather than regular, thumping iambics would.

Line 11 is a gem of caesura, metrical substitution, and enjambment:

> As **giv**-/ing it/ a **hope**/ that **there**

You should be able to see why not accenting "it" gives the line a swift movement that lands on "**hope**," hits a caesura, then, before telling Celia what that wondrous hope would be, he suspends the line with enjambment—"that there"—before finishing with another irregular line that I would scan as a pyrrhic foot, then an iamb, then an anapest:

> It could/ not **with**-/er-ed **be**.

Again, you can keep the line regularly iambic by scanning it this way:

> It **could**/ not **with**-/ered **be**

But can you see that it's more fun to be metrically playful rather than dolefully regular?

The last four lines carry the "punch" of the toast (so to speak). The poet sends her a rose wreath in the hope that only she could keep it forever fresh (is this guy for real?), but all she does is breathe on the rose (just as he asked her to put a kiss in an empty cup) and send it back to him. Lines thirteen and fourteen, which describe that exchange, are metrically regular:

> But **thou**/ there-**on**/ didst **on**-/ly **breathe**,

> And **sent-st**/ it **back**/ to **me**;

Now for the fireworks (metrically speaking)! The 15th line could be scanned as metrically regular iambic tetrameter:

> Since **when**/ it **grows**/ and **smells**,/ I **swear**,

But it's so much more playful to scan it this way:

> Since when/ it **grows**/ and **smells**,/ I **swear**,

And note how the opening quick rhythmic pace slows down into clear iambs and the great caesura that again holds our suspense—"smells"—like what?—is Celia about to be embarrassed? Oh no!—metrically flattered:

Not of/ it-**self**,/ but **thee**.

Can you see why you would never accent "of"—the word is not important, and accenting it would slow down a marvelously lilting line. By scanning the first foot as a pyrrhic rather than an iamb, the line rushes forward then—still keeping Celia guessing—hits a caesura—and finally comes down, after a metrical pirouette, on "but **thee**."

Although it's tempting to try to turn every line into a metrically regular unit, that would take all the fun out of poetic rhythm that uses playful variation. Rhythm governs all things in life and learning to be a good scanner of poetry—or a good poet—is like learning to be a good lover—knowing when to add a little variation, slowing down at some points, speeding up at others, then pausing, just a little, when things are getting most exciting.

Cavalier Poetry

Cavalier poetry took its cue from Ben Jonson. It was elegant, urbane, and seemed effortlessly tossed off, though in reality the Cavalier poets worked hard to perfect their lines as all good poets do. As we have seen, such poetry moves closer to song than speech, and Cavalier poets frequently used the tetrameter or the tetrameter/trimeter line for song-like effects. However, one of the greatest of the Cavalier poets, Robert Herrick, broke up his tetrameter and trimeter lines with frequent metrical substitutions so that they sound as much like speech as song.

Robert Herrick (1591-1674)

Like Ben Jonson, Robert Herrick was born into a middle-class London family. His father, a goldsmith, died shortly after his birth, and as a boy, Herrick was apprenticed to his uncle, also a goldsmith. In his twenties, Herrick went to Cambridge University, and in today's parlance, "hung out" with other young poets who flocked around Ben Jonson as his poetic "Sons" or "Tribe." Even after graduating with a degree in religion in 1623, Herrick continued to frequent taverns to talk poetry with Jonson and his cronies. Finally in 1629, he took a "real job" as an Episcopal clergyman in a church in Devonshire, in the rural western part of England.

On the one hand, Herrick hated being in Devonshire, which seemed to be, as we would say, "the boonies," compared to the sophistication of the City of London. On the other hand, being a rural clergyman afforded him ample time to write elegant poems in a classical style reminiscent of Ben Jonson. The boredom Herrick felt in Devonshire led him to dream—and write—about imaginary beauties from Ancient Greece and Rome. In real life, Herrick grew to be a plump, old bachelor parson. In his imaginary life, however, he was the elegant, cavalier beau of imagined beauties.

With the Puritan victory over King Charles I, Episcopalian clergymen such as Herrick lost their jobs, and in 1647, he returned to London with some 1,200 poems that he published in two volumes—one devoted to romantic, secular lyrics, the other to sacred, devotional poems. But England, under the Puritan rule of Oliver Cromwell, was in no mood for Cavalier poetry—sacred or secular—and Herrick's poetry was consigned to oblivion only to be rediscovered in the nineteenth century.

One of his most famous poems has been interpreted as his protest against Puritan precision and order in favor of Cavalier spontaneity and nonchalance:

Delight in Disorder

A sweet disorder in the dress		
Kindles in clothes a wantonness.	*sexiness*	
A lawn about the shoulders thrown	*lawn (silk shawl)*	
Into a fine distractión :	*(four syllables: dis-trac-ti-on)*	
An erring lace which here and there	*wandering lace*	5
Enthrals the crimson stomacher :	*red stomach belt*	
A cuff neglectful, and thereby	*not tucked into sleeve*	
Ribbons to flow confusedly :	*ribbons dangle in dsarray*	
A winning wave (deserving note)		
In the tempestuous petticoat :		10
A careless shoe-string, in whose tie		
I see a wild civility :		
Do more bewitch me than when art		
Is too precise in every part.		1648

How does Herrick vary the iambic tetrameter line to underscore his preference for elegant "messiness" over rigid "order?"

In 1660, after the death of Oliver Cromwell, and the return of England to monarchy with the "Restoration" of King Charles I's son as King Charles II, Herrick was reinstated as parson in his church in Devonshire. Although he lived to the, then, unusually old age of 83, he published no more poetry. His most famous poem, published in London in his secular volume *Hesperides* in 1648, probably best characterizes him, not as a dashing Cavalier lover but as the wise old parson who can counsel young maidens to *carpe diem* (Latin for "seize the day"—make the most of life while we can). The *carpe diem* argument was frequently used in poems in which men tried to seduce women by urging them to enjoy life by having sex while they were young and beautiful.

To the Virgins, to Make Much of Time

Gather ye rosebuds while ye may,
    Old time is still a-flying :
And this same flower that smiles to-day
    To-morrow will be dying.

The glorious lamp of heaven, the sun,   5
    The higher he's a-getting,
The sooner will his race be run,
    And nearer he's to setting.

That age is best which is the first,
    When youth and blood are warmer;   10
But being spent, the worse, and worst
    Times still succeed the former.

> Then be not coy, but use your time,   *(be not disdainful of love)*
>   And while ye may go marry:
> For having lost but once your prime   15
>   You may for ever tarry.   1648

Can you see how Herrick uses the ballad quatrain here but varies it so that the quatrains rhyme *abab*, rather than *abxb*? For me, the loveliest effects of metrics, caesura, feminine rhyme, and enjambment occur in these two lines:

> But **be**-/ ing **spent**,/ the **worse**,/ and **worst**
>   **Times still**/ suc-**ceed**/ the **for**-mer.

Reading as a poet, can you see what is so engaging about Herrick's handling of poetic form in these two lines?

Edmund Waller (1606–1687)

Edmund Waller was a wealthy aristocrat who supported King Charles I in Parliament. In 1643, he conspired with other "Royalists" to keep London under the control of the king, but when the plot was discovered, Waller confessed and turned in his fellow-conspirators, several of whom were arrested and executed. Waller was only fined and banished from England; he lived in France and Switzerland for the next ten years until the ban was lifted. With the Restoration of Charles II as King of England in 1660, when Waller, again, returned to Parliament.

    His most famous poem is "Song," where he works his own variation on the *carpe diem* theme, which is just another variation of the courtly love "complaint" about a woman who disdains her lover's romantic advances. Where Herrick addressed "To the Virgins, To Make Much of Time" directly to the young ladies who were rejecting the romantic advances of young men, Waller directs his poem to a rose that he sends to the beautiful woman who coldly rejects his love (and thus "wastes" both time and his life). We have seen other poems urge a young woman to give in to a man's advances while she is still young and beautiful, but notice how Waller's rhetoric (his attempt to persuade her) develops a line of argument that dramatically culminates in the last stanza when he tells the rose to "die" in the presence of the young woman. How does Waller's rhetoric resemble and differ from that of Herrick in "To the Virgins, To Make Much of Time?" Also note how Waller's poem differs in its form from Herrick's. Herrick uses the traditional ballad quatrain but how has Waller experimented with that form?

Song

> Go, lovely Rose—
> Tell her that wastes her time and me,
>   That now she knows,
> When I resemble her to thee,   *compare her*
> How sweet and fair she seems to be.   5
>
>   Tell her that 's young,
> And shuns to have her graces spied,
>   That hadst thou sprung
> In deserts where no men abide,

Thou must have uncommended died. *died without being praised* 10

   Small is the worth
Of beauty from the light retired:
   Bid her come forth,
Suffer herself to be desired,
And not blush so to be admired.   15

   Then die!—that she
The common fate of all things rare
   May read in thee;
How small a part of time they share
That are so wondrous sweet and fair!   1645

Richard Lovelace (1618–1657)

Richard Lovelace epitomized the Cavalier poet and gentleman. He came from a wealthy family, was a dashing and elegant courtier, and stood firmly behind King Charles I in the Civil War. He was imprisoned several times for supporting the king, lost his wealth and land in the Civil War, and died impoverished at the age of thirty-nine.

In this poem, written in ballad quatrains but rhyming *abab*, he tries to comfort the woman he loves before heading off to war to fight on behalf of King Charles I. The woman's real name was Lucy Sacheverell, his fiancée, who married another man when it was mistakenly reported that Lovelace had been killed. In this poem, he calls her "Lucasta," a name derived from the Latin *lux casta* ("light pure").

With daring wit, he makes it sound as if by leaving Lucasta to go to war, he is cheating on her with another woman (notice the pun on "arms" in the fourth line—a pun Ernest Hemingway would use in the title of *A Farewell to Arms*, his novel about World War I). In the third quatrain, however, he argues that even she should adore such "inconstancy" (infidelity), for just as she treasures her own "honour" (which, for women, meant their "virtue"), he joins the war out of his "honour" (a man's sense of his patriotic duty).

To Lucasta, Going to the Wars

Tell me not, Sweet, I am unkind,
   That from the nunnery
Of thy chaste breast and quiet mind
   To war and arms I fly.

True, a new mistress now I chase,   5
   The first foe in the field;
And with a stronger faith embrace
   A sword, a horse, a shield.

Yet this inconstancy is such
   As thou too shalt adore;   10
I could not love thee, Dear, so much,
   Loved I not Honour more.   1649

Notice how effectively Lovelace uses enjambment and caesura in the ballad quatrain to underscore the emotional power of what he is saying. Which four lines are enjambed? Which three lines have caesuras? How does the placement of the caesuras in line one, around "Sweet," compare to the caesuras around "Dear" in the last line? How would it affect the tone of the poem if he called Lucasta "Dear" in line 1 and "Sweet" in line twelve?

Sir John Suckling (1609-1642)

Sir John Suckling was a wealthy aristocrat who liked drinking, wenching, and gambling. In the Civil War, he epitomized the gallant but doomed Cavaliers. His army of dashing aristocrats on their horses, long hair flowing over their splendid red and white uniforms, was cut to pieces by the Puritan soldiers. Suckling fled to France, where he died in poverty, at an even younger age than Lovelace, reportedly by suicide.

Suckling's poetry is more blunt and cynical than that of the other Cavalier poets. In this poem, notice how Suckling expresses his love for a woman in a gruff, back-handed way by using *hyperbole* (exaggeration) and *understatement* (saying much less than he really feels). In our parlance, we might translate the first line as "I'll be damned! I've been in love with the same woman for three whole days!" How does Suckling vary the ballad quatrain in this poem?

The Constant Lover

Out upon it, I have loved
  Three whole days together!
And am like to love three more,
  If it prove fair weather.

Time shall moult away his wings   5
  Ere he shall discover
In the whole wide world again
  Such a constant lover.

But the spite on 't is, no praise
  Is due at all to me: 10
Love with me had made no stays,
  Had it any been but she.

Had it any been but she,
  And that very face,
There had been at least ere this   15
  A dozen dozen in her place.   1659

What's funny about this poem, is that Suckling strikes the pose of an "inconstant" (fickle, unfaithful lover), who usually doesn't love a woman for longer than a day (or a single night). Even more amazing to him is that he thinks he might actually love her for three *more* days (as long as the weather stays nice). The hyperbole comes in the second quatrain where he says time, which we sometime depict as a bird that is always flying away, will "moult" (shed and get a whole new set of feathers on its wings) before it finds any lover so faithful and constant than he is, who may well stay in love for six whole days!

In the third quatrain, Suckling neatly shifts to understatement, saying he can't take credit for such amazing fidelity to one woman. It's really that this particular woman has kept him more faithful than he has ever been to any other. With the repetition of "Had it been any but she" at the beginning of the fourth quatrain, we feel that under his casual, even flippant, remarks about his amazing constancy, he deeply adores this woman (but would never say so directly). The line "and that very face" gives another understated hint of his feelings: he doesn't go on, as other courtly lovers might, about her eyes, her lips, her hair, but just off-handedly says, "and that very face." Before he lets his true feelings show too much, he concludes with more hyperbole: that if it had been anyone but her he would have had at least a "dozen dozen" other women in the past three days. Can you see how such an understated, back-handed compliment to this woman is a more effective tribute to her power than many lines straightforwardly extolling her beauties?

Metaphysical Poetry

At the same time that the Cavalier poets were writing their elegant, seemingly effortless lyrics, another group of poets in the seventeenth century were writing a very different kind of verse. While the Cavalier poets emulated Ben Jonson as a model of classical, polished, song-like verse, these other poets looked to a very different kind of poet, John Donne, as their model. Just as the Cavalier poets called themselves the "Sons of Ben" or "Tribe of Ben," these other poets called themselves the "Tribe of Donne" or "Sons of Donne." John Donne and Ben Jonson were friends who admired one another's poetry, but their poetry was markedly different. Jonson and the Cavalier poets who followed him strove for a "cool," suave poetic style that seldom sounded impassioned, angry, or distraught. Reading their poems, it seldom sounds as if the poets even raise their voices, much less shout or scream.

John Donne, however, wrote in a highly emotional style that sounded more like heightened speech than elegant song. He and the poets who followed him frequently sound as if they are speaking out of furious anger or wrenching despair, rather than the calm, poised idiom of Jonson and the Cavalier poets. Their poetic lines are filled with sudden pauses, twists, and turns of thought, as if they were struggling to say what they mean, unlike the Cavalier poets who always sound at ease and "rehearsed" in what they say.

Another difference between these groups of poets is that while Jonson and the Cavalier poets wrote verse that was easily understood on a first reading—as song usually is—Donne and his followers wrote poetry that sometimes is extremely difficult to understand even after several readings. Remember that poetry in this era was still written, not so much for the general reading public, but for a small group of aristocratic, learned readers. Such poetry was also usually circulated among such readers in manuscript copies, rather than in books published for the general public. Poets and readers often knew each other, and poets could count on such readers to understand classical allusions, arcane scientific ideas, and a highly sophisticated vocabulary. They knew that such readers—like people today who do the mind-boggling cross-word puzzles in *The New York Times* and *The New Yorker* magazine—loved "brain teasing" puns, paradoxes, and metaphors. These poets wove such intellectual "wit" into their poems.

Many readers, however, found such difficult, intellectual poetry distasteful and dubbed Donne and poets like him "metaphysical," by which they meant that the poems required as much thoughtful understanding as reading metaphysics, the most abstruse form of philosophy. In particular, such readers, including the great eighteenth century writer Samuel Johnson, objected to the far-fetched, drawn-out metaphors of Donne and his followers, which they called "metaphysical conceits." The metaphysical poets took the old conventions of courtly love and gave them a radically "modern" twist." A metaphysical poet, for example, might describe the tears he sheds because of his beloved's disdain as snow melting on the "roof" of his head and running down the "gutter-spouts" of his eyes. While we can sometimes share Doctor Johnson's antipathy to such extravagant "metaphysical conceits," we can also delight in their cleverness when we hear them in contemporary country-western music. A country-music singer might "complain" to his beloved, "Up the elevator of your life I've been shafted," or "I've been flushed down the toilet of your heart."

John Donne (1572–1631)

John Donne was born into a Roman Catholic family in London at a time when it was dangerous to be a Catholic, for England was breaking away from the Catholic Church and establishing the Episcopal Church as the official church of the country. Donne went to both Oxford and Cambridge Universities, as well as to what today would be the equivalent of law school. He never received a degree, however, and proved to be an unruly, rebellious student, courting many young women, drinking and carousing in taverns, and writing bawdy, licentious poetry. Still, he read widely in classical literature, science, and religion. He traveled extensively in Europe and served on ships that battled the Spanish. His charm and wit earned him a place at court as the secretary of a prominent aristocrat, but he ruined his career by falling in love with and secretly marrying the niece of his patron. His bride's father had Donne fired from his position and put in prison.

For years after his release, Donne and his family struggled to survive, and he finally converted to the Episcopal Church. King James urged Donne to become an Anglican clergyman, and Donne eventually became the clerical dean of St. Paul's Cathedral in London, where his sermons drew huge crowds. One of his most famous sermons begins, "No man is an island, entire of itself. Each man is a piece of the continent, a part of the main [land]." The sermon ends with Donne's image of a funeral bell tolling a person's death, and his injunction, given that we are all part of humanity, "Never send to know for whom the bell tolls—it tolls for thee." Ernest Hemingway drew upon this sermon by John Donne for the title of his novel about the Spanish Civil War—*For Whom the Bell Tolls*.

Donne also wrote poems that delighted his circle of readers with their quick wit, intellectual rigor, and rough conversational style—a far cry from the elegant, polished verses of Ben Jonson and the Cavalier poets. While Cavalier poets wrote lines of iambic tetrameter/trimeter that come close to song, the metaphysical poets frequently used the iambic pentameter line to make their poetry sound, not like debonair song, but like impassioned, angry spoken conversation. Look at the opening lines of this poem by John Donne.

From "The Canonization"

> For God's sake hold your tongue, and let me love;
>   Or chide my palsy, or my gout;
>   My five gray hairs, or ruin'd fortune flout;
> With wealth your state, your mind with arts improve;
>   Take you a course, get you a place,   5
>   Observe his Honour, or his Grace;
> Or the king's real, or his stamp'd face
>   Contemplate ; what you will, approve,
>   So you will let me love.   1633

How would you scan those opening lines? I'd place accents, very irregularly, as such:

> For **God's**/ **sake, hold**/ your **tongue**/ and **let**/ me **love**,
> Or **chide**/ my **pal**-/ sy, or/ my **gout**,
> My **five**/ **gray hairs**,/ or **ru**-/ined **for**-/tune **flout**,

By making his meter so irregular, Donne brings poetry closer to speech than song. He's clearly talking, angrily, to a friend who has criticized him for devoting so much of his time to the woman he loves. The poem begins in the middle of their argument with Donne telling his friend, basically, "Shut up and stop criticizing me for being in love." If you want to criticize me, he suggests, point out my illnesses, such as palsy (trembling) or gout (inflammation of the joints), or that my hair is starting to turn gray. You can even, Donne says (probably drawing on his own experience as a courtier), make fun of the fact that my career has been ruined.

In the fourth line, Donne turns the tables on his friend, suggesting he could do a lot more profitable things than criticize him for being in love: make money; improve his mind with study; settle on a career ("Take you a course"); get a "place," an appointment in the royal court, where he can serve an aristocrat ("His Honor, or His Grace"); or even serve the King himself in person (or devote himself to making money, gold and silver coins that are stamped with the King's face as our coins and bills are stamped with the faces of presidents). Do any of these things, Donne says, just leave me alone so that I can love.

John Donne's most famous "metaphysical conceit" occurs in this next poem, written in iambic tetrameter. He wrote it to his wife in 1611 when he had to take an extended trip to the Continent. At this time, Donne and his wife were poor, uncertain of their future, and she was pregnant. She was very distraught that he would be going away for a long time and feared something terrible would happen to him, so he wrote this poem to comfort her. While he was gone, her baby was stillborn.

A Valediction Forbidding Mourning

As virtuous men pass mildly away,
   And whisper to their souls to go,
Whilst some of their sad friends do say,
   "Now his breath goes," and some say, "No."

So let us melt, and make no noise,   5
   No tear-floods, nor sigh-tempests move ;
'Twere profanation of our joys
   To tell the laity our love.   *laity:"lay" Christians (not holy priests)*

Moving of th' earth brings harms and fears ;   *earthquakes*
   Men reckon what it did, and meant;   10
But trepidation of the spheres,   *movement in the heavens*
   Though greater far, is innocent.   *Is less noticeable*

Dull sublunary lovers' love   *earthly ("sublunary" means beneath the moon)*
   —Whose soul is sense—cannot admit   *(who are sensual, physical lovers)*
Of absence, 'cause it doth remove   *(can't stand to be apart physically)*   15

The thing which elemented it.	*(physical attraction is the basis of their love)*
But we by a love so much refined,	*(our love is more refined and spiritual)*
That ourselves know not what it is,	
Inter-assurèd of the mind,	*(our love binds our minds together)*
Care less, eyes, lips and hands to miss.	*(we can stand being apart physically)* 20
Our two souls therefore, which are one,	
Though I must go, endure not yet	
A breach, but an expansion,	
Like gold to aery thinness beat.	*(gold hammered as thin as air)*
If they be two, they are two so	25
As stiff twin compasses are two;	
Thy soul, the fix'd foot, makes no show	
To move, but doth, if th' other do.	
And though it in the centre sit,	
Yet, when the other far doth roam,	30
It leans, and hearkens after it,	
And grows erect, as that comes home.	
Such wilt thou be to me, who must,	
Like th' other foot, obliquely run ;	
Thy firmness makes my circle just,	35
And makes me end where I begun.	1633

    A *valediction* is a farewell speech, such as is delivered by a high school or college *valedictorian* representing a graduating class that is saying farewell to its school, its *alma mater* (adopted mother). Here John Donne bids farewell to his wife and, in a series of brilliant *metaphysical conceits*, beseeches her not to cry but to say goodbye without "mourning" (as if he were going off to his death). He first says they should part from one another the way virtuous men die (knowing they will go to heaven). He then says that only "earthly" lovers cry and scream when they part, but that their love is heavenly and does not call for such tempestuous emotion. Although they may be far apart physically, their souls will still be united. He then compares their two souls to a sheet of gold metal that, through constant pounding with a hammer by a goldsmith, grows larger and larger but never separates, even as it becomes almost as thin as air.

    Donne then follows with his most famous "metaphysical conceit," comparing himself and his wife to the two legs of a compass (not a directional compass but the kind we use to draw circles). She is the leg of the compass that stays in place, and he is the other leg that moves away. But his movement away from her still keeps them in touch for she "bends" toward him as he moves away from her. When he is at his furthest remove from her, in fact, the two legs of the compass form a single horizontal line, united at their point of greatest separation. Her staying in place keeps him moving in a steady circle while he is gone, and, as he returns to her, the two legs of the compass come closer together and "grow erect" (the sexual overtones of "erection" is part of Donne's wit here).

John Donne also wrote many sonnets, which he called "Holy Sonnets," because they were about religious experience, rather than courtly love, as most previous sonnets had been. Here are two of his most famous sonnets. Can you see Donne's *metaphysical wit* at work in each of them?

Holy Sonnet 10

Death be not proud, though some have calléd thee
Mighty and dreadfull, for, thou art not so,
For, those, whom thou think'st, thou dost overthrow,
Die not, poore death, nor yet canst thou kill me.
From rest and sleepe, which but thy pictures bee,   *(rest and sleep resemble death)*   5
Much pleasure, then from thee, much more must flow,
And soonest our best men with thee doe goe,
Rest of their bones, and soules deliverie.   *(death releases their immortal souls)*
Thou art slave to Fate, Chance, kings, and desperate men,   *suicidal men*
And dost with poyson, warre, and sicknesse dwell,   10
And poppie, or charmes can make us sleepe as well,   *(poppy flowers are narcotics)*
And better then thy stroake; why swell'st thou then;   *why are yo*
One short sleepe past, wee wake eternally,
And death shall be no more; Death, thou shalt die.   1633

What is the rhyme scheme of this sonnet? Is it closer to the Italian or English sonnet structure? Does the *syntax* (the sentence pattern) follow the rhyme scheme structure or work against it?

Holy Sonnet 14

Batter my heart, three-person'd God, for you
As yet but knock, breathe, shine, and seek to mend;
That I may rise and stand, o'erthrow me, and bend
Your force to break, blow, burn, and make me new.
I, like an usurp'd town to'another due,   *conquered city that longs*   5
Labor to'admit you, but oh, to no end;   *for its rightful ruler*
Reason, your viceroy in me, me should defend,
But is captiv'd, and proves weak or untrue.
Yet dearly'I love you, and would be lov'd fain,   *be loved gladly in return*
But am betroth'd unto your enemy;   *engaged to your enemy*   10
Divorce me,'untie or break that knot again,
Take me to you, imprison me, for I,
Except you'enthrall me, never shall be free,   *imprison me*
Nor ever chaste, except you ravish me.   1633

In this "Holy Sonnet," Donne asks God to "batter" his heart as if he were a medieval walled town and an enemy force were using a battering ram to break down its massive locked doors. Notice how the "three-personed" God describes the Christian Trinity: Christ the Son who "knocks" at the poet's heart for admission; the Holy Spirit that "breathes" inspiration into him; and God the Father who shines in his glorious might. Donne is saying the three of them are not doing enough to heal him spiritually and make him "rise and stand." Donne and other metaphysical poets loved *paradoxes*— seemingly contradictory ideas that were nevertheless true. Thus, he says to the Holy Trinity, if he is to stand upright, they have to "o'erthrow me" (knock me down). He also asks Christ to "break," rather than "knock" at his heart; the Holy Spirit to "blow," rather than just "breathe;" and God to "burn" him, rather than just shine.

In the next four lines, Donne continues the comparison of himself to a medieval walled town by saying that while he would like to open up his gates and allow God to enter, his "reason" (God's "viceroy" or "governor") has been taken captive and is too weak or false to admit God. The extensive comparison takes another turn as Donne compares himself to a woman whose true love is God but has gotten engaged ("betrothed") to Satan, God's enemy. As such a woman, Donne now asks God, in his Trinitarian identity, to divorce, untie, or break that "wedding knot" with Satan. Donne's plea becomes even more urgent as he begs God to "Take" him by force, imprison him, so that, in another paradox, he can be "free" and, most paradoxical of all, "ravish" him so that he can be virginally "chaste."

Andrew Marvell (1621-1678)

Andrew Marvell went to Cambridge and was aligned with the Puritans against King Charles I in the English Civil War. He was hired to be the tutor of the daughter of one of the Puritan leaders, and in this position, he wrote many of his poems. He was later appointed an assistant to John Milton, who served as "Latin Secretary" (similar to our contemporary Secretary of State) under Oliver Cromwell. After the Restoration of King Charles II in 1660, Marvell helped save Milton from imprisonment and execution.

Marvell went on to serve as a member of Parliament during the reign of Charles II and continued to write poetry, though most of his poems were only published after his death. His most famous poem, "To His Coy Mistress," may, at first, seem like just another version of the *carpe diem* poem that urges a "coy" (coquettish) woman to stop spurning her lover's "complaints" and "seize the day" by making love while the two of them are still young. You may feel it's just a rehash of "To the Virgins to Make Much of Time" or "Go, Lovely Rose," but try to see how Marvell takes this Cavalier theme and enriches it with metaphysical qualities, such as shocking metaphors, learned allusions, and hyperbolic claims. Notice, too, how he uses the tetrameter line as smoothly and elegantly as the Cavalier poets but also makes it rough and dramatically conversational with the more varied poetic lines of the metaphysical poets.

To His Coy Mistress

Had we but world enough, and time,
This coyness, lady, were no crime.
We would sit down and think which way
To walk, and pass our long love's day;
Thou by the Indian Ganges' side   *(The Ganges River in India)*   5
Shouldst rubies find; I by the tide
Of Humber would complain. I would   *(The Humber River in England)*
Love you ten years before the Flood;   *(Noah's Flood in the Bible)*
And you should, if you please, refuse
Till the conversion of the Jews. *   10
My vegetable love should grow   *(vegetables were the lowest form of life)*
Vaster than empires, and more slow.
An hundred years should go to praise
Thine eyes, and on thy forehead gaze;

Two hundred to adore each breast,		15
But thirty thousand to the rest;		
An age at least to every part,		
And the last age should show your heart.	*finally make you love me*	
For, lady, you deserve this state,	*this eternal devotion*	
Nor would I love at lower rate.	*at any lesser intensity*	20
	But at my back I always hear	
Time's wingèd chariot hurrying near;		
And yonder all before us lie		
Deserts of vast eternity.		
Thy beauty shall no more be found,		25
Nor, in thy marble vault, shall sound		
My echoing song; then worms shall try	*worms shall attack your hymen*	
That long preserv'd virginity,		
And your quaint honour turn to dust,		
And into ashes all my lust.		30
The grave's a fine and private place,	*("private places" of the body)*	
But none, I think, do there embrace.		
	Now therefore, while the youthful	
hue Sits on thy skin like morning dew,		
And while thy willing soul transpires	*breathes out through your*	35
At every pore with instant fires,	*skin in hot passion*	
Now let us sport us while we may;		
And now, like am'rous birds of prey,		
Rather at once our time devour,		
Than languish in his slow-chapp'd power.	*(Time's) slowly devouring force*	40
Let us roll all our strength, and all		
Our sweetness, up into one ball;		
And tear our pleasures with rough strife		
Thorough the iron gates of life.		
Thus, though we cannot make our sun		45
Stand still, yet we will make him run.		1681

*Just before the end of the world, it was believed, Jews would convert to Christianity

    Like the metaphysical poets, Marvell uses puns and other ways of playing with words. In line twenty-nine, for example, he refers to his lady's "quaint honour." On the one hand, he is using the word *quaint* as we do, to mean her "charmingly old-fashioned" virginity. Yet Marvell also knew that *quaint* derived from the medieval *queynte*, which meant (and ultimately evolved into) the word *cunt*. Thus, he is grimly reminding her that both her sex organ and his ("my lust") will decay when they die (echoing the Biblical "ashes to ashes, dust to dust"). The structure of the poem is intellectual as well, developing as a syllogism in logic over the three verse paragraphs: *if* we had all the time in the world, I would court you forever, and you could coyly refuse to give in to me; *however*, time is wasting and soon we will be dead and our bodies will rot; *therefore*, let us make love while we can and, though we can't defeat time and death, we can enjoy our lives while they last.

Finally, notice how the metaphors in the third verse paragraph develop in the same quick, complex ways we saw in the metaphysical poems of Donne. First, he compares the woman and himself to "amorous birds of prey," such as hawks or eagles, who playfully bite and scratch one another with their beaks and talons when they make love. As such amorous flesh-eating birds, Marvell tells his mistress they should "devour" the time they have rather than letting time "devour" them as they languish in his huge, consuming jaws. Then Marvell shifts to a different metaphor: let's roll ourselves into a ball (suggesting a sexual position) that will smash through life as a cannon ball crashes through the iron gates of a castle fortress. In the last two lines, he alludes to instances in Greek mythology and in the Bible where gods make the sun stand still; while he and his lady cannot do that, they can, at least, live energetically and passionately enough so that the sun (and time) will have to run to keep up with them. Can you see how Marvell underscores these metaphors and ideas with metrical variation, enjambment, and caesuras in the last six lines of the poem?

The Restoration

Oliver Cromwell died in 1658. His son Richard tried to rule in his place, but after two years, Richard abdicated his position as "Lord Protector." In 1660, the son of Charles I, who had been living in exile in France, was welcomed back to England and crowned King Charles II. Englishmen who had chafed under Puritan rule angrily dug up Oliver Cromwell's corpse and hung it on a gibbet, so all could jeer at it.

This "restoration" of monarchy, however, was not a reversion to the rule of King James and King Charles I. Parliament had asserted its power, and Charles II had to deal with it shrewdly and diplomatically—unlike his father and grandfather. With the Restoration came the resurgence of the Church of England as the dominant religious force in the country. The Anglicans lashed back at the Puritans on their ideological left, as well as Roman Catholics to their right. They imposed their Episcopalian beliefs on both Puritans and Catholics, making it illegal for anyone who was not Episcopalian to hold civil office. King Charles II, who had developed Roman Catholic sympathies while he lived in France, tried to show tolerance to all religions.

A few years after Charles II ascended to the throne, the bubonic plague swept across England. In 1665, more than 70,000 people died of it in London alone. Then, in 1666, a fire destroyed most of London as it burned for five days, leaving two-thirds of the city homeless. Many people thought it had been set by Roman Catholics. One of the few blessings brought by the fire was that it cauterized the city and stopped the spread of the plague.

Another blessing from the fire was that, while many wooden buildings were destroyed, including the old church of St. Paul's, they were rebuilt in stone and still stand today. Many of these buildings, including the rebuilt St. Paul's Cathedral, were designed by a brilliant young architect, Christopher Wren, who followed the "Neoclassical" style of Ancient Greece and Rome, rather than the medieval Gothic style.

As Wren was supervising the reconstruction of the new St. Paul's, one of his workmen brought him a stone from the foundation of the old wooden cathedral. On the blackened, charred stone was the word *"Resurgens"* (Latin for "I will arise again"). This "neoclassical" style of architecture was also followed in America, where our nation's Capital, as well as many other public buildings, were modeled after the buildings of Ancient Greece and Rome.

The restoration of Charles II brought a new sense of unity to England. Exhausted by the bitter religious conflicts of the first half of the seventeenth century, many people shunned extreme ideas of any kind and dubbed those who held them "enthusiasts" or "fanatics"—people who based their beliefs on religious inspiration rather than sound reason. As the seventeenth century turned into the eighteenth century, the new era became known as the Age of Reason or The Enlightenment, since rational thinking, rather than religious enthusiasm, became a supreme value.

The discoveries of scientists, such as Sir Isaac Newton, bolstered the importance of reason, for they revealed that nature operated by simple, mathematical laws. Charles II was a great sponsor of science and, in 1662, established the Royal Society of London for the Improvement of Natural Knowledge, which promulgated many important scientific discoveries. Science and technology were also evident in the many improvements in everyday living, such as street lighting, good roads, and navigable canals. In these years, too, England emerged as a naval power and established a worldwide empire that stretched from the Americas to India.

As these enormous changes were beginning to take place, however, an older poet from the previous generation was creating his greatest work.

John Milton (1608–1674)

John Milton was born into a middle-class family in London that had converted from Roman Catholicism to Puritan Presbyterianism. From early childhood, John Milton showed a flair for languages. He learned Latin, Greek, Hebrew, and most of the European languages before he went to Cambridge University. After graduating in 1632, he spent several years dedicating himself to a career in poetry by reading virtually every book that existed at the time. He wrote poems in Latin, Italian, and English, and traveled across Europe, visiting famous literary figures. He returned to England in 1639, shortly before the Civil War broke out, and wrote many political essays on behalf of Parliament and Oliver Cromwell. When Cromwell took over as Lord Protector, Milton served as his Latin Secretary, what we would call Secretary of State, defending the beheading of King Charles and communicating with other European nations in Latin.

After the death of Cromwell and the Restoration of Charles II, Milton was imprisoned and might have been executed for his role in the Civil War. But by then, he had gone blind, so he was only severely fined (still, the fines were so heavy that he lost most of his property). In the last fourteen years of his life, he returned to poetry and created his greatest long poem—*Paradise Lost*. Because he was blind, Milton could not write; so he dictated them to his daughters, who, not always happily, wrote down his words as his *amanuensis*. When his daughters showed up late to take down his words, Milton would scold them. He felt his poetic inspiration came to him from the Holy Spirit as he slept, and when he woke up in the morning, "hee wanted to be milk'd."

Given his vast learning, the poems of Milton can be daunting in their length and abstruse range of reference, but you can get a sense of how Milton handled poetic form by first looking at one of his sonnets. Like John Donne, Milton used the sonnet to write about subjects other than courtly love. In this, his most famous sonnet, he wrote about the onset of his blindness, which he feared would keep him from writing the poetry he believed God wanted him to create. He alludes to the New Testament "Parable of the Talents," in which Christ tells the story of a master who gives three of his servants a certain number of "talents" (coins) to take care of while he is away. Two of the servants invest the money so that it doubles in value by the time the master returns. The third servant, however, buries his one talent in the ground to protect it until the return of his master. When the master returns to find that the third servant has done nothing to increase the value of his one talent, he casts him out of his household.

This sonnet takes the form of the poet's meditation on how he can possibly write great poetry if he is blind. He asks God if he would make farm laborers work in his fields at night when it was so dark they cannot see. At that point, his private meditation is answered by a *personified abstraction*. He imagines that the abstract quality of "patience" is a person who replies to his question. Such personified abstractions would become a feature of poetry that was written for more than a century after Milton

On His Blindness

When I consider how my light is spent,
   Ere half my days in this dark world and wide,
   And that one talent which is death to hide
Lodged with me useless, though my soul more bent
To serve therewith my Maker, and present   5
   My true account, lest He returning chide;   *so that God doesn't scold me*
   "Doth God exact day-labor, light denied?"
I fondly ask; but Patience, to prevent   *I foolishly ask*   *to forestall*
That murmur, soon replies, "God doth not need
   Either man's work or his own gifts. Who best   10
   Bear His mild yoke, they serve Him best. His state
Is kingly: Thousands at His bidding speed,
   And post o'er land and ocean without rest;
   They also serve who only stand and wait."   1655

Is Milton using the Italian or English sonnet form in this poem? How does the structure created by the metrical lines and the rhyme scheme compare to the structure created by the syntax—the order of words and phrases in the sentences? How does Milton use enjambment, caesura, and metrical substitutions to make the lines of this sonnet seem conversational, yet also meditative?

    Milton's greatest poetic work was *Paradise Lost*, in which he retells the Biblical story of how the archangel Lucifer led other angels in a rebellion in heaven against God. God and his righteous angels defeated the rebellious angels and cast them out of heaven into hell. There, Lucifer, now called Satan, rallied the fallen angels by telling them that they could get back at God by destroying a paradise he had just created—the Garden of Eden. Satan offered to go to the Garden of Eden secretly, and when he learned that Adam and Eve were allowed to do anything but eat of the tree of Knowledge of Good and Evil, Satan assumed the form of one of God's newly-created creatures, the serpent, and tempted Eve into eating that fruit and offering it to Adam, who eats it, as well, out of love for her.

    Milton wanted to make this Biblical story into a poem that would be an English Protestant equivalent of a great epic poem, such as Homer's *Iliad* and *Odyssey*, which recount great historical adventures about Greece's war with Troy. Those historical epic poems, which were initially oral narratives, have inspired later cultures to emulate them. During the Roman Empire, for example, the poet Virgil wrote *The Aeneid*, an epic about the founding of Rome by the Trojan hero Aeneas, which drew upon Homer's epics. In the Middle Ages, the great Italian poet Dante wrote *The Divine Comedy*, a Roman Catholic epic that drew upon Virgil (who is a character in the poem). Milton wanted to write an equally great epic poem for Protestant England.

    In undertaking such an ambitious project, particularly after he had gone blind, Milton had to think very hard about poetic form. He decided that his epic should not use rhyme. Rhyme was so associated with secular, romantic poetry that it had no place in a Christian epic poem. Yet Milton still wanted the grandeur and sweep of the iambic pentameter line, so he decided to write his poem in unrhymed iambic pentameter—*blank verse*—the same poetic line Shakespeare, Marlowe, and other Renaissance dramatists had used in their plays. In making this decision, Milton was the first poet to use blank verse for a poem, rather than a play.

Let's look at the very opening lines of *Paradise Lost* to see how Milton uses blank verse. Greek epics traditionally begin with an invocation to the muse. The oral poet would ask the muse of poetry to *inspire* (literally breathe into him) as he launched into his epic song. Milton follows this convention in *Paradise Lost*, but instead of asking the Greek muse of poetry to inspire him, he appeals to the Christian Holy Spirit to help him tell the story of the fall from grace in the Garden of Eden and the eventual salvation of humanity through the sacrifice of God's son, Jesus Christ:

from *Paradise Lost, Book I*

> Of Mans First Disobedience, and the Fruit
> Of that Forbidden Tree, whose mortal tast
> Brought Death into the World, and all our woe,
> With loss of Eden, till one greater Man
> Restore us, and regain the blissful Seat,   5
> Sing Heav'nly Muse

The poetic line—and the sentence—continue, but you can see how in these few opening lines Milton is inverting ordinary word order so that this opening sentence is *periodic*—that is, we don't get the normal subject-verb-object of ordinary English speech, but instead, an inverted syntax of prepositional phrases and clauses, and only get the subject and verb of the sentence—"Sing, Heav'nly Muse"—in the sixth line. Milton's use of enjambment and his placement of caesuras also give the lines their rolling, sublime quality.

Notice, too, how unevenly the accents fall in these lines:

Of **Mans**/ **First Dis**-/o-**bed**-/ience, and/ the **Fruit**

Such metrical irregularity mirrors what Milton is describing; the line "disobeys" the rule of iambic pentameter, just as Adam and Eve disobeyed God's rule about not eating the fruit of the Tree of Knowledge. Of course, Milton needs to avoid monotonous metrical regularity in writing such a lengthy poem.

At the conclusion of this invocation to the Holy Spirit, Milton shifts to his personal plea for inspiration:

> What in me is dark
> Illumin, what is low raise and support;
> That to the highth of this great Argument   *this great theme*
> I may assert Eternal Providence,   25
> And justifie the wayes of God to men.

Writing an epic is a daunting task, but trying to write it when you are blind is an overwhelming one. Notice how effectively he uses enjambment in this first line so that "dark" is suddenly followed by an explosive "Illumin." The last line of this passage is the only one that is perfect iambic pentameter:

And **jus**-/ti-**fy**/ the **ways**/ of **God**/ to **man**.

In writing *Paradise Lost*, Milton faced the question that so haunts believers in God: if God is omniscient ("all-knowing"), then he knew from the time he created Adam and Eve that they would violate his rule against eating from the Tree of Knowledge. Similarly, he knew that the archangel Lucifer would lead rebellious angels against him and be cast out of heaven and condemned to live in hell as Satan—for eternity. So knowing all of that, why did God bother to give life to these creatures? Milton wants his epic to persuade readers that God's decision to go ahead with creation was the right one and that the loss of paradise will ultimately be a heroic victory for humanity through the crucifixion and resurrection of Christ.

Another decision Milton made about poetic form was one that, as a later poet, T. S. Eliot observed in his influential essay, "A Note on the Verse of John Milton," put "poetry at the farthest possible remove from prose." Milton's poetry, especially in *Paradise Lost*, goes about as far as poetry can from everyday writing—and everyday human conversation. It is ornate, splendid, overwhelming—completely unlike anything else we might read—and certainly unlike what we might ever say in everyday conversation. Remember that Milton, blind, dictated this poem to his daughters who wrote it down each day, so that it has some of the formulaic character of the earliest oral poetry we looked at in the beginning of this course. Given Milton's staggering knowledge of ancient and modern languages, moreover, he could treat English as if it were Latin, Greek, Hebrew, French, Italian, or several other languages that are so much more complex, grammatically, than English. He could, for example, move words around in a sentence the way, as we saw at the beginning of the course, poets writing in German and other languages could.

Not everyone admires Milton's erudite use of poetic form. In the eighteenth century, Samuel Johnson described the language of *Paradise Lost* as a "Babylonish dialect," based on the "pedantic principle of using English words with a foreign idiom." What Johnson meant was that Milton wrote English as if it were Latin or another foreign language. In place of the simple subject-verb-object syntax of English, Milton moved words around in intricate and complex ways that resembled inflected languages, such as German, where a word's ending—its inflection—lets you know what part of speech it is, so you can place it anywhere in the sentence, and its meaning will be clear.

Look at this sentence that describes how God and his righteous angels cast Lucifer and his rebellious angels out of heaven and into hell:

> Him the Almighty Power
> Hurld headlong flaming from th' Ethereal Skie   45
> With hideous ruine and combustion down
> To bottomless perdition, there to dwell
> In Adamantine Chains and penal Fire,
> Who durst defie th' Omnipotent to Arms.   *dared to defy God in battle*

If Milton had followed normal English word order, he would have started this sentence with the subject, "the Almighy Power"(God), followed by the verb "Hurld," then the direct object "Him" (Satan). But by starting with "Him," Milton gives the sentence an unusual force, as if God is throwing Lucifer smack in the reader's face, and then, for the rest of the sentence, we follow his descent. Such convoluted syntax can be confusing, particularly when we reach the "Who" in the last line of the sentence—does "Who" refer to God or Lucifer? But the confusion clears immediately when we read to the end of the sentence (in which Milton *does* follow normal word order), for it was Lucifer "Who durst defie th'Omnipotent to Arms." The beauty of the sentence is that it starts with Lucifer as the direct object, "Him," of God's power in line forty-four, and line forty-nine starts with Lucifer as "Who," the subject who dared to defy God. Such syntax creates a sublime poetic sound that seems far above ordinary language—as if God Himself were talking.

In writing an epic about the fall, Milton faced a daunting but delightful challenge as a poet: how to take a story all of his readers knew from the Bible and transform it into an exciting poetic narrative. One of the ways he recast the Biblical story was to depict Adam and Eve in the Garden of Eden as they are seen through the eyes of Satan when he arrives from hell, intent on destroying what God has created. As Milton describes Adam and Eve eating their dinner, the perspective is that of Satan who is watching them, scheming, a point of view that makes the lovely description of their peaceful meal threatening:

from *Paradise Lost, Book IV*

So passd they naked on, nor shund the sight	
Of God or Angel, for they thought no ill:	320
So hand in hand they passd, the lovliest pair	
That ever since in loves imbraces met,	
Adam the goodliest man of men since borne	
His Sons, the fairest of her Daughters Eve.	
Under a tuft of shade that on a green	325
Stood whispering soft, by a fresh Fountain side	
They sat them down, and after no more toil	
Of thir sweet Gardning labour then suffic'd	
To recommend coole Zephyr, and made ease	*(cool west wind)*
More easie, wholsom thirst and appetite	330
More grateful, to thir Supper Fruits they fell,	
Nectarine Fruits which the compliant boughes	
Yeilded them, side-long as they sat recline	
On the soft downie Bank damaskt with flours:	
The savourie pulp they chew, and in the rinde	335
Still as they thirsted scoop the brimming stream;	
Nor gentle purpose, nor endearing smiles	*gentle conversation*
Wanted, nor youthful dalliance as beseems	*youthful lovemaking*
Fair couple, linkt in happie nuptial League,	
Alone as they. About them frisking playd	340
All Beasts of th' Earth, since wilde, and of all chase	*of all lairs*
In Wood or Wilderness, Forrest or Den;	
Sporting the Lion rampd, and in his paw	*lion reared up*
Dandl'd the Kid; Bears, Tygers, Ounces, Pards	*onyxes, leopards*
Gambold before them, th' unwieldy Elephant	345
To make them mirth us'd all his might, & wreathd	
His Lithe Proboscis; close the Serpent sly	*his supple trunk*
Insinuating, wove with Gordian twine	*the Gordian knot could not be untied*
His breaded train, and of his fatal guile	*His checkered, interwoven skin*
Gave proof unheeded; others on the grass	350
Couch't, and now fild with pasture gazing sat,	*(the animals in paradise are*
Or Bedward ruminating: for the Sun	*vegetarian so they "ruminate"--*
Declin'd was hasting now with prone carreer	*chew their cuds)*
To th' Ocean Iles, and in th' ascending Scale	

>   Of Heav'n the Starrs that usher Evening rose: 355
>   When Satan still in gaze, as first he stood,
>   Scarce thus at length faild speech recoverd sad.

Milton only reminds us at the end of this depiction of the Garden of Eden that it is seen from the point of view of Satan, and Satan's amazed, angry reaction to such a glorious spectacle renders it all the more stunning. The last line of this verse paragraph is so convoluted in its inverted word order that it mirrors Satan's speechless astonishment at the vision he has just seen of Adam and Eve in the Garden of Eden.

Although these are just a few passages from *Paradise Lost*, they give you some sense of how Milton used poetic and narrative form to create an epic poem in English blank verse that can stand beside Homer's *Iliad* and *Odyssey*, Virgil's *Aeneid*, and Dante's *Divine Comedy*. When *Paradise Lost* was published in 1667, Milton received ten pounds (about fifty dollars) for the work.

Restoration Drama

It was only with the restoration of King Charles II in 1660 that drama returned to England. During his exile in France, Charles II enjoyed French theater, and when he reopened theaters in England, they adopted French theatrical conventions. While some female parts were still played by boys, actresses took to the stage. Some theaters were built for indoor performances, had artificial lighting, and used a *proscenium* stage that receded into the back of the theater (probably like the stage in your high school auditorium). The audience sat in front of the stage, a curtain opened and closed at the end of an act, and playbills or programs identified characters in order of their appearance, noted changes of place and time, and explained where scenes were set. The stage had scenery and furnishings, creating the illusion that the audience was looking "into" a three-dimensional space, such as a room in a house where the "fourth wall" had been removed, allowing the audience to view the action inside the room. This kind of stage became the standard vehicle for presenting drama down to the present.

Chapter 5
Eighteenth-Century Literature

The "Glorious Revolution" of 1688

A major source of conflict during the reign of Charles II was the same one that had challenged his father and grandfather—the tension between the monarch and Parliament. Would England be ruled by the absolute power of its king or queen, or would a more democratic rule be exercised through Parliament, with its balance between an aristocratic House of Lords and an increasingly middle-class House of Commons? Charles II managed to work with Parliament more diplomatically than his Stuart predecessors, but still two strong political parties emerged that have opposed one another—under different names—ever since. The conservative Tory party supported the King and the landed aristocracy, as well as the "High" Episcopal Church of England. The Whig party included some aristocrats, but was primarily composed of middle-class merchants and bankers who wanted more tolerance for Puritans, Presbyterians, and other "Low Church" Protestants. For the first time in English history, writers, who had long depended on aristocratic patrons to support their work, aligned themselves with the Tory or Whig party, and writing became politicized as it had never been before.

The tensions in Restoration England focused on Charles II's brother James, the Duke of York, who was next in line for the throne. The problem was that James was a Roman Catholic. Charles II adroitly managed to resist attempts by Parliament to exclude his brother from the throne, and on his deathbed, Charles II received the last rites of the Roman Catholic Church. When James became King James II of England and Scotland in 1685, he proved to be as obstinant a monarch as his father, Charles I, and grandfather, James I. While, today, we can appreciate his efforts to show more tolerance to Roman Catholics—as well as to Puritans and other "Low Church" Protestants—the majority of English people were gravely concerned when he appointed Roman Catholics to important posts in government, the military, and universities. Concern turned to alarm when his queen gave birth to a son, and it looked as if England would be ruled by a Roman Catholic monarch for the foreseeable future.

Whig leaders in Parliament turned to a Protestant Dutch prince, William of Orange, who was married to James II's Protestant daughter Mary. In 1688, William of Orange landed in England with an army, but no bloodshed resulted in what came to be called the "Glorious Revolution." King James II fled with his family to France, but before he left London, he took the Great Seal of England, symbol of the British monarchy, and tossed it into the River Thames so that no successor could brandish it. William and Mary ascended to the throne, though for another hundred years, they and their successors had to stave off plots by *Jacobites* (supporters of James) to put James II back on the throne; then his son, who would have been James III (and was called "The Old Pretender" to the British throne); and finally, his dashing and romantic grandson Charles (called "Bonnie Prince Charlie"), who, if successful, would have ruled as King Charles III.

Under William and Mary, Parliament grew stronger, Puritans and other Low Church Protestants gained more freedom, and England enjoyed prosperity and stability. William and Mary were succeeded by Princess Anne, who was another Protestant daughter of James II. During the reign of Queen Anne, England and her Continental allies—Holland, Austria, and Bavaria—defeated France and Spain in a war that featured the leadership of John Churchill, Duke of Marlborough (ancestor of Winston Churchill), and the "Protestant Succession" was established that ensured that all subsequent kings and queens of England would be Protestant, rather than Roman Catholic. After Queen Anne, the last of the Stuart monarchs, died in 1714, the throne passed to her closest Protestant relative, a German prince of Hanover, who became King George I of Great Britain, the first of the "Hanoverian" line of British kings and queens.

The Augustan Age

During the reign of Queen Anne, the English people, particularly those in London, looked upon the impressive buildings, the prosperity of the nation, their success in foreign wars, and the spread of the British Empire with great pride. The London Stock Exchange was established in 1689 and The Bank of England in 1694, putting England on the same financial basis it resides in today. Londoners regarded themselves as the modern counterpart of the Roman empire under the reign of Caesar Augustus in the first century A.D. In what is also sometimes called the *Augustan* or *Neoclassic Age*, London emulated ancient Rome physically, as well as spiritually. Many of London's buildings, such as Christopher Wren's St. Paul's Cathedral, resemble Greek and Roman building with domes and pillars, rather than the medieval spires and arches of Gothic cathedrals. As prosperity grew, aristocratic landowners built grand mansions that still dot the English countryside.

Writers also emulated Roman authors, such as Horace and Virgil, who wrote in a clear, simple style, much like that of Ben Jonson and the Cavalier poets, as opposed to the intricate and complex style of Milton or John Donne. The Augustan Age saw itself as urbane and sophisticated; Londoners gathered in coffee houses to discuss political events reported in the newly-created newspapers and literary and philosophic essays in the equally new magazines or simply engage in witty, elegant, "gentlemanly" conversation. Several aristocratic women, such as Elizabeth Montagu, also created evening *salons*, where men and women could engage in refined discussions together. Such women, whose intellectual or literary ambitions rivaled those of men, wore plain blue or gray stockings instead of the elegant black stockings that ladies of court society wore. Ever since, women who present themselves as literary or intellectual equals of men rather than as alluring sexual objects have been called "bluestockings."

Writers regarded their audience as the sophisticated readers of London, readers who were aware of current political and social events, trained in classical literature, and appreciative of wit, grace, and ease (though writers had to work hard to achieve these qualities). During Queen Anne's reign, writers continued to depend upon aristocratic patronage, and such patronage enabled them to write pretty much as they wished. They did not, as most writers do today, have to depend on sales of their books to survive. Nor did they have to meet the demands of publishers or reach a broad audience of readers by writing works that appealed to the masses.

The English Language in the Eighteenth Century

After several centuries of expansion and absorption of words from other languages, the English language grew more refined and regular during the Restoration and eighteenth century. Charles II set a standard for English to become as polished, as grammatically correct, and as easy a vehicle for polite conversation as the French language was in the court of Louis XIV. Writers such as John Dryden tried to get the English to distinguish between "who" and "whom," to make their subjects and verbs agree, and to stop using double negatives ("He don't like her no more"). He even called for the establishment of an official academy to regulate the English language in the same way the French Academy prescribed rules for grammar, the admission of new words to the language, and proper usage. Some schools substituted the study of the English language and of literature in English for Classical Latin and Greek. Fewer words were borrowed from other languages, and consequently, some important words, such as *nature*, had several different meanings— human nature, the physical world, the essence of life, etc.

In 1755, Samuel Johnson created the first true dictionary of the English language. Although he initially intended to lay down rules for pronunciation and grammar, Johnson, over the course of preparing the dictionary, came to see that a dictionary should be *descriptive* rather than *proscriptive*; that is, it should represent the way a language evolves through usage, rather than upholding rules that current speakers of the language largely ignore. Were Johnson to write his dictionary today, he would include the word *ain't*, because many people actually use it, though he would have noted that it was a word that educated people do not employ. Writers also used capital letters only for proper nouns rather than for any word they deemed important.

It was during the eighteenth century, too, that Sir William Jones, a scholar who was fluent in thirteen languages and conversant in twenty-eight more—including Arabic, Persian, and Hindustani, discovered the relation between English and other languages. Because of his extraordinary command of many languages, Jones was able to discern that most of them were part of a large family of what we now call *Indo-European languages*. Jones militantly opposed England's war against American independence, and he was equally vehement in his protest against slavery. Because of these unpopular stands, he did not advance in his career as a lawyer and politician in England but was, instead, made a judge in India, which had become part of the growing British Empire. In India, Jones was the first Englishman to learn the ancient language of Sanskrit, and he realized that it was part of the same language family that included many European languages.

The Heroic Couplet

During the Restoration and eighteenth Century, drama was revived in England; a new literary form, the novel, developed with the spread of printing and literacy; and newspapers and magazines encouraged the writing of essays that we would now categorize as *creative nonfiction*. Poetry also underwent a change. The greatest poetry of the age was *satiric*—that is, it criticized the way people behaved in society. Tory writers, such as Alexander Pope, resented changes the Whigs were imposing on English life. As conservatives, the Whigs made fun of the middle class, which was rising to power. They also questioned the shift from England's traditional agrarian society to a mercantile economy and its transformation from an island culture, separate from the rest of Europe, to a world power. Pope, Swift, and other Tory writers upheld a standard of nobility, sophistication, and gentility against what they saw as the onslaught of middle-class vulgarity, commercialism, and stupidity. While they waged a losing battle against the ascendancy of the middle-class, these aristocratic writers produced wonderfully acerbic, trenchant, and witty satiric verse.

The form they most often used in their poetry was the *heroic couplet*. The couplet, two lines of iambic pentameter that rhyme, goes back to Chaucer, the very first major English poet to write in iambic pentameter. But Chaucer used couplets more loosely, often *enjambing* one couplet into another, as he does in *The Canterbury Tales:*

> When Zephyrus eek with his sweete breeth
> Inspired hath in every holt and heath
> The tendre croppes, and the yonge sonne
> Hath in the Ram his halve cours yronne,

In these four lines, Chaucer *enjambs* (runs two couplets together without an end-stopped line of punctuation) as he describes how the west wind ("Zephyrus") breathes on crops in the spring along with the "young" Sun (in the zodiacal sign of Aries, the ram) to bring vegetation to the earth again. Such enjambment mirrors the fecundity of nature in the spring that "spills over" the ends of lines just as nature overtakes the barren winter ground with new growth.

Chaucer's couplets are called *open couplets*, because they are frequently enjambed so that the lines run fluidly into one another. The heroic couplet, as it was developed in the Restoration and eighteenth century, was usually a *closed couplet*, because, while there might be enjambment between the two lines of the couplet, the second line of the couplet was almost never enjambed into the first line of the next couplet. Here, for example, are the first four lines of Alexander Pope's "An Essay on Criticism:"

> 'Tis hard to say, if greater want of skill
> Appear in writing or in judging ill;
> But of the two less dangerous is the offense
> To tire our patience than mislead our sense.

Pope begins by asking if it takes less skill to be a bad writer of poetry or to be a poor critic ("judge") of poetry. He poses this question in the first couplet. Notice that the two lines of the couplet are enjambed but that the second line is *end-stopped* (ends with a semi-colon) so that it does not spill over, in grammar or in sense, to the next couplet. Such a couplet is *closed*, because it presents a self-enclosed thought in just two lines. Equally closed and self-contained is the next couplet in which Pope answers his opening question by deciding that, of the two—being a bad poet or being a bad critic—the more dangerous offense is being a bad critic, because while a bad poet only bores us ("tires our patience"), a poor critic of poetry can mislead us about what a poem means. This second couplet is equally self-contained; while line three is enjambed, line four is end-stopped.

Can you see why an age that valued reason, moderation, balance, symmetry, and harmony would love poetry written in heroic couplets? No poetic form is more symmetrical and balanced than the closed couplet with its self-contained two lines. The heroic couplet is a difficult form for a poet to use, because it can easily become monotonous and repetitious. But a skilled poet like Pope varies his couplets with intricate grace, so that each seems a fresh turn of thought. One way he varies his couplets is by departing from normal word order, somewhat as Milton did, though Pope's inversions of normal word order are all contained within two lines so that they are not as convoluted as Milton's lengthy periodic sentences. Note that each couplet above starts out with a normal conversational phrase—"Tis hard to say" and "But of the two"—but then, Pope subtly shifts normal word order around. In the first couplet, the verb "Appear" does not come until the beginning of the second line. In the second couplet, he builds suspense by coming to the end of the third line without telling us which is worse—bad poetry or bad criticism. Even when he does tell us, in the fourth line, we have to pause and figure out that a bad poet only tires our patience but a bad critic can mislead us.

Another way Pope varies his couplets is through his use of *caesura*. The caesura, or pause within a line of poetry, goes all the way back to the earliest poetry in the English language, that of the Anglo-Saxons. All poets since then have used caesura artfully, but none more so than Alexander

Pope. In writing couplets, where the poet places the caesura is crucial, for it breaks up each line in different ways. In the first couplet, the caesura comes in line one after the fourth syllable—"'Tis hard to say,"). This caesura is marked by a comma, but Pope also creates caesuras that are not marked by punctuation, but rather by a pause after a phrase. In the second line, for example, can you hear the pause between "Appear in writing" and "or in judging ill." Pope reinforces that break in the line by using parallel phrases ("in writing" and "in judging"), thus giving the line symmetry and balance. The opening verb ("Appear") is followed by the first parallel phrase ("in writing"), the caesura "or," the next parallel phrase ("in judging"), and finally, the adjective "ill." The caesura in this line comes after the fifth syllable ("Appear in writing") so that it divides the line differently from the caesura that comes after the fourth syllable in the first line of the couplet.

In the second couplet, there are no punctuation marks to indicate where the caesura falls, but can you hear how the phrases divide the lines?

> But of the two   less dangerous is the offense
> To tire our patience   than mislead our sense.

It takes practice to hear such subtle caesuras, but once you do, Pope's couplets and those of the best writers of the Augustan Age will sound lively and varied. Can you also see that the caesura in line three comes after the fourth syllable, so that it neatly parallels the caesura in line one? And that the caesura in line four comes after the fifth syllable, so that it, in turn, parallels line two? Also, notice that the fourth line, like the second, breaks into parallel phrases on either side of the caesura: "tire our patience" and "mislead our sense," though these parallel phrases are not as exactly similar as "in writing" and "in judging." Another subtle touch of symmetry is Pope's internal rhyme between "patience" and "sense."

Like all poets, Pope also varied his lines by *metrical substitution*—substituting trochees, spondees, pyrrhics, and other metrical feet for iambs. The first line is perfectly iambic in its rhythms:

'Tis **hard**/ to **say,**/ if **great**-/er **want**/ of **skill**

But in the second line, Pope substitutes a pyrrhic for the third foot:

Ap-**pear**/ in **wri**-/ting or/ in **judg**-/ing **ill**

Not only does Pope make the two lines of the first couplet metrically different, the pyrrhic rushes us along so that the accent that falls on "**judg**-," giving that important word special emphasis.

The second couplet is even more intricate. Line three starts out with a trochee followed by an iamb:

But of/ the **two**/

But then, things get tricky. Although Pope spells out "dangerous" he probably wants it pronounced in two syllables ("dang-rous") rather than three ("dan-ger-ous"), so that would make the third foot a spondee:

less dange-/

Then the fourth foot would be a pyrrhic (as the *third* foot was in the preceding line, giving still more subtle variation):

-rous is/

Finally, the last foot would be an iamb, because Pope would expect us to *elide* the word "the" into the first syllable of "offence" ("th'of-fense):

th'of-**fence**

The fourth line is metrically parallel to the second (as it was syntactically with its parallel phrases) with the third foot a pyrrhic:

To **tire**/ our **pa**-/ tience than/ mis-**lead**/ our **sense**

Can you also hear the deft way the metrical variation affects that intricate internal rhyme between "**pa**-tience" and "**sense**," as the rhyme on "-tience" falls on an unaccented syllable while that on "**sense**" falls on an accented syllable?

While the heroic couplets of Pope and other writers of the Augustan Age are not as difficult as Milton or Donne's poetry, it takes practice and patience to appreciate them. Pope was a Tory who was writing for a sophisticated, learned audience of London readers who appreciated *wit*—a word that at the time meant not being funny, as it does now, but intellectual and imaginative brilliance. While heroic couplets might not sound like everyday conversation, they would have appealed to such readers for their *artifice*—another word that has changed its meaning since the eighteenth century. Today we speak of something false or shallow as *artificial*, but in the eighteenth century *artificial* would have meant *artful*, a well-crafted and designed *artifice* such as a poem by Pope, a symphony by Mozart, or a building by Christopher Wren.

It was an age that valued reason, order, balance, and in writing, it prized words that didn't sound as if they'd just been casually uttered, but that were put together with great thoughtfulness, craft, and grace. The eighteenth century was the era that gave birth to American independence, and when Thomas Jefferson wrote *The Declaration of Independence*, he wanted to impress the world with the patience, prudence, and forethought that had gone into the colonists' decision to rebel against England. Thus, he did not begin by saying, "We're sick and tired of all these damn taxes the King of England is sticking to us, and we're not taking it another day!" Instead, he wrote a very balanced, periodic, intricate sentence—a very eighteenth-century sentence:

> When, in the course of human events, it becomes necessary for one people to dissolve the political bonds which have connected them with another, and to assume among the powers of the earth, the separate and equal station to which the laws of nature and of nature's God, entitle them, a decent respect to the opinions of mankind requires that they should declare the cause which impelled them to the separation.

The subject of the sentence—"respect"—does not come until near the very end; the verb—"requires"—comes even later, and the most explosive word in the sentence—"separation"—is the very last.

Alexander Pope (1688-1744)

Alexander Pope was the son of a London merchant who retired from business the year his son was born and moved to the country outside of London. Growing up in rural surroundings was healthful for Pope, who was a sickly child. Stunted in growth (as an adult, he stood under five feet tall), deformed by tuberculosis of the spine, his eyesight ruined by perpetual reading, he grew up to be an irascible, nerve-wracked man. Because his family was Roman Catholic, Pope could not attend a university and was largely self-taught. As a Catholic, he also could not vote, hold political office, or receive the kind of patronage other writers earned. Encouraged by his father to pursue poetry, Pope was one of the few writers of his age to make a living by his writing. His translations of Homer's *Iliad* and *Odyssey*—into heroic couplets—earned him enough money to purchase an elegant villa on the Thames River above London, where he could enjoy nature, gardening, and other rural pleasures he had loved as a boy. Although he worked hard at poetry, laboriously revising his lines over and over again, he always gave the impression that he had tossed them off with gentlemanly ease.

Early success with such long poems as the *Essay on Criticism* (1711) and *The Rape of the Lock* (1712) made Pope a central figure in the London literary world of coffee houses, taverns, and literary salons. Like his friend Jonathan Swift, Pope was a Tory who regarded the middle-class Whig party as a barbaric affront to everything civilized, rational, and beautiful. Pope, Swift, and other Tory writers delighted in satirizing—in poetry as well as prose—all of the affectation, pedantry, and other foibles of middle-class society. They mocked the pursuit of commercial success, newspapers and magazines that catered to the growing reading public's love of gossip, scandal, and other manifestations of what they regarded as the increasing vulgarity of English life.

Their satire sharpened after the death of Queen Anne in 1714 and the reigns of George I and George II, when the Whigs returned to power. Their satires prompted retaliations from Whig writers who attacked Pope for his poetry, his Catholicism, and his physical deformities. Pope would then counter-attack, almost always winning the war of words with his wit, talent, and tenacity. As Samuel Holt Monk said,

> Pope assumed the role of the champion of traditional civilization: of right reason, humanistic learning, sound art, good taste, and public virtue. For him the supreme value was order—cosmic, political, social, aesthetic—which he saw (or believed he saw) threatened on all sides. It was fortunate that most of his enemies seem to have been designed by nature to illustrate various degrees of unreason, pedantry, bad art, vulgar taste, and, at best, indifferent morals. Personal malice edged his satire, but his art elevated his unhappy victims into symbols of Georgian barbarism.

Pope's first major poetic success was *An Essay on Criticism* in which he tried to do for his age what Horace, the great Roman poet, had done for his Augustan Age in his *Ars Poetica*—to lay out the fundamental principles of good poetry in simple, clear terms. Even at the age of twenty-three, Pope was already a master of the heroic couplet, and many lines from this poem have become famous quotations of the English language, such as:

A little learning is a dangerous thing

Pope realized that the couplet is a perfect form for *epigram*—a memorable, concise, witty statement. Many of the couplets from this poem are perfect epigrams:

> True wit is Nature to advantage dressed,
> What oft was thought, but ne'er so well expressed.

Pope's point here is characteristic of the Augustan Age: true wit comes not from saying something utterly original or unusual, but rather taking something from *nature*—not the physical, natural world but the universal understanding of all people (what we might call common sense)—and putting it into perfectly expressive words. Readers will be struck, not by an utterly new idea, but by hearing something they had always known to be true but never heard expressed quite so well. In this couplet, notice how Pope uses phrasing, caesuras, and meter to make his point.

Here is another famous passage from the *Essay on Criticism*:

True Ease in Writing comes from Art, not Chance,	362
As those move easiest who have learn'd to dance,	
'Tis not enough no Harshness gives Offence,	
The Sound must seem an Eccho to the Sense.	365
Soft is the Strain when Zephyr gently blows, *(the gentle west wind)*	
And the smooth Stream in smoother Numbers flows;	
But when loud Surges lash the sounding Shore,	
The hoarse, rough Verse shou'd like the Torrent roar.	
When Ajax strives, some Rocks' vast Weight to throw, *(*see note below)*	370
The Line too labours, and the Words move slow;	
Not so, when swift Camilla scours the Plain, *(*see note below)*	
Flies o'er th'unbending Corn, and skims along the Main	1711

*Ajax was the largest and strongest of the Greek warriors in the Trojan War. As such, he was also slow-moving (and slow-thinking). In addition to fighting with sword and spear, he would sometimes lift huge boulders from the battlefield and hurl them at his enemies. By contrast, Camilla, in Greek mythology, was a swift messenger for Artemis (Diana in Roman mythology), goddess of the moon, hunting, and chastity. Notice how Pope manipulates meter and *sound* to contrast the *sense* of what he is saying about Ajax and Camilla in poetry.

Lady Mary Wortley Montagu (1689–1762)

During the eighteenth-century, the rising power of the middle class, the increase in prosperity, and the growth of the reading public enabled more women to become writers. Although they could not attend universities such as Oxford and Cambridge to receive a classical education, women read widely on their own. In the eighteenth century, several women published poetry and other forms of writing, frequently addressing a readership of women.

Lady Mary Wortley Montagu was the daughter of a wealthy English duke. She taught herself Latin and was widely read in classical literature. She was one of the most beautiful women of her time, but her looks were scarred by smallpox. She eloped with her husband, who was appointed ambassador to Turkey. There she learned Turkish and did much to correct the English people's prejudiced attitudes toward the Near East. She had her son inoculated against smallpox and championed the new medical procedure of vaccination.

Returning to England, she became a central figure in intellectual and literary salons, where men and women met regularly, though most literary life was still conducted in the male-dominated coffee-houses of London. When her daughter eloped, Lady Montagu left her by then loveless marriage and went to live on the Continent. She sparkled in French salon society, where men and women met on a more equal footing. She was a champion of equality between the sexes and advised women trapped in loveless marriages to turn to lovers—as she had. Alexander Pope once proposed marriage to her, and she laughingly rejected him, for which he satirized her in one of his most bitter poems.

In the following poem, written in iambic tetrameter, she gives a prescription or recipe ("Receipt") for curing a friend of hers, who had been widowed for several years, of the "vapors," another name for "spleen," the affliction of women that supposedly made them nervous, depressed, and even hysterical. Following the Augustan convention of addressing real people by names taken from classical mythology and legend, she calls her friend, whose name was Lady Anne Irwin, "Delia" and her deceased husband "Damon."

A Receipt to Cure the Vapors

I
Why will Delia thus retire,
   And idly languish life away?
While the sighing crowd admire,
   'Tis too soon for hartshorn tea: *medicinal tea made from ammonia*

II
All those dismal looks and fretting   5
   Cannot Damon's life restore;
Long ago the worms have eat him,   *(pronounced "et him")*
   You can never see him more.

III
Once again consult your toilette,   *your make-up, hair, looks*
   In the glass your face review: *the mirror*   10
So much weeping soon will spoil it,
   And no spring your charms renew.

IV
I, like you, was born a woman,
   Well I know what vapors mean:
The disease, alas! is common;   15
   Single, we have all the spleen.   *(women alone have this ailment)*

V
All the morals that they tell us,
   Never cured the sorrow yet:
Chuse, among the pretty fellows,
   One of honor, youth, and wit.   20

VI
Prithee hear him every morning   *("Pray thee") please*

>   At least an hour or two;
>   Once again at night returning—
>   I believe the dose will do.   1748

Along with other aspects of poetic form, notice how Lady Montagu uses off rhymes, feminine rhymes, and metrical substitutions to underscore her meaning. In line sixteen, she starts off with a trochee, rather than an iamb—can you see why the metrical substitution enhances the meaning of the line?

The Later Eighteenth Century

As the eighteenth-century wore on, changes began to appear in English life, sensibility, and poetry. After the death of Queen Anne in 1714, George I became king, though he, along with his successor, George II, who ruled from 1727 until 1760, essentially remained German princes. They spoke little English, spent much of their time in Germany, and showed little interest in literature or the arts. During their reigns, Parliament, particularly the House of Commons, grew more powerful, and the country was largely ruled by the Prime Minister, who was usually a Whig rather than a Tory.

The Whig politicians were largely middle-class businessmen who had little interest in supporting writers and artists. Without the financial support of wealthy patrons, writers had to support themselves through a publisher's sales of their writing. The reading public expanded to the middle-class, especially women, who had increasing leisure time with widespread prosperity. Publishers would sometimes solicit *subscription* sales of a book before it was published, ensuring that everyone who paid a certain sum of money would receive a "deluxe edition" of the book and have his or her name listed as a *patron of literature* in the book itself. Such a system of support is still used by literary magazines and small press editions of books today. Writers also looked to other forms of publication that had been spawned by the invention of printing and the spread of literacy: newspapers, magazines, and literary reviews that were published in weekly, monthly, or other regular periods. In such *periodical* publications, writers discoursed on politics, society, and other topics that engaged a wide readership, such as scandal and gossip, that still sell magazines today (notice the pictures and headlines on the magazines at your grocery story check-out lane).

Out of this change in the reading public and support for writers came a conflict that is still with us today: should a writer address a sophisticated, literate, and cultivated group of readers with the most artful literature he or she can create or should writers seek a broader audience by lowering their literary standards in order to sell more copies of their publications?

By the time George III took the throne in 1760, English life, including the commercialization of literature, had changed irrevocably. George III, the first of the Georgian kings to be born in England, restored the Tories to power after foury-six years of Whig rule. Although he tried to weaken the power of Parliament, it was still the Prime Minister who ruled, much as he or she does today. Part of Parliament and the Prime Minister's ability to maintain control of the country stemmed from the incompetence, stubbornness, and unpopularity of George III. It was this king who was on the throne when the thirteen American colonies rebelled and declared themselves independent. In 1788, George III began suffering from mental illness, and during the last ten years of his reign, he was completely insane.

The premium placed on reason, harmony, and balance that so characterized the Augustan era of the early eighteenth century gradually gave way to a new emphasis on sentiment, and people looked to writers for literary works that would express the author's feelings and touch the emotions of their readers. The emerging emphasis on sentiment prompted such social changes as the improvement of prison conditions, the creation of hospitals for the poor, and support for other charitable causes. Religion, too, became more emotional. Most Anglicans were essentially *Deists*, who believed that God was a rational, benevolent deity whose creation reflected his simple wisdom, as discerned by scientists, such as Newton, who showed that the universe obeyed simple, mathematical laws. They looked down on religious "enthusiasts" and "fanatics" who followed their own inspiration and imposed their beliefs on others, as the Puritans had done under Oliver Cromwell. Putting little emphasis on the Christian doctrine of original sin, they regarded humans as basically good creatures who need only follow their reason and cooperate with others in society.

In the 1740s, however, John and Charles Wesley started a religious revival that became known as *Methodism*. Denied the opportunity to preach in churches, they took their evangelical message to thousands of common people in outdoor meetings, stressing the necessity of repenting from sin, seeking the "amazing grace" of a conversion experience, and worshipping with emotional zeal. One of the ways they intensified religious services was through the communal singing of hymns, a practice that had virtually disappeared from the Anglican Church. Between them, the Wesley brothers wrote nearly 7,000 hymns, many of them spirited songs, such as "Hark! The Herald Angels Sing," which have endured to the present. Methodists also joined in the social reform spirit of the latter half of the eighteenth century and helped bring about the abolition of slavery in England.

Writers, such as Pope and Swift, saw themselves as urban—and urbane—writers who addressed an equally sophisticated audience of city-dwellers. Even when people in the Augustan age did turn their attention to the natural landscape, they often preferred that it show the impress of human artifice—trees carefully pruned, shrubbery arranged in symmetrical patterns, and gardens laid out with geometric precision, as in the grounds of Versailles, the palace of French King Louis XIV.

Later in the eighteenth century, however, people sought out the natural world in its wilder and more sublime manifestations—craggy mountains, deep forests, resounding waterfalls. In such natural settings, they felt an emotional awe that bordered on spiritual ecstasy. They also revered people who were closer to such natural settings than city-dwellers: "noble savages" such as the native Americans of the New World, rural peasants who worked the land, and children who played spontaneously in the natural world. Spurred by such interests, scholars and writers began collecting and publishing fairy tales, folk tales, and medieval ballads, such as "Sir Patrick Spens," that we studied at the beginning of this course and that had only been preserved by oral tradition, since the Middle Ages.

The interest in medieval ballads was part of a renewed interest in the Middle Ages toward the end of the eighteenth century. In the early part of the century, the "Augustan" age modeled itself on classical Greece and Rome and looked on the Middle Ages as barbaric and, to use their term of derision, *Gothic*—a "dark age" of religious superstition, unscientific thinking, and widespread disorder. For the Augustan age, the confusion of the Middle Ages was epitomized by Gothic cathedrals that were often asymmetrical in structure, incompletely constructed, and confusingly ornamented with stone carvings, gargoyles, and other decorations.

The Augustan Age, as we have seen, preferred the classical simplicity of buildings like St. Paul's Cathedral, modeled on Rome's Pantheon, with an elegant dome, symmetrical columns, and little decoration. By the end of the eighteenth-century, however, the Gothic style was admired as an expression of spiritual aspiration, and the Middle Ages were regarded as an era of emotional intensity and mysticism.

These "Medieval revival" impulses partly reflected the fact that the rural and natural landscape of England was disappearing with the advent of what we now call "The Industrial Revolution" in the closing years of the eighteenth century. Inventions, such as the steam engine and the mechanical loom, replaced production of cloth and other goods by hand. At the same time, landowners who had once let rural people work their land as tenant farmers, fenced off their acreage and produced agricultural goods in a more scientific and efficient fashion. Shut out from farming, rural people moved to cities to work in factories, often in hideous conditions that included child labor. Workers lived in slums that grew up around factories in Central England, and industrial smoke and waste blackened the once beautiful countryside.

The "Graveyard" Poets

Where Pope and Swift had prided themselves on being sophisticated city dwellers who satirized the foibles of London society with reason, wit, and gentlemanly good manners, poets of the later eighteenth century often portrayed themselves as individuals isolated from society, haunted by melancholy, and fascinated with death, madness, and other macabre subjects. Many poems were actually set in rural cemeteries and indulged in nightmarish fantasies that titillated their readers. They also changed the image of a poet from a social person talking with easy elegance about public events to a lonely, tormented individual expressing private feelings in anguished verses. In the late eighteenth-century, this type of poetry was referred to as the "Graveyard School."

Thomas Gray (1716-1771)

Thomas Gray was a professor at Oxford University, well-versed in classical, as well as English, literature. He wrote very few poems, but "Elegy in a Country Churchyard" became one of the most famous poems in the English language. Although some aspects of the poem reflect the personal melancholy, the interest in the rural poor, and the fascination with death of the "Graveyard" poets, other parts of the poem adhere to the principles of the Augustan Age— balance, grandeur, and the portrait of a poet addressing a literate, social audience of readers. Although the poet portrays himself standing in a rural churchyard (a cemetery where country people are buried near their church), he is not one of the poor, ignorant people whose graves surround him, but a literate, sophisticated man of the world. An *elegy* is traditionally a poem written about a famous person who has died; Gray writes his elegy about the ordinary, poor, rural people who are buried near their country church. When the British general James Wolfe led his troops up the St. Lawrence River to mount an assault on the French stronghold of Quebec in what we call the French and Indian War of the 1760s, he stood in a boat and read the "Elegy" to his soldiers. When he finished, he told his men that he would rather have written that poem than win the battle for Quebec.

Elegy Written in a Country Churchyard

The curfew tolls the knell of parting day,	*evening church bells rings at dusk*
The lowing herd winds slowly o'er the lea,	*mooing cows come from the meadow*
The ploughman homeward plods his weary way,	
And leaves the world to darkness and to me.	

Now fades the glimmering landscape on the sight, 5
And all the air a solemn stillness holds,
Save where the beetle wheels his droning flight,
And drowsy tinklings lull the distant folds: *distant pens of sheep*

Save that from yonder ivy-mantled tower
The moping owl does to the moon complain 10

Of such as, wandering near her secret bower,
Molest her ancient solitary reign.

Beneath those rugged elms, that yew-tree's shade,   *dark pine trees*
Where heaves the turf in many a mouldering heap,   *the graves of the poor*
Each in his narrow cell for ever laid,   15
The rude Forefathers of the hamlet sleep.   *illiterate ancestors of the town*

The breezy call of incense-breathing morn,
The swallow twittering from the straw-built shed,
The cock's shrill clarion, or the echoing horn,   *hunting horn*
No more shall rouse them from their lowly bed.   20

For them no more the blazing hearth shall burn,
Or busy housewife ply her evening care:
No children run to lisp their sire's return,   *to announce "Daddy's home!"*
Or climb his knees the envied kiss to share,

Oft did the harvest to their sickle yield,   25
Their furrow oft the stubborn glebe has broke;   *the dense earth*
How jocund did they drive their team afield!   *How happily they ploughed*
How bow'd the woods beneath their sturdy stroke!

Let not Ambition mock their useful toil,
Their homely joys, and destiny obscure;   30
Nor Grandeur hear with a disdainful smile
The short and simple annals of the Poor.   *simple history*

The boast of heraldry, the pomp of power,   *boast of noble families*
And all that beauty, all that wealth e'er gave,
Awaits alike th' inevitable hour:-   35
The paths of glory lead but to the grave.

Nor you, ye Proud, impute to these the fault
If Memory o'er their tomb no trophies raise,   *no memorial statues*
Where through the long-drawn aisle and fretted vault   *decorated archway*
The pealing anthem swells the note of praise.   40

Can storied urn or animated bust   *funeral urn with epitaph or lifelike bust*
Back to its mansion call the fleeting breath?
Can Honour's voice provoke the silent dust,   *voice awaken the silent dead*
Or Flattery soothe the dull cold ear of Death?

Perhaps in this neglected spot is laid   45
Some heart once pregnant with celestial fire;
Hands, that the rod of empire might have sway'd,
Or waked to ecstasy the living lyre: *the living harp of poetry and song*

But Knowledge to their eyes her ample page,
Rich with the spoils of time, did ne'er unroll; 50
Chill Penury repress'd their noble rage, *Cold poverty*
And froze the genial current of the soul.

Full many a gem of purest ray serene
The dark unfathom'd caves of ocean bear:
Full many a flower is born to blush unseen, 55
And waste its sweetness on the desert air.

Some village-Hampden, that with dauntless breast *(see note *)*
The little tyrant of his fields withstood,
Some mute inglorious Milton here may rest,
Some Cromwell, guiltless of his country's blood. 60

Th' applause of list'ning senates to command,
The threats of pain and ruin to despise,
To scatter plenty o'er a smiling land,
And read their history in a nation's eyes,

Their lot forbad: nor circumscribed alone 65
Their growing virtues, but their crimes confined;
Forbad to wade through slaughter to a throne,
And shut the gates of mercy on mankind,

The struggling pangs of conscious truth to hide,
To quench the blushes of ingenuous shame, 70
Or heap the shrine of Luxury and Pride
With incense kindled at the Muse's flame.

Far from the madding crowd's ignoble strife, *crazed crowd's petty wars*
Their sober wishes never learn'd to stray;
Along the cool sequester'd vale of life 75
They kept the noiseless tenour of their way.

Yet e'en these bones from insult to protect
Some frail memorial still erected nigh, *(see note ** below)*
With uncouth rhymes and shapeless sculpture deck'd,
Implores the passing tribute of a sigh. 80

Their name, their years, spelt by th' unletter'd Muse, *illiterate Muse*
The place of fame and elegy supply:
And many a holy text around she strews,
That teach the rustic moralist to die.

For who, to dumb forgetfulness a prey, 85
This pleasing anxious being e'er resign'd,
Left the warm precincts of the cheerful day,

Nor cast one longing lingering look behind?

On some fond breast the parting soul relies,
Some pious drops the closing eye requires;   90
E'en from the tomb the voice of Nature cries,
E'en in our ashes live their wonted fires.   *usual fires*

For thee, who, mindful of th' unhonour'd dead,
Dost in these lines their artless tale relate:
If chance, by lonely contemplation led,   95
Some kindred spirit shall inquire thy fate, —

Haply some hoary-headed swain may say,   *gray-haired peasant*
"Oft have we seen him at the peep of dawn
Brushing with hasty steps the dews away,
To meet the sun upon the upland lawn;   100

"There at the foot of yonder nodding beech
That wreathes its old fantastic roots so high,
His listless length at noontide would he stretch,
And pore upon the brook that babbles by.

"Hard by yon wood, now smiling as in scorn,   105
Muttering his wayward fancies he would rove;
Now drooping, woeful wan, like one forlorn,
Or crazed with care, or cross'd in hopeless love.

"One morn I miss'd him on the custom'd hill,
Along the heath, and near his favourite tree;   110
Another came; nor yet beside the rill,
Nor up the lawn, nor at the wood was he;

"The next with dirges due in sad array
Slow through the church-way path we saw him borne,-
Approach and read (for thou canst read) the lay   *the poetic inscription*   115
Graved on the stone beneath yon aged thorn."   *on his tombstone*

                The Epitaph
Here rests his head upon the lap of Earth
A youth to Fortune and to Fame unknown.
Fair Science frowned not on his humble birth,
And Melancholy marked him for her own.   120

Large was his bounty, and his soul sincere,
Heaven did a recompense as largely send:
He gave to Misery all he had, a tear,
He gained from Heaven ('twas all he wish'd) a friend.

> *No farther seek his merits to disclose,*   125
> *Or draw his frailties from their dread abode*
> *(There they alike in trembling hope repose),*
> *The bosom of his Father and his God.*   1751

*John Hampden was a courageous member of Parliament who openly defied King Charles I over an unfair tax. Hampden's defiance was a symbolic gesture that helped spark the Civil War between the king's forces and those of Parliament. Hampden was killed during the war. In this passage, Gray imagines that one of the poor people buried in the churchyard might have been as courageous as John Hampden in standing up to a local bully.

**In this quatrain, Gray observes that, while the wealthy dead have fancy funeral urns, statues of themselves, and grand tombs, these rural poor have only a humble memorial nearby. Carved on it is a poorly-worded ("uncouth") poetic epitaph and a crudely-shaped statue.

    In its rural setting; its descriptions of the natural world; the poet's isolated position and dark, melancholy musings; and its reverence for the simple poor, Gray's elegy typifies poetry of the latter part of the eighteenth century and looks forward to the next great era of poetry, the Romantic Age (1798–1832). But the poem's form is still rooted in the conventions of the Augustan Age, even though it is not written in heroic couplets, but in iambic pentameter quatrains rhyming *abab*. Although the first four lines sound like everyday speech, we soon get convoluted poetic diction ("And all the air a solemn stillness holds"):

> Nor you, ye proud, impute to these the fault,
>   If Memory o'er their tomb no trophies raise,

Many of the quatrains also use the caesura and parallel phrases to create an Augustan sense of symmetry and balance:

> The boast of heraldry, the pomp of power,
>   And all that beauty, all that wealth e'er gave,

After the first few quatrains, too, Gray stops describing the natural scene around him and, instead, turns to very generalized images, such as:

> Full many a gem of purest ray serene,
>   The dark, unfathomed caves of ocean bear:

Gray is not standing at the bottom of an ocean cave where he can see these beautiful jewels; he's just imagining them with little descriptive detail.
    Throughout the poem, he also uses *personified abstractions* in which he takes an abstract idea and describes it as if it were a person:

> Let not Ambition mock their useful toil,
>   Their homely joys, and destiny obscure;
> Nor Grandeur hear with a disdainful smile
>   The short and simple annals of the poor.

Here, he portrays the abstract idea of "Ambition" as a person who mocks the rural poor and "Grandeur" as someone who condescendingly sneers at their simple lives.

Finally, Gray, although writing in quatrains, still follows the convention of the heroic couplet in keeping most of his lines end-stopped rather than enjambed. Almost every quatrain, moreover, ends on a sentence. Can you find some that don't—and see why Gray chose to have those particular sentences run over two or more quatrains?

Phyllis Wheatley (1753-1784)

Phyllis Wheatley, who was born in Senegal, Africa, was enslaved and shipped to America at the age of seven. She was bought by a Boston merchant to be a slave to his wife. The Wheatley family educated Phyllis, who learned to read Latin and Greek, as well as English. She published her first poem, an elegy on the death of a famous Puritan preacher, in a Boston newspaper. The Wheatleys sent her to London to improve her health. There, she developed a deep admiration for the poetry of John Milton and Alexander Pope and published a collection of her own poems. When she returned to Boston, she was given her freedom and married a free black man. Although she died in poverty and obscurity, Phyllis Wheatley was later hailed as the first African-American woman to have her poetry published. In this poem, she uses the iambic pentameter couplet that was such a popular poetic form in the eighteenth century.

On Being Brought from Africa to America

Twas mercy brought me from my pagan land,
Taught my beknighted soul to understand   *my darkened soul*
That there's a God, that there's a Savior too:
Once I redemption neither sought nor knew.
Some view our sable race with scornful eye,   *our gleamingly black*
"Their color is a diabolic dye."   *devilish dye*
Remember Christians; Negroes, black as Cain,   *(see note * below)*
May be refin'd, and join th' angelic train.
                                                                1773

*After Cain slew his brother Abel, as recounted in the Book of Genesis, God placed a "mark" upon Cain to indicate that he was an outcast. Many people once believed that Cain's "mark" was the blackness of his skin which he passed on to inhabitants of Africa.

The Novel

The audience for fiction changed with the invention of the printing press in 1436. Instead of writing for an oral audience, writers began to write for a *reader*, who would silently read the story to himself or herself. Since there was no oral dimension to reading a book, writers wrote in prose rather than poetry; not only was it easier to write in prose sentences than in poetic lines, writers were usually paid by the word—around three cents a word—another inducement to write in loose prose rather than concise poetry. It would take more than 200 years, however, before enough people learned to read to create a demand for books and other reading materials. The 1700s saw the emergence of newspapers, magazines, and a new kind of narrative written in prose—the *novel*.

The novel, as its name implies, is different from older prose narratives because it is *new*—set in present-day society, not in some romantic past of knights and dragons in far-off lands. Just like its stories, its prose language is more contemporary and conversational than the poetry of older narratives. The writer of a novel aimed at the individual reader, reading alone, rather than the communal audience for drama and narrative poetry. Thus, the novel was a form that grew out of a period in history when the individual, rather than the community, was growing in importance.

In the Protestant religions that spread across Northern Europe after the Reformation in the sixteenth century, each person was individually responsible for her or his salvation, as opposed to the traditional Catholic community of believers. Protestants were "people of the Book"—believers who read and interpreted the Bible for themselves, as opposed to Catholics who took their religious instruction from priests. The first book to come from Gutenberg's printing press was the Bible, and the rapid dissemination of printed bibles—in various modern European language translations—helped fuel the Reformation. A Catholic might wryly observe that the proliferation of printed bibles led to the many different religious "sects" or denominations of Protestantism, as various groups disagreed over the meaning of one or another passage of scripture.

In economics, too, capitalism made each person an individual economic unit in a business or in "selling" his or her own labor. In politics, individualism underlaid the ideas of democracy, equality, and "inalienable rights" that led to the formulation of countries such as the United States of America.

Not only was the novel part of this new movement toward individualism, it frequently focused its narrative on an individual. So, many of the titles of early novels—*Robinson Crusoe*, *Pamela*, *Joseph Andrews*—reflect their focus on how an individual struggles to overcome the opposition of nature or society.

As various writers of the eighteenth century experimented with writing novels, they tried different ways of giving form to these long, prose narratives. Novels were published as printed books and attracted a wide readership. They appealed primarily to middle-class people who had learned to read, had the money to purchase books, and—especially middle-class women—had the leisure time to devote to reading, now that servants did household chores. As Martin S. Day has observed[9],

> With the 18th century came an expansion of cities, a greater mobility of the population, an increase in trade, and a greater individual and social self-consciousness; hence the average man met more people than ever before and realized as never before the interdependence of society. The novel essentially undertook the task of helping mankind understand the position of the individual in the larger social organism.

What form did this new literary genre take? Let's look at excerpts from three early novels to see how three different novelists—Daniel Defoe, Henry Fielding, and Jane Austen—tackled the problem of creating the *form* of the novel.

Daniel Defoe (1660-1731)

Daniel Defoe began life as Daniel Foe, the son of a London butcher, but later added the Frenchified "De" to his last name. After receiving a basic high school education, he became a merchant and

---

[9] Martin S. Day, *History of English Literature to 1660* Garden City, NY: Doubleday & Company, Inc., 1963), p. 147.

traveled extensively (at one point he was captured by Algerian pirates). After several failures in business, he eked out a living as a journalist, writing for newspapers, pamphlets, and other publications in support of the middle class as it struggled for power and position against the entrenched, aristocratic landowners of England. Only in his sixties did he turn to writing novels, such as *Robinson Crusoe* (1719). His novels were popular and sold well but could not lift Defoe out of his lifelong financial woes. He died, bankrupt, hiding from his creditors.

While *Robinson Crusoe* is his most famous novel, the book that was most important in establishing the form of the novel was *The Fortunes and Misfortunes of the Famous Moll Flanders*. Defoe presents this fictional novel as the "true" autobiography of a notorious thief, prostitute, and convict. Following the form of autobiography, he creates a character Moll Flanders, who tells the story of her life in her own voice, using the *first-person* pronouns (*I*, *my*, etc.)—a very traditional way to tell a story, particularly an autobiography. Defoe simply adapted that autobiographical form of narrative to the fictional form of a novel.

Here is an excerpt from Defoe's novel, in which Moll Flanders recounts the loss of her virginity to a young man in an aristocratic house where she works as a servant.

from *Moll Flanders*

When we were together he began to talk very gravely to me, and to tell me he did not bring me there to betray me; that his passion for me would not suffer him to abuse me; that he resolved to marry me as soon as he came to his estate; that in the meantime, if I would grant his request, he would maintain me very honourably; and made me a thousand protestations of his sincerity and of his affection to me; and that he would never abandon me, and as I may say, made a thousand more preambles than he need to have done.

However, as he pressed me to speak, I told him I had no reason to question the sincerity of his love to me after so many protestations, but—and there I stopped, as if I left him to guess the rest. 'But what, my dear?' says he. 'I guess what you mean: what if you should be with child? Is not that it? Why, then,' says he, 'I'll take care of you and provide for you, and the child too; and that you may see I am not in jest,' says he, 'here's an earnest for you,' and with that he pulls out a silk purse, with an hundred guineas in it, and gave it me. 'And I'll give you such another,' says he, 'every year till I marry you.'

My colour came and went, at the sight of the purse and with the fire of his proposal together, so that I could not say a word, and he easily perceived it; so putting the purse into my bosom, I made no more resistance to him, but let him do just what he pleased, and as often as he pleased; and thus I finished my own destruction at once, for from this day, being forsaken of my virtue and my modesty, I had nothing of value left to recommend me, either to God's blessing or man's assistance.

1722

Narrative Form in Moll Flanders

By having his character, Moll, tell the story of her life in her own words, Defoe used what we now call the *first-person point of view*, a form of storytelling in which the narrator is a character in the story he or she tells. Such a point of view has its problems: characters who tell the story in their own voices cannot recount incidents in the story where they were not present; they can't tell us what other characters in the story are thinking; they are limited solely to what they have experienced of the events that make up the story. Using the first-person point of view, however, can make for a very intense way of telling a story, as it does here, where we, as readers, feel we are physically present at Moll's seduction.

The first-person point of view also gives us insight into the mind of the character who narrates the story. In this excerpt, for example, the young man who is trying to seduce Moll pleads with her, saying he will marry her once he becomes old enough to claim his inheritance. Moll confides to us as readers, however, that she was ready to sleep with him on the spot and, thus, "he made a thousand more preambles than he *need* to have done." The fact that Moll was eager to make love to him also makes us regard her hint about worrying he might get her pregnant as a ploy. When she looks reluctant about the prospect of making love, he guesses she's worried about getting pregnant, so he promises he'll take care of her and gives her a purse full of "guineas" (gold coins) to show her his intentions are, if not honorable, honest.

Moll then unintentionally betrays her own values by saying she was more excited by seeing a purse full of gold coins than she was turned on by the boy's passion for her—a kind of delicious *dramatic irony* that can be created with first-person point of view. A character may be telling the reader something with the intention of creating a positive impression, but the reader "sees through" the narrator's story to the character's unintended revelations. Moll is no innocent waif seduced by a sophisticated rake but a shrewd little minx out to get money for sexual favors. In telling the story of her first seduction years later, she regards it in hard, economic terms. As a poor servant girl in a crassly capitalistic society, she had only one economic "commodity" to sell—her virginity. When she gave it away to this wealthy boy for a sack of gold coins, she lost her chance to make him marry her.

Notice, too, how Defoe combines showing and telling in the way the narrator describes the scene of her seduction. Although it happens at a particular time and place, Moll does not really present the moment of her loss of virginity as a dramatic scene, for there is very little dialogue in *direct discourse*. In direct discourse, the writer presents what the characters say in lines of dialogue—as in a dramatic play—set off by quotation marks. Defoe uses a few passages of direct discourse, as when he writes, "'But what, my dear?' says he." Even here, however, Defoe does not put the man's lines of dialogue in a new, indented paragraph, as would become customary in later fiction. The man's words simply run together with the rest of the sentences in the paragraph.

Most of the other dialogue between Moll and her lover is given in *indirect discourse*, where Moll summarizes what was said—*telling* rather than *showing*. For example, she tells us that "However, as he pressed me to speak, I told him that I had no reason to question the sincerity of his love." If that exchange of dialogue were presented dramatically, it would appear in direct discourse, like dialogue in a play:

"Please, my darling," he said, "speak to me."
"I have no reason to question the sincerity of your love," I replied.

The distinction between direct and indirect discourse is a subtle one, but it distinguishes the form of this passage—and of Defoe's entire novel—that consists more of narrative summary than narrative scene—more *telling* than *showing*.

Henry Fielding (1707–1754)

Henry Fielding's family had aristocratic connections, but he was trained in the law and spent most of his career as a justice of the peace, prosecuting criminals and trying to help the poor. He also had some success as a playwright, but when his plays, as well as those of other dramatists, provoked government censorship, he turned to other forms of writing.

While Defoe based his novels on the form of autobiography, Fielding thought the novel should be a prose version of epic, especially those comic epic poems that supposedly were destroyed when the great library at Alexandria (in Egypt) burned in classical times. Instead of using the kind of first-person narrator Defoe used in *Moll Flanders*, Fielding made himself the narrator, much like Homer was the narrator of *The Iliad* and *The Odyssey*. Such a narrator is sometimes called *omniscient*, because he or she can tell us what is happening in various settings, what information we need to know about earlier events in the story, and even what various characters are thinking. Fielding and other eighteenth-century novelists even went so far as to have their narrators speak directly to the "dear reader," talk about the book they were writing, and describe their characters as fictional creations, rather than, as Defoe had done, pretend they were actual people.

In this passage from *Tom Jones* (1749), for example, Fielding recounts an incident that happened when Tom Jones, his girlfriend Sophia Western, and Tom's nasty cousin Blifil were children.

from Tom Jones

Tom Jones, when very young, had presented Sophia with a little bird, which he had taken from the nest, had nursed up, and taught to sing.

Of this bird, Sophia, then about thirteen years old, was so extremely fond, that her chief business was to feed and tend it, and her chief pleasure to play with it. By these means little Tommy, for so the bird was called, was become so tame, that it would feed out of the hand of its mistress, would perch upon the finger, and lie contented in her bosom, where it seemed almost sensible of its own happiness; though she always kept a small string about its leg, nor would ever trust it with the liberty of flying away.

One day, when Mr. Allworthy and his whole family dined at Mr. Western's, Master Blifil, being in the garden with little Sophia, and observing the extreme fondness that she showed for her little bird, desired her to trust it for a moment in his hands. Sophia presently complied with the young gentleman's request, and after some previous caution, delivered him her bird; of which he was no sooner in possession, than he slipt the string from its leg and tossed it into the air.

The foolish animal no sooner perceived itself at liberty, than forgetting all the favours it had received from Sophia, it flew directly from her, and perched on a bough at some distance.

Sophia, seeing her bird gone, screamed out so loud that Tom Jones, who was at a little distance, immediately ran to her assistance.

He was no sooner informed of what had happened, than he cursed Blifil for a pitiful malicious rascal; and then immediately stripping off his coat he applied himself to climbing the tree to which the bird escaped.

Tom had almost recovered his little namesake, when the branch on which it was perched, and that hung over a canal, broke, and the poor lad plumped over head and ears into the water.

Sophia's concern now changed its object. And as she apprehended the boy's life was in danger, she screamed ten times louder than before; and indeed Master Blifil himself now seconded her with all the vociferation in his power.

The company, who were sitting in a room next the garden, were instantly alarmed, and came all forth; but just as they reached the canal, Tom (for the water was luckily pretty shallow in that part) arrived safely on shore.

Thwackum fell violently on poor Tom, who stood dropping and shivering before him, when Mr. Allworthy desired him to have patience; and turning to Master Blifil, said, "Pray, child, what is the reason of all this disturbance?"

Master Blifil answered, "Indeed, uncle, I am very sorry for what I have done; I have been unhappily the occasion of it all. I had Miss Sophia's bird in my hand, and thinking the poor creature languished for liberty, I own I could not forbear giving it what it desired; for I always thought there was something very cruel in confining anything. It seemed to be against the law of nature, by which everything hath a right to liberty; nay, it is even unchristian, for it is not doing what we would be done by; but if I had imagined Miss Sophia would have been so much concerned at it, I am sure I never would have done it; nay, if I had known what would have happened to the bird itself: for when Master Jones, who climbed up that tree after it, fell into the water, the bird took a second flight, and presently a nasty hawk carried it away."

Poor Sophia, who now first heard of her little Tommy's fate (for her concern for Jones had prevented her perceiving it when it happened), shed a shower of tears. These Mr. Allworthy endeavoured to assuage, promising her a much finer bird: but she declared she would never have another. Her father chid her for crying so for a foolish bird; but could not help telling young Blifil, if he was a son of his, his backside should be well flayed.

Sophia now returned to her chamber, the two young gentlemen were sent home, and the rest of the company returned to their bottle; where a conversation ensued on the subject of the bird, so curious, that we think it deserves a chapter by itself. 1749

Narrative Form in *Tom Jones*

Fielding, despite his early experience as a playwright, renders this episode more in narrative summary than narrative scene. As the omniscient narrator, he gives us exposition about how Tom Jones had given the bird as a present to Sophia, how much she treasured the bird, and how she kept it tied on a string. When we get to a particular time—"One day"—and a particular place—the garden on the estate where Sophia lives, Fielding, like Defoe, renders the events that follow more in narrative summary than narrative scene. Almost all of the dialogue, for example, is reported in indirect discourse, such as "He was no sooner informed of what had happened than he cursed Blifil for a pitiful, malicious rascal." We don't get the actual dialogue here reported in direct discourse but, instead, a summary of the exchange among Sophia, Tom, and Blifil. We only get dialogue in direct discourse near the end of the scene as Mr. Allworthy, Tom's guardian, asks Blifil, "Pray, child, what is the reason of all this disturbance?" Blifil then replies with a long speech in dialogue in which he informs the others (and the reader) of something Fielding the narrator might have told us—that the escaped bird was attacked and carried off by a hawk.

After Blifil has spoken, however, Fielding returns to summarizing the action and reporting dialogue in indirect discourse, such as Sophia's father's telling Blifil that if the boy had been his son, he would have gotten a whipping for releasing the bird. Fielding, like Defoe, thus relies more on *telling* than *showing*, even though his omniscient narrator is very different from Defoe's first-person narrator. At the end of the episode, Fielding, as narrator, addresses the reader directly about the novel he is writing, saying that the conversation among the adults was so interesting he thinks it deserves "a chapter by itself." At the end of the next chapter, in which Fielding reports the conversation among the adults about the bird incident, he addresses the reader even more directly:

> Such was the conclusion of this adventure of the bird and the dialogue occasioned by it, which we could not help recounting to our reader, though it happened some years before that stage or period of time at which our story is now arrived.

As an omniscient narrator, Fielding apologizes to his reader for recounting an event that happened much earlier in his story.

The Novel of Manners

By the end of the eighteenth century, several novelists, most notably Jane Austen, began to write novels about everyday social life among middle-class families in England. There were few outwardly exciting actions in such novels—just the ordinary events of middle-class life. What made such everyday occurrences interesting, however, was the way characters—characters who were often intelligent, sensitive, and witty—responded to such prosaic doings as holding a dinner party, going to a dance, or visiting a friend.

Because such novels portrayed the customs, polite (and sometimes impolite) behavior, and social habits of the middle and upper classes, they are called *novels of manners*. Novels of manners are seldom about exciting adventures, physically violent conflicts, or historically significant events, such as military battles. Instead, they deal with the subtle relations among genteel people in their day-to-day social intercourse—showing *manners* in a much broader sense than knowing when you need to write a thank-you note or using the proper forks for salad and dessert.

Jane Austen (1775-1817)

Jane Austen was the daughter of an Episcopal minister, and she grew up in several cities, small and large, in the southwest of England. After the death of her father in 1805, she moved around with her mother and sisters, finally settling in the tiny village of Chawton. Except for occasional visits to London, she lived in Chawton, and her novels reflect the daily life among the middle and upper classes in such villages. Although she lived during the Napoleonic wars and the social upheaval of the Industrial Revolution, life in such villages was remarkably placid and outwardly uneventful.

As a girl, Jane Austen wrote stories, often parodies of sensational romantic fiction. When she turned to writing novels, she spent a great deal of time revising her fiction—more so than any previous novelist. She published only four novels during her lifetime—*Sense and Sensibility* (1811), *Pride and Prejudice* (1813), *Mansfield Park* (1814), and *Emma* (1815)—but each is a masterpiece of narrative craftsmanship. Several have been made, again and again, into successful movies.

In 1817, her health began to fail, and she moved to Winchester to be near her doctor, but she died within the year. After her death, two of her other novels were published, and several unfinished novels were found among her papers.

Narrative Form in Pride and Prejudice

In novels such as *Pride and Prejudice*, Jane Austen used fictional forms in ways that writers of today still employ. While Defoe and Fielding blended narrative scene with narrative summary, Jane Austen carefully demarcated these two ways of rendering a story. Look, for example, at the opening chapter of *Pride and Prejudice*. Jane Austen begins with exposition as an omniscient narrator, like Fielding in *Tom Jones*:

> It is a truth universally acknowledged, that a single man in possession of a good fortune must be in want of a wife.
> However little known the feelings or views of such a man may be on his first entering a neighbourhood, this truth is so well fixed in the minds of the surrounding families, that he is considered as the rightful property of some one or other of their daughters.

To Jane Austen's contemporary readers, these first sentences would have been amusing for the high-sounding "truth universally acknowledged" was often invoked throughout the eighteenth century to define rational laws that all people could recognize. The framers of our Constitution, for example, established as one such universal law that all men are entitled to "life, liberty, and the pursuit of happiness" (altering the original phrase of the philosopher John Locke—"life, liberty, and property"). But, the universal truth Austen mentions is that any single, wealthy young man is fair game for mothers who want to marry off their daughters.

After those opening two sentences, however, Austen almost completely disappears as narrator and presents the conversation between Mr. and Mrs. Bennet as a *narrative scene*:

``My dear Mr. Bennet,'' said his lady to him one day, ``have you heard that Netherfield Park is let at last?''

Mr. Bennet replied that he had not.

``But it is,'' returned she; ``for Mrs. Long has just been here, and she told me all about it.''

Mr. Bennet made no answer.

``Do not you want to know who has taken it?'' cried his wife impatiently.

``You want to tell me, and I have no objection to hearing it.''

This was invitation enough.

``Why, my dear, you must know, Mrs. Long says that Netherfield is taken by a young man of large fortune from the north of England; that he came down on Monday in a chaise and four to see the place, and was so much delighted with it that he agreed with Mr. Morris immediately; that he is to take possession before Michaelmas, and some of his servants are to be in the house by the end of next week.''

``What is his name?''

``Bingley.''

``Is he married or single?''

``Oh! single, my dear, to be sure! A single man of large fortune; four or five thousand a year. What a fine thing for our girls!''

``How so? how can it affect them?''

``My dear Mr. Bennet,'' replied his wife, ``how can you be so tiresome! You must know that I am thinking of his marrying one of them.''

``Is that his design in settling here?''

``Design! nonsense, how can you talk so! But it is very likely that he may fall in love with one of them, and therefore you must visit him as soon as he comes.''

``I see no occasion for that. You and the girls may go, or you may send them by themselves, which perhaps will be still better; for, as you are as handsome as any of them, Mr. Bingley might like you the best of the party.''

``My dear, you flatter me. I certainly have had my share of beauty, but I do not pretend to be any thing extraordinary now. When a woman has five grown up daughters, she ought to give over thinking of her own beauty.''

"In such cases, a woman has not often much beauty to think of."

"But, my dear, you must indeed go and see Mr. Bingley when he comes into the neighbourhood."

"It is more than I engage for, I assure you."

"But consider your daughters. Only think what an establishment it would be for one of them. Sir William and Lady Lucas are determined to go, merely on that account, for in general, you know they visit no new comers. Indeed you must go, for it will be impossible for us to visit him, if you do not."

"You are over-scrupulous, surely. I dare say Mr. Bingley will be very glad to see you; and I will send a few lines by you to assure him of my hearty consent to his marrying which ever he chuses of the girls; though I must throw in a good word for my little Lizzy."

"I desire you will do no such thing. Lizzy is not a bit better than the others; and I am sure she is not half so handsome as Jane, nor half so good humoured as Lydia. But you are always giving her the preference."

"They have none of them much to recommend them," replied he; "they are all silly and ignorant like other girls; but Lizzy has something more of quickness than her sisters."

"Mr. Bennet, how can you abuse your own children in such way? You take delight in vexing me. You have no compassion on my poor nerves."

"You mistake me, my dear. I have a high respect for your nerves. They are my old friends. I have heard you mention them with consideration these twenty years at least."

"Ah! you do not know what I suffer."

"But I hope you will get over it, and live to see many young men of four thousand a year come into the neighbourhood."

"It will be no use to us if twenty such should come, since you will not visit them."

"Depend upon it, my dear, that when there are twenty I will visit them all."

Mr. Bennet was so odd a mixture of quick parts, sarcastic humour, reserve, and caprice, that the experience of three and twenty years had been insufficient to make his wife understand his character. Her mind was less difficult to develope. She was a woman of mean understanding, little information, and uncertain temper. When she was discontented, she fancied herself nervous. The business of her life was to get her daughters married; its solace was visiting and news.

Only in this last paragraph of the chapter does Austen return as the omniscient narrator to "tell" us about Mr. and Mrs. Bennet. Everything between the first and last paragraphs of the chapter could be a dramatic scene from a play—an extraordinary way of opening a novel by primarily *showing*, rather than *telling*, her story. Almost all of the dialogue, moreover, is rendered in direct discourse—as it would be in a play. The only bit of indirect discourse is "Mr. Bennet replied that he had not."

In the course of this scene we get exposition—much as we would in a play—through dialogue. While Defoe or Fielding would have provided this exposition by having their narrator tell us about it, Austen works like a dramatist and has the information come out through the conversation between the Bennets. In fact, she handles dialogue so deftly that she frequent omits the "tags"—"Mr. Bennet said," "Mrs. Bennet said,"—but we can still follow the conversation between the two. What we learn from Mrs. Bennet is that a wealthy young bachelor named Bingley has just moved into their neighborhood and rented Netherfield, one of the fashionable mansions in the village of Meryton. Mrs. Bennet is eager to have Bingley meet their daughters, in the hope that he will marry one of them, but social propriety requires Mr. Bennet to first make a call upon Bingley and introduce himself.

The comic conflict in this scene arises from the way Mr. Bennet (who has undoubtedly already heard about the imminent arrival of Bingley) teases his wife by pretending not to understand that Bingley is a good marriage prospect for one of their daughters. He is clearly much cleverer than his wife and takes a somewhat sadistic pleasure in condescending to her. He pretends to worry that if she accompanies her daughters on a visit to meet Bingley, the young bachelor will find Mrs. Bennet more attractive than any of her daughters. She doesn't realize he's pulling her chain and instead takes his comment as a compliment to her beauty. Mr. Bennet is also sarcastic about his daughters. He considers them all silly girls, except for one, "Lizzy" (Elizabeth), thus making us eager to see this one daughter in the same way Shakespeare has people talk about his main characters, such as Othello, before he brings them on stage. Mr. Bennet frustrates his wife by saying he will not call upon Bingley, but, in the very next chapter, he makes the call without telling her.

Scene and Summary in *Pride and Prejudice*

While Defoe and Fielding blended elements of narrative summary and narrative scene—telling and showing—Jane Austen usually keeps these two ways of presenting a story distinct so that, in her novels, she creates a rhythm of fictional form as she alternates between scene and summary. The first chapter, as we have seen, is devoted, except for its opening and closing paragraphs, exclusively to narrative scene.

Here is another passage from early in the novel, which Austen renders in narrative summary, describing how Mrs. Bennet invited Mr. Bingley to dinner, how he declined because he would be going to "town" (London), but how he, in turn, promised that when he returns to Meryton, he will attend a ball at the "assembly" (a public building used for dances and other social events):

> An invitation to dinner was soon afterwards dispatched; and already had Mrs. Bennet planned the courses that were to do credit to her housekeeping, when an answer arrived which deferred it all. Mr. Bingley was obliged to be in town the following day, and consequently unable to accept the honour of their invitation, &c. Mrs. Bennet was quite disconcerted. She could not imagine what business he could have in town so soon after his arrival in Hertfordshire; and she began to fear that he might be always flying about from one place to another, and never settled at Netherfield as he ought to be. Lady Lucas quieted her fears a little by starting the idea of his being gone to London

only to get a large party for the ball; and a report soon followed that Mr. Bingley was to bring twelve ladies and seven gentlemen with him to the assembly. The girls grieved over such a large number of ladies; but were comforted the day before the ball by hearing that, instead of twelve, he had brought only six with him from London, his five sisters and a cousin. And when the party entered the assembly room, it consisted of only five altogether; Mr. Bingley, his two sisters, the husband of the oldest, and another young man.

Mr. Bingley was good looking and gentlemanlike; he had a pleasant countenance, and easy, unaffected manners. His brother-in-law, Mr. Hurst, merely looked the gentleman; but his friend Mr. Darcy soon drew the attention of the room by his fine, tall person, handsome features, noble mien; and the report which was in general circulation within five minutes after his entrance, of his having ten thousand a year. The gentlemen pronounced him to be a fine figure of a man, the ladies declared he was much handsomer than Mr. Bingley, and he was looked at with great admiration for about half the evening, till his manners gave a disgust which turned the tide of his popularity; for he was discovered to be proud, to be above his company, and above being pleased; and not all his large estate in Derbyshire could then save him from having a most forbidding, disagreeable countenance, and being unworthy to be compared with his friend.

Mr. Bingley had soon made himself acquainted with all the principal people in the room; he was lively and unreserved, danced every dance, was angry that the ball closed so early, and talked of giving one himself at Netherfield. Such amiable qualities must speak for themselves. What a contrast between him and his friend! Mr. Darcy danced only once with Mrs. Hurst and once with Miss Bingley, declined being introduced to any other lady, and spent the rest of the evening in walking about the room, speaking occasionally to one of his own party. His character was decided. He was the proudest, most disagreeable man in the world, and every body hoped that he would never come there again. Amongst the most violent against him was Mrs. Bennet, whose dislike of his general behaviour was sharpened into particular resentment by his having slighted one of her daughters.

Notice how all of the action is *described* by the narrator in *summary*—not *presented* in narrative scene. There is much conversation, but none of it is given in quoted dialogue, only in indirect discourse ("The gentlemen pronounced him to be a fine figure of a man, the ladies declared he was much handsomer than Mr. Bingley . . ."). Why do you think Jane Austen decided to present this part of her novel, which introduces her hero, Darcy, in narrative summary rather than narrative scene? Perhaps it was economy. In the course of one paragraph, the middle paragraph above, the people at the dance go from admiring Darcy for his looks and wealth at the beginning of the evening to despising him for what they regard as his haughty "pride" by the end of the dance—all in the space of a few sentences.

Point of View in Pride and Prejudice

Another of Jane Austen's innovations in fictional form was her use of what we now call the *third-person limited point of view*. Most narratives before *Pride and Prejudice* were told from the point of view of a character in the first-person (as in *Moll Flanders*) or by the storyteller himself or herself as an omniscient narrator (such as Fielding in *Tom Jones*) who can summarize or dramatize the action, go into the minds of characters to tell us what they are thinking, bring us up to date on what has happened earlier in the story, and even talk directly to us as readers. Presenting fiction from the point of view of a first-person narrator who is a character in the story or an omniscient narrator who knows everything about the characters and the plot are two ways of telling stories that go back to the earliest oral tales and epics.

But, the *third-person limited point of view* emerged with the advent of printing. Novelists, and short story writers, could present portions of their novels or an entire story through the point of view of a character but still keep that character at some distance from the reader by rendering his or her perceptions, thoughts, and feelings in third (*he* or *she*), rather than first (*I*) person. Jane Austen frequently presents her story from the point of view of her main character. In this scene, which follows the narrative summary above, we are in Elizabeth Bennet's point of view:

> Elizabeth Bennet had been obliged, by the scarcity of gentlemen, to sit down for two dances; and during part of that time, Mr. Darcy had been standing near enough for her to overhear a conversation between him and Mr. Bingley, who came from the dance for a few minutes to press his friend to join it.
>
> ``Come, Darcy,'' said he, ``I must have you dance. I hate to see you standing about by yourself in this stupid manner. You had much better dance.''
>
> ``I certainly shall not. You know how I detest it, unless I am particularly acquainted with my partner. At such an assembly as this, it would be insupportable. Your sisters are engaged, and there is not another woman in the room whom it would not be a punishment to me to stand up with.''
>
> ``I would not be so fastidious as you are,'' cried Bingley, ``for a kingdom! Upon my honour I never met with so many pleasant girls in my life, as I have this evening; and there are several of them, you see, uncommonly pretty.''
>
> ``You are dancing with the only handsome girl in the room,'' said Mr. Darcy, looking at the eldest Miss Bennet.
>
> ``Oh! she is the most beautiful creature I ever beheld! But there is one of her sisters sitting down just behind you, who is very pretty, and I dare say very agreeable. Do let me ask my partner to introduce you.''
>
> ``Which do you mean?'' and turning round, he looked for a moment at Elizabeth, till catching her eye, he withdrew his own and coldly said, ``She is tolerable; but not handsome enough to tempt me; and I am in no humour at present to give consequence to young ladies who are slighted by other men. You had better return to your partner and enjoy her smiles, for you are wasting your time with me.''
>
> Mr. Bingley followed his advice. Mr. Darcy walked off; and Elizabeth remained with no very cordial feelings towards him. She told the story however

with great spirit among her friends; for she had a lively, playful disposition, which delighted in any thing ridiculous.

By presenting the conversation between Darcy and Bingley as something overheard by Elizabeth, Austen makes us wonder how she will react to what Bingley says about her sister Jane, as well as what Darcy says about Elizabeth herself. At the end of the scene, Austen takes us into Elizabeth's mind so that we can see her reaction. It tells us a lot about her character that, while what Darcy says about her hurts her feelings, Elizabeth not only laughs it off but delights in telling the story to her friends.

If one piece of advice sometimes given to young writers is "Show, don't tell," then another is "Don't shift point of view' (though for those of you who are beginning writers, it is important to adhere to these traditional rules until you have more experience in writing fiction). Austen shifts point of view throughout this novel, usually between her omniscient narrator and the third-person point of view of Elizabeth Bennet. In Chapter 6, for example, the omniscient narrator steps in to *tell* us, in narrative summary, something that Elizabeth is completely unaware of. In this passage, Austen even uses the omniscient point of view to go into Darcy's mind and give us his thoughts:

> Occupied in observing Mr. Bingley's attentions to her sister, Elizabeth was far from suspecting that she was herself becoming an object of some interest in the eyes of his friend. Mr. Darcy had at first scarcely allowed her to be pretty; he had looked at her without admiration at the ball; and when they next met, he looked at her only to criticise. But no sooner had he made it clear to himself and his friends that she had hardly a good feature in her face, than he began to find it was rendered uncommonly intelligent by the beautiful expression of her dark eyes. To this discovery succeeded some others equally mortifying. Though he had detected with a critical eye more than one failure of perfect symmetry in her form, he was forced to acknowledge her figure to be light and pleasing; and in spite of his asserting that her manners were not those of the fashionable world, he was caught by their easy playfulness. Of this she was perfectly unaware—to her he was only the man who made himself agreeable no where, and who had not thought her handsome enough to dance with.
>
> He began to wish to know more of her, and as a step towards conversing with her himself, attended to her conversation with others. His doing so drew her notice.

Can you see why it would spoil the fun if Elizabeth were aware that Darcy was falling in love with her? Can you also see how this passage starts inside Elizabeth's point of view, "occupied in observing Mr. Bingley's attentions to her sister;" shifts to the omniscient narrator, who tells us something Elizabeth is "far from suspecting;" then in the last sentence—"His doing so drew her notice"—shifts back to Elizabeth's third-person limited point of view? Just as a good writer knows when to *show* and when to *tell*, Jane Austen knows when to shift point of view.

Creative Nonfiction

In the 1960s, the short story, which had long filled the pages of magazines such as *The New Yorker* and the *Atlantic Monthly*, gave way to a form of writing that we still find in such magazines today—nonfiction essays. The 1960s also saw a new appetite for nonfiction books—fact-based narratives—such as Rachel Carson's *Silent Spring*, a book about the destructive effect of agricultural pesticides on birds, and Ralph Nader's *Unsafe at Any Speed*, an exposé of the shoddy manufacturing practices of American automakers.

One of the biggest books of the decade was written by a southern novelist and short-story writer, Truman Capote, about two ex-convicts who robbed and murdered a family in a small town in Kansas. Capote read about the murders in *The New York Times*, then traveled to Kansas, where he interviewed the two killers, police, and people in the town. After conducting other extensive research into the case, Capote wrote what was described as a *documentary thriller* in which he blended the techniques of journalism with those of fiction. Capote was not sure what to call such a book, so he termed it a "Nonfiction Novel." *In Cold Blood* became one of the best-selling books of the decade, was made into a movie starring Robert Blake, and more recently, became the focus of the Academy-Award-winning film *Capote*.

It may be that so many exciting events took place in the 1960s—political assassinations, the moon landing, antiwar protests, civil rights and other liberation movements—that readers became as interested in reading about these real events as they were in reading fictional short stories and novels. The spread of television also fed this interest in what was happening in the real world. While television aired many fictional dramas and sitcoms, it also featured news, documentaries, and other programs based on real life. The *New York Times* had long published a list of "Best-Selling Books," but these had always been confined to novels. In the 1960s, the *Times* began running *two* lists of bestsellers: *Fiction* and *Nonfiction*.

The Form of Creative Nonfiction: Voice

The surge of interest in nonfiction continued into the 1970s with what came to be called the *new journalism* of writers such as Tom Wolfe and Hunter Thompson. These writers dropped the traditional "objective" stance of journalists and inserted themselves into their essays and books. They also told their stories through dramatic scenes and went into the minds of the people they were writing about—just as a fiction writer might do with the characters of a novel. Such journalism was sometimes called "gonzo journalism" because it flourished its style in a way traditional journalism never did—reveling in colloquial idioms, slang, even profanity. By the 1980s, these various developments in writing about real people and real events came to be called "creative nonfiction."

What sets creative nonfiction most apart from journalism is the author's "voice"—the tone which registers how she or he feels about the subject. A journalist always maintains an objective tone—the good "gray" style of *The New York Times*. But a writer of creative nonfiction incorporates his or her feelings into the writing. In memoir, one of the most popular forms of creative nonfiction, the writer frequently uses two "voices": one that of himself or herself as a character undergoing an experience earlier in life; the other that of the older person looking back upon that younger self with a different perspective—and feelings. Just as we have emphasized the line in poetry, the stage and scene in drama, and point of view in fiction, we will examine "voice" in creative nonfiction. "Voice" is created by the writer's "style"—the choice of words, patterns of phrases, and sentence structure.

It is one of the subtlest forms of creative writing and requires attentive reading to detect how a writer feels about his or her subject.

The Tradition of Creative Nonfiction

On the one hand, creative nonfiction in the 1960s was a new and exciting genre of writing, but on the other hand, such writing is as old as literature itself. Biography, history, and other forms of what we now call creative nonfiction go back to classical times with writers such as Thucydides, Herodotus, and Plutarch. The only forms of creative nonfiction that were not widespread in classical culture were what we would call today *autobiography* and *memoir*. The ancient Greeks and Romans, it seems, were not very interested in writing—or reading about—themselves.

This new concern with the personal *self* that finds expression in autobiography and memoir appears with the spread of Christianity. Works such as *The Confessions of Saint Augustine* trace the *conversion* experience of the writer from a life of profligacy to one of holiness. The individual Christian's searching examination of his or her soul, the struggle to atone for one's sins, and meditations on life after death brought a new emphasis to the experience of the individual.

Throughout the Middle Ages, the Roman Catholic Church managed to balance this new sense of individualism with the kind of *communal* identity that citizens of the Roman Empire had felt. It was the Church, with its priests, its sacraments, and its dogmas, that mediated between the individual and God. Individual Christians, like ancient Romans, felt they were not spiritually alone but part of a vast community of believers—*Christendom*.

With the Protestant Reformation of the sixteenth century, however, the individual became the central focus of religion. Along with the Reformation, the Renaissance emphasized the importance of the individual. The revival of classical humanism made the actions and thoughts of the individual paramount. The invention of printing in this same era also made the publication and circulation of the most *private* kinds of writings, such as diaries, letters, and other personal meditations, possible.

No Protestants were more intently concerned about their individual spiritual lives than the Puritans who settled in Massachusetts in the early seventeenth century. They believed that they were *predestined* to be saved or damned by an all-knowing and all-powerful God. Nothing that they did in life, for good or evil, could alter their destiny as ether "elect" or "damned." The central question of their spiritual lives, therefore, was to try to find out if they were saved by God's amazing grace so they might have the blessed assurance of salvation.

Eighteenth-Century Creative Nonfiction

It seems historically appropriate that a new genre of creative writing—creative nonfiction—should take root in one of the world's newest countries—America—where a premium has always been placed upon the life of the individual.

Jonathan Edwards (1703-1758)

Born into a family of ministers, Jonathan Edwards, after studying at Yale, became the most famous preacher of his day. His sermons ignited *The Great Awakening*, a series of emotional revival meetings across New England that started a tradition that has continued down to the present in the hands of such *evangelists* as Billy Graham.

Yet, Edwards was so insistent that Christians had to undergo the conversion experience to know that they were saved before they could be full members of his church that church leaders had him dismissed. Undaunted, Edwards took a position as minister of a small church in Western Massachusetts and became a missionary preaching to Indian tribes in the region.

His writings, which combined traditional Christian reliance on the authority of the Bible with a keen understanding of the philosophy of John Locke and other European intellectuals, eventually earned him an invitation to become the first president of what is now Princeton University. Early in his presidency, however, Edwards was given the, then, newly-invented procedure of inoculation to vaccinate him against smallpox. The serum used in his injection, however, was contaminated, and Edwards contracted smallpox and died.

As you read "Personal Narrative," notice how little Edwards tells us about his everyday life as a boy; instead he focuses on his inner, spiritual life. The point of view Edwards uses is a common one found in creative nonfiction—that of an older person looking back on himself as a young man. Edwards recounts his struggle to know if the spiritual experiences he underwent indicated whether he was truly saved. He also recounts his terror of the doctrine of *God's sovereignty*—the belief that God, in his omniscience, has always known who would be saved and who would be damned. As in a good short story, Edwards learns to overcome this fear and even rejoice in the doctrine of God's sovereignty. How does that *turning point* conversion take place?

from *Personal Narrative*

I had a variety of concerns and exercises about my soul from my childhood; but had two more remarkable seasons of awakening, before I met with that change by which I was brought to those new dispositions, and that new sense of things, that I have since had. The first time was when I was a boy, some years before I went to college, at a time of remarkable awakening in my father's congregation. I was then very much affected for many months, and concerned about the things of religion, and my soul's salvation; and was abundant in duties. I used to pray five times a day in secret, and to spend much time in religious talk with other boys; and used to meet with them to pray together. I experienced I know not what kind of delight in religion. My mind was much engaged in it, and had much self-righteous pleasure; and it was my delight to abound in religious duties. I with some of my schoolmates joined together, and built a booth in a swamp, in a very retired spot, for a place of prayer. And besides, I had particular secret places of my own in the woods, where I used to retire by myself; and was from time to time much affected. My affections seemed to be lively and easily moved, and I seemed to be in my element when engaged in religious duties. And I am ready to think, many are deceived with such affections, and such a kind of delight as I then had in religion, and mistake it for grace.

But in process of time, my convictions and affections wore off; and I entirely lost all those affections and delights and left off secret prayer, at least as to any constant performance of it; and returned like a dog to his vomit, and went on in the ways of sin. Indeed I was at times very uneasy, especially towards the latter part of my time at college; when it pleased God, to seize me with a pleurisy; in which he brought me nigh to the grave, and shook me over the pit of hell. And yet, it was not long after my recovery, before I fell again into my old ways of sin. But God would not suffer me to go on with any quietness; I had great and violent inward struggles, till, after many conflicts with wicked inclinations, repeated resolutions, and bonds that I laid myself under by a kind of vows to God,

I was brought wholly to break off all former wicked ways, and all ways of known outward sin; and to apply myself to seek salvation, and practice many religious duties; but without that kind of affection and delight which I had formerly experienced. My concern now wrought more by inward struggles and conflicts, and self-reflections. But yet, it seems to me, I sought after a miserable manner; which has made me sometimes since to question, whether ever it issued in that which was saving; being ready to doubt, whether such miserable seeking ever succeeded. I was indeed brought to seek salvation in a manner that I never was before; I felt a spirit to part with all things in the world, for an interest in Christ. My concern continued and prevailed, with many exercising thoughts and inwards struggles; but yet it never seemed to be proper to express that c concern by the name of terror.

From my childhood up, my mind had been full of objections against the doctrine of God's sovereignty, in choosing whom he would to eternal life, and rejecting whom he pleased; leaving them eternally to perish, and be everlastingly tormented in hell. It used to appear like a horrible doctrine to me. But I remember the time very well, when I seemed to be convinced, and fully satisfied, as to this sovereignty of God, and his justice in thus eternally disposing of men, according to his sovereign pleasure. But never could give an account, how, or by what means, I was thus convinced, not in the least imagining at the time, nor a long time after, that there was any extraordinary influence of God's Spirit in it; but only that now I saw further, and my reason apprehended the justice and reasonableness of it. However, my mind rested in it; and it put an end to all those cavils and objections. And there has been a wonderful alteration in my mind, in respect to the doctrine of God's sovereignty, from that day to this; so that I scarce ever have found so much as the rising of an objection against it, in the most absolute sense, in God's strewing mercy to whom he will shew mercy, and hardening whom he will. God's absolute sovereignty and justice, with respect to salvation and damnation, is what my mind seems to rest assured of, as much as of any thing that I see with my eyes; at least it is so at times. But I have often, since that first conviction, had quite another kind of sense of God's sovereignty than I had then. I have often since had not only a conviction, but a delightful conviction. The doctrine has very often appeared exceeding pleasant, bright, and sweet. Absolute sovereignty is what I love to ascribe to God. But my first conviction was not so.

The first instance that I remember of that sort of inward, sweet delight in God and divine things that I have lived much in since, was on reading those words, I Tim. 1:17. Now unto the King eternal, immortal, invisible, the only wise God, be honour and glory for ever and ever, Amen. As I read the words, there came into my soul, and was as it were diffused through it, a sense of the glory of the Divine Being; a new sense, quite different from any thing I ever experienced before Never any words of scripture seemed to me as these words did. I thought with myself, how excellent a Being that was, and how happy I should be, if I might enjoy that God, and be rapt up to him in heaven, and be as it were swallowed up in him forever! I kept saying, and as it were singing over these words of scripture to myself; and went to pray to God that I might enjoy him, and prayed in a manner quite different from what I used to do; with a new sort of affection. But it never came into my thought, that there was anything spiritual, or of a saving nature in this.

From about that time, I began to have a new kind of apprehensions and ideas of Christ. and the work of redemption, and the glorious way of salvation by him. An inward, sweet sense of these things, at times, came into my heart; and my soul was led away in pleasant views and contemplations of them. And my mind was greatly engaged to spend my time in reading and meditating on Christ, on the beauty and excellency of his person, and the lovely way of salvation by free grace in him. I found no books so delightful to me, as those that treated of these subjects. Those words Cant. 2:1, used to be abundantly with me, I am the Rose of Sharon, and the Lily of the valleys. The words seemed to me, sweetly to represent the loveliness and beauty of Jesus Christ. The whole book of Canticles used to be pleasant to me, and I used to be much in reading it, about that time; and found, from time to time, an inward sweetness, that would carry me away, in my contemplations. This I know not how to express otherwise, than by a calm, sweet abstraction of soul from all the concerns of this world; and sometimes a kind of vision, or fixed ideas and imaginations, of being alone in the mountains, or some solitary wilderness, far from all mankind, sweetly conversing with Christ, and wrapt and swallowed up in God. The sense I had of divine things, would often of a sudden kindle up, as it were, a sweet burning in my heart; an ardor of soul, that I know not how to express.

Not long after I first began to experience these things, I gave an account to my father of some things that had passed in my mind. I was pretty much affected by the discourse we had together; and when the discourse was ended, I walked abroad alone, in a solitary place in my father's pasture, for contemplation. And as I was walking there, and looking up on the sky and clouds, there came into my mind so sweet a sense of the glorious majesty and grace of God, that I know not how to express. I seemed to see them both in a sweet conjunction; majesty and meekness joined together; it was a sweet, and gentle, and holy majesty; and also a majestic meekness; an awful sweetness; a high, and great, and holy gentleness.

After this my sense of divine things gradually increased, and became more and more lively, and had more of that inward sweetness. The appearance of everything was altered; there seemed to be, as it were, a calm sweet cast, or appearance of divine glory, in almost everything. God's excellency, his wisdom, his purity and love, seemed to appear in everything; in the sun, moon, and stars; in the clouds, and blue sky; in the grass, flowers, trees; in the water, and all nature; which used greatly to fix my mind. I often used to sit and view the moon for continuance; and in the day, spent much time in viewing the clouds and sky, to behold the sweet glory of God in these things; in the mean time, singing forth, with a low voice my contemplations of the Creator and Redeemer. And scarce anything, among all the works of nature, was so sweet to me as thunder and lightning; formerly, nothing had been so terrible to me. Before, I used to be uncommonly terrified with thunder, and to be struck with terror when I saw a thunder storm rising; but now, on the contrary, it rejoiced me. I felt God, so to speak, at the first appearance of a thunder storm; and used to take the opportunity, at such times, to fix myself in order to view the clouds, and see the lightnings play, and hear the majestic and awful voice of God's thunder, which oftentimes was exceedingly entertaining, leading me to sweet contemplations of my great and glorious God. While thus engaged, it always seemed natural to me to sing, or chant for my mediations; or, to speak my thoughts in soliloquies with a singing voice.

I felt then great satisfaction, as to my good state; but that did not content me. I had vehement longings of soul after God and Christ, and after more holiness, wherewith my heart seemed to be full, and ready to break; which often brought to my mind the words of the Psalmist, Psal. 119:28. My soul breaketh for the longing it hath. I often felt a mourning and lamenting in my heart, that I had not turned to God sooner, that I might have had more time to grow in grace. My mind was greatly fixed on divine things; almost perpetually in the contemplation of them. I spent most of my time in thinking of divine things, year after year; often walking alone in the woods, and solitary places, for meditation, soliloquy, and prayer, and converse with God; and it was always my manner, at such times, to sing forth my contemplations. I was almost constantly in ejaculatory prayer, wherever I was. Prayer seemed to be natural to me, as the breath by which the inward burnings of my heart had vent. The delights which I now felt in the things of religion, were of an exceeding different kind from those before mentioned, that I had when a boy; and what I then had no more notion of, than one born blind has of pleasant and beautiful colors. They were of a more inward, pure, soul animating and refreshing nature. Those former delights never reached the heart; and did not arise from any sight of the divine excellency of the things of God; or any taste of the soul satisfying and life-giving good there is in them   1740

Benjamin Franklin (1706-1790)

Benjamin Franklin was the youngest son of a Boston candle-maker, who took Ben out of school at the age of ten to work in the family business. At twelve, he was apprenticed to his older brother, who ran a printing shop that published a newspaper. Franklin began writing for the paper, and in 1723, he set out on his own to Philadelphia, where he established his own printing shop and began publishing *Poor Richard's Almanac*, a periodical whose clever *aphorisms*, such as "A Penny Saved is a Penny Earned" and "Fish and Visitors Smell after Three Days," became enormously popular in colonial America.

Franklin's fame and success led him into politics, and he became a leader in the movement for American independence. He served on the committee that framed the *Declaration of Independence* and on the commission that negotiated with France for its support of the American colonies in the Revolutionary War. As the war drew to a close, Franklin helped frame the peace treaty with England. When he returned to America, he was one of Pennsylvania's delegates to the Constitutional Convention and, in his eighties, helped to bring the divided delegates together to give the constitution unanimous support.

Beyond his accomplishments in politics and diplomacy, Franklin was an inventor who created the "Franklin stove," bifocal eyeglasses, the lightning rod, and many other inventions. He helped establish the first public library in America, volunteer fire companies and militias, an academy that became the University of Pennsylvania, and other civic institutions. Despite all that he had achieved in his spectacular rise from humble origins, Franklin chose for his gravestone the simple epitaph "Benjamin Franklin, Printer."

Franklin wrote only one complete book during his busy lifetime—an autobiography that he worked on as his other enterprises gave him brief periods of time to write. As you read the excerpts from that autobiography below, compare Franklin's sense of his life to that of Jonathan Edwards in "Personal Narrative." Although Jonathan Edwards and Benjamin Franklin were born within three years of one another in the Massachusetts colony, they were more than a century apart in sensibility. Edwards was very much a product of the seventeenth century—a passionate, zealous, religious man, who, while interested in philosophy and science, focused on his spiritual life. By contrast, Benjamin Franklin was a supreme example of the eighteenth-century man of reason—enlightened, tolerant, and fully engaged in the politics, business, and culture of his day.

One difference that might not be immediately apparent from reading just a short excerpt from Franklin's autobiography is that, while Jonathan Edwards writes with whole-hearted sincerity, Franklin often adopts the ironic "deadpan" stance of a humorist who pretends not to see anything funny in what he says. In the following paragraph from the autobiography, for example, Franklin describes his attempt to maintain his commitment to being a vegetarian, like his employer (Tryon), during a voyage from Boston to Philadelphia. In those days, ships did not have restaurants, so when the winds dropped and the ship was stuck at sea near Rhode Island (Block Island), the hungry passengers fished for cod and cooked their catch on the deck of the ship.

> I believe I have omitted mentioning that, in my first voyage from Boston, being becalm'd off Block Island, our people set about catching cod, and hauled up a great many. Hitherto I had stuck to my resolution of not eating animal food, and on this occasion consider'd, with my master Tryon, the taking every fish as a

kind of unprovoked murder, since none of them had, or ever could do us any injury that might justify the slaughter. All this seemed very reasonable. But I had formerly been a great lover of fish, and, when this came hot out of the frying-pan, it smelt admirably well. I balanc'd some time between principle and inclination, till I recollected that, when the fish were opened, I saw smaller fish taken out of their stomachs; then thought I, "If you eat one another, I don't see why we mayn't eat you." So I din'd upon cod very heartily, and continued to eat with other people, returning only now and then occasionally to a vegetable diet. So convenient a thing it is to be a reasonable creature, since it enables one to find or make a reason for everything one has a mind to do.

Can you see how Franklin appears to be the rational thinker who decides to abandon vegetarianism on principle but is really laughing at himself for rationalizing his longing to eat the wonderful-smelling fried fish? Keep that tricky "deadpan" narrator in mind as you read this next episode from Franklin's autobiography. This passage is one of the few extended parts of the book in which Franklin deals with his inner as opposed to his outer life of accomplishments. As Franklin records his religious and moral beliefs, notice how different his account is from Jonathan Edwards' impassioned description of his religious terror and ecstasy in "Personal Narrative."

from *The Autobiography of Benjamin Franklin*

I had been religiously educated as a Presbyterian; and though some of the dogmas of that persuasion, such as the eternal decrees of God, election, reprobation, etc., appeared to me unintelligible, others doubtful, and I early absented myself from the public assemblies of the sect, Sunday being my studying day, I never was without some religious principles. I never doubted, for instance, the existence of the Deity; that he made the world, and govern'd it by his Providence; that the most acceptable service of God was the doing good to man; that our souls are immortal; and that all crime will be punished, and virtue rewarded, either here or hereafter. These I esteem'd the essentials of every religion; and, being to be found in all the religions we had in our country, I respected them all, tho' with different degrees of respect, as I found them more or less mix'd with other articles, which, without any tendency to inspire, promote, or confirm morality, serv'd principally to divide us, and make us unfriendly to one another. This respect to all, with an opinion that the worst had some good effects, induc'd me to avoid all discourse that might tend to lessen the good opinion another might have of his own religion; and as our province increas'd in people, and new places of worship were continually wanted, and generally erected by voluntary contribution, my mite for such purpose, whatever might be the sect, was never refused.

Tho' I seldom attended any public worship, I had still an opinion of its propriety, and of its utility when rightly conducted, and I regularly paid my annual subscription for the support of the only Presbyterian minister or meeting we had in Philadelphia. He us'd to visit me sometimes as a friend, and admonished me to attend his administrations, and I was now and then prevail'd on to do so, once for five Sundays successively. Had he been in my opinion a good preacher, perhaps I might have continued, notwithstanding the occasion I had for the Sunday's leisure in my course of study; but his discourses were chiefly either polemic arguments, or explications of the peculiar doctrines of our sect, and were all to me very dry, uninteresting, and unedifying, since not a single moral principle was inculcated or enforc'd, their aim seeming to be rather to make us Presbyterians than good citizens.

At length he took for his text that verse of the fourth chapter of Philippians, "Finally, brethren, whatsoever things are true, honest, just, pure, lovely, or of good report, if there be any virtue, or any praise, think on these things." And I imagin'd, in a sermon on such a text, we could not miss of having some morality. But he confin'd himself to five points only, as meant by the apostle, viz.: 1. Keeping holy the Sabbath day. 2. Being diligent in reading the holy Scriptures. 3. Attending duly the publick worship. 4. Partaking of the Sacrament. 5. Paying a due respect to God's ministers. These might be all good things; but, as they were not the kind of good things that I expected from that text, I despaired of ever meeting with them from any other, was disgusted, and attended his preaching no more. I had some years before compos'd a little Liturgy, or form of prayer, for my own private use (viz., in 1728), entitled, Articles of Belief and Acts of Religion. I return'd to the use of this, and went no more to the public assemblies. My conduct might be blameable, but I leave it, without attempting further to excuse it; my present purpose being to relate facts, and not to make apologies for them.

PLAN FOR ATTAINING MORAL PERFECTION

It was about this time I conceived the bold and arduous project of arriving at moral perfection. I wish'd to live without committing any fault at any time; I would conquer all that either natural inclination, custom, or company might lead me into. As I knew, or thought I knew, what was right and wrong, I did not see why I might not always do the one and avoid the other. But I soon found I had undertaken a task of more difficulty than I had imagined While my care was employ'd in guarding against one fault, I was often surprised by another; habit took the advantage of inattention; inclination was sometimes too strong for reason. I concluded, at length, that the mere speculative conviction that it was our interest to be completely virtuous, was not sufficient to prevent our slipping; and that the contrary habits must be broken, and good ones acquired and established, before we can have any dependence on a steady, uniform rectitude of conduct. For this purpose I therefore contrived the following method.

In the various enumerations of the moral virtues I had met with in my reading, I found the catalogue more or less numerous, as different writers included more or fewer ideas under the same name. Temperance, for example, was by some confined to eating and drinking, while by others it was extended to mean the moderating every other pleasure, appetite, inclination, or passion, bodily or mental, even to our avarice and ambition. I propos'd to myself, for the sake of clearness, to use rather more names, with fewer ideas annex'd to each, than a few names with more ideas; and I included under thirteen names of virtues all that at that time occurr'd to me as necessary or desirable, and annexed to each a short precept, which fully express'd the extent I gave to its meaning.

These names of virtues, with their precepts, were:

1. Temperance.

Eat not to dullness; drink not to elevation.

2. Silence.

Speak not but what may benefit others or yourself; avoid trifling conversation.

3. Order.

Let all your things have their places; let each part of your business have its time.

4. Resolution.

Resolve to perform what you ought; perform without fail what you resolve.

5. Frugality.

Make no expense but to do good to others or yourself; i. e., waste nothing.

6. Industry.

Lose no time; be always employ'd in something useful; cut off all unnecessary actions.

7. Sincerity.

Use no hurtful deceit; think innocently and justly; and, if you speak, speak accordingly.

8. Justice.

Wrong none by doing injuries, or omitting the benefits that are your duty.

9. Moderation.

Avoid extreams; forbear resenting injuries so much as you think they deserve.

10. Cleanliness.

Tolerate no uncleanliness in body, cloaths, or habitation.

11. Tranquillity.

Be not disturbed at trifles, or at accidents common or unavoidable.

12. Chastity.

Rarely use venery but for health or offspring, never to dullness, weakness, or the injury of your own or another's peace or reputation.

13. Humility.

Imitate Jesus and Socrates.

My intention being to acquire the habitude of all these virtues, I judg'd it would be well not to distract my attention by attempting the whole at once, but to fix it on one of them at a time; and, when I should be master of that, then to proceed to another, and so on, till I should have gone thro' the thirteen; and, as the previous acquisition of some might facilitate the acquisition of certain others, I arrang'd them with that view, as they stand above. Temperance first, as it tends to procure that coolness and clearness of head, which is so necessary where constant vigilance was to be kept up, and guard maintained against the unremitting attraction of ancient habits, and the force of perpetual temptations. This being acquir'd and establish'd, Silence would be more easy; and my desire being to gain knowledge at the same time that I improv'd in virtue, and considering that in conversation it was obtain'd rather by the use of the ears than of the tongue, and therefore wishing to break a habit I was getting into of prattling, punning, and joking, which only made me acceptable to trifling company, I gave Silence the second place. This and the next, Order, I expected would allow me more time for attending to my project and my studies. Resolution, once become habitual, would keep me firm in my endeavours to obtain all the subsequent virtues; Frugality and Industry freeing me from my remaining debt, and producing affluence and independence, would make more easy the practice of Sincerity and Justice, etc., etc. Conceiving then, that, agreeably to the advice of Pythagoras in his Golden Verses, daily examination would be necessary, I contrived the following method for conducting that examination.

I made a little book, in which I allotted a page for each of the virtues. I rul'd each page with red ink, so as to have seven columns, one for each day of the week, marking each column with a letter for the day. I cross'd these columns with thirteen red lines, marking the beginning of each line with the first letter of one of the virtues, on which line, and in its proper column, I might mark, by a little black spot, every fault I found upon examination to have been committed respecting that virtue upon that day.

I determined to give a week's strict attention to each of the virtues successively. Thus, in the first week, my great guard was to avoid every the least offense against Temperance, leaving the other virtues to their ordinary chance, only marking every evening the faults of the day. Thus, if in the first week I could keep my first line, marked T, clear of spots, I suppos'd the habit of that virtue so much strengthen'd, and its opposite weaken'd, that I might venture extending my attention to include the next, and for the following week keep both lines clear of spots. Proceeding thus to the last, I could go thro' a course compleat in thirteen weeks, and four courses in a year. And like him who, having a garden to weed, does not attempt to eradicate all the bad herbs at once, which would exceed his reach and his strength, but works on one of the beds at a time, and, having accomplish'd the first, proceeds to a second, so I should have, I hoped, the encouraging pleasure of seeing on my pages the progress I made in virtue, by clearing successively my lines of their spots, till in the end, by a number of courses, I should be happy in viewing a clean book, after a thirteen weeks' daily examination.

The precept of Order requiring that every part of my business should have its allotted time, one page in my little book contain'd the following scheme of employment for the twenty-four hours of a natural day.

5:00	Rise, wash, and address Powerful Goodness. The Morning Question: What good shall I do this day?
6:00	Contrive day's business, and take the resolution of the day.
7:00	Prosecute the present study, and breakfast.
8:00	Work
9:00	"
10:00	"
11:00	"
12:00	Read, or overlook my accounts, and dine.
1:00	Work
2:00	"
3:00	"
4:00	"
5:00	"
6:00	Put things in their places.

7:00   Supper.
8:00   Music or diversion, or conversation
9:00   Examination of the day. Evening Question. What good have I done today?
10:00 Sleep

    I enter'd upon the execution of this plan for self-examination, and continu'd it with occasional intermissions for some time. I was surpris'd to find myself so much fuller of faults than I had imagined; but I had the satisfaction of seeing them diminish. To avoid the trouble of renewing now and then my little book, which, by scraping out the marks on the paper of old faults to make room for new ones in a new course, became full of holes, I transferr'd my tables and precepts to the ivory leaves of a memorandum book, on which the lines were drawn with red ink, that made a durable stain, and on those lines I mark'd my faults with a black-lead pencil, which marks I could easily wipe out with a wet sponge. After a while I went thro' one course only in a year, and afterward only one in several years, till at length I omitted them entirely, being employ'd in voyages and business abroad, with a multiplicity of affairs that interfered; but I always carried my little book with me.

    My scheme of Order gave me the most trouble; and I found that, tho' it might be practicable where a man's business was such as to leave him the disposition of his time, that of a journeyman printer, for instance, it was not possible to be exactly observed by a master, who must mix with the world, and often receive people of business at their own hours. Order, too, with regard to places for things, papers, etc., I found extreamly difficult to acquire. I had not been early accustomed to it, and, having an exceeding good memory, I was not so sensible of the inconvenience attending want of method. This article, therefore, cost me so much painful attention, and my faults in it vexed me so much, and I made so little progress in amendment, and had such frequent relapses, that I was almost ready to give up the attempt, and content myself with a faulty character in that respect, like the man who, in buying an ax of a smith, my neighbour, desired to have the whole of its surface as bright as the edge. The smith consented to grind it bright for him if he would turn the wheel; he turn'd, while the smith press'd the broad face of the ax hard and heavily on the stone, which made the turning of it very fatiguing. The man came every now and then from the wheel to see how the work went on, and at length would take his ax as it was, without farther grinding. "No," said the smith, "turn on, turn on; we shall have it bright by-and-by; as yet, it is only speckled." "Yes," says the man, "but I think I like a speckled ax best." And I believe this may have been the case with many, who, having, for want of some such means as I employ'd, found the difficulty of obtaining good and breaking bad habits in other points of vice and virtue, have given up the struggle, and concluded that "a speckled ax was best"; for something, that pretended to be reason, was every now and then suggesting to me that such extream nicety as I exacted of myself might be a kind of foppery in morals, which, if it were known, would make me ridiculous; that a perfect character might be attended with the inconvenience of being envied and hated; and that a benevolent man should allow a few faults in himself, to keep his friends in countenance.

In truth, I found myself incorrigible with respect to Order; and now I am grown old, and my memory bad, I feel very sensibly the want of it. But, on the whole, tho' I never arrived at the perfection I had been so ambitious of obtaining, but fell far short of it, yet I was, by the endeavour, a better and a happier man than I otherwise should have been if I had not attempted it; as those who aim at perfect writing by imitating the engraved copies, tho' they never reach the wish'd-for excellence of those copies, their hand is mended by the endeavour, and is tolerable while it continues fair and legible.

It may be well my posterity should be informed that to this little artifice, with the blessing of God, their ancestor ow'd the constant felicity of his life, down to his 79th year, in which this is written. What reverses may attend the remainder is in the hand of Providence; but, if they arrive, the reflection on past happiness enjoy'd ought to help his bearing them with more resignation. To Temperance he ascribes his long-continued health, and what is still left to him of a good constitution; to Industry and Frugality, the early easiness of his circumstances and acquisition of his fortune, with all that knowledge that enabled him to be a useful citizen, and obtained for him some degree of reputation among the learned; to Sincerity and Justice, the confidence of his country, and the honorable employs it conferred upon him; and to the joint influence of the whole mass of the virtues, even in the imperfect state he was able to acquire them, all that evenness of temper, and that cheerfulness in conversation, which makes his company still sought for, and agreeable even to his younger acquaintance. I hope, therefore, that some of my descendants may follow the example and reap the benefit.

It will be remark'd that, tho' my scheme was not wholly without religion, there was in it no mark of any of the distinguishing tenets of any particular sect. I had purposely avoided them; for, being fully persuaded of the utility and excellency of my method, and that it might be serviceable to people in all religions, and intending some time or other to publish it, I would not have anything in it that should prejudice anyone, of any sect, against it. I purposed writing a little comment on each virtue, in which I would have shown the advantages of possessing it, and the mischiefs attending its opposite vice; and I should have called my book The Art of Virtue, because it would have shown the means and manner of obtaining virtue, which would have distinguished it from the mere exhortation to be good, that does not instruct and indicate the means, but is like the apostle's man of verbal charity, who only without showing to the naked and hungry how or where they might get clothes or victuals, exhorted them to be fed and clothed.—James ii. 15, 16.

But it so happened that my intention of writing and publishing this comment was never fulfilled. I did, indeed, from time to time, put down short hints of the sentiments, reasonings, etc., to be made use of in it, some of which I have still by me; but the necessary close attention to private business in the earlier part of my life, and public business since, have occasioned my postponing it; for, it being connected in my mind with a great and extensive project, that required the whole man to execute, and which an unforeseen succession of employs prevented my attending to, it has hitherto remain'd unfinish'd.

In this piece it was my design to explain and enforce this doctrine, that vicious actions are not hurtful because they are forbidden, but forbidden because they are hurtful, the nature of man alone considered; that it was, therefore, everyone's interest to be virtuous who wish'd to be happy even in this world; and I should, from this circumstance (there being always in the world a number of rich merchants, nobility, states, and princes, who have need of honest instruments for the management of their affairs, and such being so rare), have endeavoured to convince young persons that no qualities were so likely to make a poor man's fortune as those of probity and integrity.

My list of virtues contain'd at first but twelve; but a Quaker friend having kindly informed me that I was generally thought proud; that my pride show'd itself frequently in conversation; that I was not content with being in the right when discussing any point, but was overbearing, and rather insolent, of which he convinc'd me by mentioning several instances; I determined endeavouring to cure myself, if I could, of this vice or folly among the rest, and I added Humility to my list, giving an extensive meaning to the word.

I cannot boast of much success in acquiring the reality of this virtue, but I had a good deal with regard to the appearance of it. I made it a rule to forbear all direct contradiction to the sentiments of others, and all positive assertion of my own. I even forbid myself, agreeably to the old laws of our Junto, the use of every word or expression in the language that imported a fix'd opinion, such as certainly, undoubtedly, etc., and I adopted, instead of them, I conceive, I apprehend, or I imagine a thing to be so or so; or it so appears to me at present. When another asserted something that I thought an error, I deny'd myself the pleasure of contradicting him abruptly, and of showing immediately some absurdity in his proposition; and in answering I began by observing that in certain cases or circumstances his opinion would be right, but in the present case there appear'd or seem'd to me some difference, etc. I soon found the advantage of this change in my manner; the conversations I engag'd in went on more pleasantly. The modest way in which I propos'd my opinions procur'd them a readier reception and less contradiction; I had less mortification when I was found to be in the wrong, and I more easily prevail'd with others to give up their mistakes and join with me when I happened to be in the right.

And this mode, which I at first put on with some violence to natural inclination, became at length so easy, and so habitual to me, that perhaps for these fifty years past no one has ever heard a dogmatical expression escape me. And to this habit (after my character of integrity) I think it principally owing that I had early so much weight with my fellow-citizens when I proposed new institutions, or alterations in the old, and so much influence in public councils when I became a member; for I was but a bad speaker, never eloquent, subject to much hesitation in my choice of words, hardly correct in language, and yet I generally carried my points.

In reality, there is, perhaps, no one of our natural passions so hard to subdue as pride. Disguise it, struggle with it, beat it down, stifle it, mortify it as much as one pleases, it is still alive, and will every now and then peep out and show itself; you will see it, perhaps, often in this history; for, even if I could conceive that I had compleatly overcome it, I should probably be proud of my humility.   1771

Chapter 6
The Romantic Age (1785–1832)

At the end of the eighteenth century, another great shift in sensibility took hold of Western Europe, ushering out the *Age of Reason* and ushering in the *Romantic Age*. One of its first signs, as we have seen, was a new interest in the common people, particularly the rural folk. Pope and Swift had been urbane, witty poets interested in London society, but, beginning with poems such as Gray's "Elegy in a Country Churchyard," later in the eighteenth century, we saw a new interest in what Gray calls "the simple annals of the poor." Part of that interest, as we have also seen, reflected the fact that much of rural England was disappearing in the wake of the Industrial Revolution, where machine-made goods from factories replaced handmade ones crafted in homes in small rural communities. People who had once farmed the land or worked in such *cottage industries* now crowded into large cities to work in factories and live in slums. As better and better machines were developed to manufacture goods, many of these workers lost their jobs, and their attempts to protest their wretched condition were met with brutal government repression.

Political power was shifting as well, from a small group of aristocratic landowners to a larger group of merchants, bankers, and factory owners. At the bottom of society, those who worked in the factories, including many children, and the peasants who remained on the land were virtually powerless. An even worse discrepancy in wealth and power in France led to the French Revolution in 1789, which, inspired by the American Revolution, had begun as an assertion of "Liberty, Equality, and Fraternity." But, the French Revolution quickly turned into the *Reign of Terror* in which King Louis XVI, Queen Marie Antoinette, and even many of the early leaders of the revolution were guillotined in bloody public spectacles. The ruling classes in England and other European countries were alarmed when the French rebels offered to assist any other country that wanted to overthrow its government.

Even more alarming was the rise to power of Napoleon Bonaparte, who proclaimed himself Emperor of France in 1804. Napoleon led his powerful army against the rest of Europe. To many English, including several poets, such as Robert Burns, William Blake, William Wordsworth, and Percy Bysshe Shelley, the French Revolution initially sparked hopes for a complete transformation of society that would do away with class distinctions, spread democracy, and improve the lives of the poor. Some even had hopes that Napoleon would liberate the oppressed masses of Europe, but as he conquered and, in turn, oppressed such countries as Spain, most liberals lost faith in Napoleon. For more than ten years, Napoleon waged war across Europe, winning many stunning victories. Though the French navy was defeated by Admiral Nelson at the Battle of Trafalgar in 1805, Napoleon's armies continued to advance across the Continent.

In 1814, however, Napoleon's invasion of Russia proved disastrous, his army was defeated at the battle of Leipzig, and British troops, led by the Duke of Wellington, poured into France from Spain. Although Napoleon was exiled to the Island of Elba, he escaped in 1815, gathered his army around him, and triumphantly entered Paris. Britain, Austria, Prussia (now Germany), and Russia joined forces against him with an army of more than a million soldiers. Napoleon and his *Grand Armée* were decisively defeated by the allied forces in the Battle of Waterloo on June 18, 1815.

In reaction to threats from the French Revolution and the rise to power of Napoleon, the victorious European countries became even more conservative and oppressive. Poetry gave expression to this new concern for the common people, as we have seen in Thomas Gray's "Elegy in a Country Churchyard." But while Gray evinces sympathy with the rural folk, he is clearly a sophisticated and educated gentleman, and the *form* of his poem has the poetic inversions, balanced phrases, and learned allusions of much eighteenth-century poetry. Near the end of the eighteenth century, a very different kind of poet appeared, one who, though sophisticated and self-educated, chose to speak more simply.

Robert Burns (1759–1796)

As a boy, Robert Burns worked hard on his father's farm in Southwest Scotland, so hard, in fact, that he developed a heart condition that would kill him at age thirty-seven. Although he occasionally attended school, he was largely self-taught through his wide reading. At fifteen, he fell in love and wrote his first poetry. From then on, he had affairs with many women, produced a string of illegitimate children, and wrote many great poems. When his poems were published, he was hailed as a "ploughman poet"—a "natural" poet who spoke from pure inspiration. Burns went along with this image, concealing the fact that he had studied poetry assiduously for most of his life. Many of his poems were actually song lyrics, which he set to traditional Scottish melodies or "airs," using the form of the ballad.

Burns was also outspoken in his support of the American and French revolutions, a radical democrat who wanted to eliminate class distinctions. He was a rebel against the strict Calvinism under which he was raised—especially its sexual constraints. He became a notorious literary figure in Edinburgh and received government patronage, but he still struggled to support himself as a farmer. He married one of his many mistresses, settled down in a small Scottish town, and became a devoted family man beset with money problems and declining health.

Burns spent the last few years of his short life collecting, editing, and writing new lyrics to traditional Scottish folk songs. Although many of these became popular, he refused to accept any payment for this "labor of love." In these songs, Burns expressed his love of drinking with his comrades, romancing the ladies, and flaunting the rigid moral tenets of Scottish Presbyterianism. His most famous song lyric was this one that we sing on New Year's Eve:

Auld Lang Syne (Old Long Ago)

Should auld acquaintance be forgot,
    And never brought to min'?
Should auld acquaintance be forgot,
    And auld lang syne?

Chorus (repeated after each verse):
For auld lang syne, my dear,
    For auld lang syne,
We'll tak a cup o' kindness yet,   *a drink of friendship*
    For auld lang syne!

And surely ye'll be your pint-stowp,   *you'll pay for your pint cup of beer*

5

And surely I'll be mine,		10
And we'll tak a cup o kindness yet,		
For auld lang syne!		

We twa hae run about the braes,	*We two have run about the hills*	
And pou'd the gowans fine,	*And pulled the daisies fine*	
But we've wander'd monie a weary fit,	*many a weary foot (away)*	15
Sin auld lang syne.		

We twa hae paidl'd in the burn	*paddled in the stream*	
Frae morning sun till dine,	*till dinner (at noon)*	
But seas between us braid hae roar'd	*broad (distant) have roared*	
Sin auld lang syne.		

And there's a hand my trusty fiere,	*here's a hand, my trusty friend*	20
And gie's a hand o thine,	*give us a hand of yours*	
And we'll tak a right guid-willie waught,	*good-will swig (of beer)*	
For auld lang syne		1796

Notice the form of this song. If you're going to write poetry about simple country folk, what form would you use? Not the sophisticated, intricate, heroic couplet of Pope but the simple poetic form of the ballad that had been passed along, orally, for centuries. By the end of the eighteenth century, scholars and poets were regarding the ballad form with new respect.

But, you may wonder, why such lines as "Sin auld lang syne" are not in iambic trimeter; their four syllables would be scanned in this way:

For **auld/ lang syne**

They form a line of iambic dimeter with the first foot an iamb and the second foot a spondee. But remember that Robert Burns was setting new lyrics to traditional Scottish songs, and, as a lyricist, he could take liberties in matching words to musical notes. One of the liberties afforded lyricists was *melisma*, which allows a single syllable to be sung over more than one note. Sing "Auld Lang Syne" aloud to yourself. You will find that you sing the line like this, drawing the single syllables of "auld" and "lang" over two notes:

For **au**-/ld **la**-/ng **syne**

Singing it in that way makes it a line of iambic trimeter. We use melisma when we sing many songs, such as our national anthem, which begins with the word "Oh" sung over two notes—"O-oh say can you see"—and ends in a burst of melisma:

ba-an-ne-er ye-et wa-ve

Burns varied the ballad quatrain in other song lyrics to fit the music. In this next poem, he adds an "O" at the end of some lines to make the words fit the music and uses several feminine rhymes, appropriately so, in a poem that praises women. Although Burns was a staunch atheist, he uses the story of creation from the Book of Genesis to praise women by alluding to the biblical account of the creation of Eve from Adams's rib. Burns substitutes "Nature" for God, but cleverly suggests the creation of Adam was nature's "apprentice" (practice) effort; having made man, Nature then went on to do her more important "finished product" by creating woman. Like many traditional songs, the form of "Green Grow the Rashes" is *strophic*, alternating between verses and a *chorus* or *refrain*. Since the chorus or refrain is always the same, musically and lyrically, it appears only once below.

Green Grow the Rashes

Chorus (repeated after each verse):

Green grow the rashes, O;	*the rushes (tall grasses)*
Green grow the rashes, O;	
The sweetest hours that e'er I spend,	
Are spent amang the lasses, O.	

Verses

There's nought but care on ev'ry han',		5
In ev'ry hour that passes, O;		
What signifies the life o' man,		
An' 'twere na for the lasses, O.		
The warly race may riches chase,	*the worldly*	
An' riches still may fly them, O;	*elude them*	10
An' tho' at last they catch them fast,		
Their hearts can ne'er enjoy them, O.		
But gie me a canny hour at e'en,	*give me a quiet hour at evening*	
My arms about my Dearie, O;		
An' warly cares an' warly men,		15
May a' gae tapsalteerie, O!	*May all go topsy-turvy*	
For you sae douse, ye sneer at this,	*For those of you so serious*	
Ye're nought but senseless asses, O;		
The wisest Man the warl' saw,	*King Solomon had many wives*	
He dearly lov'd the lasses, O.		20
Auld Nature swears, the lovely Dears	*Old (Mother) Nature*	
Her noblest work she classes, O;		
Her prentice han' she try'd on man,	*Her apprentice (amateur) hand*	
An' then she made the lasses, O.		1787

Another of Robert Burns' song lyrics begins, like so many courtly love poems, by praising his beloved in fairly conventional similes—my love is like a rose; my love is like a melody. But after the initial quatrain of this ballad, Burns turns from celebrating his lady to describing the power of his love in fresh, hyperbolic images.

A Red, Red Rose

O My Luve 's like a red, red rose
    That 's newly sprung in June: *newly bloomed*
O my Luve 's like the melodie
    That's sweetly play'd in tune!

As fair art thou, my bonnie lass,   5
    So deep in luve am I:
And I will luve thee still, my dear,
    Till a' the seas gang dry: *all the seas go dry*

Till a' the seas gang dry, my dear,
    And the rocks melt wi' the sun;   10
I will luve thee still, my dear,
    While the sands o' life shall run.

And fare thee weel, my only Luve,   *fare thee well*
    And fare thee weel a while!
And I will come again, my Luve,   15
    Tho' it were ten thousand mile.   1796

William Blake (1757–1827)

William Blake is probably the most formidable poet in the English language. Born and raised in London, he went to art school and was apprenticed to an engraver. Combining poetry with painting and engraving, he produced several books in which he illustrated his own poems.

William Blake's most famous poem, "The Tyger," celebrates a creator who could fashion such different animals as a lamb and a tiger. While Blake hated established religion, he was a deeply spiritual man. He saw himself as a visionary prophet and developed a complex and elaborate system of religious mythology. Some of that mythology informs this poem, as when stars, symbolizing the power of human reason, "throw down their spears" in a confession of the impotence of rationality to comprehend the awesome creation of an animal such as the tiger. Even without understanding Blake's complex mythology, however, readers can feel his sublime awe before such a creature.

The Tyger

Tyger Tyger, burning bright,
In the forests of the night;
What immortal hand or eye,
Could frame thy fearful symmetry

In what distant deeps or skies.   5
Burnt the fire of thine eyes!
On what wings dare he aspire?
What the hand, dare seize the fire!

    And what shoulder, & what art.
    Could twist the sinews of thy heart?   10
    And when thy heart began to beat,
    What dread hand! & what dread feet!

    What the hammer! what the chain,
    In what furnace was thy brain?
    What the anvil, what dread grasp,   15
    Dare its deadly terrors clasp!

    When the stars threw down their spears
    And water'd heaven with their tears:
    Did he smile his work to see
    Did he who made the Lamb make thee!   20

    Tyger Tyger burning bright,
    In the forests of the night:
    What immortal hand or eye,
    Dare frame thy fearful symmetry!   1794

Blake's use of metaphor can be challenging, but can you see why he describes a tiger as "burning bright" in a "forest of the night?" What metaphor does he use to describe the creation of the tiger?

    Why does Blake use trochaic tetrameter ("**Ty**-ger/ **Ty**-ger/. **Burn**-/ing **bright**") in this poem to celebrate the power of the tiger? How does the trochaic rhythm accent such normally unimportant words, such as "in" and "and?" How does Blake avoid the problem posed by trochaic meters that would end each line on an unaccented syllable?

Another of Blake's poems is a protest against several social injustices:

London

I wander thro' each charter'd street,	*constricted street*
Near where the charter'd Thames does flow,	*London's River Thames*
And mark in every face I meet	
Marks of weakness, marks of woe.	
In every cry of every Man,	5
In every Infant's cry of fear,	
In every voice, in every ban,	*law or penalty against something*
The mind-forg'd manacles I hear.	
How the Chimney-sweeper's cry	
Every black'ning Church appalls;	*(see note* below)* 10
And the hapless Soldier's sigh	
Runs in blood down Palace walls.	
But most thro' midnight streets I hear	
How the youthful Harlot's curse	

Blasts the new born Infant's tear,	*(see note ** below)*	15
And blights with plagues the Marriage hearse.	1794	

*Here Blake protests the use of children as chimney sweeps. Churches turn black from the city's smoke and dirt, but Blake describes them as "blackly" evil, because they do not put a stop to such child abuse. He believes that the cries of the children—"Sweep! Sweep!"—should horrify people in the churches (with a pun on "appall," which literally means "to whiten or turn pale"), but such cries go ignored.

**Blake also protests the city's widespread prostitution, which entrapped young girls from the slums. He puns on "curse," which means both the profanity used by such prostitutes but also the "curse" they impose on their clients—venereal disease. Prostitutes were frequented by many "proper" middle-class men, and once those men had acquired syphilis, they passed the disease to their wives. When these wives gave birth, the venereal disease infected their babies, blinding them. The curse of venereal disease would, thus, transform the carriage, in which newlyweds rode after their wedding, into a funeral hearse.

The Poetry of Nature

The Romantic Age also ushered in a new interest in the natural world. In the eighteenth century, the word *nature*, as we have seen, referred to all of the world, including human society, so that when Pope says "True Wit is Nature to advantage dressed," he means the order of all things as it is captured, accurately and aptly, in poetry. By the end of the eighteenth century, however, *nature* had come to mean, as it does now, the physical world of mountains, forests, and rivers, a world set apart from human society. In the Romantic Age, poets sought out this nature in its most sublime and spectacular forms—craggy mountains, plunging waterfalls, desolate moors, and secluded forests. They went to contemplate such natural scenes, and many felt that they could commune with a spiritual presence in nature.

As Martin S. Day has observed, "Perhaps only at this point in human history could such a taste develop, for the Age of Reason had removed the superstitious dread from natural phenomena and the Industrial Revolution threatened to tame their savagery." Even when landscape architects designed gardens, they sought to capture the wildness of nature. In the eighteenth century, gardens were designed with geometric precision, and trees and foliage were often trimmed to give them symmetrical shapes (much in the way people trim their hedges in neat columns today). In the Romantic Age, however, gardens were designed to appear wild and irregular, with trees and shrubbery retaining their natural shapes.

William Wordsworth (1770–1850)

William Wordsworth grew up in the picturesque Lake District of Northwestern England. As a boy, he roamed among mountains, lakes, and forests and got to know the rural farmers, shepherds, and hermits who lived in this sparsely-populated area. Though his parents died when he was young, Wordsworth was able to attend Cambridge University, where he read widely and wrote poetry. During the summer of 1790, after his junior year, he and a friend took a walking tour of France and Switzerland. After graduating from Cambridge in 1791, Wordsworth returned to France, which was reveling in the aftermath of the French Revolution.

Wordsworth became a supporter of the revolutionary cause and looked forward to the imminent transformation of Western society. He also fell in love with a young French woman, who bore his illegitimate daughter. As the French Revolution turned into the bloody Reign of Terror, Wordsworth became disillusioned. Shortly after the birth of his daughter, England and France went to war, and that war, along with his own financial problems, forced Wordsworth to return to England. On the verge of a nervous breakdown, he settled in a cottage in the Lake District with his sister Dorothy. With her help and with frequent walks in the surrounding woods, his mental health was restored.

He also became close friends with Samuel Taylor Coleridge, a poet who had also gone to Cambridge. The two young men (Wordsworth was twenty-eight; Coleridge twenty-six) spent their time reading each other's poetry and discussing their ideas about the current state of poetry. Together, in 1798, they published what became one of the most revolutionary books of poetry in English—*Lyrical Ballads, With a Few Other Poems*. To readers at the time, the poems seemed strange: why would two Cambridge-educated young men be writing in the ballad form about the English countryside, poor farmers and shepherds, and even of retarded children, crazed peasants, and wandering beggars? Although this collection of ordinary, "democratic" poems was assailed by critics, it became popular, and in 1800, Wordsworth and Coleridge published a new edition.

For this second edition, Wordsworth wrote a *preface* that was even more provocative than the poems. In it, he attacked most eighteenth-century poetry as artificial, contrived, and lifeless. Even when eighteenth-century poets tried to write about the natural world, Wordsworth argued, they didn't seem to be looking very closely at what they were describing. He stated that his aim was to write about the most common and ordinary things but to describe them so accurately that they would seem extraordinary. Wordsworth also lambasted the poetic inversions, the strained diction, and the hackneyed imagery of much eighteenth-century poetry. Instead of the artificial intricacies of the heroic couplet, he vowed to write in the simple, plain language of ordinary people.

The final poem in the first edition of *Lyrical Ballads* exemplifies how radically different Wordsworth's poetry was from the poetry of the eighteenth-century. The very first word of the title of the poem, "Lines," indicates not the carefully crafted artifice of Pope's heroic couplets, but an informal, conversational, spontaneous effusion of poetic lines.

Lines
Composed a Few Miles Above Tintern Abbey
On Revisiting the Banks of the Wye
During a Tour, July 13, 1798

The rest of the title indicates that Wordsworth composed the poem "on the spot" as he took a walking tour of Wales and revisited a sight he had seen five years before—the Gothic ruins of a medieval abbey above the Wye River. During this second visit, accompanied by his sister Dorothy, Wordsworth was inspired by the setting and began formulating the poem in his mind over the course of four or five days. Only then did he write it down. Notice how casually conversational the opening lines are.

> Five years have past; five summers, with the length
> Of five long winters! and again I hear
> These waters, rolling from their mountain-springs
> With a soft inland murmur. Once again
> Do I behold these steep and lofty cliffs,
> That on a wild secluded scene impress

> Thoughts of more deep seclusion; and connect
> The landscape with the quiet of the sky.
> The day is come when I again repose
> Here, under this dark sycamore, and view 10
> These plots of cottage-ground, these orchard-tufts,
> Which at this season, with their unripe fruits,
> Are clad in one green hue, and lose themselves
> 'Mid groves and copses. Once again I see
> These hedge-rows, hardly hedge-rows, little lines
> Of sportive wood run wild: these pastoral farms,
> Green to the very door; and wreaths of smoke
> Sent up, in silence, from among the trees!
> With some uncertain notice, as might seem
> Of vagrant dwellers in the houseless woods, 20
> Or of some Hermit's cave, where by his fire
> The Hermit sits alone.
>
> These beauteous forms,
> Through a long absence, have not been to me
> As is a landscape to a blind man's eye:

His form is blank verse, that unrhymed iambic pentameter that is so close to English speech, but Wordsworth makes the lines seem even more colloquial with his chatty phrases ("hardly hedgerows"), his deft shifting of caesura, and his use of enjambment. But, notice too how, as the poem develops through Wordsworth's recollections of what nature meant to him at various points in his life, the poem soars to the kind of sublime language that we have seen in Milton, especially in such passages as that beginning with line 35 ("Nor less, I trust ... ") where Wordsworth describes a mystical experience in nature, and the passage beginning in line 93 ("And I have felt/ A presence that disturbs me ... "), where he describes his sense of a spiritual presence that "rolls through" both nature and humanity. Like Milton, Wordsworth also writes blank-verse paragraphs, so that line twenty-one is split over one iambic pentameter line

> The **Her**-/mit **sits**/ a-**lone**.
> These **beaut**-/ous **forms**/

As Wordsworth recounts the ways his love of nature has changed and developed since he was a boy, he describes how, in childhood, nature was "all in all" to him: he simply took an unthinking, "animal" delight in its spectacular mountains, waterfalls, and deep woods. As he grew older and more experienced, however, he brought to his experience of nature what he had learned from his life with people. What he "perceived" in nature with his eye and ear was, thus, tinged by what his mind "half-created" as he remembered things that had happened to him and brought those thoughts to bear on what he looked at in nature. At times, he even feels a spiritual power that unites nature with humanity:

And now, with gleams of half-extinguished thought,
With many recognitions dim and faint,
And somewhat of a sad perplexity, 60
The picture of the mind revives again:
While here I stand, not only with the sense
Of present pleasure, but with pleasing thoughts
That in this moment there is life and food
For future years. And so I dare to hope,
Though changed, no doubt, from what I was when first
I came among these hills; when like a roe
I bounded o'er the mountains, by the sides
Of the deep rivers, and the lonely streams,
Wherever nature led: more like a man 70
Flying from something that he dreads, than one
Who sought the thing he loved. For nature then
(The coarser pleasures of my boyish days,
And their glad animal movements all gone by)
To me was all in all.--I cannot paint
What then I was. The sounding cataract
Haunted me like a passion: the tall rock,
The mountain, and the deep and gloomy wood,
Their colours and their forms, were then to me
An appetite; a feeling and a love, 80
That had no need of a remoter charm,
By thought supplied, nor any interest
Unborrowed from the eye.--That time is past,
And all its aching joys are now no more,
And all its dizzy raptures. Not for this
Faint I, nor mourn nor murmur, other gifts
Have followed; for such loss, I would believe,
Abundant recompence. For I have learned
To look on nature, not as in the hour
Of thoughtless youth; but hearing oftentimes 90
The still, sad music of humanity,
Nor harsh nor grating, though of ample power
To chasten and subdue. And I have felt
A presence that disturbs me with the joy
Of elevated thoughts; a sense sublime
Of something far more deeply interfused,
Whose dwelling is the light of setting suns,
And the round ocean and the living air,
And the blue sky, and in the mind of man;
A motion and a spirit, that impels 100
All thinking things, all objects of all thought,
And rolls through all things. Therefore am I still
A lover of the meadows and the woods,
And mountains; and of all that we behold

> From this green earth; of all the mighty world
> Of eye, and ear,--both what they half create,
> And what perceive; well pleased to recognise
> In nature and the language of the sense,
> The anchor of my purest thoughts, the nurse,
> The guide, the guardian of my heart, and soul   110
> Of all my moral being.

In addition to writing in blank verse, Wordsworth wrote many poems using the ballad form. Some of his ballads, known as the "Lucy poems," are about a young woman who has never been identified. Whether "Lucy" was someone Wordsworth loved or a country lass he had only heard about, these poems show what a simple but powerful form the ballad could be.

A Slumber Did My Spirit Seal

> A Slumber did my spirit seal;
>   I had no human fears:
> She seem'd a thing that could not feel
>   The touch of earthly years.
>
> No motion has she now, no force;   5
>   She neither hears nor sees;
> Roll'd round in earth's diurnal course   *daily rotation*
>   With rocks, and stones, and trees   1800

Why does Wordsworth compress this simple elegy into two ballad quatrains? What do you think he means by "a slumber did my spirit seal" and "human fears?" Why does he refer to Lucy in line three as a "thing?" What is ironic about the fact that she seemed impervious to the touch of "earthly years?" How does Wordsworth use alliteration in the second quatrain, as well as metrical substitution? Is there any difference between "rocks" and "stones" or is Wordsworth just using those words for the way they sound?

Just as Wordsworth and other Romantic poets revived the ballad form, they also wrote sonnets, which had largely been ignored during the eighteenth century. In this sonnet, he laments the fact that most people of his modern, industrialized, urbanized age look upon the natural world without imagination. He wishes that he had been raised a primitive pagan so that, at least, when he looked at the ocean, he would think he was seeing the Greek god Proteus, who was an embodiment of the shifting shapes of ocean waves, or hear, in the sound of the surf, another Greek god, Triton, blowing his circular ("wreathed") conch shell.

The World Is Too Much with Us

> The world is too much with us; late and soon,
> Getting and spending, we lay waste our powers;
> Little we see in Nature that is ours;
> We have given our hearts away, a sordid boon!
> This Sea that bares her bosom to the moon;   5
> The winds that will be howling at all hours,
> And are up-gathered now like sleeping flowers,

>   For this, for everything, we are out of tune;
>   It moves us not.--Great God! I'd rather be
>   A pagan suckled in a creed outworn;   10
>   So might I, standing on this pleasant lea,
>   Have glimpses that would make me less forlorn;
>   Have sight of Proteus rising from the sea;
>   Or hear old Triton blow his wreathèd horn.   1807

Is this a Petrarchan or a Shakespearean sonnet? How does Wordsworth alter the traditional form of the sonnet to express his frustration? What has he learned from Milton's sonnets?

Samuel Taylor Coleridge (1772–1834)

Although most of the poems in *Lyrical Ballads* were written by Wordsworth, the longest and most ambitious poem in the collection, "The Rime of the Ancient Mariner," was written by Samuel Taylor Coleridge. Coleridge was a brilliant student at Cambridge University but was so bored with his studies he turned to drinking and carousing. When he met Wordsworth in 1795, Coleridge worked closely on poetry and produced several magnificent poems that were part of *Lyrical Ballads*. In "The Rime of the Ancient Mariner," Coleridge tried to create a kind of elaborate medieval ballad, using archaic vocabulary and adding explanatory notes, as if this "relic" of an ancient poem needed scholarly glosses.

The poem is too long to include in its entirety here, but its first section will give you a sense of its story and poetic form. "The Rime of the Ancient Mariner" is a *frame narrative*—a story in which someone tells somebody else a story. The told story is, thus, "framed" by the story about its telling. Frame narratives were frequently used for stories that involved fantastical or supernatural elements that might seem unbelievable if not contained (and distanced) within a realistic frame. Many ghost stories, for example, are framed by narratives about a group of people sitting around a campfire who decide to entertain themselves by telling stories about ghosts. These fantastical ghost stories are then framed by the realistic story about people sitting around a campfire. In Homer's *Odyssey*, too, the most bizarre adventures, such as Odysseus' encounter with the one-eyed Cyclops, are not narrated directly as they occur but retold many years later in a frame narrative as Odysseus recounts all that has happened to him in his voyages.

In the frame narrative of "The Rime of the Ancient Mariner," an old sailor stops one of three young men about to enter a hall to attend a wedding feast and starts to tell the narrative of his strange voyage. Coleridge creates an intriguing *conflict* in the frame narrative by having the wedding guest try to resist the old sailor and go into the wedding hall. But the mariner and his story are so compelling that the wedding guest cannot resist listening to it. Notice, as you read, how Coleridge begins with a fairly traditional ballad quatrain of alternating iambic tetrameter and trimeter lines rhyming *abxb*, but he soon begins experimenting with that form, adding lines, playing with caesura and enjambment, changing metrical feet, and using internal and off-rhymes.

from *The Rime of the Ancient Mariner*

Part I

>   It is an ancient Mariner,
>   And he stoppeth one of three.

`By thy long grey beard and glittering eye,
Now wherefore stopp'st thou me?   *"Now why do you stop me?*

The bridegroom's doors are opened wide,   5
And I am next of kin;
The guests are met, the feast is set:
Mayst hear the merry din.'

He holds him with his skinny hand,
"There was a ship," quoth he.   10
`Hold off! unhand me, grey-beard loon!'
Eftsoons his hand dropped he.   *At once*

He holds him with his glittering eye -
The Wedding-Guest stood still,
And listens like a three years' child: 15
The Mariner hath his will.

The Wedding-Guest sat on a stone:
He cannot choose but hear;
And thus spake on that ancient man,
The bright-eyed Mariner.   20

"The ship was cheered, the harbour cleared,
Merrily did we drop
Below the kirk, below the hill,   *Below (out of sight of) the church*
Below the lighthouse top.

The sun came up upon the left,   25
Out of the sea came he!
And he shone bright, and on the right
Went down into the sea.

Higher and higher every day,
Till over the mast at noon –   *sun is directly overhead (at the Equator)*   30
The Wedding-Guest here beat his breast,
For he heard the loud bassoon.   *(music at the wedding feast)*

The bride hath paced into the hall,
Red as a rose is she;
Nodding their heads before her goes   35
The merry minstrelsy.

The Wedding-Guest he beat his breast,
Yet he cannot choose but hear;
And thus spake on that ancient man,
The bright-eyed Mariner.   40

"And now the storm-blast came, and he
Was tyrannous and strong:
He struck with his o'ertaking wings,
And chased us south along.   *(toward the South Pole)*

With sloping masts and dipping prow,   45
As who pursued with yell and blow
Still treads the shadow of his foe,
And foward bends his head,
The ship drove fast, loud roared the blast,
And southward aye we fled.   50

And now there came both mist and snow,
And it grew wondrous cold:
And ice, mast-high, came floating by,
As green as emerald.

And through the drifts the snowy clifts   *snowy cliffs*   55
Did send a dismal sheen:
Nor shapes of men nor beasts we ken   *we could see*
The ice was all between.

The ice was here, the ice was there,
The ice was all around: 60
It cracked and growled, and roared and howled,
Like noises in a swound!   *in a swoon (fit)*

At length did cross an Albatross,
Thorough the fog it came;   *Through*
As it had been a Christian soul,   65
We hailed it in God's name.

It ate the food it ne'er had eat,
And round and round it flew.
The ice did split with a thunder-fit;
The helmsman steered us through!   70

And a good south wind sprung up behind;
The Albatross did follow,
And every day, for food or play,
Came to the mariner's hollo!

In mist or cloud, on mast or shroud,   *shroud: rope holding the mast*   75
It perched for vespers nine;   *for evening church service at nine*
Whiles all the night, through fog-smoke white,
Glimmered the white moonshine."

`God save thee, ancient Mariner,

>   From the fiends that plague thee thus! -   80
>   Why look'st thou so?' -"With my crossbow
>   I shot the Albatross."

Here at the end of the first part of the poem, the mariner's story is interrupted by the wedding guest, suddenly pulling us back into the frame narrative. Evidently, in telling about the albatross, the mariner's face became so horrifying that the wedding guest interrupts the tale to ask what fiends torment the old man. That interruption makes all the more dramatic the mariner's confession that he shot the bird with his crossbow. The interruption also conveniently relieves the mariner (and Coleridge) from explaining why he would kill such a friendly creature. The murder has no apparent motive but is just a pointless act of cruelty. As in the ballads of the Middle Ages that we read at the beginning of the course, much is left out of the simple, spare narrative.

Can you see how simply, yet powerfully, Coleridge handles the ballad line? Lines such as "As green as emerald," "The ice was here, the ice was there," and "I shot the albatross" may look like *primitive* poetry, but they are the work of a polished craftsman trying to appear as "artless" as a folk poet. How would you describe the rhyme between "cold" and "emerald?" The use of caesura in "The ice was here, the ice was there?" The enjambment after "crossbow?" The metrical effect of "I shot the albatross?"

Percy Bysshe Shelley (1792–1822)

No poet epitomized the Romantic Age more than Percy Bysshe Shelley. Like his close friend and fellow poet Lord Byron, he was born into a wealthy, aristocratic family. Sent to Eton, a fashionable prep school, he was bullied by boys who loomed over his slight frame and hectored by teachers who were used to making even the biggest boys cower. Tough and resilient despite his size, Shelley developed a lifelong hatred of tyranny, injustice, and oppression. Going on to college at Oxford, he was expelled for a pamphlet he published, "The Necessity of Atheism." Moving to London, he defended the daughter of an oppressive tavern-keeper, then married her, even though he believed marriage was an institution that oppressed women. Together, the eighteen-year-old husband and sixteen-year-old bride devoted themselves to helping poor people in England and Ireland.

Shelley began to publish poetry and fell in love with Mary Wollstonecraft Godwin (who would write the Gothic novel *Frankenstein*), moved to France, and abandoned his first wife, though he invited her to live with them as a sister (instead, she committed suicide). Shelley then married Mary Godwin, and realizing that he was regarded as immoral, atheistic, and politically radical back in England, spent the rest of his life on the Continent. In the poetry he wrote in France and Italy, Shelley emerged as the quintessential *Romantic poet*, isolated and in rebellion against society, striving to revolutionize the world by making it more democratic, and committed to the fullest blossoming of himself as an individual. That commitment prompted Shelley, along with other Romantic poets, to write about his most anguished personal feelings. In doing so, Romantic poets gave rise to the idea, widely held among readers today, that a writer must suffer deeply and pour out that suffering in poetry. Such a notion would have seemed absurd to an eighteenth-century writer, such as Pope.

Shelley's agony is not merely personal, but extends to all of humanity. Deeply sympathetic with the French Revolution, he grew disheartened with political repression in England and with the defeat of revolutionary hopes in Europe. Still, he never gave up working for radical change in society, as he expressed in one of his greatest poems, "Ode to the West Wind."

Ode to the West Wind

I

O wild West Wind, thou breath of Autumn's being,
Thou from whose unseen presence the leaves dead
Are driven like ghosts from an enchanter fleeing,

Yellow, and black, and pale, and hectic red,
Pestilence-stricken multitudes! O thou   *(like crowds of plague victims)*   5
Who chariotest to their dark wintry bed

The wingèd seeds, where they lie cold and low,
Each like a corpse within its grave, until
Thine azure sister of the Spring shall blow   *The west wind that brings spring*

Her clarion o'er the dreaming earth, and fill   *Her trumpet call*
(Driving sweet buds like flocks to feed in air)   10
With living hues and odours plain and hill;

Wild Spirit, which art moving everywhere;
Destroyer and preserver; hear, O hear!

II

Thou on whose stream, 'mid the steep sky's commotion,   15
Loose clouds like earth's decaying leaves are shed,
Shook from the tangled boughs of Heaven and Ocean,

Angels of rain and lightning! there are spread
On the blue surface of thine aëry surge,   *airy, windy*
Like the bright hair uplifted from the head   20

Of some fierce Mænad, even from the dim verge   *(see note ** below)*
Of the horizon to the zenith's height,
The locks of the approaching storm. Thou dirge

Of the dying year, to which this closing night
Will be the dome of a vast sepulchre,   25
Vaulted with all thy congregated might

Of vapours, from whose solid atmosphere
Black rain, and fire, and hail, will burst: O hear!

III

Thou who didst waken from his summer dreams
The blue Mediterranean, where he lay,   30
Lull'd by the coil of his crystàlline streams,   *(see note *** below)*

Beside a pumice isle in Baiæ's bay,

And saw in sleep old palaces and towers
Quivering within the wave's intenser day,

All overgrown with azure moss, and flowers 35
So sweet, the sense faints picturing them! Thou
For whose path the Atlantic's level powers

Cleave themselves into chasms, while far below
The sea-blooms and the oozy woods which wear
The sapless foliage of the ocean, know 40

Thy voice, and suddenly grow gray with fear,
And tremble and despoil themselves: O hear!

IV

If I were a dead leaf thou mightest bear;
If I were a swift cloud to fly with thee;
A wave to pant beneath thy power, and share 45

The impulse of thy strength, only less free
Than thou, O uncontrollable! If even
I were as in my boyhood, and could be

The comrade of thy wanderings over Heaven,
As then, when to outstrip thy skiey speed 50
Scarce seem'd a vision—I would ne'er have striven

As thus with thee in prayer in my sore need.
O! lift me as a wave, a leaf, a cloud!
I fall upon the thorns of life! I bleed!

A heavy weight of hours has chain'd and bow'd 55
One too like thee—tameless, and swift, and proud.

V

Make me thy lyre, even as the forest is: *(see note **** below)*
What if my leaves are falling like its own?
The tumult of thy mighty harmonies

Will take from both a deep autumnal tone, 60
Sweet though in sadness. Be thou, Spirit fierce,
My spirit! Be thou me, impetuous one!

Drive my dead thoughts over the universe,
Like wither'd leaves, to quicken a new birth;
And, by the incantation of this verse, 65

Scatter, as from an unextinguish'd hearth

> Ashes and sparks, my words among mankind!
> Be through my lips to unawaken'd earth
>
> The trumpet of a prophecy! O Wind,
>   If Winter comes, can Spring be far behind?

1820

* The wind tears clouds apart just as it tears leaves from trees. The clouds themselves are formed from both air and water vapor ("the tangled boughs of Heaven and Ocean").

** A Maenad was a woman worshipper of the Greek god Dionysus. Dionysus was the god of fertility, as well as of wine. As a fertility god, he died every autumn and was resurrected, with crops and other vegetation, the following spring. In rituals that celebrated his death and rebirth, worshippers drank wine until they lost all sense of themselves and danced in a wild frenzy. By comparing the west wind moving across the sky to a "fierce Maenad," Shelley is portraying it metaphorically as a crazed worshipper of Dionysus, flinging her long hair backwards as she runs.

***Shelley, who lived in various places around the Mediterranean Sea, noticed that the sea had currents of different colors. Baie's Bay, near Naples in Southern Italy, was where many Roman emperors built lavish villas out of "pumice," a volcanic rock. He imagines these lovely villas reflected in the Mediterranean, and he felt that colors reflected in water were more vivid and harmoniously blended. A few lines later, when he describes the wind moving out in the Atlantic Ocean, he notes how "sea blooms and the oozy woods" at the bottom of the ocean undergo the same autumnal loss of foliage that trees on land do. "The vegetation at the bottom of the sea," he explained in a note to the poem, "sympathizes with that of the land in change of seasons."

**** Many Romantic poets placed an *Aeolian lute* or *lyre*, a kind of wind harp (Aeolus was the Greek god of the winds) on their open windowsills so that the wind could blow over it and produce natural, spontaneous music that was the furthest kind of music imaginable from the formal, intricate, structured compositions of the eighteenth century. Here, Shelley is asking to be an Aeolian lyre so that the west wind can blow through him and help him give voice to its inspiring power in poetic song.

The Romantic Ode

The *ode*, a popular poetic form among Romantic poets, was based on the songs sung by the chorus in Ancient Greek tragedy. An ode frequently involves an *apostrophe*—not the mark of punctuation, but an *address* to the subject of the poem—in this case the west wind—as if it were a person. By thus *personifying* the west wind, Shelley can converse with it in his poem as if it were a human being.

    Shelley wrote this poem while he was living in Italy, and he borrowed the form of *terza rima*, which the great medieval Italian poet Dante had used for his *Divinia Commedia*. Terza rima is an extremely difficult form to use in English, since it is so heavily dependent upon rhyme (just as the Petrarchan or Italian sonnet is harder to write, given its rhyme scheme, than the English or Shakespearean sonnet). In terza rima, each stanza consists of three lines, rhyming, initially *aba*, but then, the *b* rhyme from that stanza or *tercet* becomes the initial rhyme of the next tercet, rhyming *bcb*, with the next tercet rhyming *cdc*, then the next tercet rhyming *ded*, then the stanza concluding with a couplet *ee*. Can you see why terza rima is an appropriate form to use in this poem, given the scenes Shelley is describing?

Not only did Shelley handle the individual lines of terza rima brilliantly in this poem, he gave an overall *tripartite* structure to the ode. In Italy, the western wind brings in seasonal change, and Shelley writes about the coming of autumn in three manifestations: in the first stanza, he describes autumn coming to the land as the wind sweeps the colored leaves from the trees; in the second stanza, he describes how autumn comes to the sky with wind and rain that blow the clouds about; in the third stanza, he describes a lesser-known phenomenon of how autumn winds affect the sea by changing the leaves of underwater foliage in a way that alters the surface color of the ocean.

At the beginning of stanza four, he asks the wind to lift him in the same way as he has described it moving "a dead leaf," "a swift cloud," and "a wave," thus extending the three-part structure of the poem. Literally, he is asking the wind to *inspire* him, much as epic poets, such as Homer, began their poems by praying to the goddess or muse of poetry to infuse them with the inspiration to sing poetically. Notice how in the opening line of the poem, "O wild West Wind, thou breath of Autumn's being," Shelley underscores the idea of breathing in the wind's spirit and breathing out inspired poetry with alliteration. Not only does the *w* sound, which we can feel with our own lips as we read the line aloud, run through *wild*, *west*, and *wind*, we place our lips in the same position to say *O* and *thou*.

Shelley's description of himself as a creature like the west wind, "tameless, and swift, and proud" has seemed to many readers the height of Romantic self-aggrandizement, just as an earlier line, "I fall upon the thorns of life! I bleed" seems the depth of self-pity. Even more audacious was Shelley's plea to the wind to inspire him to write poetry that will bring on a great revolution: "Be thou me!" At the end of this poem, Shelley remains purely Romantic in his unyielding belief that social revolution will indeed come, and the concluding line has become one of the most familiar quotations in the English language. Shelley himself, however, never lived to see the gradual spread of freedom, equality, and democracy. He died in a shipwreck off the coast of Italy, barely 30 years old. When his body was recovered, searchers found Shelley was carrying a volume of his friend John Keats' poetry with him.

Along with other Romantic poets, Shelley revived the form of the sonnet, which had languished during the eighteenth century. The sonnet below gives expression to Shelley's hatred of tyrants. "Ozymandias" was the Greek name for the Egyptian pharaoh Ramses II, a proud, overbearing ruler of the thirteenth century B.C. He had the largest statue in Egypt erected to himself, but none of it remains.

Ozymandias

I met a traveller from an antique land
Who said: "Two vast and trunkless legs of stone
Stand in the desert. Near them on the sand,
Half sunk, a shattered visage lies, whose frown
And wrinkled lip and sneer of cold command   5
Tell that its sculptor well those passions read
Which yet survive, stamped on these lifeless things,
The hand that mocked them and the heart that fed.
And on the pedestal these words appear:
`My name is Ozymandias, King of Kings: 10
Look on my works, ye mighty, and despair!'
Nothing beside remains. Round the decay
Of that colossal wreck, boundless and bare,
The lone and level sands stretch far away".   1818

How does Shelley vary the rhyme scheme and sentence-pattern divisions of traditional sonnets?

John Keats (1795–1821)

While other Romantic poets came from aristocratic or well-to-do middle-class families and attended universities such as Oxford or Cambridge, John Keats was born into a lower-class *Cockney* family from London's East End. His father took care of horses in a livery stable but married the stable owner's daughter and moved up in social station when the owner died and the couple inherited the business. Keats was sent to private school where, despite his rambunctious behavior (though small in stature he got into a lot of fights), teachers encouraged his love of literature, music, and theater. His father and mother died when he was young, and his guardian took him out of school at fifteen and had him apprenticed to a surgeon and pharmacist. While, today, becoming a surgeon or pharmacist requires extensive education, in Keats' day these were trades one learned through an apprenticeship, much as one learned to become a carpenter or blacksmith. Keats then went on to train in a London hospital, but he abandoned medicine to devote himself to poetry.

Although he did not start writing poetry until he was eighteen, Keats was encouraged by prominent writers and editors. In 1818, he fell in love with Fanny Brawne, but Keats was too poor to marry her. His poetic output during 1819 was stupendous, and he produced some of the greatest poems in the English language. Such glorious years of creativity are deemed an *annis mirabilis* (Latin for *miraculous year*). Even before the year was out, however, Keats was suffering from the onset of tuberculosis, the lung disease that had killed his mother and one of his brothers. His medical training told him that the blood he coughed up on his pillow presaged his death. He moved to the warmer climate of Italy to try to improve his health, but he died in Rome at barely twenty-six years old.

One of Keats' first great poems was this sonnet. Because he had not studied classical Greek, as other poets had, he could not read Homer in the original language. But he had become friends with one of his former teachers, who showed Keats an English translation of Homer's *Iliad* by the Renaissance poet George Chapman. Keats was so entranced by the translation that he stayed up all night to read it and composed this sonnet the next morning.

In the sonnet, he compares his discovery of Chapman's translation of Homer, after reading many other translations, to that of a traveler who has been in many places around the world ("realms of gold" are, literally, wealthy countries but, metaphorically, classic books whose covers were often decorated with gold leaf). When Keats says he has been to many "western islands … Which bards in fealty to Apollo hold," he is referring not only to beautiful islands in the Western Mediterranean but, metaphorically, to books of poetry whose "bards" (poets) owe their inspiration to Apollo, the Greek god of poetry. This traveler/reader finally reaches the "demesne" (realm) of Homer, which he has long heard about but never fully experienced until he read Chapman's translation.

That extended metaphor takes up the entire octave of this Petrarchan sonnet, then, in the sestet, Keats compares his discovery of Chapman's translation to an astronomer who, with his telescope, discovers a new planet in the universe (at the time, Herschel's telescope had just found the new planet of Uranus). Keats then compares his discovery of Chapman's Homer to the Spanish conquistador who was the first European to "discover" the Pacific Ocean. Every school child knows that Cortez conquered Mexico but that it was Balboa who first saw the Pacific Ocean. Keats never corrected his mistake, and the passage, with its deft enjambment, caesuras, and metrical substitutions, still renders the thrilling moment of a great discovery when the explorers are speechless as they gaze upon the new ocean from a mountain peak (what we now call the Isthmus of Panama—the site of the Panama Canal—was once called the Isthmus of Darien).

On First Looking into Chapman's Homer

Much have I travell'd in the realms of gold,
    And many goodly states and kingdoms seen;
    Round many western islands have I been
Which bards in fealty to Apollo hold.
Oft of one wide expanse had I been told   5
    That deep-brow'd Homer ruled as his demesne: *domain*
    Yet did I never breathe its pure serene
Till I heard Chapman speak out loud and bold:
Then felt I like some watcher of the skies
    When a new planet swims into his ken;   10
Or like stout Cortez, when with eagle eyes
    He stared at the Pacific—and all his men
Look'd at each other with a wild surmise—
    Silent, upon a peak in Darien.   1816

Like other Romantic poets, Keats used the ballad form, and he tried, like Coleridge, to make his ballads sound archaic, as if they had been written in the Middle Ages. As with many medieval ballads, he tells the story through repetitive dialogue, using a frame narrative to distance the supernatural events related by the knight narrator. Keats also uses the ballad quatrain, but alters it in subtle ways, sometimes making the second line of the quatrain a line of iambic tetrameter, rather than iambic trimeter, and shortening the fourth line of each quatrain to iambic dimeter, sometimes by substituting an anapest for the first metrical foot in the line. Consider the effects of these alterations in ballad form as you read "La Belle Dame sans Merci" ("The Beautiful Lady without Pity").

La Belle Dame Sans Merci

"O what can ail thee, knight-at-arms,
    Alone and palely loitering?
The sedge has wither'd from the Lake,
    And no birds sing.

O what can ail thee, knight-at-arms!   5
    So haggard and so woe-begone?
The squirrel's granary is full,
    And the harvest's done.

I see a lily on thy brow   *(His forehead is white)*
    With anguish moist and fever dew,   10
And on thy cheeks a fading rose   *(His cheeks also are losing color)*
    Fast withereth too."

"I met a lady in the meads,   *(Here the knight begins to tell his tale)*
    Full beautiful—a faery's child,
Her hair was long, her foot was light,   15
    And her eyes were wild.

I made a garland for her head,   *a wreath of flowers*
    And bracelets too, and fragrant zone;   *and flowery girdle (belt)*
She look'd at me as she did love,
    And made sweet moan.   20

I set her on my pacing steed,   *prancing horse*
    And nothing else saw all day long,
For sidelong would she bend, and sing
    A faery's song.

She found me roots of relish sweet,   25
    And honey wild, and manna dew,
And sure in language strange she said—
    "I love thee true."

She took me to her elfin grot,   *her fairy cave*
    And there she wept, and sigh'd fill sore,   30
And there I shut her wild wild eyes
    With kisses four.

And there she lulléd me asleep,
    And there I dream'd—Ah! woe betide!
The latest dream I ever dream'd   *The most recent dream*   35
    On the cold hill's side.

I saw pale kings and princes too,
    Pale warriors, death-pale were they all;
They cried—'La Belle Dame sans Merci
    Hath thee in thrall!'   *(Has bewitched, enchanted you)*   40

I saw their starved lips in the gloam,   *in the twilight*
    With horrid warning gapéd wide,
And I awoke and found me here,
    On the cold hill's side.

And this is why I sojourn here,   45
    Alone and palely loitering,
Though the sedge is wither'd from the Lake,
    And no birds sing."   1819

This poem treats a theme similar to that of "Bright Star:" the knight transcends the everyay world and, led by the mysterious lady, enters a magical world of fantasy, but then, he returns to this world. How is Keats' treatment of this theme different in "La Belle Dame Sans Merci?"

The greatest poems of Keats' *annis mirabilis* were his odes. While Shelley used terza rima for his "Ode to the West Wind," Keats developed a stanza form that was closer to the poetic stanzas chanted by the chorus in Greek tragedy. Those stanzas often alternated between *strophes*, which developed one idea, and *antistrophes*, which developed a counter-idea in the same meter, lines, and rhyme scheme. These Greek choric odes sometimes also included an *epode*, a stanza of a different length and rhyme scheme that developed a new idea. Keats' odes follow the pattern of these choric odes from ancient Greek tragedy. Can you see how he also derived the form of his stanzas from the sonnet form?

"To Autumn" is one of his great odes, addressed, in an apostrophe, to the season. Notice the way Keats gradually personifies the season of autumn, first as a "bosom-friend" of the sun that actively ripens fruits and other vegetation, then, in the second stanza, as a young woman going about her chores on a farm ("thy store")—yet not really working, just sitting on the floor of a barn as wheat is tossed into the air to let the wind "winnow" the grain from the chaff (the same "winnowing wind" lifts her hair), sleeping in the fields beside her scythe ("thy hook"), laying her head over a brook like a "gleaner" (a farm worker who picks up the leftover bits of corn or wheat after the reapers have harvested a field of grain), or simply watching apple juice slowly drip from a cider press.

To Autumn

Season of mists and mellow fruitfulness!
  Close bosom-friend of the maturing sun;
Conspiring with him how to load and bless
  With fruit the vines that round the thatch-eaves run;
To bend with apples the moss'd cottage-trees,   5
  And fill all fruit with ripeness to the core;
    To swell the gourd, and plump the hazel shells
  With a sweet kernel; to set budding more,
And still more, later flowers for the bees,
Until they think warm days will never cease,   10
  For Summer has o'er-brimm'd their clammy cells.

Who hath not seen thee oft amid thy store?
  Sometimes whoever seeks abroad may find
Thee sitting careless on a granary floor,
  Thy hair soft-lifted by the winnowing wind;   15
Or on a half-reap'd furrow sound asleep,
  Drowsed with the fume of poppies, while thy hook
    Spares the next swath and all its twinèd flowers;
And sometimes like a gleaner thou dost keep
  Steady thy laden head across a brook;   20
  Or by a cider-press, with patient look,
    Thou watchest the last oozings hours by hours.

Where are the songs of Spring? Ay, where are they?
  Think not of them, thou hast thy music too,—
While barrèd clouds bloom the soft-dying day,   25
  And touch the stubble-plains with rosy hue;
Then in a wailful choir the small gnats mourn
  Among the river sallows, borne aloft   *willow trees along a river*
    Or sinking as the light wind lives or dies;
And full-grown lambs loud bleat from hilly bourn   *hilllside field*   30
  Hedge-crickets sing; and now with treble soft

> The redbreast whistles from a garden-croft; *small field near a house*
> And gathering swallows twitter in the skies.
>
> 1819-1820

Lord Byron (1788–1824)

Lord Byron, whose family name was George Gordon, was one of the most notorious figures of the Romantic Age. Born in London to an aristocratic family that could trace its ancestry back to King James I of Scotland, Byron was brought up in the strictest tradition of Calvinist Protestantism. He had a club foot, which his mother tried to have corrected by surgery many times before dismissing him as a "lame brat." In prep school, boys made fun of his awkward walk, but he became an excellent boxer and swimmer and got into many fights, most of which he won. Early in life, he fell in love, hopelessly, with several beautiful women, and became the object of the affections—and sexual favors—of many others.

Rejecting his Calvinist upbringing, he became a radical free-thinker, and upon assuming his hereditary position in Parliament's House of Lords, he spoke out against the oppression of the working class. After rumors of an incestuous affair with his half-sister, Augusta Leigh, Byron left England, never to return, and lived on the Continent, where he befriended Percy Bysshe Shelley. He became involved with Italian revolutionary movements, then moved to Greece to join the struggle of that country to free itself from Turkish rule. He died of a fever during the struggle, and his body was brought back to England for burial. The young poet Alfred Lord Tennyson, upon learning of the death of Byron, said, "It is as if the sun had gone out."

Byron was the most famous, flamboyant, and audacious figure of the Romantic Age. He performed daring deeds, such as swimming across the treacherous Hellespont between Greece and Turkey. Although of aristocratic lineage, he was a staunch radical who defended the rights of oppressed people everywhere. As a poet, he portrayed himself as the epitome of the Romantic rebel, outcast, and sinner.

Byron was most famous for long poems about characters based upon himself, such as "Childe Harold's Pilgrimage" (1812), a young dissolute hero who rejects English society for a life of adventure and sensuality in the Mediterranean. The poem was an instant success; "I awoke one morning," Byron said, "and found myself famous." Childe Harold's Pilgrimage inaugurated *Byronism*, a cult of youthful adventure, rebellion, and *Weltschmerz* (suffering for the grief of the world) that spread across Europe. Here is one of the final stanzas from "Childe Harold's Pilgrimage," one in which he addresses the ocean in an apostrophe:

from *Childe Harold's Pilgrimage*

> Roll on, thou deep and dark blue Ocean—roll!
> Ten thousand fleets sweep over thee in vain:
> Man marks the earth with ruin—his control
> Stops with the shore; upon the watery plain
> The wrecks are all thy deed, nor doth remain
> A shadow of man's ravage, save his own,
> When, for a moment, like a drop of rain,
> He sinks into thy depths with bubbling groan,
> Without a grave, unknelled, uncoffined, and unknown.
>
> 1812

Notice the rhyme scheme, Byron's use of caesura and enjambment, and the concluding alexandrine (a line of nine iambic feet).

Byron also wrote elegant short lyrics such as this, inspired by seeing a beautiful widow wearing a black dress of mourning but with glittering spangles in the fabric, inspiring his metaphor of stars glistening in the night sky.

She Walks in Beauty

> She walks in beauty, like the night
>   Of cloudless climes and starry skies,
> And all that's best of dark and bright
>   Meet in her aspect and her eyes;
> Thus mellow'd to that tender light   5
>   Which Heaven to gaudy day denies.
>
> One shade the more, one ray the less,
>   Had half impair'd the nameless grace
> Which waves in every raven tress
>   Or softly lightens o'er her face,   10
> Where thoughts serenely sweet express
>   How pure, how dear their dwelling-place.
>
> And on that cheek and o'er that brow
>   So soft, so calm, yet eloquent,
> The smiles that win, the tints that glow,   15
>   But tell of days in goodness spent,—
> A mind at peace with all below,
>   A heart whose love is innocent.   1815

How does Byron use enjambment and caesura to underscore the beauty he praises? What is effective about the metrical substitution at the beginning of line four? The caesuras in lines seven, twelve, and fourteen?

Leigh Hunt (1784–1859)

People think of Romantic poetry as passionate and intense, but many poets of the era wrote witty light verse, as well. Leigh Hunt was a leading liberal journalist whose weekly newspaper, the *Examiner*, attacked the repressive Tory government so sharply that Hunt and his brother and co-editor were imprisoned for two years. A close friend of Shelley and Byron, Hunt was the first writer to praise Keats, who, for a while, became Hunt's disciple. This charming poem was supposedly inspired by a kiss from Mrs. Jane Welsh Carlyle, wife of the philosopher and writer Thomas Carlyle. Hunt had come to tell Carlyle that he had found a publisher for one of Carlyle's books, and Jane ("Jenny") was so pleased with Hunt's news that she kissed him.

Jenny Kissed Me

> Jenny kiss'd me when we met,
>   Jumping from the chair she sat in;
> Time, you thief, who love to get
>   Sweets into your list, put that in!

  Say I'm weary, say I'm sad,   5
  Say that health and wealth have miss'd me,
  Say I'm growing old, but add,
  Jenny kiss'd me.   1838

How does Hunt use trochaic meter, feminine rhymes, caesura, and enjambment in this poem?

Chapter 7
The American Short Story

It was during the Romantic Age that American Literature first gained international recognition for its achievement in the short story. Just as the novel was a written narrative made possible by the invention of printing and the creation of books for a large reading public, new forms of print in the eighteenth century, such as newspapers and magazines, helped make possible the rise of *short stories* that appealed to a new reading public. The short story is a written form that addresses itself, as the novel does, to a solitary reader. The reader of a novel completes the book over a series of readings, but the reader of a short story usually completes the story in a single sitting.

Writers' understanding of that difference between how readers read novels and how they read short stories makes the short story much more focused and concise than the novel. A novel such as *Pride and Prejudice* takes place over a long stretch of time, involves many characters, and traces several related conflicts and resolutions. A short story often takes place over a brief course of time, focuses on a single character, and involves a single conflict that results in a change within that character. There are, of course, many stories that are exceptions to this description. The first story we will study, "Rip Van Winkle," takes place over twenty years, a much longer stretch of time than *Pride and Prejudice*, and Rip himself does not undergo a change but remains pretty much the same character at the end of the story as he was at the beginning..

The short story was the first major form of creative writing to bring recognition to an American writer. Although Americans had been writing poetry, fiction, and drama ever since colonial times, a British reviewer early in the nineteenth century could scornfully ask, in print, "Who in the world reads an American book?" The first American writer to win international recognition was Washington Irving, in 1820, with a collection of tales and essays called *The Sketch Book*. *The Sketch Book* included two stories, "Rip Van Winkle" and "The Legend of Sleepy Hollow," which have become classics. Irving's success with the short story inspired other American writers to work in this form.

The popularity of the short story with American writers in the nineteenth century also reflected the fact that America was then not a participant in the international copyright law. American publishers could print pirated copies of novels by popular British writers such as Charles Dickens and William Makepeace Thackeray without paying those authors royalties on the sales of their books. Why would such publishers try to develop young American novelists, to whom they *would* have to pay royalties, when they could publish books by such established British writers for free? Dickens made it a great point in his reading tour of America late in the nineteenth century to say that no Americans who bought his books contributed to his royalties. Dickens helped raise the awareness of the American reading public about copyright law, and by the beginning of the twentieth century, America became a participant in the international copyright law. Until then, however, American writers usually had to write short stories for magazines in order to establish themselves; only then would publishers consider bringing out their novels.

Washington Irving (1783–1859)

Washington Irving was born into a prosperous family in New York and began his literary career by editing a magazine with his brothers and other writers. Writing under various pseudonyms, he published several stories and essays and, in 1809, a comic history of New York that was very popular in America and England. After his fiancée died of tuberculosis, Irving spent several decades travelling in England and Europe. In 1820, he established his international literary reputation—and respect for American writers—with *The Sketch Book*, which included "Rip Van Winkle."

Rip Van Winkle

A Posthumous Writing of Diedrich Knickerbocker

The following Tale was found among the papers of the late Diedrich Knickerbocker, an old gentleman of New York, who was very curious in the Dutch history of the province, and the manners of the descendants from its primitive settlers. His historical researches, however, did not lie so much among books as among men; for the former are lamentably scanty on his favorite topics; whereas he found the old burghers, and still more their wives, rich in that legendary lore, so invaluable to true history. Whenever, therefore, he happened upon a genuine Dutch family, snugly shut up in its low-roofed farmhouse, under a spreading sycamore, he looked upon it as a little clasped volume of black-letter, and studied it with the zeal of a book-worm.

The result of all these researches was a history of the province during the reign of the Dutch governors, which he published some years since. There have been various opinions as to the literary character of his work, and, to tell the truth, it is not a whit better than it should be. Its chief merit is its scrupulous accuracy, which indeed was a little questioned on its first appearance, but has since been completely established; and it is now admitted into all historical collections, as a book of unquestionable authority.

The old gentleman died shortly after the publication of his work, and now that he is dead and gone, it cannot do much harm to his memory to say that his time might have been better employed in weightier labors. He, however, was apt to ride his hobby his own way; and though it did now and then kick up the dust a little in the eyes of his neighbors, and grieve the spirit of some friends, for whom he felt the truest deference and affection; yet his errors and follies are remembered "more in sorrow than in anger," and it begins to be suspected, that he never intended to injure or offend. But however his memory may be appreciated by critics, it is still held dear by many folks, whose good opinion is well worth having; particularly by certain biscuit-bakers, who have gone so far as to imprint his likeness on their new-year cakes; and have thus given him a chance for immortality, almost equal to the being stamped on a Waterloo Medal, or a Queen Anne's Farthing.

Whoever has made a voyage up the Hudson must remember the Kaatskill mountains. They are a dismembered branch of the great Appalachian family, and are seen away to the west of the river, swelling up to a noble height, and lording it over the surrounding country. Every change of season, every change of weather, indeed, every hour of the day, produces some change in the magical hues and shapes of these mountains, and they are regarded by all the good wives, far and near, as perfect barometers. When the weather is fair and settled, they are clothed in blue and purple, and print their bold outlines on the clear evening sky, but, sometimes, when the rest of the landscape is cloudless, they will gather a hood of gray vapors about their summits, which, in the last rays of the setting sun, will glow and light up like a crown of glory.

At the foot of these fairy mountains, the voyager may have descried the light smoke curling up from a village, whose shingle-roofs gleam among the trees, just where the blue tints of the upland melt away into the fresh green of the nearer landscape. It is a little village of great antiquity, having been founded by some of the Dutch colonists, in the early times of the province, just about the beginning of the government of the good Peter Stuyvesant, (may he rest in peace!) and there were some of the houses of the original settlers standing within a few years, built of small yellow bricks brought from Holland, having latticed windows and gable fronts, surmounted with weather-cocks.

In that same village, and in one of these very houses (which, to tell the precise truth, was sadly time-worn and weather-beaten), there lived many years since, while the country was yet a province of Great Britain, a simple good-natured fellow of the name of Rip Van Winkle. He was a descendant of the Van Winkles who figured so gallantly in the chivalrous days of Peter Stuyvesant, and accompanied him to the siege of Fort Christina. He inherited, however, but little of the martial character of his ancestors. I have observed that he was a simple good-natured man; he was, moreover, a kind neighbor, and an obedient hen-pecked husband. Indeed, to the latter circumstance might be owing that meekness of spirit which gained him such universal popularity; for those men are most apt to be obsequious and conciliating abroad, who are under the discipline of shrews at home. Their tempers, doubtless, are rendered pliant and malleable in the fiery furnace of domestic tribulation; and a curtain lecture is worth all the sermons in the world for teaching the virtues of patience and long-suffering. A termagant wife may, therefore, in some respects, be considered a tolerable blessing; and if so, Rip Van Winkle was thrice blessed.

Certain it is, that he was a great favorite among all the good wives of the village, who, as usual, with the amiable sex, took his part in all family squabbles; and never failed, whenever they talked those matters over in their evening gossipings, to lay all the blame on Dame Van Winkle. The children of the village, too, would shout with joy whenever he approached. He assisted at their sports, made their playthings, taught them to fly kites and shoot marbles, and told them long stories of ghosts, witches, and Indians. Whenever he went dodging about the village, he was surrounded by a troop of them, hanging on his skirts, clambering on his back, and playing a thousand tricks on him with impunity; and not a dog would bark at him throughout the neighborhood.

The great error in Rip's composition was an insuperable aversion to all kinds of profitable labor. It could not be from the want of assiduity or perseverance; for he would sit on a wet rock, with a rod as long and heavy as a Tartar's lance, and fish all day without a murmur, even though he should not be encouraged by a single nibble. He would carry a fowling-piece on his shoulder for hours together, trudging through woods and swamps, and up hill and down dale, to shoot a few squirrels or wild pigeons. He would never refuse to assist a neighbor even in the roughest toil, and was a foremost man at all country frolics for husking Indian corn, or building stone-fences; the women of the village, too, used to employ him to run their errands, and to do such little odd jobs as their less obliging husbands would not do for them. In a word Rip was ready to attend to anybody's business but his own; but as to doing family duty, and keeping his farm in order, he found it impossible.

In fact, he declared it was of no use to work on his farm; it was the most pestilent little piece of ground in the whole country; every thing about it went wrong, and would go wrong, in spite of him. His fences were continually falling to pieces; his cow would either go astray, or get among the cabbages; weeds were sure to grow quicker in his fields than anywhere else; the rain always made a point of setting in just as he had some out-door work to do; so that though his patrimonial estate had dwindled away under his management, acre by acre, until there was little more left than a mere patch of Indian corn and potatoes, yet it was the worst conditioned farm in the neighborhood.
His children, too, were as ragged and wild as if they belonged to nobody. His son Rip, an urchin begotten in his own likeness, promised to inherit the habits, with the old clothes of his father. He was generally seen trooping like a colt at his mother's heels, equipped in a pair of his father's cast-off galligaskins, which he had much ado to hold up with one hand, as a fine lady does her train in bad weather.

Rip Van Winkle, however, was one of those happy mortals, of foolish, well-oiled dispositions, who take the world easy, eat white bread or brown, whichever can be got with least thought or trouble, and would rather starve on a penny than work for a pound. If left to himself, he would have whistled life away in perfect contentment; but his wife kept continually dinning in his ears about his idleness, his carelessness, and the ruin he was bringing on his family. Morning, noon, and night, her tongue was incessantly going, and everything he said or did was sure to produce a torrent of household eloquence. Rip had but one way of replying to all lectures of the kind, and that, by frequent use, had grown into a habit. He shrugged his shoulders, shook his head, cast up his eyes, but said nothing. This, however, always provoked a fresh volley from his wife; so that he was fain to draw off his forces, and take to the outside of the house - the only side which, in truth, belongs to a hen-pecked husband.

Rip's sole domestic adherent was his dog Wolf, who was as much hen-pecked as his master; for Dame Van Winkle regarded them as companions in idleness, and even looked upon Wolf with an evil eye, as the cause of his master's going so often astray. True it is, in all points of spirit befitting an honorable dog, he was as courageous an animal as ever scoured the woods - but what courage can withstand the ever-during and all-besetting terrors of a woman's tongue? The moment Wolf entered the house his crest fell, his tail drooped to the ground, or curled between his legs, he sneaked about with a gallows air, casting many a sidelong glance at Dame Van Winkle, and at the least flourish of a broom-stick or ladle, he would fly to the door with yelping precipitation.

Times grew worse and worse with Rip Van Winkle as years of matrimony rolled on; a tart temper never mellows with age, and a sharp tongue is the only edged tool that grows keener with constant use. For a long while he used to console himself, when driven from home, by frequenting a kind of perpetual club of the sages, philosophers, and other idle personages of the village; which held its sessions on a bench before a small inn, designated by a rubicund portrait of His Majesty George the Third. Here they used to sit in the shade through a long lazy summer's day, talking listlessly over village gossip, or telling endless sleepy stories about nothing. But it would have been worth any statesman's money to have heard the profound discussions that sometimes took place, when by chance an old newspaper fell into their hands from some passing traveller. How solemnly they would listen to the contents, as drawled out by Derrick Van Bummel, the schoolmaster, a dapper learned little man, who was not to be daunted by the most gigantic word in the dictionary; and how sagely they would deliberate upon public events some months after they had taken place.

The opinions of this junto were completely controlled by Nicholas Vedder, a patriarch of the village, and landlord of the inn, at the door of which he took his seat from morning till night, just moving sufficiently to avoid the sun and keep in the shade of a large tree; so that the neighbors could tell the hour by his movements as accurately as by a sundial. It is true he was rarely heard to speak, but smoked his pipe incessantly. His adherents, however (for every great man has his adherents), perfectly understood him, and knew how to gather his opinions. When anything that was read or related displeased him, he was observed to smoke his pipe vehemently, and to send forth short, frequent and angry puffs; but when pleased, he would inhale the smoke slowly and tranquilly, and emit it in light and placid clouds; and sometimes, taking the pipe from his mouth, and letting the fragrant vapor curl about his nose, would gravely nod his head in token of perfect approbation.

From even this stronghold the unlucky Rip was at length routed by his termagant wife, who would suddenly break in upon the tranquillity of the assemblage and call the members all to naught; nor was that august personage, Nicholas Vedder himself, sacred from the daring tongue of this terrible virago, who charged him outright with encouraging her husband in habits of idleness.

Poor Rip was at last reduced almost to despair; and his only alternative, to escape from the labor of the farm and clamor of his wife, was to take gun in hand and stroll away into the woods. Here he would sometimes seat himself at the foot of a tree, and share the contents of his wallet with Wolf, with whom he sympathized as a fellow-sufferer in persecution. "Poor Wolf," he would say, "thy mistress leads thee a dog's life of it; but never mind, my lad, whilst I live thou shalt never want a friend to stand by thee!" Wolf would wag his tail, look wistfuly in his master's face, and if dogs can feel pity I verily believe he reciprocated the sentiment with all his heart.

In a long ramble of the kind on a fine autumnal day, Rip had unconsciously scrambled to one of the highest parts of the Kaatskill mountains. He was after his favorite sport of squirrel shooting, and the still solitudes had echoed and re-echoed with the reports of his gun. Panting and fatigued, he threw himself, late in the afternoon, on a green knoll, covered with mountain herbage, that crowned the brow of a precipice. From an opening between the trees he could overlook all the lower country for many a mile of rich woodland. He saw at a distance the lordly Hudson, far, far below him, moving on its silent but majestic course, with the reflection of a purple cloud, or the sail of a lagging bark, here and there sleeping on its glassy bosom, and at last losing itself in the blue highlands.

On the other side he looked down into a deep mountain glen, wild, lonely, and shagged, the bottom filled with fragments from the impending cliffs, and scarcely lighted by the reflected rays of the setting sun. For some time Rip lay musing on this scene; evening was gradually advancing; the mountains began to throw their long blue shadows over the valleys; he saw that it would be dark long before he could reach the village, and he heaved a heavy sigh when he thought of encountering the terrors of Dame Van Winkle.

As he was about to descend, he heard a voice from a distance, hallooing, "Rip Van Winkle! Rip Van Winkle!" He looked round, but could see nothing but a crow winging its solitary flight across the mountain. He thought his fancy must have deceived him, and turned again to descend, when he heard the same cry ring through the still evening air: "Rip Van Winkle! Rip Van Winkle!" - at the same time Wolf bristled up his back, and giving a low growl, skulked to his master's side, looking fearfully down into the glen. Rip now felt a vague apprehension stealing over him; he looked anxiously in the same direction, and perceived a strange figure slowly toiling up the rocks, and bending under the weight of something he carried on his back. He was surprised to see any human being in this lonely and unfrequented place, but supposing it to be some one of the neighborhood in need of his assistance, he hastened down to yield it.

On nearer approach he was still more surprised at the singularity of the stranger's appearance. He was a short square-built old fellow, with thick bushy hair, and a grizzled beard. His dress was of the antique Dutch fashion - a cloth jerkin strapped round the waist - several pair of breeches, the outer one of ample volume, decorated with rows of buttons down the sides, and bunches at the knees. He bore on his shoulder a stout keg, that seemed full of liquor, and made signs for Rip to approach and assist him with the load. Though rather shy and distrustful of this new acquaintance, Rip complied with his usual alacrity; and mutually relieving one another, they clambered up a narrow gully, apparently the dry bed of a mountain torrent. As they ascended, Rip every now and then heard long rolling peals, like distant thunder, that seemed to issue out of a deep ravine, or rather cleft, between lofty rocks, toward which their rugged path conducted. He paused for an instant, but supposing it to be the muttering of one of those transient thunder-showers which often take place in mountain heights, he proceeded. Passing through the ravine, they came to a hollow, like a small amphitheatre, surrounded by perpendicular precipices, over the brinks of which impending trees shot their branches, so that you only caught glimpses of the azure sky and the bright evening cloud. During the whole time Rip and his companion had labored on in silence; for though the former marvelled greatly what could be the object of carrying a keg of liquor up this wild mountain, yet there was something strange and incomprehensible about the unknown, that inspired awe and checked familiarity.

On entering the amphitheatre, new objects of wonder presented themselves. On a level spot in the centre was a company of odd-looking personages playing at nine-pins. They were dressed in a quaint outlandish fashion; some wore short doublets, others jerkins, with long knives in their belts, and most of them had enormous breeches, of similar style with that of the guide's. Their visages, too, were peculiar: one had a large beard, broad face, and small piggish eyes: the face of another seemed to consist entirely of nose, and was surmounted by a white sugar-loaf hat set off with a little red cock's tail. They all had beards, of various shapes and colors. There was one who seemed to be the commander. He was a stout old gentleman, with a weather-beaten countenance; he wore a laced doublet, broad belt and hanger, high-crowned hat and feather, red stockings, and high-heeled shoes, with roses in them. The whole group reminded Rip of the figures in an old Flemish painting, in the parlor of Dominie Van Shaick, the village parson, and which had been brought over from Holland at the time of the settlement.

What seemed particularly odd to Rip was, that though these folks were evidently amusing themselves, yet they maintained the gravest faces, the most mysterious silence, and were, withal, the most melancholy party of pleasure he had ever witnessed. Nothing interrupted the stillness of the scene but the noise of the balls, which, whenever they were rolled, echoed along the mountains like rumbling peals of thunder.

As Rip and his companion approached them, they suddenly desisted from their play, and stared at him with such fixed statue-like gaze, and such strange, uncouth, lack-lustre countenances, that his heart turned within him, and his knees smote together. His companion now emptied the contents of the keg into large flagons, and made signs to him to wait upon the company. He obeyed with fear and trembling; they quaffed the liquor in profound silence, and then returned to their game.

By degrees Rip's awe and apprehension subsided. He even ventured, when no eye was fixed upon him, to taste the beverage, which he found had much of the flavor of excellent Hollands. He was naturally a thirsty soul, and was soon tempted to repeat the draught. One taste provoked another; and he reiterated his visits to the flagon so often that at length his senses were overpowered, his eyes swam in his head, his head gradually declined, and he fell into a deep sleep.

On waking, he found himself on the green knoll whence he had first seen the old man of the glen. He rubbed his eyes - it was a bright sunny morning. The birds were hopping and twittering among the bushes, and the eagle was wheeling aloft, and breasting the pure mountain breeze. "Surely," thought Rip, "I have not slept here all night." He recalled the occurrences before he fell asleep. The strange man with a keg of liquor - the mountain ravine - the wild retreat among the rocks - the woe-begone party at ninepins - the flagon - "Oh! that flagon! that wicked flagon!" thought Rip - "what excuse shall I make to Dame Van Winkle!"

He looked round for his gun, but in place of the clean well-oiled fowling-piece, he found an old firelock lying by him, the barrel incrusted with rust, the lock falling off, and the stock worm-eaten. He now suspected that the grave roysterers of the mountain had put a trick upon him, and having dosed him with liquor, had robbed him of his gun. Wolf, too, had disappeared, but he might have strayed away after a squirrel or partridge. He whistled after him and shouted his name, but all in vain; the echoes repeated his whistle and shout, but no dog was to be seen.

He determined to revisit the scene of the last evening's gambol, and if he met with any of the party, to demand his dog and gun. As he rose to walk, he found himself stiff in the joints, and wanting in his usual activity. "These mountain beds do not agree with me," thought Rip; "and if this frolic should lay me up with a fit of the rheumatism, I shall have a blessed time with Dame Van

Winkle." With some difficulty he got down into the glen: he found the gully up which he and his companion had ascended the preceding evening; but to his astonishment a mountain stream was now foaming down it, leaping from rock to rock, and filling the glen with babbling murmurs. He, however, made shift to scramble up its sides, working his toilsome way through thickets of birch, sassafras, and witch-hazel, and sometimes tripped up or entangled by the wild grapevines that twisted their coils or tendrils from tree to tree, and spread a kind of network in his path.

At length he reached to where the ravine had opened through the cliffs to the amphitheatre; but no traces of such opening remained. The rocks presented a high impenetrable wall over which the torrent came tumbling in a sheet of feathery foam, and fell into a broad deep basin, black from the shadows of the surrounding forest. Here, then, poor Rip was brought to a stand. He again called and whistled after his dog; he was only answered by the cawing of a flock of idle crows, sporting high in air about a dry tree that overhung a sunny precipice; and who, secure in their elevation, seemed to look down and scoff at the poor man's perplexities. What was to be done? the morning was passing away, and Rip felt famished for want of his breakfast. He grieved to give up his dog and gun; he dreaded to meet his wife; but it would not do to starve among the mountains. He shook his head, shouldered the rusty firelock, and, with a heart full of trouble and anxiety, turned his steps homeward.

As he approached the village he met a number of people, but none whom he knew, which somewhat surprised him, for he had thought himself acquainted with every one in the country round. Their dress, too, was of a different fashion from that to which he was accustomed. They all stared at him with equal marks of surprise, and whenever they cast their eyes upon him, invariably stroked their chins. The constant recurrence of this gesture induced Rip, involuntarily, to do the same, when to his astonishment, he found his beard had grown a foot long!

He had now entered the skirts of the village. A troop of strange children ran at his heels, hooting after him, and pointing at his gray beard. The dogs, too, not one of which he recognized for an old acquaintance, barked at him as he passed. The very village was altered; it was larger and more populous. There were rows of houses which he had never seen before, and those which had been his familiar haunts had disappeared. Strange names were over the doors - strange faces at the windows - every thing was strange. His mind now misgave him; he began to doubt whether both he and the world around him were not bewitched. Surely this was his native village, which he had left but the day before. There stood the Kaatskill mountains - there ran the silver Hudson at a distance - there was every hill and dale precisely as it had always been - Rip was sorely perplexed - "That flagon last night," thought he, "has addled my poor head sadly!"

It was with some difficulty that he found the way to his own house, which he approached with silent awe, expecting every moment to hear the shrill voice of Dame Van Winkle. He found the house gone to decay - the roof fallen in, the windows shattered, and the doors off the hinges. A half-starved dog that looked like Wolf was skulking about it. Rip called him by name, but the cur snarled, showed his teeth, and passed on. This was an unkind cut indeed - "My very dog," sighed poor Rip, "has forgotten me!"

He entered the house, which, to tell the truth, Dame Van Winkle had always kept in neat order. It was empty, forlorn, and apparently abandoned. This desolateness overcame all his connubial fears - he called loudly for his wife and children - the lonely chambers rang for a moment with his voice, and then all again was silence.

He now hurried forth, and hastened to his old resort, the village inn - but it too was gone. A large rickety wooden building stood in its place, with great gaping windows, some of them broken and mended with old hats and petticoats, and over the door was painted, "the Union Hotel, by Jonathan Doolittle." Instead of the great tree that used to shelter the quiet little Dutch inn of yore, there now was reared a tall naked pole, with something on the top that looked like a red night-cap, and from it was fluttering a flag, on which was a singular assemblage of stars and stripes - all this was strange and incomprehensible. He recognized on the sign, however, the ruby face of King George, under which he had smoked so many a peaceful pipe; but even this was singularly metamorphosed. The red coat was changed for one of blue and buff, a sword was held in the hand instead of a sceptre, the head was decorated with a cocked hat, and underneath was painted in large characters, GENERAL WASHINGTON.

There was, as usual, a crowd of folk about the door, but none that Rip recollected. The very character of the people seemed changed. There was a busy, bustling, disputatious tone about it, instead of the accustomed phlegm and drowsy tranquillity. He looked in vain for the sage Nicholas Vedder, with his broad face, double chin, and fair long pipe, uttering clouds of tobacco-smoke instead of idle speeches; or Van Bummel, the schoolmaster, doling forth the contents of an ancient newspaper. In place of these, a lean, bilious-looking fellow, with his pockets full of handbills, was haranguing vehemently about rights of citizens - elections - members of congress - liberty - Bunker's Hill - heroes of seventy-six - and other words, which were a perfect Babylonish jargon to the bewildered Van Winkle.

The appearance of Rip, with his long grizzled beard, his rusty fowling-piece, his uncouth dress, and an army of women and children at his heels, soon attracted the attention of the tavern politicians. They crowded round him, eyeing him from head to foot with great curiosity. The orator bustled up to him, and, drawing him partly aside, inquired "on which side he voted?" Rip stared in vacant stupidity. Another short but busy little fellow pulled him by the arm, and, rising on tiptoe, inquired in his ear, "Whether he was Federal or Democrat?" Rip was equally at a loss to comprehend the question; when a knowing, self-important old gentleman, in a sharp cocked hat, made his way through the crowd, putting them to the right and left with his elbows as he passed, and planting himself before Van Winkle, with one arm akimbo, the other resting on his cane, his keen eyes and sharp hat penetrating, as it were, into his very soul, demanded in an austere tone, "what brought him to the election with a gun on his shoulder, and a mob at his heels, and whether he meant to breed a riot in the village?" - "Alas! gentlemen," cried Rip, somewhat dismayed, "I am a poor quiet man, a native of the place, and a loyal subject of the king, God bless him!"

Here a general shout burst from the by-standers - "A tory! a tory! a spy! a refugee! hustle him! away with him!" It was with great difficulty that the self-important man in the cocked hat restored order; and, having assumed a tenfold austerity of brow, demanded again of the unknown culprit, what he came there for, and whom he was seeking? The poor man humbly assured him that he meant no harm, but merely came there in search of some of his neighbors, who used to keep about the tavern.

"Well--who are they?--name them."

Rip bethought himself a moment, and inquired, "Where's Nicholas Vedder?"

There was a silence for a little while, when an old man replied, in a thin piping voice, "Nicholas Vedder! why, he is dead and gone these eighteen years! There was a wooden tombstone in the church-yard that used to tell all about him, but that's rotten and gone too."

Where's Brom Dutcher?"

"Oh, he went off to the army in the beginning of the war; some say he was killed at the storming of Stony Point - others say he was drowned in a squall at the foot of Antony's Nose. I don't know - he never came back again."

"Where's Van Bummel, the schoolmaster?"

"He went off to the wars too, was a great militia general, and is now in congress."

Rip's heart died away at hearing of these sad changes in his home and friends, and finding himself thus alone in the world. Every answer puzzled him too, by treating of such enormous lapses of time, and of matters which he could not understand: war - congress - Stony Point; - he had no courage to ask after any more friends, but cried out in despair, "Does nobody here know Rip Van Winkle?"

"Oh, Rip Van Winkle!" exclaimed two or three, "Oh, to be sure! that's Rip Van Winkle yonder, leaning against the tree."

Rip looked, and beheld a precise counterpart of himself, as he went up the mountain: apparently as lazy, and certainly as ragged. The poor fellow was now completely confounded. He doubted his own identity, and whether he was himself or another man. In the midst of his bewilderment, the man in the cocked hat demanded who he was, and what was his name?

"God knows," exclaimed he, at his wit's end; "I'm not myself - I'm somebody else - that's me yonder - no - that's somebody else got into my shoes - I was myself last night, but I fell asleep on the mountain, and they've changed my gun, and every thing's changed, and I'm changed, and I can't tell what's my name, or who I am!"

The by-standers began now to look at each other, nod, wink significantly, and tap their fingers against their foreheads. There was a whisper also, about securing the gun, and keeping the old fellow from doing mischief, at the very suggestion of which the self-important man in the cocked hat retired with some precipitation. At this critical moment a fresh comely woman pressed through the throng to get a peep at the gray-bearded man. She had a chubby child in her arms, which, frightened at his looks, began to cry. "Hush, Rip," cried she, "hush, you little fool; the old man won't hurt you." The name of the child, the air of the mother, the tone of her voice, all awakened a train of recollections in his mind. "What is your name, my good woman?" asked he.

"Judith Gardenier."

"And your father's name?"

"Ah, poor man, Rip Van Winkle was his name, but it's twenty years since he went away from home with his gun, and never has been heard of since - his dog came home without him; but whether he shot himself, or was carried away by the Indians, nobody can tell. I was then but a little girl."

Rip had but one question more to ask; but he put it with a faltering voice:

"Where's your mother?"

"Oh, she too had died but a short time since; she broke a blood-vessel in a fit of passion at a New-England peddler."

There was a drop of comfort, at least, in this intelligence. The honest man could contain himself no longer. He caught his daughter and her child in his arms. "I am your father!" cried he - "Young Rip Van Winkle once - old Rip Van Winkle now! - Does nobody know poor Rip Van Winkle?"

All stood amazed, until an old woman, tottering out from among the crowd, put her hand to her brow, and peering under it in his face for a moment, exclaimed, "Sure enough! it is Rip Van Winkle - it is himself! Welcome home again, old neighbor - Why, where have you been these twenty long years?"

Rip's story was soon told, for the whole twenty years had been to him but as one night. The neighbors stared when they heard it; some were seen to wink at each other, and put their tongues in their cheeks: and the self-important man in the cocked hat, who, when the alarm was over, had returned to the field, screwed down the corners of his mouth, and shook his head - upon which there was a general shaking of the head throughout the assemblage.

It was determined, however, to take the opinion of old Peter Vanderdonk, who was seen slowly advancing up the road. He was a descendant of the historian of that name, who wrote one of the earliest accounts of the province. Peter was the most ancient inhabitant of the village, and well versed in all the wonderful events and traditions of the neighborhood. He recollected Rip at once, and corroborated his story in the most satisfactory manner. He assured the company that it was a fact, handed down from his ancestor the historian, that the Kaatskill mountains had always been haunted by strange beings. That it was affirmed that the great Hendrick Hudson, the first discoverer of the river and country, kept a kind of vigil there every twenty years, with his crew of the Half-moon; being permitted in this way to revisit the scenes of his enterprise, and keep a guardian eye upon the river, and the great city called by his name. That his father had once seen them in their old Dutch dresses playing at nine-pins in a hollow of the mountain; and that he himself had heard, one summer afternoon, the sound of their balls, like distant peals of thunder.

To make a long story short, the company broke up, and returned to the more important concerns of the election. Rip's daughter took him home to live with her; she had a snug, well-furnished house, and a stout cheery farmer for a husband, whom Rip recollected for one of the urchins that used to climb upon his back. As to Rip's son and heir, who was the ditto of himself, seen leaning against the tree, he was employed to work on the farm; but evinced an hereditary disposition to attend to anything else but his business.

Rip now resumed his old walks and habits; he soon found many of his former cronies, though all rather the worse for the wear and tear of time; and preferred making friends among the rising generation, with whom he soon grew into great favor.

Having nothing to do at home, and being arrived at that happy age when a man can be idle with impunity, he took his place once more on the bench at the inn door, and was reverenced as one of the patriarchs of the village, and a chronicle of the old times "before the war." It was some time before he could get into the regular track of gossip, or could be made to comprehend the strange events that had taken place during his torpor. How that there had been a revolutionary war - that the country had thrown off the yoke of old England - and that, instead of being a subject of his Majesty George the Third, he was now a free citizen of the United States. Rip, in fact, was no politician; the changes of states and empires made but little impression on him; but there was one species of despotism under which he had long groaned, and that was - petticoat government. Happily that was at an end; he had got his neck out of the yoke of matrimony, and could go in and out whenever he pleased, without dreading the tyranny of Dame Van Winkle. Whenever her name was mentioned, however, he shook his head, shrugged his shoulders, and cast up his eyes; which might pass either for an expression of resignation to his fate, or joy at his deliverance.

He used to tell his story to every stranger that arrived at Mr. Doolittle's hotel. He was observed, at first, to vary on some points every time he told it, which was, doubtless, owing to his having so recently awaked. It at last settled down precisely to the tale I have related, and not a man, woman, or child in the neighborhood, but knew it by heart. Some always pretended to doubt the reality of it, and insisted that Rip had been out of his head, and that this was one point on which he always remained flighty. The old Dutch inhabitants, however, almost universally gave it full credit. Even to this day they never hear a thunderstorm of a summer afternoon about the Kaatskill, but they say Hendrick Hudson and his crew are at their game of nine-pins; and it is a common wish of all hen-pecked husbands in the neighborhood, when life hangs heavy on their hands, that they might have a quieting draught out of Rip Van Winkle's flagon.

NOTE: The foregoing Tale, one would suspect, had been suggested to Mr. Knickerbocker by a little German superstition about the Emperor Frederick der Rothbart, and the Kypphauser mountain: the subjoined note, however, which he had appended to the tale, shows that it is an absolute fact, narrated with his usual fidelity:

"The story of Rip Van Winkle may seem incredible to many, but nevertheless I give it my full belief, for I know the vicinity of our old Dutch settlements to have been very subject to marvellous events and appearances. Indeed, I have heard many stranger stories than this, in the villages along the Hudson; all of which were too well authenticated to admit of a doubt. I have even talked with Rip Van Winkle myself who, when last I saw him, was a very venerable old man, and so perfectly rational and consistent on every other point, that I think no conscientious person could refuse to take this into the bargain; nay, I have seen a certificate on the subject taken before a country justice and signed with a cross, in the justice's own handwriting. The story, therefore, is beyond the possibility of doubt. D. K."   1819

Narrative Form in "Rip Van Winkle"

One of the first things to notice about the form of "Rip Van Winkle" is that it is a *frame narrative*. That is, the story of Rip is framed by—told within—a story about a character named Diedrich Knickerbocker, among whose posthumous papers, Irving tells us, the story of Rip was found. There was, of course, no such person as Diedrich Knickerbocker—Irving just invents that person as a literary device to explain where he learned the story of Rip Van Winkle.

Frame narratives are very old devices in storytelling. In *The Odyssey*, for example, most of the exciting portions of the story, such as Odysseus' encounter with the one-eyed Cyclops and his descent into the underworld, are told not in the present-time of the narrative but as tales Odysseus later tells people about his adventures after the Trojan War. Using a frame narrative, Homer makes stories that might seem fantastical more realistic by presenting them not directly but indirectly—as stories told by one character to other characters about something that happened in the past.

Many ghost stories are framed by a narrative of ordinary people sitting around a campfire. One of the people offers to tell a story about the terrifying ghost who is said to haunt the part of the forest where the group is camping. The ghost story the camper tells to other campers is thus framed by the story of their sitting around the campfire. At the end of the camper's story about the ghost, the teller then returns us to the frame by describing the framed story's effect on the other campers. The effect is usually terrifying enough to keep the young campers from wandering in the woods at night.

In a similar way, Irving gives the story of Rip Van Winkle's twenty-year sleep a little more credibility by saying it was recorded by Diedrich Knickerbocker, a historian of the Dutch colonies in upstate New York. Even as he distances himself from the story of Rip by saying he found it in Knickerbocker's papers, Irving jokes with the reader, saying that Knickerbocker relied for his history on oral tales he heard from the Dutch settlers, particularly older women (old wives' tales). Irving also says, tongue in cheek, that when Knickerbocker's history was first published, a lot of readers were skeptical about its fantastical elements, but now it is revered for its "scrupulous accuracy." Irving is pulling our leg here, just as he does at the end of the story when he returns to the "frame" and prints Knickerbocker's testimony that the story must be true because he heard it from Rip Van Winkle himself.

Once Irving shifts from the *frame* narrative to the *framed* narrative, with its beautiful description of the Kaatskill Mountains, we supposedly get Diedrich Knickerbocker's account of the story of Rip Van Winkle. Which parts of the story are told in narrative summary and which are told in dramatic scene? What point of view does Irving use to render this story? Does the point of view change in the course of the narrative? How does Irving handle plot and character in this story? If a short story usually focuses on a single change, what changes in the course of this story?

Gothic Tales

You may recall that, when we studied Romantic poetry, we talked about the great shift in sensibility from the eighteenth century—variously called the *Age of Reason*, the *Enlightenment*, the *Neoclassical*, or *Augustan Age*—to the *Romantic Age* that followed it, from approximately 1795 to 1830. The eighteenth century was an era of trust in human reason, when scientists such as Isaac Newton discovered that the natural world obeyed simple mathematical laws such as that of gravity and acceleration. Philosophers such as John Locke, in turn, tried to emulate that symmetry and balance in human society. After the Great Fire of London in 1666, architects such as Christopher Wren rebuilt the city along the lines of such classical structures as the Pantheon so that London seemed to be a grand reincarnation of Rome under the emperor Augustus. Art and literature centered on the city, on urban life, on how people interacted in society. In poetry, the predominant literary form was the balanced, symmetrical couplet of Pope and Swift. We even see these values reflected in the stately homes and gardens of the eighteenth century with their simple, clean, symmetrical lines.

It is one of the great ironies of history that the Age of Reason ended when the most culturally enlightened country in the world was plunged into upheaval in the French Revolution of 1789. The ensuing bloody *Reign of Terror* followed, in which countless people were executed at the guillotine—including some of the leaders of the revolution itself. In the wake of the French Revolution, a new era of sensibility, which had been developing during the late 1700s, swept across England and Europe. Reason and science were challenged by feeling and imagination. In place of literature that reflected sophisticated urban life, writers celebrated the natural world, particularly in its wildest manifestations such as craggy mountains, gloomy woods, and spectacular waterfalls. In place of wit and urbanity, writers focused on simple, rural folk who lived close to the natural world (think of Gray's "Elegy" and Burns' rustic poems). There was a new interest in the supernatural and the mystical (think of Coleridge and Blake), and the tightly-balanced couplets of Pope and other eighteenth-century poets gave way to the loosely flowing blank verse of Wordsworth's "Tintern Abbey" and Coleridge's simple ballad quatrains in "The Rime of the Ancient Mariner."

Another aspect of this change of sensibility was that in place of the eighteenth century love of Greek and Roman classical culture, literature, and architecture, Romantics embraced the medieval culture of spirituality and mysticism. "Gothic" had been a term of disparagement in the eighteenth century, which regarded Gothic cathedrals—with their a-symmetrical, unbalanced design, their frenzied ornaments of gargoyles and stone carvings, and their uneven array of turrets and spires—as barbaric, when compared to the simple, unadorned symmetrical architecture of the Parthenon, the Pantheon, and other buildings of ancient Greece and Rome. In the Romantic Age, however, Gothic style was celebrated for its spontaneity, irregularity, and mystical power.

In fiction, Gothic novels, such as *Frankenstein* and *Dracula*, were very different from the novel of manners. For one thing, Gothic fiction was not set in the everyday social world of its readers but in some locale remote in place or time. Gothic fiction might even be set in a medieval castle in some remote part of the country where eerie things happen, such as bookcases turning and opening onto staircases that wind down into dungeons, where the eyes of portraits move, where mad scientists conduct hideous experiments in secret laboratories—conventions that persist today in horror movies.

The stories themselves were not about the simple everyday events Jane Austen describes but involve violent actions—tortures, rapes, and murders—frequently with supernatural characters such as ghosts and vampires. The characters in Gothic fiction are not the polished, debonair people we meet in the novel of manners but isolated, anti-social, often deranged creatures obsessed with strange compulsions. Given how unrealistic the settings, events, and characters of Gothic fiction are, it is not surprising that writers frequently use a frame narrative to distance the stories.

The American short story came into international recognition when the popularity of Gothic fiction was at its height in England and Europe, so several American writers, notably Edgar Allan Poe, used some of the forms of Gothic fiction for their short stories. While Poe and other Gothic writers relished the "horror" elements in Gothic fiction, they also saw such fiction as a way to portray the strange, twisted depths of the human mind that could never be directly presented in the world of polite society in the novel of manners.

Edgar Allan Poe (1809-1849)

In addition to his poetry, Edgar Allan Poe wrote many short stories, essays, and reviews for magazines, several of which he edited. In 1839, he published a collection of short stories, *Tales of the Grotesque and Arabesque*, which contained what today we would call "horror" stories, "mystery" stories, and "detective" stories. Poe also wrote about the nature of the short story, which he thought was a literary form in which the writer tried to *affect* a reader in the brief span it took to read the tale—to shock, terrify, and surprise the reader. As you read the following story, think about how its form differs from that of "Rip Van Winkle."

The Cask of Amontillado*

wine barrel of a kind of sherry

The thousand injuries of Fortunato I had borne as I best could, but when he ventured upon insult, I vowed revenge. You, who so well know the nature of my soul, will not suppose, however, that I gave utterance to a threat. At length I would be avenged; this was a point definitively settled -- but the very definitiveness with which it was resolved precluded the idea of risk. I must not only punish, but punish with impunity. A wrong is unredressed when retribution overtakes its redresser. It is equally unredressed when the avenger fails to make himself felt as such to him who has done the wrong.

It must be understood that neither by word nor deed had I given Fortunato cause to doubt my good will. I continued as was my wont, to smile in his face, and he did not perceive that my smile NOW was at the thought of his immolation.

He had a weak point -- this Fortunato -- although in other regards he was a man to be respected and even feared. He prided himself on his connoisseurship in wine. Few Italians have the true virtuoso spirit. For the most part their enthusiasm is adopted to suit the time and opportunity to practise imposture upon the British and Austrian millionaires. In painting and gemmary, Fortunato, like his countrymen, was a quack, but in the matter of old wines he was sincere. In this respect I did not differ from him materially; I was skilful in the Italian vintages myself, and bought largely whenever I could.

It was about dusk, one evening during the supreme madness of the carnival season, that I encountered my friend. He accosted me with excessive warmth, for he had been drinking much. The man wore motley. He had on a tight-fitting parti-striped dress and his head was surmounted by the conical cap and bells. I was so pleased to see him, that I thought I should never have done wringing his hand.

I said to him -- "My dear Fortunato, you are luckily met. How remarkably well you are looking to-day! But I have received a pipe of what passes for Amontillado, and I have my doubts."

"How?" said he, "Amontillado? A pipe? Impossible ? And in the middle of the carnival?"

"I have my doubts," I replied; "and I was silly enough to pay the full Amontillado price without consulting you in the matter. You were not to be found, and I was fearful of losing a bargain."

"Amontillado!"

"I have my doubts."

"Amontillado!"

"And I must satisfy them."

"Amontillado!"

"As you are engaged, I am on my way to Luchesi. If any one has a critical turn, it is he. He will tell me" --

"Luchesi cannot tell Amontillado from Sherry."

"And yet some fools will have it that his taste is a match for your own."

"Come let us go."

"Whither?"

"To your vaults."

"My friend, no; I will not impose upon your good nature. I perceive you have an engagement Luchesi" --

"I have no engagement; come."

"My friend, no. It is not the engagement, but the severe cold with which I perceive you are afflicted . The vaults are insufferably damp. They are encrusted with nitre."

"Let us go, nevertheless. The cold is merely nothing. Amontillado! You have been imposed upon; and as for Luchesi, he cannot distinguish Sherry from Amontillado."

Thus speaking, Fortunato possessed himself of my arm. Putting on a mask of black silk and drawing a roquelaire closely about my person, I suffered him to hurry me to my palazzo.

There were no attendants at home; they had absconded to make merry in honour of the time. I had told them that I should not return until the morning and had given them explicit orders not to stir from the house. These orders were sufficient, I well knew, to insure their immediate disappearance , one and all, as soon as my back was turned.

I took from their sconces two flambeaux, and giving one to Fortunato bowed him through several suites of rooms to the archway that led into the vaults. I passed down a long and winding staircase, requesting him to be cautious as he followed. We came at length to the foot of the descent, and stood together on the damp ground of the catacombs of the Montresors.

The gait of my friend was unsteady, and the bells upon his cap jingled as he strode.

"The pipe," said he.

"It is farther on," said I; "but observe the white webwork which gleams from these cavern walls."

He turned towards me and looked into my eyes with two filmy orbs that distilled the rheum of intoxication .

"Nitre?" he asked, at length

"Nitre," I replied. "How long have you had that cough!"

"Ugh! ugh! ugh! -- ugh! ugh! ugh! -- ugh! ugh! ugh! -- ugh! ugh! ugh! -- ugh! ugh! ugh!

My poor friend found it impossible to reply for many minutes.

"It is nothing," he said, at last.

"Come," I said, with decision, we will go back; your health is precious. You are rich, respected, admired, beloved; you are happy as once I was. You are a man to be missed. For me it is no matter. We will go back; you will be ill and I cannot be responsible. Besides, there is Luchesi" --

"Enough," he said; "the cough is a mere nothing; it will not kill me. I shall not die of a cough."

"True--true," I replied; "and, indeed, I had no intention of alarming you unnecessarily -- but you should use all proper caution. A draught of this Medoc will defend us from the damps."

Here I knocked off the neck of a bottle which I drew from a long row of its fellows that lay upon the mould.

"Drink," I said, presenting him the wine.

He raised it to his lips with a leer. He paused and nodded to me familiarly, while his bells jingled.

"I drink," he said, "to the buried that repose around us."

"And I to your long life."

He again took my arm and we proceeded.

"These vaults," he said, are extensive."

"The Montresors," I replied, "were a great numerous family."

"I forget your arms."

"A huge human foot d'or, in a field azure; the foot crushes a serpent rampant whose fangs are imbedded in the heel."

"And the motto?"

"Nemo me impune lacessit."*   *("No one crosses me with impunity")*

"Good!" he said.

The wine sparkled in his eyes and the bells jingled. My own fancy grew warm with the Medoc. We had passed through walls of piled bones, with casks and puncheons intermingling, into the inmost recesses of the catacombs. I paused again, and this time I made bold to seize Fortunato by an arm above the elbow.

"The nitre!" I said: "see it increases. It hangs like moss upon the vaults. We are below the river's bed. The drops of moisture trickle among the bones. Come, we will go back ere it is too late. Your cough" --

"It is nothing" he said; "let us go on. But first, another draught of the Medoc."

I broke and reached him a flagon of De Grave. He emptied it at a breath. His eyes flashed with a fierce light. He laughed and threw the bottle upwards with a gesticulation I did not understand.

I looked at him in surprise. He repeated the movement -- a grotesque one.

"You do not comprehend?" he said.

"Not I," I replied.

"Then you are not of the brotherhood."

"How?"

"You are not of the masons."   *(Freemasons were a secret fraternity of stone carvers)*

"Yes, yes," I said "Yes! yes."

"You? Impossible! A mason?"

"A mason," I replied.

"A sign," he said.

"It is this," I answered, producing a trowel from beneath the folds of my roquelaire.   *(Montresor takes out a swtone mason's trowel from under his cloak)*

"You jest," he exclaimed, recoiling a few paces. "But let us proceed to the Amontillado."

"Be it so," I said, replacing the tool beneath the cloak, and again offering him my arm. He leaned upon it heavily. We continued our route in search of the Amontillado. We passed through a range of low arches, descended, passed on, and descending again, arrived at a deep crypt, in which the foulness of the air caused our flambeaux rather to glow than flame.

At the most remote end of the crypt there appeared another less spacious. Its walls had been lined with human remains piled to the vault overhead , in the fashion of the great catacombs of Paris. Three sides of this interior crypt were still ornamented in this manner. From the fourth the bones had been thrown down, and lay promiscuously upon the earth, forming at one point a mound of some size. Within the wall thus exposed by the displacing of the bones, we perceived a still interior recess, in depth about four feet, in width three, in height six or seven. It seemed to have been constructed for no especial use in itself, but formed merely the interval between two of the colossal supports of the roof of the catacombs, and was backed by one of their circumscribing walls of solid granite.

It was in vain that Fortunato, uplifting his dull torch, endeavoured to pry into the depths of the recess. Its termination the feeble light did not enable us to see.

"Proceed," I said; "herein is the Amontillado. As for Luchesi" --

"He is an ignoramus," interrupted my friend, as he stepped unsteadily forward, while I followed immediately at his heels. In an instant he had reached the extremity of the niche, and finding his progress arrested by the rock, stood stupidly bewildered . A moment more and I had fettered him to the granite. In its surface were two iron staples, distant from each other about two feet, horizontally. From one of these depended a short chain. from the other a padlock. Throwing the links about his waist, it was but the work of a few seconds to secure it. He was too much astounded to resist . Withdrawing the key I stepped back from the recess.

"Pass your hand," I said, "over the wall; you cannot help feeling the nitre. Indeed it is very damp. Once more let me implore you to return. No? Then I must positively leave you. But I must first render you all the little attentions in my power."

"The Amontillado!" ejaculated my friend, not yet recovered from his astonishment.

"True," I replied; "the Amontillado."

As I said these words I busied myself among the pile of bones of which I have before spoken. Throwing them aside, I soon uncovered a quantity of building stone and mortar. With these materials and with the aid of my trowel, I began vigorously to wall up the entrance of the niche.

I had scarcely laid the first tier of my masonry when I discovered that the intoxication of Fortunato had in a great measure worn off. The earliest indication I had of this was a low moaning cry from the depth of the recess. It was NOT the cry of a drunken man. There was then a long and obstinate silence. I laid the second tier, and the third, and the fourth; and then I heard the furious vibrations of the chain. The noise lasted for several minutes, during which, that I might hearken to it with the more satisfaction, I ceased my labours and sat down upon the bones. When at last the clanking subsided , I resumed the trowel, and finished without interruption the fifth, the sixth, and the seventh tier. The wall was now nearly upon a level with my breast. I again paused, and holding the flambeaux over the mason-work, threw a few feeble rays upon the figure within.

A succession of loud and shrill screams, bursting suddenly from the throat of the chained form, seemed to thrust me violently back. For a brief moment I hesitated -- I trembled. Unsheathing my rapier, I began to grope with it about the recess; but the thought of an instant reassured me. I placed my hand upon the solid fabric of the catacombs , and felt satisfied. I reapproached the wall. I replied to the yells of him who clamoured. I reechoed -- I aided -- I surpassed them in volume and in strength. I did this, and the clamourer grew still.

It was now midnight, and my task was drawing to a close. I had completed the eighth, the ninth, and the tenth tier. I had finished a portion of the last and the eleventh; there remained but a single stone to be fitted and plastered in. I struggled with its weight; I placed it partially in its destined position. But now there came from out the niche a low laugh that erected the hairs upon my head. It was succeeded by a sad voice, which I had difficulty in recognising as that of the noble Fortunato. The voice said --

"Ha! ha! ha! -- he! he! -- a very good joke indeed -- an excellent jest. We will have many a rich laugh about it at the palazzo -- he! he! he! -- over our wine -- he! he! he!"

"The Amontillado!" I said.

"He! he! he! -- he! he! he! -- yes, the Amontillado . But is it not getting late? Will not they be awaiting us at the palazzo, the Lady Fortunato and the rest? Let us be gone."

"Yes," I said "let us be gone."

"*For the love of God, Montresor!*"

"Yes," I said, "for the love of God!"

But to these words I hearkened in vain for a reply. I grew impatient. I called aloud –

"Fortunato!"

No answer. I called again --

"Fortunato!"

No answer still. I thrust a torch through the remaining aperture and let it fall within. There came forth in return only a jingling of the bells. My heart grew sick -- on account of the dampness of the catacombs. I hastened to make an end of my labour. I forced the last stone into its position; I plastered it up. Against the new masonry I reerected the old rampart of bones. For the half of a century no mortal has disturbed them.

In pace requiescat!   *(May he rest in peace)*   1846

Narrative Form in "A Cask of Amontillado"

Compare the compact first sentence of Poe's story to the leisurely first paragraph of Irving's "Rip Van Winkle" ("Whoever has made a voyage up the Hudson . . ."). How many more elements of fictional form does Poe compress into that sentence? Yet just as important as what Poe puts in is what he leaves out. What does the narrator *not* tell us about himself, his antagonist, and the events that led up to his moment of resolve for revenge? What were the "thousand injuries" Fortunato committed? What was his "insult"? Were these injuries and insults simply imagined by the super-sensitive Montresor?

In what way is this story a frame narrative? The setting of this story—in a remote place and an indefinite time (carnival time in Venice)—is typical of Gothic fiction, but also typical of Gothic fiction is the descent of Montresor and Fortunato into the winding, cavernous catacombs—underground tunnels—beneath Montresor's palace. What conflict emerges between Montresor—a French name—and Fortunato—an Italian name? Is it significant that both names mean nearly the same thing: "treasure" and "fortune"? How does Poe make use of that setting to heighten the horror of the action? Finally, to whom is Montresor telling this story? He says the walling-up of Fortunato happened fifty years earlier, so how old would he be now that he is finally telling of his murder of Fortunato? Who would the "you" be "who so well knows the nature of my soul" that Montresor addresses at the beginning of the tale?

Chapter 8
The Victorian Age (1832–1901)

Although Queen Victoria did not accede to the throne until 1837, the period that bears her name is marked by the year 1832 because it was then that Parliament passed the First Reform Bill. The Reform Bill gave the right to vote to all men in the middle class. Up until then, only wealthy landowners, factory owners, bankers, and other members of the upper- and middle-classes could vote. The Reform Bill also gave more representation in Parliament to cities such as Manchester and Birmingham, which had grown enormously in population during the Industrial Revolution but had remained largely unrepresented in Parliament because of outmoded laws that sent representatives to Parliament from sparsely populated districts ("rotten boroughs") or from districts where representatives were hand-picked by the local aristocrat ("pocket boroughs").

The Reform Bill did not extend voting rights to the working class, did not alleviate conditions in the hideous slums of large cities, nor did it put an end to children working in coal mines for sixteen hours a day. Still, it was a turning point in English history, transferring power from the aristocratic land-holding gentry to the middle class. When Victoria became Queen of England in 1837, she was alert to this change in British society, and she and her husband, Prince Albert, lived a life that was more in accord with middle-class mores than the aristocratic hedonism of monarchs before her.

As the first country to become industrialized, England enjoyed prosperity during the nineteenth century. Railway service drew people more closely together, the invention of the telegraph facilitated communication, and medical advances such as anesthetics and vaccination improved the health of the population. Understandably, many Victorians came to embrace the notion of progress—the idea that civilization, particularly British civilization, was destined to grow better and better. English factory goods, such as textiles, were sold around the world. The colonies of the British Empire stretched so far around the globe that it was literally true that "the sun never set on the Union Jack [the British flag]." London became the center of banking, the stock market, and the insurance business.

Still, amid all of this prosperity and progress, millions suffered in poverty, lived in wretched slums, and slaved in mines and factories. Through much of the era, the upper and middle classes feared that the working class might rise in bloody rebellion, and for many years that fear led to more and more repression. Not until the middle of the century were protective tariffs lifted so that prices of basic goods dropped and working conditions became more humane Not until the middle of the century was the right to vote extended to some working-class men.

Even as these social and economic reforms calmed the threat of class war, Victorian society faced more spiritual and intellectual threats. Discoveries by astronomers, geologists, and biologists (especially Charles Darwin's publication of *The Origin of the Species* in 1859) shook traditional Christian belief in the literal truth of the biblical account of creation, the existence of God, and the uniqueness of the human race. Science had long provided so many benefits to society and underscored the idea that civilization was progressing onward and upward. Now, with such ideas as

193

evolution, science shook the basis of religious beliefs that had existed for almost two thousand years. Most Victorians, however, responded to these problems and challenges with such typically middle-class virtues as hard work, sober living, and moral earnestness.

Writers who addressed such an audience of middle-class readers had to respect the premium placed on respectability, the family, and female innocence. Knowing that their works had to appeal to a diverse public, ranging from well-educated and sophisticated businessmen to servant girls, who, with the spread of compulsory education, could read, many writers took their cue from the theater. Seeing that successful plays appealed to a widespread audience, novelists such as Charles Dickens stressed dramatic narratives. Because they often wrote for *serial* publication, in which chapters of a novel were published in monthly installments in magazines or newspapers, novelists constructed their stories so that each installment ended with a dramatic *cliff-hanger* scene that made readers eagerly await the next installment. A novelist friend advised Dickens how to handle his audience of serial readers: "Make 'em laugh, make 'em cry, make 'em wait!"

The Dramatic Monologue

The theater also inspired the development of the *dramatic monologue*, the one major new poetic form of the Victorian Age. Earlier poetry, except for some of the medieval ballads, had been the lyrical expression of the poet in her or his own voice. The audience addressed by the poet, moreover, was the reader. In the dramatic monologue, however, the poem is spoken by a particular character, as if it were an extended segment of dialogue in a play. The audience for such a speech was another character or characters in the poem. Most of the major poets of the Victorian Age wrote dramatic monologues, and some of the best poems of the era are cast in this form. Frequently, such dramatic monologues were written in blank verse, which Shakespeare and other Elizabethan playwrights had used for their plays.

Alfred Lord Tennyson (1809-1892)

The leading poet of the Victorian Age, whose books were in practically every middle-class household, was Alfred Lord Tennyson. The son of an alcoholic clergyman, Tennyson attended Cambridge University, where he made several friends who encouraged him to write poetry. One of these, Arthur Hallam, was engaged to Tennyson's sister; Hallam's early death haunted Tennyson for the rest of his life and inspired one of his greatest long poems, the elegy *In Memoriam* (1850). Tennyson himself had fallen in love with Emily Sellwood, but for many years they could not marry because he was too poor. Financial problems also forced him to withdraw from Cambridge, but he continued to write and publish poetry. When his first volume of poetry was attacked by critics, Tennyson absorbed the criticism and worked hard at his craft. In 1842, the collection of poems he had been working on for many years proved enormously successful. Several of the poems in the collection were dramatic monologues, and one of the most famous is "Ulysses" (the Roman name for the Greek Odysseus, the hero of *The Odyssey*).

Ulysses

It little profits that an idle king,
By this still hearth, among these barren crags,
Match'd with an aged wife, I mete and dole   *I reward and punish*
Unequal laws unto a savage race,
That hoard, and sleep, and feed, and know not me.   *(don't know my greatness)*   5

I cannot rest from travel; I will drink
Life to the lees. All times I have enjoy'd
Greatly, have suffer'd greatly, both with those
That loved me, and alone; on shore, and when
Thro' scudding drifts the rainy Hyades   *(the Hyades were a group of stars*   10
Vext the dim sea. I am become a name;   *whose rising brought on rain at sea)*
For always roaming with a hungry heart
Much have I seen and known,-- cities of men
And manners, climates, councils, governments,
Myself not least, but honor'd of them all,--   15
And drunk delight of battle with my peers,
Far on the ringing plains of windy Troy.
I am a part of all that I have met;
Yet all experience is an arch wherethro'
Gleams that untravell'd world whose margin fades   20
For ever and for ever when I move.
How dull it is to pause, to make an end,
To rust unburnish'd, not to shine in use!
As tho' to breathe were life! Life piled on life
Were all too little, and of one to me   25
Little remains; but every hour is saved
From that eternal silence, something more,
A bringer of new things; and vile it were
For some three suns to store and hoard myself,
And this gray spirit yearning in desire   30
To follow knowledge like a sinking star,
Beyond the utmost bound of human thought.

This is my son, mine own Telemachus,
to whom I leave the sceptre and the isle,--
Well-loved of me, discerning to fulfill   35
This labor, by slow prudence to make mild
A rugged people, and thro' soft degrees
Subdue them to the useful and the good.
Most blameless is he, centred in the sphere
Of common duties, decent not to fail   40
In offices of tenderness, and pay
Meet adoration to my household gods,
When I am gone. He works his work, I mine.

There lies the port; the vessel puffs her sail;
There gloom the dark, broad seas. My mariners, 45
Souls that have toil'd, and wrought, and thought with me,--
That ever with a frolic welcome took
The thunder and the sunshine, and opposed
Free hearts, free foreheads,-- you and I are old;
Old age hath yet his honor and his toil. 50
Death closes all; but something ere the end,
Some work of noble note, may yet be done,
Not unbecoming men that strove with Gods.
The lights begin to twinkle from the rocks;
The long day wanes; the slow moon climbs; the deep   55
Moans round with many voices. Come, my friends.
'T is not too late to seek a newer world.
Push off, and sitting well in order smite
The sounding furrows; for my purpose holds
To sail beyond the sunset, and the baths   *(to sail beyond the western end of the* 60
Of all the western stars, until I die.   *Mediterranean—then the end of the world)*

It may be that the gulfs will wash us down;
It may be we shall touch the Happy Isles,   *(the Islands where dead heroes*
And see the great Achilles, whom we knew.   *enjoyed their afterlife*
Tho' much is taken, much abides; and tho' 65
We are not now that strength which in old days
Moved earth and heaven, that which we are, we are,--
One equal temper of heroic hearts,
Made weak by time and fate, but strong in will
To strive, to seek, to find, and not to yield. 1842

Notice how, as the monologue develops, we get a sense of character, setting, and audience, so that the poem becomes a miniature drama. Ulysses is speaking to his old shipmates and urging them to make one final voyage with him before they die. Tennyson based his portrait of Ulysses not on Homer's *Odyssey* but on Dante's *Inferno*, where Ulysses is placed in hell as punishment for deserting his family and country in old age and leading his sailors on a foolhardy voyage.

Tennyson had one of the greatest ears of any poet writing in English. Attuned to vowel and consonant sounds, he could craft lines that subtly wove the "i" sound together in the poem's opening lines:

> *It l*i*ttle prof*i*ts that an* i*dle k*i*ng*
> *By th*i*s st*i*ll hearth.*

Then shift to long *e* sounds:

> *I m*e*te and dole*
> *Un*e*qual laws unto a savage race,*
> *That hoard, and sl*ee*p, and f*ee*d, and know not m*e*.*

He also skillfully uses internal rhyme in lines such as

The sounding *fur*rows; for my *pur*pose holds

Throughout the poem, notice how Tennyson uses caesura and enjambment to underscore the appeal Ulysses makes to his old shipmates to join him in one final voyage. Tennyson said he started working on this poem, almost ten years before it was published, as a way to go on with life after his friend Arthur Hallam died. Can you see how the form of dramatic monologue can offer a poet a way to express personal feeling indirectly—through the words of a character, other than himself, in a dramatic context different from the poet's own real-life situation?

Robert Browning (1812–1889)

No poet used the dramatic monologue more creatively than Robert Browning. If you compare "My Last Duchess" to Tennyson's "Ulysses," you will see how Browning captures the sound of casual, everyday speech—someone chatting with somebody else—while Tennyson's Ulysses delivers a grandiloquent address to his mariners. In Browning's dramatic monologue, too, although only the main character, the Italian Duke of Ferrara speaks, we can infer how the other character in the scene reacts to what Ferrara is saying. The fact that both poems are written in iambic pentameter should also indicate what a flexible poetic line that can be.

Robert Browning grew up in a London suburb, the son of middle-class, highly-educated parents. Although he attended school, most of his extensive knowledge was acquired at home and went into his poetry, making some of his poems seem arcane and obscure to many readers. Browning's first book of poetry, published in 1833, contained passionate, soul-bearing personal poems in the manner of Shelley and other Romantic poets. When critics assailed such "confessional" poems, Browning turned to the dramatic monologue, where he wrote not in his own voice but in that of a fictional or real character from history.

Browning's marriage to Elizabeth Barrett was one of the world's great love stories. After falling in love with Elizabeth, then a semi-invalid under the domination of a stern, possessive father, Browning persuaded her to elope with him to Italy. There Elizabeth recovered her health and became a significant poet in her own right. Browning found in Italian history, particularly the Renaissance, many subjects for his dramatic monologues, such as painters, musicians, and clergymen.

One of Browning's most brilliant (and appalling) characters is the Duke of Ferrara in "My Last Duchess." Based upon an actual Renaissance duke, whose first wife mysteriously died after only three years of marriage, Ferrara in this poem is speaking to an emissary of the Count of Tyrol about the prospect of marrying the Count's daughter. The poem begins when the Duke pulls back a curtain that hangs over the portrait of his first wife ("My last Duchess"), a curtain that he alone is allowed to open and close. As the Duke talks about his first wife, he reveals himself as a truly arrogant, repulsive, but also frighteningly powerful person. We can only wonder what the emissary's response to the duke's monologue is and what he will tell the Count about the prospect of marrying his daughter to such a monster. Although Browning uses iambic pentameter, he writes not in blank verse but in couplets. But his couplets are not "closed heroic couplets," such as Pope used, but "open couplets," such as Chaucer used in *The Canterbury Tales*, in which the second line of one couplet can be "enjambed" into the first line of the following couplet. Such open couplets give the poem a chatty, conversational quality.

My Last Duchess

Ferrara

That's my last Duchess painted on the wall,
Looking as if she were alive. I call
That piece a wonder, now: Frà Pandolf's hands   *(fictional portrait painter)*
Worked busily a day, and there she stands.
Will 't please you sit and look at her? I said   5
"Frà Pandolf" by design, for never read
Strangers like you that pictured countenance,   *painted likeness of her face*
The depth and passion of its earnest glance,
But to myself they turned (since none puts by
The curtain I have drawn for you, but I)   10
And seemed as they would ask me, if they durst,
How such a glance came there; so, not the first   *the emissary has asked the*
Are you to turn and ask thus. Sir, 'twas not   *same question others have*
Her husband's presence only, called that spot   *(that blush in her cheeks)*
Of joy into the Duchess' cheek: perhaps   15
Frà Pandolf chanced to say, "Her mantle laps
Over my Lady's wrist too much," or "Paint
Must never hope to reproduce the faint
Half-flush that dies along her throat"; such stuff   *such compliments*
Was courtesy, she thought, and cause enough   20
For calling up that spot of joy. She had
A heart . . . how shall I say? . . . too soon made glad,
Too easily impressed; she liked whate'er
She looked on, and her looks went everywhere.   25
Sir, 'twas all one! My favour at her breast,   *my gift of a necklace*
The dropping of the daylight in the West,
The bough of cherries some officious fool   *some servant gave her*
Broke in the orchard for her, the white mule
She rode with round the terrace--all and each   30
Would draw from her alike the approving speech,
Or blush, at least. She thanked men,--good; but thanked
Somehow . . . I know not how . . . as if she ranked
My gift of a nine-hundred-years-old name   *of an ancient royal title*
With anybody's gift. Who'd stoop to blame   35
This sort of trifling? Even had you skill
In speech--(which I have not)--to make your will
Quite clear to such an one, and say, "Just this
Or that in you disgusts me; here you miss,
Or there exceed the mark"--and if she let   40
Herself be lessoned so, nor plainly set
Her wits to yours, forsooth, and made excuse,
--E'en then would be some stooping; and I chuse   *I choose not to lower myself*
Never to stoop. Oh, sir, she smiled, no doubt,   *by asking her to change*
Whene'er I passed her; but who passed without   45

> Much the same smile? This grew; I gave commands; *(see note * below)*
> Then all smiles stopped together. There she stands
> As if alive. Will 't please you rise? We'll meet
> The company below, then. I repeat,
> The Count your Master's known munificence 50
> Is ample warrant that no just pretence
> Of mine for dowry will be disallowed;
> Though his fair daughter's self, as I avowed
> At starting, is my object. Nay, we'll go
> Together down, Sir! Notice Neptune, though, 55
> Taming a sea-horse, thought a rarity,
> Which Claus of Innsbruck cast in bronze for me. 1842

*Browning once explained that the line "I gave commands" meant that Duke had either had his wife murdered or imprisoned in a convent. When he says "Will 't please you rise," it's not clear whether he is ordering the emissary to stand and leave or whether the emissary has been so appalled by the way the Duke has treated his last Duchess that he wants no more marital negotiations and plans to warn his master (the Count) not to let his daughter marry this fiendish duke.

Whatever the case, the Duke takes charge and says they will "meet the company below"—presumably other guests at a dinner party downstairs. The lines that follow are the Duke's convoluted way of telling the emissary that he expects the Count (who ranks below a duke in the aristocratic pecking order) will pay a large amount of money as a dowry to have his daughter marry into so eminent a family as the Duke's. After hinting about the money he wants as a dowry, however, the Duke tries to back-track and say that, of course, it's not the dowry he wants but the Count's daughter herself. The very way he phrases the restatement, however, reveals how sinister he is: "his fair daughter's self . . . is my object"— just as he has turned his last duchess into an "object"—the portrait.

As the two men start down the stairs, the emissary, in deference to the Duke's higher rank, steps aside to let Ferrara go down the stairs first, but the Duke jovially says, "Nay, we'll go/ Together down, sir." As they descend the stairs, the Duke makes his point once more that the Count's daughter had better be a lot more obedient an "object" than his last Duchess was. He points to a statue of Neptune, the Roman name for Poseidon, the Greek god of the ocean, taming a sea horse (riding the sea horse the way cowboys "broke" a bucking bronco) and notes that Claus of Innsbruck (another fictional artist) "cast in bronze for me." Although Browning has varied his iambic pentameter line throughout the poem, this last line is strongly iambic and ends, pointedly, on words that indicate how selfish and mean-spirited Ferrara is: "Which **Claus/** of **Inns-**/bruck **cast/** in **bronze/** for **me.**"

Matthew Arnold (1822–1888)

Matthew Arnold was the son of a clergyman and teacher. He attended Rugby, a fashionable prep school, where his father was headmaster. While he behaved himself under his father's stern discipline and moral guidance, when Arnold went to college at Oxford, he became a jokester and dandy who barely passed his exams. Nevertheless, for thirty-five years he was a school administrator who visited schools in England and on the Continent and suggested many educational reforms. During these years he also wrote poetry, and the success of his poems earned him the position of Professor of Poetry at Oxford in 1857. A few years later, however, he gave up writing poetry and devoted himself to literary, religious, and social criticism. His most famous poem is this dramatic monologue, "Dover Beach." With its huge white cliffs rising above the English Channel, Dover is England's equivalent of Niagara Falls as a site for honeymoons and other romantic trysts. It's only in the sixth line of this poem, when the speaker says, "Come to the window" that we realize the poem is a dramatic monologue spoken to a woman, presumably his bride or mistress.

Dover Beach

The sea is calm to-night.
The tide is full, the moon lies fair
Upon the straits; on the French coast the light
Gleams and is gone; the cliffs of England stand;
Glimmering and vast, out in the tranquil bay.   5
Come to the window, sweet is the night-air!
Only, from the long line of spray
Where the sea meets the moon-blanched land,   *moon-lit*
Listen! you hear the grating roar
Of pebbles which the waves draw back, and fling,   *Dover has a pebbled rather*   10
At their return, up the high strand,   *than sandy beach*
Begin, and cease, and then again begin,
With tremulous cadence slow, and bring
The eternal note of sadness in.

Sophocles long ago   *(see note* below)*   15
Heard it on the Aegaean, and it brought
Into his mind the turbid ebb and flow
Of human misery; we
Find also in the sound a thought,
Hearing it by this distant northern sea.   *(The North Sea)*   20

The Sea of Faith   *(see note** below)*
Was once, too, at the full, and round earth's shore
Lay like the folds of a bright girdle furled.
But now I only hear
Its melancholy, long, withdrawing roar,   25
Retreating, to the breath
Of the night-wind, down the vast edges drear
And naked shingles of the world.   *And stony, pebbly beaches*

Ah, love, let us be true
To one another! for the world, which seems   30
To lie before us like a land of dreams,
So various, so beautiful, so new,
Hath really neither joy, nor love, nor light,
Nor certitude, nor peace, nor help for pain;
And we are here as on a darkling plain   35
Swept with confused alarms of struggle and flight,

Where ignorant armies clash by night. *(see note *** below)* 1867

* Sophocles was the Greek dramatist of *Oedipus Rex, Antigone*, and many other tragic plays. In *Antigone*, he compares the suffering of a family to the pounding of the sea's waves upon the shore. The Aegean Sea surrounds the peninsula of Greece.

** "The Sea of Faith" is Arnold's metaphor for the time, from the Middle Ages to the middle of the nineteenth century, when most Europeans believed in the literal truth of the Bible. He compares that comforting belief to the sea at high tide, which wraps the land in a safe, protective "girdle" (garment belt). But with the discoveries of astronomy, geology, and biology in the mid nineteenth century (particularly Darwin's *Origins of the Species*), the biblical account of creation was thrown into doubt and, for many people, the whole basis for Christianity as well as belief in God, an afterlife, and a divine mandate for morality. Arnold compares that loss of faith to the sea retreating from the land at ebb tide, withdrawing its protective "girdle" and leaving people spiritually "naked" and vulnerable.

***Arnold, who was well-versed in classical literature, may be alluding here to a battle described by the Greek historian Thucydides, where fighting between two armies continued into the night, when soldiers could not distinguish enemy soldiers from their own comrades.

Notice how Arnold uses enjambment, caesura, and metrical substitution to give this dramatic monologue the feel of spoken conversation. Also notice how he varies the iambic pentameter line, sometimes shortening it to lines of iambic tetrameter, trimeter, and even dimeter. How does Arnold's handling of the iambic pentameter line resonate with what he is saying in "Dover Beach"?

While the dramatic monologue was the major new poetic form developed by Victorian poets, other forms, both traditional and new, flourished during the ninettenth century.

Elizabeth Barrett Browning (1806–1861)

During her lifetime, Elizabeth Barrett Browning was a much more popular poet than her husband, Robert Browning. After eloping with him to Italy, she embraced many radical causes, urging the unification of Italy as a nation and attacking the oppressed condition of women. Her most famous poems are a sequence of sonnets she wrote about her developing love for Robert Browning, which she tried to disguise, with Victorian modesty, by presenting them as translations of sonnets by a Portuguese writer, *Sonnets from the Portuguese*. This is the most famous of her "Portuguese" sonnets:

How Do I Love Thee?

How do I love thee? Let me count the ways.
I love thee to the depth and breadth and height
My soul can reach, when feeling out of sight
For the ends of Being and ideal Grace.
I love thee to the level of everyday's   5
Most quiet need, by sun and candle-light.
I love thee freely, as men strive for Right;
I love thee purely, as they turn from Praise.

    I love thee with a passion put to use
    In my old griefs, and with my childhood's faith.   10
    I love thee with a love I seemed to lose
    With my lost saints,---I love thee with the breath,
    Smiles, tears, of all my life!---and, if God choose,
    I shall but love thee better after death.   1850

Is this a Petrarchan or Shakespearean sonnet? Does the rhyme scheme fit or run counter to the syntactic structure of the sentences? Which rhymes are *slant*, or *near* rhymes?

Edward Fitzgerald (1809–1883)

Edward Fitzgerald was born into a well-to-do family and attended Cambridge University, where he befriended Alfred Lord Tennyson and other young writers. Rather than write his own poetry, he devoted himself to translating Greek and Latin. In the 1850s, he began studying Near-Eastern languages and came across a manuscript that contained poems by Omar Khayyám, a Persian (Iranian) mathematician and astronomer of the twelfth century. The poems were written in a verse form called *rubâ'i*, which consists of quatrains rhyming *aaba*. In 1859, Fitzgerald published a free translation of a collection of these poems called *The Rubáiyát of Omar Khayyám of Naishápúr*. He published his translation anonymously, and at first it was barely noticed. A few years later, however, the translation was discovered by several young poets who found that its themes of sensuality, atheism, and living for the pleasure of the moment expressed their disenchantment with the Victorian Age's emphasis on hard work, pious faith, and moral earnestness. Fitzgerald revised and republished his translation several times, and it has become one of the most popular poems in the English language. Below are some of its more famous quatrains.

from *The Rubáiyát of Omar Khayyám*

        1
Awake! for Morning in the Bowl of Night
Has flung the Stone that puts the Stars to Flight:
    And Lo! the Hunter of the East has caught   *(the sun)*
The Sultan's Turret in a Noose of Light.

        7
Come, fill the Cup, and in the Fire of Spring
The Winter Garment of Repentance fling:
    The Bird of Time has but a little way
To fly---and Lo! the Bird is on the Wing.

        12
A Book of Verses underneath the Bough,
A Jug of Wine, a Loaf of Bread---and Thou
    Beside me singing in the Wilderness---
Ah, Wilderness were Paradise enow.   *enough of paradise*

        13
Some for the glories of This World; and some

Sigh for the Prophet's Paradise to come;　　　　　　　　　*(Mohammed's promised heaven)*
　　　Ah, take the Cash and let the Credit go,
Nor heed the rumble of a distant Drum!
　　　24
Ah, make the most of what we yet may spend,
Before we too into the Dust descend;
　　　Dust into Dust, and under Dust, to lie,
Sans Wine, sans Song, sans Singer, and---sans End!　　　　　*Farewell Wine . . .*

　　　71
The Moving Finger writes; and, having writ,
Moves on: nor all thy Piety nor Wit
　　　Shall lure it back to cancel half a Line,
Nor all thy Tears wash out a Word of it.

　　　72
And that inverted Bowl we call The Sky,
Whereunder crawling coop't we live and die,
　　　Lift not thy hands to *It* for help---for It
Rolls impotently on as Thou or I.

　　　99
Ah Love! could thou and I with Fate conspire
To grasp this sorry Scheme of Things entire,
　　　Would not we shatter it to bits---and then
Re-mould it nearer to the Heart's Desire!

　　　TAMAM SHUD　　　　　*(It is completed)*　　　1859, 1879

Thomas Hardy (1840–1928)

Thomas Hardy grew up in Dorsetshire, in the southwestern part of England. He was trained as an architect, but he gave up that career to pursue writing. After he had published a series of successful novels, most of which were set in the rustic countryside of his youth, one of his novels, *Jude the Obscure* (1896), was attacked as immoral and nihilistic. Hardy thereupon abandoned fiction and spent the rest of his career writing poetry. In his poetry, too, Hardy wrote about his native region (which he called by its medieval name, "Wessex"—the country of the 'West Saxons') and frequently used variations of the ballad form.

　　　When England sent troops to fight against the Dutch colonists of South Africa in the Boer War (1899-1902), one of the English soldiers who was killed was a young man from Hardy's region whose name was Hodge and who had been a drummer in his army unit. Hardy imagines how the boy was buried in such unfamiliar, foreign surroundings, where even the constellations in the sky would have been strange to him. Hardy underscores the foreign world that surrounds Hodge by using terms from the language of Afrikaans (South African Dutch).

Drummer Hodge

They throw in Drummer Hodge, to rest
    Uncoffined--just as found:
His landmark is a kopje-crest   *a small hill*
    That breaks the veldt around: *the open plain, prairie*
And foreign constellations west   *set in the southern hemisphere*   5
    Each night above his mound.

Young Hodge the drummer never knew--
    Fresh from his Wessex home--
The meaning of the broad Karoo,   *broad, arid plateau*
    The Bush, the dusty loam,   *British colonial term for "the wilds"*   10
And why uprose to nightly view
    Strange stars amid the gloom.   *amid the twilight*

Yet portion of that unknown plain
    Will Hodge for ever be;
His homely Northern breast and brain   15
    Grow to some Southern tree,
And strange-eyed constellations reign
    His stars eternally.   1902

Hardy wrote this next poem on New Year's Eve 1899, in the waning hours of the nineteenth century with its belief in progress, the rewards of hard work, and moral earnestness. "Darkling" means that he hears the thrush in the darkness.

The Darkling Thrush

I leant upon a coppice gate   *gate to a small woodland area*
When Frost was spectre-gray,
And Winter's dregs made desolate
The weakening eye of day.   *the dying sunlight*
The tangled bine-stems scored the sky   *leafless twigs of shrubs that*   5
Like strings of broken lyres,   *seemed to scratch the sky above*
And all mankind that haunted nigh
Had sought their household fires.   *their hearths (fireplaces)*

The land's sharp features seemed to be
The Century's corpse outleant,   *outstretched corpse*   10
His crypt the cloudy canopy,
The wind his death-lament.
The ancient pulse of germ and birth   *(nature's fertility)*
Was shrunken hard and dry,
And every spirit upon earth   15
Seemed fervourless as I.   *as depressed, listless, despondent*

At once a voice arose among
The bleak twigs overhead
In a full-hearted evensong
Of joy illimited; *limitless joy* 20
An agèd thrush, frail, gaunt, and small,
In blast-beruffled plume, *(feathers by the wind)*
Had chosen thus to fling his soul
Upon the growing gloom.

So little cause for carolings 25
Of such ecstatic sound
Was written on terrestrial things
Afar or nigh around,
That I could think there trembled through
His happy good-night air 30
Some blessed Hope, whereof he knew
And I was unaware. 1902

There have been many poems, such as Keats' "Ode to A Nightingale" and Shelley's "To a Skylark," in which a poet takes joyous inspiration from hearing the song of a bird. Hardy's poem plays off these earlier Romantic poems by describing the landscape as bleak and lifeless, comparing it to the nineteenth century, which had started out so gloriously but was ending so despondently. Where Keats' nightingale and Shelley's skylark were youthful, vital birds who sang beautifully, Hardy's thrush is old, battered, and frail. (Note how Hardy uses caesuras in the line that describes the bird.) In his comparison of the twigs in the branches of the bushes overhead to "strings of broken lyres," Hardy suggests that, as a poet (whose traditional stringed instrument for accompanying his poetry was a lyre or harp), his poetic soul is broken and has nothing to "sing" about as a new century dawns. The word "That," which begins the fourth line from the end of the poem is ambiguous: on the one hand, Hardy may be saying that, while he himself sees no cause for rejoicing, the thrush knows something hopeful that Hardy is unaware of; or Hardy could be using "That" in the sense of "That I could be such a fool!" and suggesting it would be absurd to think that just because an old, haggard bird could sing rapturously doesn't mean there was anything to justify such optimism for humans.

Hardy wrote this next poem just as World War I was about to break out in Europe. The title refers to the British navy conducting gunnery practice in the English Channel, near Hardy's home in Dorsetshire. With macabre wit, Hardy imagines that the sound of those huge guns off the coast have awakened the corpses in a nearby churchyard (cemetery). At first, the dead think that the hour of the Last Judgment has come, but then God laughs, explaining that it's just humanity going to war again, and, almost sadistically, suggests that there may never be a Judgment Day.

Channel Firing

That night your great guns, unawares,
Shook all our coffins as we lay,
And broke the chancel window-squares, *church windows near altar*
We thought it was the Judgement-day

And sat upright. While drearisome 5
Arose the howl of wakened hounds:

The mouse let fall the altar-crumb,
The worm drew back into the mounds,

The glebe cow drooled. Till God cried, "No; *The cow in a small field*
It's gunnery practice out at sea
Just as before you went below;
The world is as it used to be:

"All nations striving strong to make
Red war yet redder. Mad as hatters
They do no more for Christés sake *(archaic spelling of "Christ's")*
Than you who are helpless in such matters.

"That this is not the judgment-hour
For some of them's a blessed thing,
For if it were they'd have to scour
Hell's floor for so much threatening. . . .

"Ha, ha. It will be warmer when
I blow the trumpet (if indeed
I ever do; for you are men,
And rest eternal sorely need)."

So down we lay again. "I wonder,
Will the world ever saner be,"
Said one, "than when He sent us under
In our indifferent century!"

And many a skeleton shook his head.
"Instead of preaching forty year,"
My neighbour Parson Thirdly said,
"I wish I had stuck to pipes and beer."

Again the guns disturbed the hour,
Roaring their readiness to avenge,
As far inland as Stourton Tower, *(see note * below)*
And Camelot, and starlit Stonehenge.

1914

*By invoking these place names from his region of England, Hardy underscores how long warfare has been going on. Stourton Tower was nicknamed "Alfred's Tower" to commemorate the Anglo-Saxon King Alfred who fought the Vikings in the eighth century A.D. Camelot was the legendary realm of King Arthur of the Celts, who preceded the Anglo-Saxons in England. Still earlier, were the primitive people who built the circle of huge stones in southwestern England called Stonehenge.

Gerard Manly Hopkins (1844–1889)

As a student of Greek and Latin at Oxford University, Gerard Manly Hopkins was deeply influenced by the *Oxford Movement*, a campaign, led by the Anglican priest and Oxford professor John Henry Newman, to make the Anglican Church more dogmatic and ritualistic—in effect, more like the Roman Catholic Church. When Newman himself converted to Roman Catholicism and then became a Catholic priest (and, later, a cardinal), young, deeply religious men like Hopkins followed his lead. Hopkins converted to Roman Catholicism in 1866 and later became a Jesuit priest. As part of his new priestly role, he gave up the writing of poetry and burned copies of his early poems. Encouraged by literary friends, Hopkins resumed writing poetry in the mid-1870s, but he would not publish his poems for fear the church authorities would disapprove. He served as a parish priest in several churches in England and in 1884 became a professor of classics at University College in Dublin. It was only in 1918, many years after Hopkins' death, that his friend Robert Bridges, who had become England's Poet Laureate, published an edition of Hopkins' verse.

The publication of his poems in 1918 made Hopkins seem more of a modern poet than a Victorian one—especially to many young twentieth-century poets. Hopkins' experiments with language and poetic rhythm seemed startlingly fresh even in an era of radical experimentation in poetry. As is often the case, poetry such as Hopkins' that seems so *avant-garde* is based upon far older, even ancient, poetic forms. Hopkins had been fascinated by the discovery, early in the nineteenth-century, of manuscripts of Anglo-Saxon poetry, most notably an almost complete manuscript of *Beowulf*. As scholars studied the Old English language and deciphered the form of Anglo-Saxon poetry—which we covered at the beginning of this course with such poems as "The Seafarer" and "Caedmon's Hymn"—it became clear that the oldest poetry in English had not been written in iambic pentameter or any other metrical lines but in accentual, alliterative verse. Hopkins developed a poetic line that, like Anglo-Saxon verse, was strongly accentual and alliterative but did not have a set numbers of syllables per line. Hopkins called this form *sprung rhythm* and frequently placed accent marks over words to make sure the reader stressed them. He also used rhyme and even wrote in such traditional forms as the sonnet, though his innovations in language and line made such sonnets seem experimental. Here, for example, is a fourteen line poem that celebrates the flight of a windhover, a small hawk that flies with its head into the wind and thus swirls and glides spectacularly. Can you see how in this poem Hopkins radically alters the form of the sonnet?

The Windhover

To Christ Our Lord

I caught this morning morning's minion, king-	*morning's darling*
dom of daylight's dauphin, dapple-dawn-drawn Falcon, in his riding	*prince*
Of the rolling level underneath him steady air, and striding	
High there, how he rung upon the rein of a wimpling wing	*rippling wing*
In his ecstasy! then off, off forth on swing,	5
As a skate's heel sweeps smooth on a bow-bend: the hurl and gliding	
Rebuffed the big wind. My heart in hiding	
Stirred for a bird,—the achieve of; the mastery of the thing!	
Brute beauty and valour and act, oh, air, pride, plume, here	
Buckle! AND the fire that breaks from thee then, a billion	10
Times told lovelier, more dangerous, O my chevalier!	*my knight, champion*

  No wonder of it: shéer plód makes plough down sillion   *plowed earth*
Shine, and blue-bleak embers, ah my dear,
  Fall, gall themselves, and gash gold-vermillion.   1877

  Such a poem gave twentieth-century readers problems when it was published in 1918, and it would have truly baffled readers of the nineteenth century when it was written. At the end of the first line, Hopkins splits the word "king-dom" so that "king" rhymes with the next seven lines that follow but also, internally, with the "-ing" of "morning." By starting the second line with "-dom" the syllable alliterates with the other *d* words in the line (including "ri*d*ing"). Even more innovative is the way Hopkins compresses words in striking combinations. Instead of saying that he watched the bird fly against the dappled sky of the dawn, he compresses that idea into a compound adjective: "dapple-dawn-drawn Falcon" (creating a triple internal rhyme on "*dawn*," "*drawn*," and "Fal-*con*"). Similarly, instead of saying that, while the wind was turbulently rolling, the bird's body was steady and level, Hopkins says, "his riding/Of the rolling level underneath him steady air," as if he were trying to twist the order of the words to reflect the dynamic movement of the bird in the wind. Equally daring is the way Hopkins suddenly shifts from comparing the bird to a horse swerving on a "rein" pulled by the wind to the heel of an ice skate as the skater cuts a curve, a "bow bend." In the eighth line, Hopkins' breathless admiration for the bird's flight impels him to shorten the word "achievement" to "the achieve of" the falcon.

  Did you notice that the first eight lines constitute something like the octave of a Pertrarchan sonnet? What is the rhyme scheme? Which rhymes are feminine and which are masculine? How does the sentence structure of the octave follow or run counter to the rhyme scheme? Which lines are enjambed and which are end-stopped? How does Hopkins use caesura?

  In the sestet, how does the form of the poem change its tone? A critical word is "Buckle," which can mean two very different things. On the one hand, as in "buckle" a belt, it can mean to join two things together On the other hand, as in "the bridge buckled," it can mean that something breaks in half. At the beginning of the sestet, Hopkins seems to be asking the "Brute beauty" of the bird to "buckle" in the sense of "join together" with the power and beauty the poet feels for Christ so that the bird becomes a spiritual revelation to the poet. In the last three lines of the sestet, however, Hopkins seems to be using "buckle" in the sense of break open. He describes how a plow, when it cuts through a clod of dull brown dirt, splits it into gleaming black pieces. Similarly, when dull gray coals fall through a fireplace grate, they split ("gall themselves") into gleaming red embers. In this sense, Hopkins may be suggesting that the physical beauty of the bird "breaks open" to reveal its even more dazzling inner spirit.

  In this next poem, Hopkins praises God for his creation of "imperfect" things. "Pied Beauty" is beauty that is made of various colors in spots or streaks, like a leopard or zebra. Through the poem, Hopkins weaves synonyms for such "dappled" beauty—"brinded" (streaked), "stipple" (spotted)"counter" (contrasted)—and he depicts images of things that possess such "freckled" beauty—multi-colored skies, brindled cows, stippled trout, and chestnuts that show their spotted seeds after roasting has burned off their shells. He also expresses love for landscapes that look like a crazy quilt. For example, fields that have crops next to fields that are just ploughed up next to other fields that lie fallow to restore nutrients. Similarly, he loves the "pied" look of tools of carpenters, blacksmiths, and other tradespeople that have been worn (and stained) over long use.

Pied Beauty

Glory be to God for dappled things—
For skies of couple-colour as a brinded cow;
For rose-moles all in stipple upon trout that swim;
Fresh-firecoal chestnut-falls; finches' wings;
Landscape plotted and pieced—fold, fallow, and plough   5
And áll trades, their gear and tackle and trim,

All things counter, original, spare, strange;
Whatever is fickle, frecklèd (who knows how?)
With swíft, slów; sweet, sóur; adázzle, dím;
He fathers-forth whose beauty is pást change: 10
Práise him.   1877

Notice the rhyme scheme of this poem. In what ways could it be an instance of "pied beauty" itself?

In these next two poems, we see Hopkins in his role as a priest to his community. In the first, he comforts a young girl, Margaret, who is upset by the sight of leaves turning color and falling off the trees in autumn. In typical Hopkins fashion, he describes the falling leaves in a brilliantly twisted phrase: instead of saying the golden leaves of trees in a grove are falling from their branches, he compresses that idea into "Goldengrove unleaving." At first, he tries to comfort the child by saying that, as she grows older, she will find much worse things to cry about than the fact that falling leaves turn trees pale ("wan") and bare in autumn ("though worlds of wanwood leafmeal lie"). Yet as the little girl continues to cry, Hopkins realizes that, while intellectually she does not understand the concept of death, her spirit intuited ("ghost guessed") that the falling autumn leaves are a portent of her own mortality.

Spring and Fall: To a Young Child

Márgarét, are you gríeving
Over Goldengrove unleaving?
Leáves, líke the things of man, you
With your fresh thoughts care for, can you?
Ah! ás the heart grows older   5
It will come to such sights colder
By and by, nor spare a sigh
Though worlds of wanwood leafmeal lie;
And yet you wíll weep and know why.
Now no matter, child, the name: 10
Sórrow's spríngs áre the same.
Nor mouth had, no nor mind, expressed
What heart heard of, ghost guessed:
It ís the blight man was born for,
It is Margaret you mourn for.   1893

How does Hopkins use rhyme in this poem? Where does he shift from couplets to a tercet?

As a priest, Hopkins was wracked by spiritual anguish, and he wrote several "dark sonnets" that portray his religious despair. In this sonnet, he describes a psychological agony that could grip anyone, religious or not. He feels that his mental pains have been "schooled" by previous pains in how to make him suffer more effectively. He also feels that "force" ("perforce" —because) such mental torment has only a little while to work on him, it strives to be all the more "fell" (brutal). Hopkins underscores the intensity of his mental pain grammatically by saying it gets, comparatively, "worse" and "worse" but that there is no superlative "worst" after which it subsides.

No Worst, There is None

No worst, there is none. Pitched past pitch of grief,
More pangs will, schooled at forepangs, wilder wring.
Comforter, where, where is your comforting?
Mary, mother of us, where is your relief?
My cries heave, herds-long; huddle in a main, a chief   5
Woe, world-sorrow; on an age-old anvil wince and sing—
Then lull, then leave off. Fury had shrieked 'No lingering! Let me be fell: force I must be brief.'

O the mind, mind has mountains; cliffs of fall
Frightful, sheer, no-man-fathomed. Hold them cheap   10
May who ne'er hung there. Nor does long our small
Durance deal with that steep or deep. Here! creep,   *(power of endurance)*
Wretch, under a comfort serves in a whirlwind: all
Life death does end and each day dies with sleep.   1885

A. E. Housman (1859-1936)

In turning from the intense, experimental verse of Gerard Manly Hopkins to the classically simple and elegant poems of our last poet of the late Victorian Age, A. E. (Alfred Edward) Housman, we find the same contrast we did in the seventeenth century between the intellectual, impassioned verse of Donne and other "Metaphysical" poets and the easy elegance of such "Cavalier" poets as Jonson, Herrick, and Lovelace. Like Hopkins, Housman attended Oxford University as a student of the classics, but his shame over his homosexual affection for a fellow student brought on mental problems that led to his failing his examinations.

Housman took a job as a government clerk but pursued his classical studies on his own and ultimately became a professor of Latin at Cambridge University. Striving to achieve the limpidity of classical Greek and Roman verse, he wrote *A Shropshire Lad* in 1896, a volume of poetry about his childhood in the rural, mid-western region of England. In keeping with his rustic—but still sophisticated—subject matter, Housman chose the tetrameter line or the ballad quatrain for most of his poems. Unlike the poems of Hopkins, almost none of Housman's poems require interpretation or explanatory footnotes, though this first, his most famous poem, alludes to the biblical prediction that most people will have a lifespan of seventy years. Can you tell how old the speaker of the poem is?

Loveliest of Trees, the Cherry Now

Loveliest of trees, the cherry now
Is hung with bloom along the bough,
And stands about the woodland ride
Wearing white for Eastertide.

Now, of my threescore years and ten,   5
Twenty will not come again,
And take from seventy springs a score,
It only leaves me fifty more.

And since to look at things in bloom
Fifty springs are little room,   10
About the woodlands I will go
To see the cherry hung with snow.   1896

Notice how Housman uses the ballad quatrain in this next poem:

When I Was One-and-Twenty

When I was one-and-twenty
    I heard a wise man say,
'Give crowns and pounds and guineas   *(British money denominations)*
    But not your heart away;

Give pearls away and rubies   5
    But keep your fancy free.'
But I was one-and-twenty,
    No use to talk to me.

When I was one-and-twenty
    I heard him say again,   10
'The heart out of the bosom
    Was never given in vain;
'Tis paid with sighs a plenty
    And sold for endless rue.'   *endless regret*
And I am two-and-twenty,   15
    And oh, 'tis true, 'tis true   1896

In the next poem, Housman uses the tetrameter line. How does it create a different effect from the ballad quatrain?

To an Athlete Dying Young

The time you won your town the race
We chaired you through the market-place; *We carried you on our shoulders*
Man and boy stood cheering by,
And home we brought you shoulder-high.

To-day, the road all runners come, 5
Shoulder-high we bring you home, *we carry your casket to the grave*
And set you at your threshold down,
Townsman of a stiller town.

Smart lad, to slip betimes away
From fields where glory does not stay, 10
And early though the laurel grows *(see note * below)*
It withers quicker than the rose.

Eyes the shady night has shut
Cannot see the record cut,
And silence sounds no worse than cheers 15
After earth has stopped the ears:

Now you will not swell the rout
Of lads that wore their honours out,
Runners whom renown outran
And the name died before the man. 20

So set, before its echoes fade,
The fleet foot on the sill of shade,
And hold to the low lintel up
The still-defended challenge-cup.

And round that early-laurelled head 25
Will flock to gaze the strengthless dead, *(see note ** below)*
And find unwithered on its curls
The garland briefer than a girl's. 1896

*Athletes in ancient Greece and Rome were crowned with a wreath made of laurel leaves.

** In these last two quatrains, Houseman imagines the dead athlete's townspeople leaving his body in the graveyard, where his tombstone ("lintel") still displays his racing trophy ("challenge cup"). Then, in the last quatrain, he imagines the ghost of the athlete entering the classical underworld where the spirits ("shades") of the many other "strengthless dead" flock to greet him and marvel at the laurel wreath he wears.

Victorian Drama

It was only with the restoration of King Charles II in 1660 that drama returned to England after being banned by the Puritans for nearly twenty years. During his exile in France, Charles II enjoyed French theater, and when he reopened theaters in England, they adopted French theatrical conventions. While some female parts were still played by boys, actresses took to the stage for the first time. Some theaters were built for indoor performances, had artificial lighting, and used a *proscenium* stage that receded into the back of the theater (probably like the stage in your high school auditorium). The audience sat in front of the stage, a curtain opened and closed at the end of an act, and playbills or programs identified characters in order of their appearance, noted changes of place and time, and explained where scenes were set. The stage had scenery and furnishings, creating the illusion that the audience was looking "into" a three-dimensional space, such as a room in a house where the "fourth wall" had been removed, allowing the audience to view the action inside the room. This kind of stage became the standard vehicle for presenting drama down to the present. Oscar Wilde used this kind of stage in *The Importance of Being Earnest*, setting his story in different places and times in a series of acts and scenes. The first act of the play takes place in a London residence, but in the second act we move to a house in the countryside, and the time jumps ahead to a later day. Even in the country house, the stage changes from a room inside the house to an outside garden—and back again.

Oscar Wilde (1854–1900)

Oscar Wilde was born in Ireland, majored in classical studies at Trinity College, Dublin, and won a scholarship to Oxford University where he was influenced by the Aesthetic ("art for art's sake") movement led by Walter Pater. Settling in London, he became the center of a group of painters, writers, and other creative people, such as playwright George Bernard Shaw, poet William Butler Yeats, and the American painter James McNeill Whistler. Even these people were dazzled by Wilde's wit and his flamboyant, colorful dress at a time when most men wore Victorian gray and black attire. In addition to his successful dramatic career, Wilde wrote poetry, fiction, and criticism.

Wilde's career took a disastrous turn when the father of a young poet accused Wilde of homosexuality—at the time a criminal offense. Wilde sued the man for libel but lost the case and was arrested and jailed for two years. During his years in jail, Wilde lost his wife and children in a divorce as well as most of what money he had. Upon his release, he left England for France, where he lived under an assumed name, dependent on the charity of friends. After three miserable years, he died and was buried in Le Père Lachaise, the Parisian cemetery where so many famous people, from Frédéric Chopin to Jim Morrison, are interred.

Wilde is poking fun at the Victorian Age in this play, making one of its most important values—moral "earnestness"—a pun on a man's name. He also sends up a lot of theatrical clichés, such as confused identities, lost children, and last-minute "discoveries." Wilde was a brilliant conversationalist, who could come up with witty remarks at, as they say, a drop of the hat, and his dialogue in this play sparkles with clever *repartee*. But Wilde was also a shrewd dramatist who knew how to use the stage and props for visual comedy. The tea party scene between Gwendolyn and Cecily is one of the great comic moments in theater. Thinking as a playwright, try to see how Wilde crafted this scene, particularly in his use of props.

Chapter 9
Nineteenth-Century American Creative Nonfiction

Frederick Douglass (1818–1895)

Frederick Douglass was born Frederick Bailey, the son of a black slave and a white man. As a boy, he was raised on a Maryland plantation and was then sent to Baltimore, where the lady of the house was kind to him and began to teach him how to read. Her husband stopped the lessons, however, saying, "Learning would spoil the best nigger in the world."

That taste of reading fired Douglass' spirit, and he secretly continued to teach himself to read even though he was sent back to the plantation. There he worked in the fields under a harsh foreman who liked to beat young slaves to break their spirit. However, Douglass was able to read newspapers, in which he learned about abolitionists, northerners who risked their lives to help slaves escape.

After enduring many floggings from the plantation foreman, one day Douglass, who had grown to be large and powerful, stood up to the foreman, who backed down. With that victory, Douglass, at twenty-one, planed his escape to the North. With the help of abolitionists, he found work, married, and became a popular lecturer on antislavery and other causes.

In 1845, he published *Narrative of the Life of Frederick Douglass, an American Slave, Written by Himself*. The book was a commercial and critical success, though Douglass had to conceal much information, such as how he had escaped, in order to protect people who had helped him. He also feared that the publication would lead to his recapture as a "fugitive slave," so he left America for England where he became an acclaimed lecturer. British friends raised the $700 he needed to officially "buy" his freedom from his old master. When he moved back to the United States, Douglass started a weekly newspaper in which he supported not only the antislavery movement but other causes, such as women's rights. On the masthead of his newspaper was the slogan "Right is of no sex—Truth is of no color."

One of the most powerful features of Douglass' autobiography is its *tone*—the emotional way he tells his story, as if we could hear his own voice talking to us. How would you describe his tone of voice? Is Douglass passionate, angry, or bitter as he recounts his life as a slave? Or is he calm, dispassionate, even clinical? Which emotional tone better enhances the story he tells?

from *Narrative of the Life of Frederick Douglass*

Chapter I

I was born in Tuckahoe, near Hillsborough, and about twelve miles from Easton, in Talbot County, Maryland. I have no accurate knowledge of my age, never having seen any authentic record containing it. By far the larger part of the slaves know as little of their ages as horses know of theirs, and it is the wish of most masters within my knowledge to keep their slaves thus ignorant. I do not remember to have ever met a slave who could tell of his birthday. They seldom come nearer to it than planting-time, harvest-time, cherry-time, spring-time, or fall-time. A want of information concerning my own was a source of unhappiness to me even during childhood. The white children could tell their ages. I could not tell why I ought to be deprived of the same privilege. I was not allowed to make any inquiries of my master concerning it. He deemed all such inquiries on the part of a slave improper and impertinent, and evidence of a restless spirit. The nearest estimate I can give makes me now between twenty-seven and twenty-eight years of age. I come to this, from hearing my master say, some time during 1835, I was about seventeen years old.

My mother was named Harriet Bailey. She was the daughter of Isaac and Betsey Bailey, both colored, and quite dark. My mother was of a darker complexion than either my grandmother or grand-father.

My father was a white man. He was admitted to be such by all I ever heard speak of my parentage.

The opinion was also whispered that my master was my father; but of the correctness of this opinion, I know nothing; the means of knowing was withheld from me. My mother and I were separated when I was but an infant -- before I knew her as my mother. It is a common custom, in the part of Maryland from which I ran away, to part children from their mothers at a very early age. Frequently, before the child has reached its twelfth month, its mother is taken from it, and hired out on some farm a considerable distance off, and the child is placed under the care of an old woman, too old for field labor. For what this separation is done, I do not know, unless it be to hinder the development of the child's affection toward its mother, and to blunt and destroy the natural affection of the mother for the child. This is the inevitable result.

I never saw my mother, to know her as such, more than four or five times in my life; and each of these times was very short in duration, and at night. She was hired by a Mr. Stewart, who lived about twelve miles from my home. She made her journeys to see me in the night, travelling the whole distance on foot, after the performance of her day's work. She was a field hand, and a whipping is the penalty of not being in the field at sunrise, unless a slave has special permission from his or her master to the contrary -- a permission which they seldom get, and one that gives to him that gives it the proud name of being a kind master. I do not recollect of ever seeing my mother by the light of day. She was with me in the night. She would lie down with me, and get me to sleep, but long before I waked she was gone. Very little communication ever took place between us. Death soon ended what little we could have while she lived, and with it her hardships and suffering. She died when I was about seven years old, on one of my master's farms, near Lee's Mill. I was not allowed to be present during her illness, at her death, or burial. She was gone long before I knew anything about it. Never having enjoyed, to any considerable extent, her soothing presence, her tender and watchful care, I received the tidings of her death with much the same emotions I should have probably felt at the death of a stranger.

Called thus suddenly away, she left me without the slightest intimation of who my father was. The whisper that my master was my father, may or may not be true; and, true or false, it is of but little consequence to my purpose whilst the fact remains, in all its glaring odiousness, that slaveholders have ordained, and by law established, that the children of slave women shall in all cases follow the condition of their mothers; and this is done too obviously to administer to their own lusts, and make a gratification of their wicked desires profitable as well as pleasurable; for by this cunning arrangement, the slaveholder, in cases not a few, sustains to his slaves the double relation of master and father.

I know of such cases; and it is worthy of remark that such slaves invariably suffer greater hardships, and have more to contend with, than others. They are, in the first place, a constant offence to their mistress. She is ever disposed to find fault with them; they can seldom do any thing to please her; she is never better pleased than when she sees them under the lash, especially when she suspects her husband of showing to his mulatto children favors which he withholds from his black slaves. The master is frequently compelled to sell this class of his slaves, out of deference to the feelings of his white wife; and, cruel as the deed may strike any one to be, for a man to sell his own children to human flesh-mongers, it is often the dictate of humanity for him to do so; for, unless he does this, he must not only whip them himself, but must stand by and see one white son tie up his brother, of but few shades darker complexion than himself, and ply the gory lash to his naked back; and if he lisp one word of disapproval, it is set down to his parental partiality, and only makes a bad matter worse, both for himself and the slave whom he would protect and defend.

Every year brings with it multitudes of this class of slaves. It was doubtless in consequence of a knowledge of this fact, that one great statesman of the south predicted the downfall of slavery by the inevitable laws of population. Whether this prophecy is ever fulfilled or not, it is nevertheless plain that a very different-looking class of people are springing up at the south, and are now held in slavery, from those originally brought to this country from Africa; and if their increase do no other good, it will do away the force of the argument, that God cursed Ham, and therefore American slavery is right. If the lineal descendants of Ham are alone to be scripturally enslaved, it is certain that slavery at the south must soon become unscriptural; for thousands are ushered into the world, annually, who, like myself, owe their existence to white fathers, and those fathers most frequently their own masters.

I have had two masters. My first master's name was Anthony. I do not remember his first name. He was generally called Captain Anthony--a title which, I presume, he acquired by sailing a craft on the Chesapeake Bay. He was not considered a rich slaveholder. He owned two or three farms, and about thirty slaves. His farms and slaves were under the care of an overseer. The overseer's name was Plummer. Mr. Plummer was a miserable drunkard, a profane swearer, and a savage monster. He always went armed with a cowskin and a heavy cudgel. I have known him to cut and slash the women's heads so horribly, that even master would be enraged at his cruelty, and would threaten to whip him if he did not mind himself. Master, however, was not a humane slaveholder. It required extraordinary barbarity on the part of an overseer to affect him. He was a cruel man, hardened by a long life of slaveholding. He would at times seem to take great pleasure in whipping a slave. I have often been awakened at the dawn of day by the most heart-rending shrieks of an own aunt of mine, whom he used to tie up to a joist, and whip upon her naked back till she was literally covered with blood. No words, no tears, no prayers, from his gory victim, seemed to move his iron heart from its bloody purpose. The louder she screamed, the harder he whipped; and where the blood ran fastest, there he whipped longest. He would whip her to make her scream, and whip her to make her hush; and not until overcome by fatigue, would he cease to swing the blood-clotted cowskin. I remember the first time I ever witnessed this horrible exhibition. I was quite a child, but I well remember it. I never shall forget it whilst I remember anything. It was the first of a long series of such outrages, of which I was doomed to be a witness and a participant. It struck me with awful force. It was the blood-stained gate, the entrance to the hell of slavery, through which I was about to pass. It was a most terrible spectacle. I wish I could commit to paper the feelings with which I beheld it.

This occurrence took place very soon after I went to live with my old master, and under the following circumstances. Aunt Hester went out one night--where or for what I do not know--and happened to be absent when my master desired her presence. He had ordered her not to go out evenings, and warned her that she must never let him catch her in company with a young man, who was paying attention to her belonging to Colonel Lloyd. The young man's name was Ned Roberts, generally called Lloyd's Ned. Why master was so careful of her, may be safely left to conjecture. She was a woman of noble form, and of graceful proportions, having very few equals, and fewer superiors, in personal appearance, among the colored or white women of our neighborhood.

Aunt Hester had not only disobeyed his orders in going out, but had been found in company with Lloyd's Ned; which circumstance, I found, from what he said while whipping her, was the chief offence. Had he been a man of pure morals himself, he might have been thought interested in protecting the innocence of my aunt; but those who knew him will not suspect him of any such virtue. Before he commenced whipping Aunt Hester, he took her into the kitchen, and stripped her from neck to waist, leaving her neck, shoulders, and back, entirely naked. He then told her to cross her hands, calling her at the same time a d -- -d b -- -h. After crossing her hands, he tied them with a strong rope, and led her to a stool under a large hook in the joist, put in for the purpose. He made her get upon the stool, and tied her hands to the hook. She now stood fair for his infernal purpose. Her arms were stretched up at their full length, so that she stood upon the ends of her toes. He then said to her, "Now, you d -- -d b -- -h, I'll learn you how to disobey my orders!" and after rolling up his sleeves, he commenced to lay on the heavy cowskin, and soon the warm, red blood (amid heart-rending shrieks from her, and horrid oaths from him) came dripping to the floor. I was so terrified and horror-stricken at the sight, that I hid myself in a closet, and dared not venture out till long after the bloody transaction was over. I expected it would be my turn next. It was all new to me. I had never seen anything like it before. I had always lived with my grandmother on the outskirts of the plantation, where she was put to raise the children of the younger women. I had therefore been, until now, out of the way of the bloody scenes that often occurred on the plantation.

Chapter XI

I now come to that part of my life during which I planned, and finally succeeded in making, my escape from slavery. But before narrating any of the peculiar circumstances, I deem it proper to make known my intention not to state all the facts connected with the transaction. My reasons for pursuing this course may be understood from the following: First, were I to give a minute statement of all the facts, it is not only possible, but quite probable, that others would thereby be involved in the most embarrassing difficulties. Secondly, such a statement would most undoubtedly induce greater vigilance on the part of slaveholders than has existed heretofore among them; which would, of course, be the means of guarding a door whereby some dear brother bond- man might escape his galling chains. I deeply regret the necessity that impels me to suppress anything of importance connected with my experience in slavery. It would afford me great pleasure indeed, as well as materially add to the interest of my narrative, were I at liberty to gratify a curiosity, which I know exists in the minds of many, by an accurate statement of all the facts pertaining to my most fortunate escape. But I must deprive myself of this pleasure, and the curious of the gratification which such a statement would afford. I would allow myself to suffer under the greatest imputations which evil-minded men might suggest, rather than exculpate myself, and thereby run the hazard of closing the slightest avenue by which a brother slave might clear himself of the chains and fetters of slavery.

I have never approved of the very public manner in which some of our western friends have conducted what they call the "Underground Railroad," but which I think, by their open declarations, has been made most emphatically the "Upper Ground Railroad." I honor those good men and women for their noble daring, and applaud them for willingly subjecting them- selves to bloody persecution, by openly avowing their participation in the escape of slaves. I, however, can see very little good resulting from such a course, either to themselves or the slaves escaping; while, upon the other hand, I see and feel assured that those open declarations are a positive evil to the slaves remaining, who are seeking to escape. They do nothing towards enlightening the slave, whilst they do much towards enlightening the master. They stimulate him to greater watchfulness, and enhance his power to capture his slave. We owe something to the slave south of the line as well as to those north of it; and in aiding the latter on their way to freedom, we should be careful to do nothing which would be likely to hinder the former from escaping from slavery. I would keep the merciless slaveholder profoundly ignorant of the means of flight adopted by the slave. I would leave him to imagine himself surrounded by myriads of invisible tormentors, ever ready to snatch from his infernal grasp his trembling prey. Let him be left to feel his way in the dark; let darkness commensurate with his crime hover over him; and let him feel that at every step he takes, in pursuit of the flying bondman, he is running the frightful risk of having his hot brains dashed out by an invisible agency. Let us render the tyrant no aid; let us not hold the light by which he can trace the footprints of our flying brother. But enough of this. I will now proceed to the statement of those facts, connected with my escape, for which I am alone responsible, and for which no one can be made to suffer but myself.

In the early part of the year 1838, I became quite restless. I could see no reason why I should, at the end of each week, pour the reward of my toil into the purse of my master. When I carried to him my weekly wages, he would, after counting the money, look me in the face with a robber-like fierceness, and ask, "Is this all?" He was satisfied with nothing less than the last cent. He would, however, when I made him six dollars, sometimes give me six cents, to encourage me. It had the opposite effect. I regarded it as a sort of admission of my right to the whole. The fact that he gave me any part of my wages was proof, to my mind, that he believed me entitled to the whole of them. I always felt worse for having received any thing; for I feared that the giving me a few cents would ease his conscience, and make him feel himself to be a pretty honorable sort of robber. My discontent grew upon me. I was ever on the look-out for means of escape; and, finding no direct means, I determined to try to hire my time, with a view of getting money with which to make my escape. In the spring of 1838, when Master Thomas came to Baltimore to purchase his spring goods, I got an opportunity, and applied to him to allow me to hire my time. He unhesitatingly refused my request, and told me this was another stratagem by which to escape. He told me I could go nowhere but that he could get me; and that, in the event of my running away, he should spare no pains in his efforts to catch me. He exhorted me to content myself, and be obedient. He told me, if I would be happy, I must lay out no plans for the future. He said, if I behaved myself properly, he would take care of me. Indeed, he advised me to complete thoughtlessness of the future, and taught me to depend solely upon him for happiness. He seemed to see fully the pressing necessity of setting aside my intellectual nature, in order to contentment in slavery. But in spite of him, and even in spite of myself, I continued to think, and to think about the injustice of my enslavement, and the means of escape.

    Things went on without very smoothly indeed, but within there was trouble. It is impossible for me to describe my feelings as the time of my contemplated start drew near. I had a number of warm-hearted friends in Baltimore, --friends that I loved almost as I did my life--and the thought of being separated from them forever was painful beyond expression. It is my opinion that thousands would escape from slavery, who now remain, but for the strong cords of affection that bind them to their friends. The thought of leaving my friends was decidedly the most painful thought with which I had to contend. The love of them was my tender point, and shook my decision more than all things else. Besides the pain of separation, the dread and apprehension of a failure exceeded what I had experienced at my first attempt. The appalling defeat I then sustained returned to torment me. I felt assured that, if I failed in this attempt, my case would be a hopeless one--it would seal my fate as a slave forever. I could not hope to get off with anything less than the severest punishment, and being placed beyond the means of escape. It required no very vivid imagination to depict the most frightful scenes through which I should have to pass, in case I failed. The wretchedness of slavery, and the blessedness of freedom, were perpetually before me. It was life and death with me. But I remained firm, and, according to my resolution, on the third day of September, 1838, I left my chains, and succeeded in reaching New York without the slightest interruption of any kind. How I did so,--what means I adopted--what direction I travelled, and by what mode of conveyance,--I must leave unexplained, for the reasons before mentioned.

I have been frequently asked how I felt when I found myself in a free State. I have never been able to answer the question with any satisfaction to my- self. It was a moment of the highest excitement I ever experienced. I suppose I felt as one may imagine the unarmed mariner to feel when he is rescued by a friendly man-of-war from the pursuit of a pirate. In writing to a dear friend, immediately after my arrival at New York, I said I felt like one who had escaped a den of hungry lions. This state of mind, however, very soon subsided; and I was again seized with a feeling of great insecurity and loneliness. I was yet liable to be taken back, and subjected to all the tortures of slavery. This in itself was enough to damp the ardor of my enthusiasm. But the loneliness overcame me. There I was in the midst of thousands, and yet a perfect stranger; without home and without friends, in the midst of thousands of my own brethren--children of a common Father, and yet I dared not to unfold to any one of them my sad condition. I was afraid to speak to any one for fear of speaking to the wrong one, and thereby falling into the hands of money-loving kidnappers, whose business it was to lie in wait for the panting fugitive, as the ferocious beasts of the forest lie in wait for their prey. The motto which I adopted when I started from slavery was this--"Trust no man!" I saw in every white man an enemy, and in almost every colored man cause for distrust. It was a most painful situation; and, to understand it, one must needs experience it, or imagine himself in similar circumstances. Let him be a fugitive slave in a strange land--a land given up to be the hunting-ground for slaveholder--whose inhabitants are legalized kidnappers--where he is every moment subjected to the terrible liability of being seized upon by his fellowmen, as the hideous crocodile seizes upon his prey!--I say, let him place himself in my situation--without home or friends--without money or credit--wanting shelter, and no one to give it--wanting bread, and no money to buy it,--and at the same time let him feel that he is pursued by merciless men-hunters, and in total darkness as to what to do, where to go, or where to stay,--perfectly help less both as to the means of defence and means of escape,--in the midst of plenty, yet suffering the terrible gnawings of hunger,--in the midst of houses, yet having no home,--among fellow-men, yet feeling as if in the midst of wild beasts, whose greediness to swallow up the trembling and half-famished fugitive is only equalled by that with which the monsters of the deep swallow up the helpless fish upon which they subsist,--I say, let him be placed in this most trying situation,--the situation in which I was placed,--then, and not till then, will he fully appreciate the hardships of, and know how to sympathize with, the toil-worn and whip-scarred fugitive slave.

Thank Heaven, I remained but a short time in this distressed situation. I was relieved from it by the humane hand of Mr. David Ruggles, whose vigilance, kindness, and perseverance, I shall never forget. I am glad of an opportunity to express, as far as words can, the love and gratitude I bear him. Mr. Ruggles is now afflicted with blindness, and is him- self in need of the same kind offices which he was once so forward in the performance of toward others. I had been in New York but a few days, when Mr. Ruggles sought me out, and very kindly took me to his boarding-house at the corner of Church and Lespenard Streets. Mr. Ruggles was then very deeply engaged in the memorable Darg case, as well as attending to a number of other fugitive slaves, devising ways and means for their successful escape; and, though watched and hemmed in on almost every side, he seemed to be more than a match for his enemies.

Very soon after I went to Mr. Ruggles, he wished to know of me where I wanted to go; as he deemed it unsafe for me to remain in New York. I told him I was a calker, and should like to go where I could get work. I thought of going to Canada; but he decided against it, and in favor of my going to New Bedford, thinking I should be able to get work there at my trade. At this time, Anna,* my intended wife, came on; for I wrote to her immediately after my arrival at New York, (notwithstanding my homeless, houseless, and helpless condition) informing her of my successful flight, and wishing her to come on forthwith. In a few days after her arrival, Mr. Ruggles called in the Rev. J. W. C. Pennington, who, in the presence of Mr. Ruggles, Mrs. Michaels, and two or three others, performed the marriage ceremony, and gave us a certificate, of which the following is an exact copy:

--

"This may certify, that I joined together in holy matrimony Frederick Johnson+ and Anna Murray, as man and wife, in the presence of Mr. David Ruggles and Mrs. Michaels. "James W. C. Pennington

"New York, Sept. 15, 1838"

[*NOTE: Anna was a free black woman. Douglass had formerly been named Frederick Bailey but changed his name to Frederick Johnson]

Upon receiving this certificate, and a five-dollar bill from Mr. Ruggles, I shouldered one part of our baggage, and Anna took up the other, and we set out forthwith to take passage on board of the steamboat John W. Richmond for Newport, on our way to New Bedford. Mr. Ruggles gave me a letter to a Mr. Shaw in Newport, and told me, in case my money did not serve me to New Bedford, to stop in Newport and obtain further assistance; but upon our arrival at Newport, we were so anxious to get to a place of safety, that, notwithstanding we lacked the necessary money to pay our fare, we decided to take seats in the stage, and promise to pay when we got to New Bedford. We were encouraged to do this by two excellent gentlemen, residents of New Bedford, whose names I afterward ascertained to be Joseph Ricketson and William C. Taber. They seemed at once to understand our circumstances, and gave us such assurance of their friendliness as put us fully at ease in their presence. It was good indeed to meet with such friends, at such a time. Upon reaching New Bedford, we were directed to the house of Mr. Nathan Johnson, by whom we were kindly received, and hospitably provided for. Both Mr. and Mrs. Johnson took a deep and lively interest in our welfare. They proved themselves quite worthy of the name of abolitionists. When the stage-driver found us unable to pay our fare, he held on upon our bag- gage as security for the debt. I had but to mention the fact to Mr. Johnson, and he forthwith advanced the money.

We now began to feel a degree of safety, and to prepare ourselves for the duties and responsibilities of a life of freedom. On the morning after our arrival at New Bedford, while at the breakfast-table, the question arose as to what name I should be called by. The name given me by my mother was, "Frederick Augustus Washington Bailey." I, however, had dispensed with the two middle names long before I left Maryland so that I was generally known by the name of "Frederick Bailey." I started from Baltimore bearing the name of "Stanley." When I got to New York, I again changed my name to "Frederick Johnson," and thought that would be the last change. But when I got to New Bedford, I found it necessary again to change my name. The reason of this necessity was, that there were so many Johnsons in New Bedford, it was already quite difficult to distinguish between them. I gave Mr. Johnson the privilege of choosing me a name, but told him he must not take from me the name of "Frederick." I must hold on to that, to preserve a sense of my identity. Mr. Johnson had just been reading the "Lady of the Lake," and at once suggested that my name be "Douglass." From that time until now I have been called "Frederick Douglass;" and as I am more widely known by that name than by either of the others, I shall continue to use it as my own.

I was quite disappointed at the general appearance of things in New Bedford. The impression which I had received respecting the character and condition of the people of the north, I found to be singularly erroneous. I had very strangely supposed, while in slavery, that few of the comforts, and scarcely any of the luxuries, of life were enjoyed at the north, compared with what were enjoyed by the slaveholders of the south. I probably came to this conclusion from the fact that northern people owned no slaves. I supposed that they were about upon a level with the non-slaveholding population of the south. I knew they were exceedingly poor, and I had been accustomed to regard their poverty as the necessary consequence of their being non-slaveholders. I had somehow imbibed the opinion that, in the absence of slaves, there could be no wealth, and very little refinement. And upon coming to the north, I expected to meet with a rough, hard-handed, and uncultivated population, living in the most Spartan-like simplicity, knowing nothing of the ease, luxury, pomp, and grandeur of southern slaveholders. Such being my conjectures, any one acquainted with the appearance of New Bedford may very readily infer how palpably I must have seen my mistake.

In the afternoon of the day when I reached New Bedford, I visited the wharves, to take a view of the shipping. Here I found myself surrounded with the strongest proofs of wealth. Lying at the wharves, and riding in the stream, I saw many ships of the finest model, in the best order, and of the largest size. Upon the right and left, I was walled in by granite warehouses of the widest dimensions, stowed to their utmost capacity with the necessaries and comforts of life. Added to this, almost everybody seemed to be at work, but noiselessly so, compared with what I had been accustomed to in Baltimore. There were no loud songs heard from those engaged in loading and unloading ships. I heard no deep oaths or horrid curses on the laborer. I saw no whipping of men; but all seemed to go smoothly on. Every man appeared to understand his work, and went at it with a sober, yet cheerful earnestness, which betokened the deep interest which he felt in what he was doing, as well as a sense of his own dignity as a man. To me this looked exceedingly strange. From the wharves I strolled around and over the town, gazing with wonder and admiration at the splendid churches, beautiful dwellings, and finely-cultivated gardens; evincing an amount of wealth, comfort, taste, and refinement, such as I had never seen in any part of slaveholding Maryland.

Everything looked clean, new, and beautiful. I saw few or no dilapidated houses, with poverty- stricken inmates; no half-naked children and bare-footed women, such as I had been accustomed to see in Hillsborough, Easton, St. Michael's, and Baltimore. The people looked more able, stronger, healthier, and happier, than those of Maryland. I was for once made glad by a view of extreme wealth, without being saddened by seeing extreme poverty. But the most astonishing as well as the most interesting thing to me was the condition of the colored people, a great many of whom, like myself, had escaped thither as a refuge from the hunters of men. I found many, who had not been seven years out of their chains, living in finer houses, and evidently enjoying more of the comforts of life, than the average of slaveholders in Maryland. I will venture to assert, that my friend Mr. Nathan Johnson (of whom I can say with a grateful heart, "I was hungry, and he gave me meat; I was thirsty, and he gave me drink; I was a stranger, and he took me in") lived in a neater house; dined at a better table; took, paid for, and read, more newspapers; better understood the moral, religious, and political character of the nation,--than nine tenths of the slaveholders in Talbot county Maryland. Yet Mr. Johnson was a working man. His hands were hardened by toil, and not his alone, but those also of Mrs. Johnson. I found the colored people much more spirited than I had supposed they would be. I found among them a determination to protect each other from the blood-thirsty kidnapper, at all hazards. Soon after my arrival, I was told of a circumstance which illustrated their spirit. A colored man and a fugitive slave were on unfriendly terms. The former was heard to threaten the latter with informing his master of his whereabouts. Straightway a meeting was called among the colored people, under the stereotyped notice, "Business of importance!" The betrayer was invited to attend. The people came at the appointed hour, and organized the meeting by appointing a very religious old gentleman as president, who, I believe, made a prayer, after which he addressed the meeting as follows: "Friends, we have got him here, and I would recommend that you young men just take him outside the door and kill him!" With this, a number of them bolted at him; but they were intercepted by some more timid than themselves, and the betrayer escaped their vengeance, and has not been seen in New Bedford since. I believe there have been no more such threats, and should there be hereafter, I doubt not that death would be the consequence.

 I found employment, the third day after my arrival, in stowing a sloop with a load of oil. It was new, dirty, and hard work for me; but I went at it with a glad heart and a willing hand. I was now my own master. It was a happy moment, the rapture of which can be understood only by those who have been slaves. It was the first work, the reward of which was to be entirely my own. There was no Master Hugh standing ready, the moment I earned the money, to rob me of it. I worked that day with a pleasure I had never before experienced. I was at work for myself and newly-married wife. It was to me the starting-point of a new existence. When I got through with that job, I went in pursuit of a job of calking; but such was the strength of prejudice against color, among the white calkers, that they re- fused to work with me, and of course I could get no employment. Finding my trade of no immediate benefit, I threw off my calking habiliments, and pre- pared myself to do any kind of work I could get to do. Mr. Johnson kindly let me have his wood-horse and saw, and I very soon found myself a plenty of work. There was no work too hard--none too dirty. I was ready to saw wood, shovel coal, carry wood, sweep the chimney, or roll oil casks,--all of which I did for nearly three years in New Bedford, before I became known to the anti-slavery world.   1845

Mark Twain (1835-1910)

In addition to writing fiction, Mark Twain also wrote creative nonfiction. One evening, over dinner with a friend, Twain reminisced about his boyhood in Hannibal, Missouri during the days of the steamboat. He also recounted his experience learning how to become a steamboat pilot under the stern, demanding mentorship of Horace Bixby, one of the finest steamboat pilots on the Mississippi River. The friend was charmed by Twain's account of his adolescence, the demands of piloting a steamboat, and, most of all, Twain's poetic evocation of the great Mississippi River.

 At the friend's urging, Twain wrote to William Dean Howells, then editor of the *Atlantic Monthly*, to see if Howells would be interested in publishing a memoir about his experiences. Howells was enthusiastic, and Twain set down his memories in "Old Times on the Mississippi," which ran in the *Atlantic* in seven installments, excerpts of which are reprinted below. Occasionally, Twain uses what may now seem like technical terms but were familiar to most people of his time. In the second paragraph, for example, he refers to the ornate wooden carvings of the pilot house atop the "Texas deck"—the deck over the officer's quarters that was called the Texas deck because it was the largest on the ship.

from *Old Times on the Mississippi*

I. "Cub" Wants to Be a Pilot

When I was a boy, there was but one permanent ambition among my comrades in our village on the west bank of the Mississippi River. That was, to be a steamboatman. We had transient ambitions of other sorts, but they were only transient. When a circus came and went, it left us all burning to become clowns; the first negro minstrel show that came to our section left us all suffering to try that kind of life; now and then we had a hope that if we lived and were good, God would permit us to be pirates. These ambitions faded out, each in its turn; but the ambition to be a steamboatman always remained.

Once a day a cheap, gaudy packet arrived upward from St. Louis, and another downward from Keokuk. Before these events had transpired, the day was glorious with expectancy; after they had transpired, the day was a dead and empty thing. Not only the boys, but the whole village, felt this. After all these years I can picture that old time to myself now, just as it was then: the white town drowsing in the sunshine of a summer's morning; the streets empty, or pretty nearly so; one or two clerks in front of the Water Street stores, with their splint-bottomed chairs tilted back against the wall, chins on breasts, hats slouched over their faces, asleep--with shingle-shavings enough around to show what broke them down; a sow and a litter of pigs loafing along the sidewalk, doing a good business in water-melon rinds and seeds; two or three lonely little freight piles scattered about the "levee;" a pile of "skids" on the slope of the stone-paved wharf, and the fragrant town drunkard asleep in the shadow of them; two or three wood flats at the head of the wharf, but nobody to listen to the peaceful lapping of the wavelets against them; the great Mississippi, the majestic, the magnificent Mississippi, rolling its mile-wide tide along, shining in the sun; the dense forest away on the other side; the "point" above the town, and the "point" below, bounding the river-glimpse and turning it into a sort of sea, and withal a very still and brilliant and lonely one. Presently a film of dark smoke appears above one of those remote "points;" instantly a negro drayman, famous for his quick eye and prodigious voice, lifts up the cry, "S-t-e-a-m-boat a-comin'!" and the scene changes! The town drunkard stirs, the clerks wake up, a furious clatter of drays follows, every house and store pours out a human contribution, and all in a twinkling the dead town is alive and moving. Drays, carts, men, boys, all go hurrying from many quarters to a common centre, the wharf. Assembled there, the people fasten their eyes upon the coming boat as upon a wonder they are seeing for the first time. And the boat is rather a handsome sight, too. She is long and sharp and trim and pretty; she has two tall, fancy-topped chimneys, with a gilded device of some kind swung between them; a fanciful pilot-house, all glass and "gingerbread," perched on top of the "texas" deck behind them; the paddle-boxes are gorgeous with a picture or with gilded rays above the boat's name; the boiler deck, the hurricane deck, and the texas deck are fenced and ornamented with clean white railings; there is a flag gallantly flying from the jack-staff; the furnace doors are open and the fires flaring bravely; the upper decks are black with passengers; the captain stands by the big bell, calm, imposing, the envy of all; great volumes of the blackest smoke are rolling and tumbling out of the chimneys--a husbanded grandeur created with a bit of pitch pine just before arriving at a town; the crew are grouped on the forecastle; the broad stage is run far out over the port bow, and an envied deck-hand stands picturesquely on the end of it with a coil of rope in his hand; the pent steam is screaming through the gauge-cocks; the captain lifts his hand, a bell rings, the wheels stop; then they turn back, churning the water to foam, and the steamer is at rest. Then such a scramble as there is to get aboard, and to get ashore, and to take in freight and to discharge freight, all at one and the same time; and such a yelling and cursing as the mates facilitate it all with! Ten minutes later the steamer is under way again, with no flag on the jack-staff and no black smoke issuing from the chimneys. After ten more minutes the town is dead again, and the town drunkard asleep by the skids once more.

    My father was a justice of the peace, and I supposed he possessed the power of life and death over all men and could hang anybody that offended him. This was distinction enough for me as a general thing; but the desire to be a steamboatman kept intruding, nevertheless. I first wanted to be a cabin-boy, so that I could come out with a white apron on and shake a table-cloth over the side, where all my old comrades could see me; later I thought I would rather be the deck-hand who stood on the end of the stage-plank with the coil of rope in his hand, because he was particularly conspicuous. But these were only day-dreams-- they were too heavenly to be contemplated as real possibilities. By and by one of our boys went away. He was not heard of for a long time. At last he turned up as apprentice engineer or "striker" on a steamboat. This thing shook the bottom out of all my Sunday-school teachings. That boy had been notoriously worldly, and I just the reverse, yet he was exalted to this eminence, and I left in obscurity and misery. There was nothing generous about this fellow in his greatness. He would always manage to have a rusty bolt to scrub while his boat tarried at our town, and he would sit on the inside guard and scrub it, where we could all see him and envy him and loathe him. And whenever his boat was laid up he would come home and swell around the town in his blackest and greasiest clothes, so that nobody could help remembering that he was a steamboatman; and he used all sorts of steamboat technicalities in his talk, as if he were so used to them that he forgot common people could not understand them. He would speak of the "labboard" side of a horse in an easy, natural way that would make one wish he was dead. And he was always talking about "St. Looy" like an old citizen, he would refer casually to occasions when he "was coming down Fourth Street," or when he was "passing by the Planter's House," or when there was a fire and he took a turn on the brakes of "the old Big Missouri;" and then he would go on and lie about how many towns the size of ours were burned down there that day. Two or three of the boys had long been persons of consideration among us because they had been to St. Louis once and had a vague general knowledge of its wonders, but the day of their glory was over now. They lapsed into a humble silence, and learned to disappear when the ruthless "cub"-engineer approached. This fellow had money, too, and hair oil. Also an ignorant silver watch and a showy brass watch chain. He wore a leather belt and used no suspenders. If ever a youth was cordially admired and hated by his comrades, this one was. No girl could withstand his charms. He "cut out" every boy in the village. When his boat blew up at last, it diffused a tranquil contentment among us such as we had not known for months. But when he came home the next week, alive, renowned, and appeared in church all battered up and bandaged, a shining hero, stared at and wondered over by everybody, it seemed to us that the partiality of Providence for an undeserving reptile had reached a point where it was open to criticism.

This creature's career could produce but one result, and it speedily followed, Boy after boy managed to get on the river. The minister's son became an engineer. The doctor's and the postmaster's sons became "mud clerks;" the wholesale liquor dealer's son became a bar-keeper on a boat; four sons of the chief merchant, and two sons of the county judge, became pilots. Pilot was the grandest position of all. The pilot, even in those days of trivial wages, had a princely salary--from a hundred and fifty to two hundred and fifty dollars a month, and no board to pay. Two months of his wages would pay a preacher's salary for a year. Now some of us were left disconsolate. We could not get on the river--at least our parents would not let us.

So by and by I ran away. I said I never would come home again till I was a pilot and could come in glory. But somehow I could not manage it. I went meekly aboard a few of the boats that lay packed together like sardines at the long St. Louis wharf, and very humbly inquired for the pilots, but got only a cold shoulder and short words from mates and clerks. I had to make the best of this sort of treatment for the time being, but I had comforting day-dreams of a future when I should be a great and honored pilot, with plenty of money, and could kill some of these mates and clerks and pay for them.

Months afterward the hope within me struggled to a reluctant death, and I found myself without an ambition. But I was ashamed to go home. I was in

Cincinnati, and I set to work to map out a new career. I had been reading about the recent exploration of the river Amazon by an expedition sent out by our government. It was said that the expedition, owing to difficulties, had not thoroughly explored a part of the country lying about the head-waters, some four thousand miles from the mouth of the river. It was only about fifteen hundred miles from Cincinnati to New Orleans, where I could doubtless get a ship. I had thirty dollars left; I would go and complete the exploration of the Amazon. This was all the thought I gave to the subject. I never was great in matters of detail. I packed my valise, and took passage on an ancient tub called the Paul Jones, for New Orleans. For the sum of sixteen dollars I had the scarred and tarnished splendors of "her" main saloon principally to myself, for she was not a creature to attract the eye of wiser travelers.

When we presently got under way and went poking down the broad Ohio, I became a new being, and the subject of my own admiration. I was a traveler! A word never had tasted so good in my mouth before. I had all exultant sense of being bound for mysterious lands and distant climes which I never have felt in so uplifting a degree since. I was in such a glorified condition that all ignoble feelings departed out of me, and I was able to look down and pity the untraveled with a compassion that had hardly a trace of contempt in it. Still, when we stopped at villages and wood-yards, I could not help lolling carelessly upon the railings of the boiler duck to enjoy the envy of the country boys on the bank. If they did not seem to discover me, I presently sneezed to attract their attention, or moved to a position where they could not help seeing me. And as soon as I knew they saw me I gaped and stretched, and gave other signs of being mightily bored with traveling.

I kept my hat off all the time, and stayed where the wind and the sun could strike me, because I wanted to get the bronzed and weather-beaten look of an old traveler. Before the second day was half gone, I experienced a joy which filled me with the purest gratitude; for I saw that the skin had begun to blister and peel off my face and neck. I wished that the boys and girls at home could see me now.

We reached Louisville in time--at least the neighborhood of it. We stuck hard and fast on the rocks in the middle of the river and lay there four days. I was now beginning to feel a strong sense of being a part of the boat's family, a sort of infant son to the captain and younger brother to the officers. There is no estimating the pride I took in this grandeur, or the affection that began to swell and grow in me for those people. I could not know how the lordly steamboatman scorns that sort of presumption in a mere landsman. I particularly longed to acquire the least trifle of notice from the big stormy mate, and I was on the alert for an opportunity to do him a service to that end. It came at last. The riotous powwow of setting a spar was going on down on the forecastle, and I went down there and stood around in the way--or mostly skipping out of it-- till the mate suddenly roared a general order for somebody to bring him a capstan bar. I sprang to his side and said: "Tell me where it is--I'll fetch it!"

If a rag-picker had offered to do a diplomatic service for the Emperor of Russia, the monarch could not have been more astounded than the mate was. He even stopped swearing. He stood and stared down at me. It took him ten seconds to scrape his disjointed remains together again. Then he said impressively: "Well, if this don't beat hell!" and turned to his work with the air of a man who had been confronted with a problem too abstruse for solution.

I crept away, and courted solitude for the rest of the day. I did not go to dinner; I stayed away from supper until everybody else had finished. I did not feel so much like a member of the boat's family now as before. However, my spirits returned, in installments, as we pursued our way down the river. I was sorry I hated the mate so, because it was not in (young) human nature not to admire him. He was huge and muscular, his face was bearded and whiskered all over; he had a red woman and a blue woman tattooed on his right arm--one on each side of a blue anchor with a red rope to it; and in the matter of profanity he was perfect. When he was getting out cargo at a landing, I was always where I could see and hear. He felt all the sublimity of his great position, and made the world feel it, too. When he gave even the simplest order, he discharged it like a blast of lightning, and sent a long, reverberating peal of profanity thundering after it. I could not help contrasting the way in which the average landsman would give an order, with the mate's way of doing it. If the landsman should wish the gang-plank moved a foot farther forward, he would probably say: "James, or William, one of you push that plank forward, please;" but put the mate in his place, and he would roar out: "Here, now, start that gang-plank for'ard! Lively, now! What're you about! Snatch it! snatch it! There! there! Aft again! aft again! Don't you hear me? Dash it to dash! are you going to sleep over it! 'Vast heaving. 'Vast heaving, I tell you! Going to heave it clear astern? Where're you going with that barrel! for'ard with it 'fore I make you swallow it, you dash-dash-dash-dashed split between a tired mud-turtle and a crippled hearse-horse!"

I wished I could talk like that.

When the soreness of my adventure with the mate had somewhat worn off, I began timidly to make up to the humblest official connected with the boat-- the night watchman. He snubbed my advances at first, but I presently ventured to offer him a new chalk pipe, and that softened him. So he allowed me to sit with him by the big bell on the hurricane deck, and in time he melted into conversation. He could not well have helped it, I hung with such homage on his words and so plainly showed that I felt honored by his notice. He told me the names of dim capes and shadowy islands as we glided by them in the solemnity of the night, under the winking stars, and by and by got to talking about himself.

He seemed over-sentimental for a man whose salary was six dollars a week--or rather he might have seemed so to an older person than I. But I drank in his words hungrily, and with a faith that might have moved mountains if it had been applied judiciously. What was it to me that he was soiled and seedy and fragrant with gin? What was it to me that his grammar was bad, his construction worse, and his profanity so void of art that it was an element of weakness rather than strength in his conversation? He was a wronged man, a man who had seen trouble, and that was enough for me. As he mellowed into his plaintive history his tears dripped upon the lantern in his lap, and I cried, too, from sympathy. He said he was the son of an English nobleman--either an earl or an alderman, he could not remember which, but believed he was both; his father, the nobleman, loved him, but his mother hated him from the cradle; and so while he was still a little boy he was sent to "one of them old, ancient colleges"-- he couldn't remember which; and by and by his father died and his mother seized the property and "shook" him, as he phrased it. After his mother shook him, members of the nobility with whom he was acquainted used their influence to get him the position of "loblolly-boy in a ship;" and from that point my watchman threw off all trammels of date and locality and branched out into a narrative that bristled all along with incredible adventures; a narrative that was so reeking with bloodshed and so crammed with hair-breadth escapes and the most engaging and unconscious personal villainies, that I sat speechless, enjoying, shuddering, wondering, worshiping.

It was a sore blight to find out afterwards that he was a low, vulgar, ignorant, sentimental, half-witted humbug, an untraveled native of the wilds of Illinois, who had absorbed wildcat literature and appropriated its marvels, until in time he had woven odds and ends of the mess into this yarn, and then gone on, telling it to fledgelings like me, until he had come to believe it himself.

II.A "Cub" Pilot's Experience; or, Learning the River.

What with lying on the rocks four days at Louisville, and some other delays, the poor old Paul Jones fooled away about two weeks in making the voyage from Cincinnati to New Orleans. This gave me a chance to get acquainted with one of the pilots, and he taught me how to steer the boat, and thus made the fascination of river life more potent than ever for me.

It also gave me a chance to get acquainted with a youth who had taken deck passage--more 's the pity; for he easily borrowed six dollars of me on a promise to return to the boat and pay it back to me the day after we should arrive. But he probably died or forgot, for he never came. It was doubtless the former, since he had said his parents were wealthy, and he only traveled deck passage because it was cooler.

I soon discovered two things. One was that a vessel would not be likely to sail for the mouth of the Amazon under ten or twelve years; and the other was that the nine or ten dollars still left in my pocket would not suffice for so imposing an exploration as I had planned, even if I could afford to wait for a ship. Therefore it followed that I must contrive a new career. The Paul Jones was now bound for St. Louis. I planned a siege against my pilot, and at the end of three hard days he surrendered. He agreed to teach me the Mississippi River from New Orleans to St. Louis for five hundred dollars, payable out of the first wages I should receive after graduating. I entered upon the small enterprise of "learning" twelve or thirteen hundred miles of the great Mississippi River with the easy confidence of my time of life. If I had really known what I was about to require of my faculties, I should not have had the courage to begin. I supposed that all a pilot had to do was to keep his boat in the river, and I did not consider that that could be much of a trick, since it was so wide.

The boat backed out from New Orleans at four in the afternoon, and it was "our watch" until eight. Mr. B--, my chief, "straightened her up," plowed her along past the sterns of the other boats that lay at the Levee, and then said, "Here, take her; shave those steamships as close as you 'd peel an apple." I took the wheel, and my heart went down into my boots; for it seemed to me that we were about to scrape the side off every ship in the line, we were so close. I held my breath and began to claw the boat away from the danger; and I had my own opinion of the pilot who had known no better than to get us into such peril, but I was too wise to express it. In half a minute I had a wide margin of safety intervening between the Paul Jones and the ships; and within ten seconds more I was set aside in disgrace, and Mr. B-- was going into danger again and flaying me alive with abuse of my cowardice. I was stung, but I was obliged to admire the easy confidence with which my chief loafed from side to side of his wheel, and trimmed the ships so closely that disaster seemed ceaselessly imminent. When he had cooled a little he told me that the easy water was close ashore and the current outside, and therefore we must hug the bank, up-stream, to get the benefit of the former, and stay well out, down-stream, to take advantage of the latter. In my own mind I resolved to be a down-stream pilot and leave the up-streaming to people dead to prudence.

Now and then Mr. B-- called my attention to certain things. Said he, "This is Six-Mile Point." I assented. It was pleasant enough information, but I could not see the bearing of it. I was not conscious that it was a matter of any interest to me. Another time he said. "This is Nine-Mile Point." Later he said, "This is Twelve-Mile Point." They were all about level with the water's edge; they all looked about alike to me; they were monotonously unpicturesque. I hoped Mr. B-- would change the subject. But no; he would crowd up around a point, hugging the shore with affection, and then say: "The slack water ends here, abreast this bunch of China-trees; now we cross over." So he crossed over.

He gave me the wheel once or twice, but I had no luck. I either came near chipping off the edge of a sugar plantation, or else I yawed too far from shore, and so I dropped back into disgrace again and got abused.

The watch was ended at last, and we took supper and went to bed. At midnight the glare of a lantern shone in my eyes, and the night watchman said:

"Come!; turn out!"

And then he left. I could not understand this extraordinary procedure; so I presently gave up trying to, and dozed off to sleep. Pretty soon the watchman was back again, and this time he was gruff. I was annoyed. I said:--

"What do you want to come bothering around here in the middle of the night for? Now as like as not I'll not get to sleep again to-night."

The watchman said:--

"Well, if this ain't good, I 'm blest."

The "off-watch" was just turning in, and I heard some brutal laughter from them, and such remarks as "Hello, watchman! ain't the new cub turned out yet? He's delicate, likely. Give him some sugar in a rag and send for the chambermaid to sing rock-a-by-baby to him."

About this time Mr. B-- appeared on the scene. Something like a minute later I was climbing the pilot-house steps with some of my clothes on and the rest in my arms. Mr. B-- was close behind, commenting. Here was something fresh-- this thing of getting up in the middle of the night to go to work. It was a detail in piloting that had never occurred to me at all. I knew that boats ran all night, but somehow I had never happened to reflect that somebody had to get up out of a warm bed to run them. I began to fear that piloting was not quite so romantic as I had imagined it was; there was something very real and work-like about this new phase of it.

It was a rather dingy night, although a fair number of stars were out. The big mate was at the wheel, and he had the old tub pointed at a star and was holding her straight up the middle of the river. The shores on either hand were not much more than a mile apart, but they seemed wonderfully far away and ever so vague and indistinct. The mate said:--

"We've got to land at Jones's plantation, sir."

The vengeful spirit in me exulted. I said to myself, I wish you joy of your job, Mr. B--; you'll have a good time finding Mr. Jones's plantation such a night as this; and I hope you never will find it as long as you live.

Mr. B-- said to the mate:

"Upper end of the plantation, or the lower?"

"Upper."

"I can't do it. The stumps there are out of water at this stage. It's no great distance to the lower, and you 'll have to get along with that."

"All right, sir. If Jones don't like it he'll have to lump it, I reckon."

And then the mate left. My exultation began to cool and my wonder to come up. Here was a man who not only proposed to find this plantation on such a night, but to find either end of it you preferred. I dreadfully wanted to ask a question, but I was carrying about as many short answers as my cargo-room would admit of, so I held my peace. All I desired to ask Mr. B--was the simple question whether he was ass enough to really imagine he was going to find that plantation on a night when all plantations were exactly alike and all the same color. But I held in. I used to have fine inspirations of prudence in those days.

Mr. B--made for the shore and soon was scraping it, just the same as if it had been daylight. And not only that, but singing--

"Father in heaven the day is declining," etc.

It seemed to me that I had put my life in the keeping of a peculiarly reckless outcast. Presently he turned on me and said:--

"What's the name of the first point above New Orleans?"

I was gratified to be able to answer promptly, and I did. I said I didn't know.

"Don't know?"

This manner jolted me. I was down at the foot again, in a moment. But I had to say just what I had said before.

"Well, you're a smart one," said Mr. B--. "What's the name of the next point?"

Once more I didn't know.

"Well this beats anything. Tell me the name of any point or place I told you."

I studied a while and decided that I couldn't.

"Look-a-here! What do you start out from, above Twelve-Mile Point, to cross over?"

"I--I--don't know."

"You--you--don't know?" mimicking my drawling manner of speech. "What do you know?"

"I--I--nothing, for certain."

"By the great Cæsar's ghost I believe you! You're the stupidest dunderhead I ever saw or ever heard of, so help me Moses! The idea of you being a pilot--you! Why, you don't know enough to pilot a cow down a lane."

Oh, but his wrath was up! He was a nervous man, and he shuffled from one side of his wheel to the other as if the floor was hot. He would boil a while to himself, and then overflow and scald me again.

"Look-a-here! What do you suppose I told you the names of those points for?"

I tremblingly considered a moment, and then the devil of temptation provoked me to say:--

"Well--to--to--be entertaining, I thought."

This was a red rag to the bull. He raged and stormed so (he was crossing the river at the time) that I judge it made him blind, because he ran over the steering-oar of a trading-scow. Of course the traders sent up a volley of red-hot profanity. Never was a man so grateful as Mr. B--was: because he was brim full, and here were subjects who would talk back. He threw open a window, thrust his head out; and such an irruption followed as I never had heard before. The fainter and farther away the scowmen's curses drifted, the higher Mr. B--lifted his voice and the weightier his adjectives grew. When he closed the window he was empty. You could have drawn a seine through his system and not caught curses enough to disturb your mother with. Presently he said to me in the gentlest way:--

"My boy, you must get a little memorandum-book, and every time I tell you a thing, put it down right away. There's only one way to be a pilot, and that is to get this entire river by heart. You have to know it just like A B C."

That was a dismal revelation to me; for my memory was never loaded with anything but blank cartridges. However, I did not feel discouraged long. I judged that it was best to make some allowances, for doubtless Mr. B--was "stretching." Presently he pulled a rope and struck a few strokes on the big bell. The stars were all gone now, and the night was as black as ink. I could hear the wheels churn along the bank, but I was not entirely certain that I could see the shore. The voice of the invisible watchman called up from the hurricane deck:--

"What's this, sir?"

"Jones's plantation."

I said to myself, I wish I might venture to offer a small bet that it isn't. But I did not chirp. I only waited to see. Mr. B--handled the engine bells, and in due time the boat's nose came to the land, a torch glowed from the forecastle, a man skipped ashore, a darky's voice on the bank said. "Gimme de carpet-bag, Mars' Jones," and the next moment we were standing up the river again, all serene. I reflected deeply a while, and then said,--but not aloud,--Well, the finding of that plantation was the luckiest accident that ever happened; but it couldn't happen again in a hundred years. And I fully believed it was an accident, too.

By the time we had gone seven or eight hundred miles up the river, I had learned to be a tolerably plucky up-stream steersman in daylight, and before we reached St. Louis I had made a trifle of progress in night-work, but only a trifle. I had a note-book that fairly bristled with the names of towns, "points," bars, islands, bends, reaches, etc.: but the information was to be found only in the note-book--none of it was in my head. It made my heart ache to think I had only got half of the river set down; for as our watch was four hours off and four hours on, day and night, there was a long four-hour gap in my book for every time I had slept since the voyage began.

My chief was presently hired to go on a big New Orleans boat, and I packed my satchel and went with him. She was a grand affair. When I stood in her pilot-house I was so far above the water that I seemed perched on a mountain; and her decks stretched so far away, fore and aft, below me, that I wondered how I could ever have considered the little Paul Jones a large craft. There were other differences, too. The Paul Jones's pilot-house was a cheap, dingy, battered rattle-trap, cramped for room: but here was a sumptuous glass temple; room enough to have a dance in; showy red and gold window-curtains; an imposing sofa; leather cushions and a back to the high bench where visiting pilots sit, to spin yarns and "look at the river;" bright, fanciful "cuspadores" instead of a broad wooden box filled with sawdust; nice new oil-cloth on the floor; a hospitable big stove for winter; a wheel as high as my head, costly with inlaid work; a wire tiller-rope; bright brass knobs for the bells; and a tidy, white-aproned, black "texas-tender," to bring up tarts and ices and coffee during mid-watch, day and night. Now this was "something like;" and so I began to take heart once more to believe that piloting was a romantic sort of occupation after all. The moment we were under way I began to prowl about the great steamer and fill myself with joy. She was as clean and as dainty as a drawing-room; when I looked down her long, gilded saloon, it was like gazing through a splendid tunnel; she had an oil-picture, by some gifted sign-painter, on every state-room door; she glittered with no end of prism-fringed chandeliers; the clerk's office was elegant, the bar was marvelous, and the bar-keeper had been barbered and upholstered at incredible cost. The boiler deck (i. e., the second story of the boat, so to speak) was as spacious as a church, it seemed to me; so with the forecastle; and there was no pitiful handful of deck-hands, firemen, and roustabouts down there, but a whole battalion of men. The fires were fiercely glaring from a long row of furnaces, and over them were eight huge boilers! This was unutterable pomp. The mighty engines--but enough of this. I had never felt so fine before. And when I found that the regiment of natty servants respectfully "sir'd" me, my satisfaction was complete.

When I returned to the pilot-house St. Louis was gone and I was lost. Here was a piece of river which was all down in my book, but I could make neither head nor tail of it: you understand, it was turned around. I had seen it, when coming up-stream, but I had never faced about to see how it looked when it was behind me. My heart broke again, for it was plain that I had got to learn this troublesome river both ways.

III. The Continued Perplexities of "Cub" Piloting

At the end of what seemed a tedious while, I had managed to pack my head full of islands, towns, bars, "points," and bends; and a curiously inanimate mass of lumber it was, too. However, inasmuch as I could shut my eyes and reel off a good long string of these names without leaving out more than ten miles of river in every fifty, I began to feel that I could take a boat down to New Orleans if I could make her skip those little gaps. But of course my complacency could hardly get start enough to lift my nose a trifle into the air, before Mr. B-- would think of something to fetch it down again. One day he turned on me suddenly with this settler:--

"What is the shape of Walnut Bend?"

He might as well have asked me my grandmother's opinion of protoplasm. I reflected respectfully, and then said I didn't know it had any particular shape. My gunpowdery chief went off with a bang, of course, and then went on loading and firing until he was out of adjectives.

I had learned long ago that he only carried just so many rounds of ammunition, and was sure to subside into a very placable and even remorseful old smooth-bore as soon as they were all gone. That word "old" is merely affectionate; he was not more than thirty-four. I waited. By and by he said,--

"My boy, you've got to know the shape of the river perfectly. It is all there is left to steer by on a very dark night. Everything else is blotted out and gone. But mind you, it hasn't the same shape in the night that it has in the day-time."

"How on earth am I ever going to learn it, then?"

"How do you follow a hall at home in the dark? Because you know the shape of it. You can't see it."

"Do you mean to say that I've got to know all the million trifling variations of shape in the banks of this interminable river as well as I know the shape of the front hall at home?"

"On my honor you've got to know them better than any man ever did know the shapes of the halls in his own house."

"I wish I was dead!"

"Now I don't want to discourage you, but"--

"Well, pile it on me; I might as well have it now as another time."

"You see, this has got to be learned; there isn't any getting around it. A clear starlight night throws such heavy shadows that if you didn't know the shape of a shore perfectly you would claw away from every bunch of timber, because you would take the black shadow of it for a solid cape; and you see you would be getting scared to death every fifteen minutes by the watch. You would be fifty yards from shore all the time when you ought to be within twenty feet of it. You can't see a snag in one of those shadows, but you know exactly where it is, and the shape of the river tells you when you are coming to it. Then there's your pitch dark night; the river is a very different shape on a pitch dark night from what it is on a starlight night. All shores seem to be straight lines, then, and mighty dim ones, too; and you'd run them for straight lines, only you know better. You boldly drive your boat right into what seems to be a solid, straight wall (you knowing very well that in reality there is a curve there), and that wall falls back and makes way for you. Then there's your gray mist. You take a night when there's one of these grisly, drizzly, gray mists, and then there isn't any particular shape to a shore. A gray mist would tangle the head of the oldest man that ever lived. Well, then, different kinds of moonlight change the shape of the river in different ways. You see"--

"Oh, don't say any more, please! Have I got to learn the shape of the river according to all these five hundred thousand different ways? If I tried to carry all that cargo in my head it would make me stoop-shouldered."

"No! you only learn the shape of the river; and you learn it with such absolute certainty that you can always steer by the shape that 's in your head, and never mind the one that 's before your eyes."

"Very well, I'll try it; but after I have learned it can I depend on it? Will it keep the same form and not go fooling around?"

Before Mr. B-- could answer, Mr. W--came in to take the watch and he said,--

"B--, you'll have to look out for President's Island and all that country clear away up above the Old Hen and Chickens. The banks are caving and the shape of the shores changing like everything. Why, you wouldn't know the point above 40. You can go up inside the old sycamore snag, now."

So that question was answered. Here were leagues of shore changing shape. My spirits were down in the mud again. Two things seemed pretty apparent to me. One was, that in order to be a pilot a man had got to learn more than any one man ought to be allowed to know; and the other was, that he must learn it all over again in a different way every twenty-four hours.

That night we had the watch until twelve. Now it was an ancient river custom for the two pilots to chat a bit when the watch changed. While the relieving pilot put on his gloves and lit his cigar, his partner, the retiring pilot, would say something like this:--

"I judge the upper bar is making down a little at Hale's Point; had quarter twain with the lower lead and mark twain [note: two fathoms] with the other."

"Yes, I thought it was making down a little, last trip. Meet any boats?"

"Met one abreast the head of 21, but she was away over hugging the bar, and I couldn't make her out entirely. I took her for the Sunny South--hadn't any skylights forward of the chimneys."

And so on. And as the relieving pilot took the wheel his partner would mention that we were in such-and-such bend, and say we were abreast of such-and-such a man's wood-yard or plantation. This was courtesy; I supposed it was necessity. But Mr. W-- came on watch full twelve minutes late, on this particular night--a tremendous breach of etiquette; in fact, it is the unpardonable sin among pilots. So Mr. B-- gave him no greeting whatever, but simply surrendered the wheel and marched out of the pilot-house without a word. I was appalled; it was a villainous night for blackness, we were in a particularly wide and blind part of the river, where there was no shape or substance to anything, and it seemed incredible that Mr. B-- should have left that poor fellow to kill the boat trying to find out where he was. But I resolved that I would stand by him any way. He should find that he was not wholly friendless. So I stood around, and waited to be asked where we were. But Mr. W-- plunged on serenely through the solid firmament of black cats that stood for an atmosphere, and never opened his mouth. Here is a proud devil, thought I; here is a limb of Satan that would rather send us all to destruction than put himself under obligations to me, because I am not yet one of the salt of the earth and privileged to snub captains and lord it over everything dead and alive in a steamboat. I presently climbed up on the bench; I did not think it was safe to go to sleep while this lunatic was on watch.

However, I must have gone to sleep in the course of time, because the next thing I was aware of was the fact that day was breaking, Mr. W--gone, and Mr. B--at the wheel again. So it was four o'clock and all well--but me; I felt like a skinful of dry bones and all of them trying to ache at once.

Mr. B--asked me what I had stayed up there for. I confessed that it was to do Mr. W--a benevolence: tell him where he was. It took five minutes for the entire preposterousness of the thing to filter into Mr. B--'s system, and then I judge it filled him nearly up to the chin; because he paid me a compliment--and not much of a one either. He said,--

"Well, taking you by-and-large, you do seem to be more different kinds of an ass than any creature I ever saw before. What did you suppose he wanted to know for?"

I said I thought it might be a convenience to him.

"Convenience! Dash! Didn't I tell you that a man's got to know the river in the night the same as he'd know his own front hall?"

"Well, I can follow the front hall in the dark if I know it is the front hall; but suppose you set me down in the middle of it in the dark and not tell me which hall it is; how am I to know?"

"Well, you've got to, on the river!"

"All right. Then I'm glad I never said anything to Mr. W--."

"I should say so. Why, he'd have slammed you through the window and utterly ruined a hundred dollars' worth of window-sash and stuff."

I was glad this damage had been saved, for it would have made me unpopular with the owners. They always hated anybody who had the name of being careless, and injuring things.

I went to work, now, to learn the shape of the river; and of all the eluding and ungraspable objects that ever I tried to get mind or hands on, that was the chief. I would fasten my eyes upon a sharp, wooded point that projected far into the river some miles ahead of me, and go to laboriously photographing its shape upon my brain; and just as I was beginning to succeed to my satisfaction, we would draw up toward it and the exasperating thing would begin to melt away and fold back into the bank! If there had been a conspicuous dead tree standing upon the very point of the cape, I would find that tree inconspicuously merged into the general forest, and occupying the middle of a straight shore, when I got abreast of it! No prominent hill would stick to its shape long enough for me to make up my mind what its form really was, but it was as dissolving and changeful as if it had been a mountain of butter in the hottest corner of the tropics. Nothing ever had the same shape when I was coming down-stream that it had borne when I went up. I mentioned these little difficulties to Mr. B--. He said,--

"That's the very main virtue of the thing. If the shapes didn't change every three seconds they wouldn't be of any use. Take this place where we are now, for instance. As long as that hill over yonder is only one hill, I can boom right along the way I'm going; but the moment it splits at the top and forms a V, I know I've got to scratch to starboard in a hurry, or I'll bang this boat's brains out against a rock; and then the moment one of the prongs of the V swings behind the other, I've got to waltz to larboard again, or I'll have a misunderstanding with a snag that would snatch the keelson out of this steamboat as neatly as if it were a sliver in your hand. If that hill didn't change its shape on bad nights there would be an awful steamboat grave-yard around here inside of a year."

It was plain that I had got to learn the shape of the river in all the different ways that could be thought of,--upside down, wrong end first, inside out, fore-and-aft, and "thortships," and then know what to do on gray nights when it hadn't any shape at all. So I set about it. In the course of time I began to get the best of this knotty lesson, and my self-complacency moved to the front once more. Mr. B--was all fixed, and ready to start it to the rear again. He opened on me after this fashion:--

"How much water did we have in the middle crossing at Hole-in-the-Wall, trip before last?"

I considered this an outrage. I said:

"Every trip, down and up, the leadsmen are singing through that tangled place for three quarters of an hour on a stretch. How do you reckon I can remember such a mess as that?"

"My boy, you've got to remember it. You've got to remember the exact spot and the exact marks the boat lay in when we had the shoalest water, in every one of the two thousand shoal places between St. Louis and New Orleans; and you mustn't get the shoal soundings and marks of one trip mixed up with the shoal soundings and marks of another, either, for they're not often twice alike. You must keep them separate."

When I came to myself again, I said,--

"When I get so that I can do that, I'll be able to raise the dead, and then I won't have to pilot a steamboat in order to make a living. I want to retire from this business. I want a slush-bucket and a brush; I'm only fit for a roustabout. I haven't got brains enough to be a pilot; and if I had I wouldn't have strength enough to carry them around, unless I went on crutches."

"Now drop that! When I say I'll learn 1 a man the river, I mean it. And you can depend on it I'll learn him or kill him."

There was no use in arguing with a person like this. I promptly put such a strain on my memory that by and by even the shoal water and the countless crossing-marks began to stay with me. But the result was just the same. I never could more than get one knotty thing learned before another presented itself. Now I had often seen pilots gazing at the water and pretending to read it as if it were a book; but it was a book that told me nothing. A time came at last, however, when Mr. B--seemed to think me far enough advanced to hear a lesson on water-reading. So he began:--

"Do you see that long slanting line on the face of the water? Now that's a reef. Moreover, it's a bluff reef. There is a solid sand-bar under it that is nearly as straight up and down as the side of a house. There is plenty of water close up to it, but mighty little on top of it. If you were to hit it you would knock the boat's brains out. Do you see where the line fringes out at the upper end and begins to fade away?"

"Yes, sir."

"Well, that is a low place; that is the head of the reef. You can climb over there, and not hurt anything. Cross over, now, and follow along close under the reef--easy water there-- not much current."

I followed the reef along till I approached the fringed end. Then Mr. B-- said,--

"Now get ready. Wait till I give the word. She won't want to mount the reef; a boat hates shoal water. Stand by--wait--wait--keep her well in hand. Now cramp her down! Snatch her! snatch her!"

He seized the other side of the wheel and helped to spin it around until it was hard down, and then we held it so. The boat resisted and refused to answer for a while, and next she came surging to starboard, mounted the reef, and sent a long, angry ridge of water foaming away from her bows.

"Now watch her; watch her like a cat, or she'll get away from you. When she fights strong and the tiller slips a little, in a jerky, greasy sort of way, let up on her a trifle; it is the way she tells you at night that the water is too shoal; but keep edging her up, little by little, toward the point. You are well up on the bar, now; there is a bar under every point, because the water that comes down around it forms an eddy and allows the sediment to sink. Do you see those fine lines on the face of the water that branch out like the ribs of a fan? Well, those are little reefs; you want to just miss the ends of them, but run them pretty close. Now look out--look out! Don't you crowd that slick, greasy-looking place; there ain't nine feet there; she won't stand it. She begins to smell it; look sharp, I tell you! Oh blazes, there you go! Stop the starboard wheel! Quick! Ship up to back! Set her back!"

The engine bells jingled and the engines answered promptly, shooting white columns of steam far aloft out of the scape pipes, but it was too late. The boat had "smelt" the bar in good earnest; the foamy ridges that radiated from her bows suddenly disappeared, a great dead swell came rolling forward and swept ahead of her, she careened far over to larboard, and went tearing away toward the other shore as if she were about scared to death. We were a good mile from where we ought to have been, when we finally got the upper hand of her again.

During the afternoon watch the next day, Mr. B--asked me if I knew how to run the next few miles. I said:--

"Go inside the first snag above the point, outside the next one, start out from the lower end of Higgins's wood-yard, make a square crossing and"--

"That's all right. I'll be back before you close up on the next point."

But he wasn't. He was still below when I rounded it and entered upon a piece of river which I had some misgivings about. I did not know that he was hiding behind a chimney to see how I would perform. I went gayly along, getting prouder and prouder, for he had never left the boat in my sole charge such a length of time before. I even got to "setting" her and letting the wheel go, entirely, while I vaingloriously turned my back and inspected the stern marks and hummed a tune, a sort of easy indifference which I had prodigiously admired in B--and other great pilots. Once I inspected rather long, and when I faced to the front again my heart flew into my mouth so suddenly that if I hadn't clapped my teeth together I would have lost it. One of those frightful bluff reefs was stretching its deadly length right across our bows! My head was gone in a moment; I did not know which end I stood on; I gasped and could not get my breath; I spun the wheel down with such rapidity that it wove itself together like a spider's web; the boat answered and turned square away from the reef, but the reef followed her! I fled, and still it followed--still it kept right across my bows! I never looked to see where I was going, I only fled. The awful crash was imminent--why didn't that villain come! If I committed the crime of ringing a bell, I might get thrown overboard. But better that than kill the boat. So in blind desperation I started such a rattling "shivaree" down below as never had astounded an engineer in this world before, I fancy. Amidst the frenzy of the bells the engines began to back and fill in a furious way, and my reason forsook its throne --we were about to crash into the woods on the other side of the river. Just then Mr. B-- stepped calmly into view on the hurricane deck. My soul went out to him in gratitude. My distress vanished; I would have felt safe on the brink of Niagara, with Mr. B-- on the hurricane deck. He blandly and sweetly took his tooth-pick out of his mouth between his fingers, as if it were a cigar,--we were just in the act of climbing an overhanging big tree, and the passengers were scudding astern like rats,--and lifted up these commands to me ever so gently:--

"Stop the starboard. Stop the larboard. Set her back on both."

The boat hesitated, halted, pressed her nose among the boughs a critical instant, then reluctantly began to back away.

"Stop the larboard. Come ahead on it. Stop the starboard. Come ahead on it. Point her for the bar."

I sailed away as serenely as a summer's morning. Mr. B--came in and said, with mock simplicity,--

"When you have a hail, my boy, you ought to tap the big bell three times before you land, so that the engineers can get ready."

I blushed under the sarcasm, and said I hadn't had any hail.

"Ah! Then it was for wood, I suppose. The officer of the watch will tell you when he wants to wood up."

I went on consuming, and said I wasn't after wood.

"Indeed? Why, what could you want over here in the bend, then? Did you ever know of a boat following a bend up-stream at this stage of the river?"

"No, sir,--and I wasn't trying to follow it. I was getting away from a bluff reef."

"No, it wasn't a bluff reef; there isn't one within three miles of where you were."

"But I saw it. It was as bluff as that one yonder."

"Just about. Run over it!"

"Do you give it as an order?"

"Yes. Run over it."

"If I don't, I wish I may die."

"All right; I am taking the responsibility."

I was just as anxious to kill the boat, now, as I had been to save her before. I impressed my orders upon my memory, to be used at the inquest, and made a straight break for the reef. As it disappeared under our bows I held my breath; but we slid over it like oil. "Now don't you see the difference? It wasn't anything but a wind reef. The wind does that."

"So I see. But it is exactly like a bluff reef. How am I ever going to tell them apart?"

"I can't tell you. It is an instinct. By and by you will just naturally know one from the other, but you never will be able to explain why or how you know them apart."

It turned out to be true. The face of the water, in time, became a wonderful book--a book that was a dead language to the uneducated passenger, but which told its mind to me without reserve, delivering its most cherished secrets as clearly as if it uttered them with a voice. And it was not a book to be read once and thrown aside, for it had a new story to tell every day. Throughout the long twelve hundred miles there was never a page that was void of interest, never one that you could leave unread without loss, never one that you would want to skip, thinking you could find higher enjoyment in some other thing. There never was so wonderful a book written by man; never one whose interest was so absorbing, so unflagging, so sparklingly renewed with every re-perusal. The passenger who could not read it was charmed with a peculiar sort of faint dimple on its surface (on the rare occasions when he did not overlook it altogether); but to the pilot that was an italicized passage; indeed, it was more than that, it was a legend of the largest capitals with a string of shouting exclamation points at the end of it; for it meant that a wreck or a rock was buried there that could tear the life out of the strongest vessel that ever floated. It is the faintest and simplest expression the water ever makes, and the most hideous to a pilot's eye. In truth, the passenger who could not read this book saw nothing but all manner of pretty pictures in it, painted by the sun and shaded by the clouds, whereas to the trained eye these were not pictures at all, but the grimmest and most dead-earnest of reading-matter.

Now when I had mastered the language of this water and had come to know every trifling feature that bordered the great river as familiarly as I knew the letters of the alphabet, I had made a valuable acquisition. But I had lost something, too. I had lost something which could never be restored to me while I lived. All the grace, the beauty, the poetry had gone out of the majestic river! I still keep in mind a certain wonderful sunset which I witnessed when steam-boating was new to me. A broad expanse of the river was turned to blood; in the middle distance the red hue brightened into gold, through which a solitary log came floating, black and conspicuous; in one place a long, slanting mark lay sparkling upon the water; in another the surface was broken by boiling, tumbling rings, that were as many-tinted as an opal; where the ruddy flush was faintest, was a smooth spot that was covered with graceful circles and radiating lines, ever so delicately traced; the shore on our left was densely wooded, and the sombre shadow that fell from this forest was broken in one place by a long, ruffled trail that shone like silver; and high above the forest wall a clean-stemmed dead tree waved a single leafy bough that glowed like a flame in the unobstructed splendor that was flowing from the sun. There were graceful curves, reflected images, woody heights, soft distances; and over the whole scene, far and near, the dissolving lights drifted steadily, enriching it, every passing moment, with new marvels of coloring.

I stood like one bewitched. I drank it in, in a speechless rapture. The world was new to me, and I had never seen anything like this at home. But as I have said, a day came when I began to cease noting the glories and the charms which the moon and the sun and the twilight wrought upon the river's face;

another day came when I ceased altogether to note them. Then, if that sunset scene had been repeated, I would have looked upon it without rapture, and would have commented upon it, inwardly, after this fashion: This sun means that we are going to have wind tomorrow: that floating log means that the river is rising, small thanks to it; that slanting mark on the water refers to a bluff reef which is going to kill somebody's steamboat one of these nights, if it keeps on stretching out like that; those tumbling "boils" show a dissolving bar and a changing channel there; the lines and circles in the slick water over yonder are a warning that that execrable place is shoaling up dangerously; that silver streak in the shadow of the forest is the "break" from a new snag, and he has located himself in the very best place he could have found to fish for steamboats; that tall, dead tree, with a single living branch, is not going to last long, and then how is a body ever going to get through this blind place at night without the friendly old landmark?

No, the romance and the beauty were all gone from the river. All the value any feature of it had for me now was the amount of usefulness it could furnish toward compassing the safe piloting of a steamboat. Since those days, I have pitied doctors from my heart. What does the lovely flush in a beauty's cheek mean to a doctor but a "break" that ripples above some deadly disease? Are not all her visible charms sown thick with what are to him the signs and symbols of hidden decay? Does he ever see her beauty at all, or doesn't he simply view her professionally, and comment upon her unwholesome condition all to himself? And doesn't he sometimes wonder whether he has gained most or lost most by learning his trade?   1875

Chapter 10
Nineteenth-Century American Poetry

Most American poets of the nineteenth century used the same poetic forms as their British counterparts (but usually did not handle them as artfully). Two American poets of the century, however—Walt Whitman, and Emily Dickinson—used poetic form in distinctively new ways.

Walt Whitman (1819–1892)

No poet altered the form of poetry more radically than Walt Whitman did with his *free verse* line, though it was not until the twentieth century that other American poets would write in free, rather than metrical, verse. Whitman was born in rural Long Island, the son of a Quaker carpenter. After a few years of school in Brooklyn, he quit to learn the printing trade and then became a journalist in New York. He read voraciously, but the poetry he wrote at first was traditional and mediocre.

In 1855, however, at the age of thirty-six, Whitman suddenly transformed himself—and the form of poetry—when he published a book of poetry entitled *Leaves of Grass*. Drawing his inspiration from the Bible, the epic poetry of Homer, Virgil, and Milton, the plays of Shakespeare, Italian opera, contemporary orators, and even the sound of waves breaking on the seashore, he created lines of poetry that were expansive, lyrical, and elegantly patterned, even though they did not follow a regular rhythm, meter or rhyme.

Although in his own lifetime, Whitman received only moderate recognition, he devoted the rest of his life to revising and expanding *Leaves of Grass*. The centerpiece of that volume of poetry has always been the long, effusive "Song of Myself," one of the most revolutionary poems ever written. What follows is a selection of segments from "Song of Myself":

from *Song of Myself*

1

I celebrate myself, and sing myself,
And what I assume you shall assume,
For every atom belonging to me as good belongs to you.

I loafe and invite my soul,
I lean and loafe at my ease observing a spear of summer grass.   5

My tongue, every atom of my blood, form'd from this soil, this air,
Born here of parents born here from parents the same, and their
parents the same,
I, now thirty-seven years old in perfect health begin,

Hoping to cease not till death.

Creeds and schools in abeyance, 10
Retiring back a while sufficed at what they are, but never forgotten,
I harbor for good or bad, I permit to speak at every hazard,
Nature without check with original energy.

5

I believe in you my soul, the other I am must not abase itself to you,
And you must not be abased to the other.

Loafe with me on the grass, loose the stop from your throat,
Not words, not music or rhyme I want, not custom or lecture, not
even the best, 85
Only the lull I like, the hum of your valvéd voice.

I mind how once we lay such a transparent summer morning,
How you settled your head athwart my hips and gently turn'd over upon me,
And parted the shirt from my bosom-bone, and plunged your tongue
to my bare-stript heart,
And reach'd till you felt my beard, and reach'd till you held my feet. 90

Swiftly arose and spread around me the peace and knowledge that pass
all the argument of the earth,
And I know that the hand of God is the promise of my own,
And I know that the spirit of God is the brother of my own,
And that all the men ever born are also my brothers, and the women
my sisters and lovers,
And that a kelson of the creation is love, *(the keel that balances a ship)* 95
And limitless are leaves stiff or drooping in the fields,
And brown ants in the little wells beneath them,
And mossy scabs of the worm fence, heap'd stones, elder, mullein and
poke-weed.   *(different shrubs, herbs, and weeds)*

6

A child said What is the grass? fetching it to me with full hands;
How could I answer the child? I do not know what it is any more than he. 100

I guess it must be the flag of my disposition, out of hopeful green
stuff woven.

Or I guess it is the handkerchief of the Lord,
A scented gift and remembrancer designedly dropt,
Bearing the owner's name someway in the corners, that we may see
and remark, and say Whose?

Or I guess the grass is itself a child, the produced babe of the vegetation. 105

Or I guess it is a uniform hieroglyphic,
And it means, Sprouting alike in broad zones and narrow zones,
Growing among black folks as among white,
Kanuck, Tuckahoe, Congressman, Cuff, I give them the same, I *(see note * below)*
receive them the same.

And now it seems to me the beautiful uncut hair of graves. 110

Tenderly will I use you curling grass,
It may be you transpire from the breasts of young men,
It may be if I had known them I would have loved them,
It may be you are from old people, or from offspring taken soon out
of their mothers' laps,
And here you are the mothers' laps. 115

This grass is very dark to be from the white heads of old mothers,
Darker than the colorless beards of old men,
Dark to come from under the faint red roofs of mouths.

O I perceive after all so many uttering tongues,
And I perceive they do not come from the roofs of mouths for nothing. 120

I wish I could translate the hints about the dead young men and women,
And the hints about old men and mothers, and the offspring taken
soon out of their laps.

What do you think has become of the young and old men?
And what do you think has become of the women and children?

They are alive and well somewhere, 125
The smallest sprout shows there is really no death,
And if ever there was it led forward life, and does not wait at the
end to arrest it,
And ceas'd the moment life appear'd.

All goes onward and outward, nothing collapses,
And to die is different from what any one supposed, and luckier. 130

* "Kanuck" was a nickname for French Canadians; "Tuckahoe" for Virginians; "Cuff" for African Americans

8

The little one sleeps in its cradle,
I lift the gauze and look a long time, and silently brush away flies
with my hand.

The youngster and the red-faced girl turn aside up the bushy hill, 150
I peeringly view them from the top.

The suicide sprawls on the bloody floor of the bedroom,
I witness the corpse with its dabbled hair, I note where the pistol
has fallen.

The blab of the pave, tires of carts, sluff of boot-soles, talk of
the promenaders,
The heavy omnibus, the driver with his interrogating thumb, the
clank of the shod horses on the granite floor, 155
The snow-sleighs, clinking, shouted jokes, pelts of snow-balls,
The hurrahs for popular favorites, the fury of rous'd mobs,
The flap of the curtain'd litter, a sick man inside borne to the hospital,
The meeting of enemies, the sudden oath, the blows and fall,
The excited crowd, the policeman with his star quickly working his
passage to the centre of the crowd, 160
The impassive stones that receive and return so many echoes,
What groans of over-fed or half-starv'd who fall sunstruck or in fits,
What exclamations of women taken suddenly who hurry home and
give birth to babes,
What living and buried speech is always vibrating here, what howls
restrain'd by decorum,
Arrests of criminals, slights, adulterous offers made, acceptances,
rejections with convex lips, 165
I mind them or the show or resonance of them--I come and I depart.

11

Twenty-eight young men bathe by the shore,
Twenty-eight young men and all so friendly; 200
Twenty-eight years of womanly life and all so lonesome.

She owns the fine house by the rise of the bank,
She hides handsome and richly drest aft the blinds of the window.

Which of the young men does she like the best?
Ah the homeliest of them is beautiful to her. 205

Where are you off to, lady? for I see you,
You splash in the water there, yet stay stock still in your room.

Dancing and laughing along the beach came the twenty-ninth bather,
The rest did not see her, but she saw them and loved them.

The beards of the young men glisten'd with wet, it ran from their
long hair, 210
Little streams pass'd all over their bodies.

An unseen hand also pass'd over their bodies,
It descended tremblingly from their temples and ribs.

The young men float on their backs, their white bellies bulge to the
sun, they do not ask who seizes fast to them,
They do not know who puffs and declines with pendant and
bending arch, 215
They do not think whom they souse with spray.

12

The butcher-boy puts off his killing-clothes, or sharpens his knife
at the stall in the market,
I loiter enjoying his repartee and his shuffle and break-down.

Blacksmiths with grimed and hairy chests environ the anvil,
Each has his main-sledge, they are all out, there is a great heat in
the fire. 220

From the cinder-strew'd threshold I follow their movements,
The lithe sheer of their waists plays even with their massive arms,
Overhand the hammers swing, overhand so slow, overhand so sure,
They do not hasten, each man hits in his place.

13

The negro holds firmly the reins of his four horses, the block swags
underneath on its tied-over chain, 225
The negro that drives the long dray of the stone-yard, steady and *support for the load*
tall he stands pois'd on one leg on the string-piece,
His blue shirt exposes his ample neck and breast and loosens over
his hip-band,
His glance is calm and commanding, he tosses the slouch of his hat
away from his forehead,
The sun falls on his crispy hair and mustache, falls on the black of
his polish'd and perfect limbs.

I behold the picturesque giant and love him, and I do not stop there, 230
I go with the team also.

In me the caresser of life wherever moving, backward as well as
forward sluing, *forward turning*
To niches aside and junior bending, not a person or object missing,
Absorbing all to myself and for this song.

Oxen that rattle the yoke and chain or halt in the leafy shade, what
is that you express in your eyes? 235

It seems to me more than all the print I have read in my life.

My tread scares the wood-drake and wood-duck on my distant and
day-long ramble,
They rise together, they slowly circle around.

I believe in those wing'd purposes,
And acknowledge red, yellow, white, playing within me,   240
And consider green and violet and the tufted crown intentional,
And do not call the tortoise unworthy because she is not something else,
And the in the woods never studied the gamut,   *musical scale*
    yet trills pretty well to me
And the look of the bay mare shames silliness out of me.

24

Walt Whitman, a kosmos, of Manhattan the son,
Turbulent, fleshy, sensual, eating, drinking and breeding,
No sentimentalist, no stander above men and women or apart from them,
No more modest than immodest.   500

Unscrew the locks from the doors!
Unscrew the doors themselves from their jambs!

Whoever degrades another degrades me,
And whatever is done or said returns at last to me.

Through me the afflatus surging and surging, through me   *inspiration*
    the current and index.   505

I speak the pass-word primeval, I give the sign of democracy,
By God! I will accept nothing which all cannot have their
counterpart of on the same terms.

Through me many long dumb voices,
Voices of the interminable generations of prisoners and slaves,
Voices of the diseas'd and despairing and of thieves and dwarfs,   510
Voices of cycles of preparation and accretion,
And of the threads that connect the stars, and of wombs and of the
father-stuff,
And of the rights of them the others are down upon,
Of the deform'd, trivial, flat, foolish, despised,
Fog in the air, beetles rolling balls of dung.   515

Through me forbidden voices,
Voices of sexes and lusts, voices veil'd and I remove the veil,
Voices indecent by me clarified and transfigur'd.

I do not press my fingers across my mouth,
I keep as delicate around the bowels as around the head and heart,
Copulation is no more rank to me than death is.

I believe in the flesh and the appetites,
Seeing, hearing, feeling, are miracles, and each part and tag of me
is a miracle.

Divine am I inside and out, and I make holy whatever I touch or am
touch'd from,
The scent of these arm-pits aroma finer than prayer,
This head more than churches, bibles, and all the creeds.

If I worship one thing more than another it shall be the spread of
my own body, or any part of it,
Translucent mould of me it shall be you!
Shaded ledges and rests it shall be you!
Firm masculine colter it shall be you!   *(cutting edge of a plow-- phallus)*
Whatever goes to the tilth of me it shall be you!   *the cultivated soil*
You my rich blood! your milky stream pale strippings of my life!
Breast that presses against other breasts it shall be you!
My brain it shall be your occult convolutions!
Root of wash'd sweet-flag! timorous pond-snipe! nest of guarded
duplicate eggs! it shall be you!
Mix'd tussled hay of head, beard, brawn, it shall be you!
Trickling sap of maple, fibre of manly wheat, it shall be you!
Sun so generous it shall be you!
Vapors lighting and shading my face it shall be you!
You sweaty brooks and dews it shall be you!
Winds whose soft-tickling genitals rub against me it shall be you!
Broad muscular fields, branches of live oak, loving lounger in my
winding paths, it shall be you!
Hands I have taken, face I have kiss'd, mortal I have ever touch'd,
it shall be you.

I dote on myself, there is that lot of me and all so luscious,
Each moment and whatever happens thrills me with joy,
I cannot tell how my ankles bend, nor whence the cause of my faintest wish,
Nor the cause of the friendship I emit, nor the cause of the
friendship I take again.

That I walk up my stoop, I pause to consider if it really be,
A morning-glory at my window satisfies me more than the metaphysics
of books.

To behold the day-break!
The little light fades the immense and diaphanous shadows,
The air tastes good to my palate.

Hefts of the moving world at innocent gambols silently rising, freshly exuding,
    Scooting obliquely high and low.

Something I cannot see puts upward libidinous prongs,   555
Seas of bright juice suffuse heaven.

The earth by the sky staid with, the daily close of their junction,
The heav'd challenge from the east that moment over my head,
The mocking taunt, See then whether you shall be master!

52

The spotted hawk swoops by and accuses me, he complains of my gab
and my loitering.

I too am not a bit tamed, I too am untranslatable,
I sound my barbaric yawp over the roofs of the world.

The last scud of day holds back for me,   *last clouds driven by the wind*
It flings my likeness after the rest and true as any on the shadow'd wilds,   1335
It coaxes me to the vapor and the dusk.

I depart as air, I shake my white locks at the runaway sun,
I effuse my flesh in eddies, and drift it in lacy jags.

I bequeath myself to the dirt to grow from the grass I love,
If you want me again look for me under your boot-soles.   1340

You will hardly know who I am or what I mean,
But I shall be good health to you nevertheless,
And filter and fibre your blood.

Failing to fetch me at first keep encouraged,
Missing me one place search another,   1345
I stop somewhere waiting for you.   1855

    Even though Whitman altered the poetic line more radically than any poet before him by abandoning meter, he still gave his poetic line pattern and balance. Consider the various ways Whitman gives form to his free-verse line. Where does he use repeated phrases? Where does he list "catalogs" of images to portray the bustle of people working in New York City?
    Notice, too, that some of his "free- verse" lines actually have metrical patterns. The following line, for example, consists of alternating anapests and iambs:

    I be-**queath**/ my-**self**/ to the **dirt**/ to **grow**/ from the **grass**/ I **love**

One of the ironies of Whitman's use of "free verse" is that all of his lines are end-stopped (though some are so long they must be indented). Never does he avail himself of enjambment, which poets such as Milton and Wordsworth used so effectively to create variation in their blank verse poems.

While most of Whitman's most famous poems are long, free-verse meditations, such as his elegy for the assassination of Abraham Lincoln, "When Lilacs Last in the Dooryard Bloom'd" (1865), he also wrote many short poems. When the Civil War broke out in 1861, Whitman traveled to Virginia to find his brother George, who had been wounded. When Whitman saw the misery of wounded soldiers and the poor medical care they received, he stayed on the battlefield voluntarily to attend to them. Close to the battlefront, he wrote many poems that captured images of men at war, such as this snapshot of cavalry soldiers riding across a shallow part of a stream.

Cavalry Crossing a Ford

A line in long array where they wind betwixt green islands,
They take a serpentine course, their arms flash in the sun--hark to
    the musical clank,
Behold the silvery river, in it the splashing horses loitering stop
    to drink,
Behold the brown-faced men, each group, each person a picture, the
    negligent rest on the saddles,
Some emerge on the opposite bank, others are just entering the
    ford--while,   5
Scarlet and blue and snowy white,
The guidon flags flutter gayly in the wind.
    signal flags   1865

In some of his shorter poems, Whitman displayed his keen eye for the natural world and the flexibility of his free-verse line to record it.

The Dalliance of the Eagles

Skirting the river road, (my forenoon walk, my rest,)
Skyward in air a sudden muffled sound, the dalliance of the eagles,
The rushing amorous contact high in space together,
The clinching interlocking claws, a living, fierce, gyrating wheel,
Four beating wings, two beaks, a swirling mass tight grappling,   5
In tumbling turning clustering loops, straight downward falling,
Till o'er the river pois'd, the twain yet one, a moment's lull,
A motionless still balance in the air, then parting, talons loosing,
Upward again on slow-firm pinions slanting, their separate diverse flight,
She hers, he his, pursuing.
    1880

As in much of his poetry, Whitman's free-verse line was as shocking to nineteenth-century readers as his emphasis upon sensuality. Just as he had broken with the convention of metrical verse, Whitman opened up poetry to deal with sexuality. In this poem, he passionately describes two eagles copulating—or perhaps only "dallying"—in the air.

Emily Dickinson (1830–1886)

While Walt Whitman revolutionized poetry by breaking with metrical verse, Emily Dickinson altered poetic form by subverting the traditional form of the ballad. The ballad formed the basis of many Protestant hymns, and Dickinson's subversion of that form reflected her rejection of religion. She stemmed from a family that traced its ancestry back to the original Puritan colony of Massachusetts, and she spent virtually her entire life in Amherst, Massachusetts. Despite the fact that most people in her family and in her community were avowed Christians, Emily Dickinson remained a religious skeptic. Withdrawn and reclusive, she read widely and wrote poems, which she copied by hand and sewed together in little paper booklets called *fascicles*. She gave no titles to her poems, so they are referred to by their first lines.

In 1862, she responded to an article in the *Atlantic Monthly* by Thomas Wentworth Higginson, a literary critic, giving advice to young poets. Dickinson sent Higginson some of her poems, and he was immediately struck by the freshness and originality of her work. He responded with suggestions and criticisms, and eventually visited her in Amherst. They corresponded for years, and, after Dickinson's death, Higginson, other friends, and members of her family prepared some of her poems for publication. In doing so, however, they "corrected" what they thought were Dickinson's uneven rhythms, grammatical errors, and false rhymes. Only in the twentieth century were her poems restored to their original, unconventional form, replete with the dashes she used to punctuate and break up her lines.

This first poem illustrates how artfully Dickinson used dashes. In the manner of one of John Donne's "metaphysical conceits," she compares the onset of madness to a funeral service for her sanity that takes place in her brain. At the very end of the poem, as she plunges into madness, she says she "Finished knowing" but closes with the word "then" surrounded by dashes. While one could simply read the last line as the conclusive "Finished knowing then," the dashes suggest that "then" is the beginning of a new experience, but, because she has lost her sanity, she cannot describe it.

I Felt a Funeral, in My Brain

I felt a Funeral, in my Brain,
And Mourners to and fro
Kept treading--treading--till it seemed
That Sense was breaking through--

And when they all were seated,   5
A Service, like a Drum--
Kept beating--beating--till I thought
My Mind was going numb--

And then I heard them lift a Box
And creak across my Soul   10
With those same Boots of Lead, again,
Then Space--began to toll,

As all the Heavens were a Bell,
And Being, but an Ear,
And I, and Silence, some strange Race   15

Wrecked, solitary, here--

And then a Plank in Reason, broke,
And I dropped down, and down--
And hit a World, at every plunge,
And Finished knowing--then--   1862

A Bird Came Down the Walk

A Bird, came down the Walk –
He did not know I saw –
He bit an Angleworm in halves
And ate the fellow, raw,

And then he drank a Dew   5
From a convenient Grass –
And then hopped sidewise to the Wall
To let a Beetle pass –

He glanced with rapid eyes
That hurried all around –   10
They looked like frightened Beads, I thought –
He stirred his Velvet Head

Like one in danger, Cautious,
I offered him a Crumb
And he unrolled his feathers   15
And rowed him softer home –

Than Oars divide the Ocean,
Too silver for a seam –
Or Butterflies, off Banks of Noon
Leap, plashless as they swim.   *Leap without splashing*   1862

How does Dickinson vary the ballad quatrain in this poem? Consider her metrical substitutions, the number of syllables in each line, and her rhymes. In what ways does the bird seem like a civilized human, and in what ways does it seem like a wild creature? Our association of robins with the coming of spring may make us overlook the fact that these pretty little birds are carnivores that eat worms.

In this next poem, Dickinson retells the Greek myth of Persephone, the daughter of Ceres, goddess of the earth and vegetation (from whose name we get the word "cereal"). When Persephone was picking daffodils one morning, Hades, the god of death and the underworld (whose Roman name was Pluto), rode by in his chariot and carried her off with him to the kingdom of the dead. Ceres protested the abduction of her daughter to Zeus, king of the gods. Zeus told her that Persephone could only return if she had eaten nothing in the underworld. When they learned that Persephone had eaten three pomegranate seeds, Zeus reached a compromise between Ceres and Hades: Persephone could return to her mother for half of each year, but for the other half she had to remain with Hades in the underworld. Ceres then made vegetation flourish during the half of the year Persephone returned to her (spring and summer) but let vegetation die when her daughter went back to the land of the dead (fall and winter).

Because I Could Not Stop for Death

Because I could not stop for Death-
He kindly stopped for me-
The Carriage held but just Ourselves-
And Immortality.

We slowly drove-He knew no haste   5
And I had put away
My labor and my leisure too,
For His Civility-

We passed the School, where Children strove
At Recess-in the Ring-   10
We passed the Fields of Gazing Grain-
We passed the Setting Sun-

Or rather-He passed Us-
The Dews drew quivering and chill-
For only Gossamer, my Gown-   15
My Tippet-only Tulle-   *My cape was made of only sheer silk net*

We paused before a House that seemed
A Swelling of the Ground-
The Roof was scarcely visible-
The Cornice-in the Ground-   20

Since then-'tis Centuries-and yet
Feels shorter than the Day
I first surmised the Horses' Heads
Were toward Eternity-   1862

How does Dickinson characterize Death in this poem? Do his kindly demeanor, civil behavior, and relaxed pace make him more or less terrifying? In the fifth quatrain, how does Dickinson describe her grave as a house? The word "surmised" in the next-to-last line is richly ambiguous. Does it suggest that she was wrong in thinking that Death was taking her to "Eternity?"

I Heard a Fly Buzz—When I Died

I heard a Fly buzz -- when I died --
The Stillness in the Room
Was like the Stillness in the Air --
Between the Heaves of Storm -- 5

The Eyes around -- had wrung them dry --
And Breaths were gathering firm
For that last Onset -- when the King
Be witnessed -- in the Room --

I willed my Keepsakes -- Signed away 10
What portion of me be
Assignable -- and then it was
There interposed a Fly --

With Blue -- uncertain stumbling Buzz --
Between the light -- and me --
And then the Windows failed -- and then
I could not see to see -- 1862

Part of the horror in this poem comes at the end when, at the moment of death, a fly that had been buzzing around the room, alights on the eye of the dying person, who cannot brush it away.

I Started Early—Took My Dog

I started Early - Took my Dog -
And visited the Sea -
The Mermaids in the Basement
Came out to look at me -

And Frigates - in the Upper Floor 5
Extended Hempen Hands -
Presuming Me to be a Mouse -
Aground - upon the Sands -

But no Man moved Me - till the Tide
Went past my simple Shoe - 10
And past my Apron - and my Belt
And past my Bodice - too -

And made as He would eat me up -
As wholly as a Dew
Upon a Dandelion's Sleeve - 15
And then - I started - too -

And He - He followed - close behind -

I felt His Silver Heel
Upon my Ankle - Then my Shoes
Would overflow with Pearl -   20

Until We met the Solid Town -
No One He seemed to know
And bowing - with a Mighty look -
At me - The Sea withdrew   1862

How does the sea behave toward the speaker in polite but terrifying ways that resemble the behavior of Death in "Because I Could Not Stop for Death"?

Chapter 11
American Realistic Fiction

Gothic fiction was usually set in places and times remote from the world of its readers. These stories often described unusual, even supernatural events involving strange characters such as Poe's Montresor. By the middle of the nineteenth century, however, there was a push to return to the kind of fiction Jane Austen wrote—stories about ordinary people in the same everyday society the readers of such fiction inhabited. In England, writers such as George Eliot (whose real name was Mary Ann Evans) and William Makepeace Thackeray set their novels in their contemporary social milieu. In France, Honore Balzac and Gustav Flaubert did the same, respectively, in novels such as *Pere Goriot* ("Old Man Goriot") and *Madame Bovary*. In America, in the latter half of the nineteenth century, this return to *realism* was led by two writers, William Dean Howells and Henry James.

William Dean Howells (1837–1920)

William Dean Howells was one of the most famous writers and editors of his day, editing such distinguished magazines as the *Atlantic Monthly* and *Harper's*, which are still published today. Howells championed realism in fiction and was close friends with Mark Twain and Henry James, but he also used his enormous prestige and influence to support younger writers, such as Stephen Crane, who challenged realism with *naturalism*, a form of fiction we will study in our next unit.

This "literary lion," as such powerful "men of letters" were called, grew up in a small town in Ohio where his father was a printer and newspaper editor. Although William received little formal education, he read voraciously and helped his father with the newspaper. With the instinct of a good editor, he published a campaign biography of presidential candidate Abraham Lincoln in 1860, beating all competing biographers to the punch. Lincoln appointed Howells the diplomatic consul to Venice, where he had plentiful time to write.

When he returned to America after the Civil War, Howells settled in Boston and became editor first of the *Atlantic Monthly*, then of *Harper's*, putting him at the center of the American literary scene. Even with his editorial duties, Howells was incredibly productive: he wrote 135 books, 35 of which were novels. Like other realists, Howells was interested in social interactions among people in middle-class society, but he also took up social reform in his fiction, protesting the oppression of the working classes.

In the short story, "Editha," Howells criticizes America's involvement in the Spanish-American War of 1898, which he and other writers regarded as naked imperialism on America's part to wrest Cuba from Spain. He tells the story largely from the third-person limited point of view of his main character, but he occasionally shifts to an omniscient narrator. Be alert to the way Howells handles that third-person point of view. Ask yourself if Editha understands herself and her situation. For example, Editha is a fervid supporter of the Spanish-American War, but Howells was opposed to it. How does he use the point of view of such a character to tell his story? As always in realistic fiction, study not only the events that occur in the story but the *impression* those events make—or fail to make—upon the character through whose point of view the story is told.

Editha

The air was thick with the war feeling, like the electricity of a storm which had not yet burst. Editha sat looking out into the hot spring afternoon, with her lips parted, and panting with the intensity of the question whether she could let him go. She had decided that she could not let him stay, when she saw him at the end of the still leafless avenue, making slowly up towards the house, with his head down and his figure relaxed. She ran impatiently out on the veranda, to the edge of the steps, and imperatively demanded greater haste of him with her will before she called aloud to him: "George!"

He had quickened his pace in mystical response to her mystical urgency, before he could have heard her; now he looked up and answered, "Well?"

"Oh, how united we are!" she exulted, and then she swooped down the steps to him, "What is it?" she cried.

"It's war," he said and he pulled her up to him and kissed her.

She kissed him back intensely, but irrelevantly, as to their passion, and uttered from deep in her throat. "How glorious!"

"It's war," he repeated, without consenting to her sense of it; and she did not know just what to think at first. She never knew what to think of him; that made his mystery, his charm. All through their courtship, which was contemporaneous with the growth of the war feeling, she had been puzzled by his want of seriousness about it. He seemed to despise it even more than he abhorred it. She could have understood his abhorring any sort of bloodshed; that would have been a survival of his old life when he thought he would be a minister, and before he changed and took up the law. But making light of a cause so high and noble seemed to show a want of earnestness at the core of his being. Not but that she felt herself able to cope with a congenital defect of that sort, and make his love for her save him from himself. Now perhaps the miracle was already wrought in him. In the presence of the tremendous fact that he announced, all triviality seemed to have gone out of him; she began to feel that. He sank down on the top step, and wiped his forehead with his handkerchief, while she poured out upon him her question of the origin and authenticity of his news.

All the while, in her duplex emotioning, she was aware that now at the very beginning she must put a guard upon herself against urging him, by any word or act, to take the part that her whole soul willed him to take, for the completion of her ideal of him. He was very nearly perfect as he was, and he must be allowed to perfect himself.

But he was peculiar, and he might very well be reasoned out of his peculiarity. Before her reasoning went her emotioning: her nature pulling upon his nature, her womanhood upon his manhood, without her knowing the means she was using to the end she was willing. She had always supposed that the man who won her would have done something to win her; she did not know what, but something. George Gearson had simply asked her for her love, on the way home from a concert, and she gave her love to him, without, as it were, thinking. But now, it flashed upon her, if he could do something worthy to have won her-- be a hero, her hero--it would be even better than if he had done it before asking her; it would be grander. Besides, she had believed in the war from the beginning.

"But don't you see, dearest," she said, "that it wouldn't have come to this if it hadn't been in the order of Providence? And I call any war glorious that is for the liberation of people who have been struggling for years against the cruelest oppression. Don't you think so, too?"

"I suppose so," he returned, languidly. "But war! Is it glorious to break the peace of the world?"

"That ignoble peace! It was no peace at all, with that crime and shame at our very gates." She was conscious of parroting the current phrases of the newspapers, but it was no time to pick and choose her words. She must sacrifice anything to the high ideal she had for him, and after a good deal of rapid argument she ended with the climax: "But now it doesn't matter about the how or why. Since the war has come, all that is gone. There are no two sides any more. There is nothing now but our country."

He sat with his eyes closed and his head leant back against the veranda, and he remarked, with a vague smile, as if musing aloud, "Our country--right or wrong."

"Yes, right or wrong!" she returned, fervidly. "I'll go and get you some lemonade." She rose rustling, and whisked away; when she came back with two tall glasses of clouded liquid on a tray, and the ice clucking in them, he still sat as she had left him, and she said, as if there had been no interruption: "But there is no question of wrong in this case. I call it a sacred war. A war for liberty and humanity, if ever there was one. And I know you will see it just as I do, yet."

He took half the lemonade at a gulp, and he answered as he set the glass down: "I know you always have the highest ideal. When I differ from you I ought to doubt myself."

A generous sob rose in Editha's throat for the humility of a man, so very nearly perfect, who was willing to put himself below her.

Besides, she felt, more subliminally, that he was never so near slipping through her fingers as when he took that meek way.

"You shall not say that! Only, for once I happen to be right." She seized his hand in her two hands, and poured her soul from her eyes into his. "Don't you think so?" she entreated him.

He released his hand and drank the rest of his lemonade, and she added, "Have mine, too," but he shook his head in answering, "I've no business to think so, unless I act so, too."

Her heart stopped a beat before it pulsed on with leaps that she felt in her neck. She had noticed that strange thing in men: they seemed to feel bound to do what they believed, and not think a thing was finished when they said it, as girls did. She knew what was in his mind, but she pretended not, and she said, "Oh, I am not sure," and then faltered.

He went on as if to himself, without apparently heeding her: "There's only one way of proving one's faith in a thing like this."

She could not say that she understood, but she did understand.

He went on again. "If I believed--if I felt as you do about this war-- Do you wish me to feel as you do?"

Now she was really not sure; so she said: "George, I don't know what you mean."

He seemed to muse away from her as before. "There is a sort of fascination in it. I suppose that at the bottom of his heart every man would like at times to have his courage tested, to see how he would act."

"How can you talk in that ghastly way?"

"It is rather morbid. Still, that's what it comes to, unless you're swept away by ambition or driven by conviction. I haven't the conviction or the ambition, and the other thing is what it comes to with me. I ought to have been a preacher, after all; then I couldn't have asked it of myself, as I must, now I'm a lawyer. And you believe it's a holy war, Editha?" he suddenly addressed her. "Oh, I know you do! But you wish me to believe so, too?"

She hardly knew whether he was mocking or not, in the ironical way he always had with her plainer mind. But the only thing was to be outspoken with him.

"George, I wish you to believe whatever you think is true, at any and every cost. If I've tried to talk you into anything, I take it all back."

"Oh, I know that, Editha. I know how sincere you are, and how-- I wish I had your undoubting spirit! I'll think it over; I'd like to believe as you do. But I don't, now; I don't, indeed. It isn't this war alone; though this seems peculiarly wanton and needless; but it's every war--so stupid; it makes me sick. Why shouldn't this thing have been settled reasonably?"

"Because," she said, very throatily again, "God meant it to be war."

"You think it was God? Yes, I suppose that is what people will say."

"Do you suppose it would have been war if God hadn't meant it?"

"I don't know. Sometimes it seems as if God had put this world into men's keeping to work it as they pleased."

"Now, George, that is blasphemy."

"Well, I won't blaspheme. I'll try to believe in your pocket Providence," he said, and then he rose to go.

"Why don't you stay to dinner?" Dinner at Balcom's Works was at one o'clock.

"I'll come back to supper, if you'll let me. Perhaps I shall bring you a convert."

"Well, you may come back, on that condition."

"All right. If I don't come, you'll understand."

He went away without kissing her, and she felt it a suspension of their engagement. It all interested her intensely; she was undergoing a tremendous experience, and she was being equal to it. While she stood looking after him, her mother came out through one of the long windows onto the veranda, with a catlike softness and vagueness.

"Why didn't he stay to dinner?"

"Because--because--war has been declared," Editha pronounced, without turning.

Her mother said, "Oh, my!" and then said nothing more until she had sat down in one of the large Shaker chairs and rocked herself for some time. Then she closed whatever tacit passage of thought there had been in her mind with the spoken words: "Well, I hope he won't go."

"And I hope he will," the girl said, and confronted her mother with a stormy exaltation that would have frightened any creature less unimpressionable than a cat.

Her mother rocked herself again for an interval of cogitation. What she arrived at in speech was: "Well, I guess you've done a wicked thing, Editha Balcom."

The girl said, as she passed indoors through the same window her mother had come out by: "I haven't done anything--yet."

In her room, she put together all her letters and gifts from Gearson, down to the withered petals of the first flower he had offered, with that timidity of his veiled in that irony of his. In the heart of the packet she enshrined her engagement ring which she had restored to the pretty box he had brought it her in. Then she sat down, if not calmly yet strongly, and wrote:

"GEORGE:--I understood when you left me. But I think we had better emphasize your meaning that if we cannot be one in everything we had better be one in nothing. So I am sending these things for your keeping till you have made up your mind.

"I shall always love you, and therefore I shall never marry any one else. But the man I marry must love his country first of all, and be able to say to me,

"'I could not love thee, dear, so much,
Loved I not honor more.'

"There is no honor above America with me. In this great hour there is no other honor.

"Your heart will make my words clear to you. I had never expected to say so much, but it has come upon me that I must say the utmost. Editha."

She thought she had worded her letter well, worded it in a way that could not be bettered; all had been implied and nothing expressed.

She had it ready to send with the packet she had tied with red, white, and blue ribbon, when it occurred to her that she was not just to him, that she was not giving him a fair chance. He had said he would go and think it over, and she was not waiting. She was pushing, threatening, compelling. That was not a woman's part. She must leave him free, free, free. She could not accept for her country or herself a forced sacrifice.

In writing her letter she had satisfied the impulse from which it sprang; she could well afford to wait till he had thought it over. She put the packet and the letter by, and rested serene in the consciousness of having done what was laid upon her by her love itself to do, and yet used patience, mercy, justice.

She had her reward. Gearson did not come to tea, but she had given him till morning, when, late at night there came up from the village the sound of a fife and drum, with a tumult of voices, in shouting, singing, and laughing. The noise drew nearer and nearer; it reached the street end of the avenue; there it silenced itself, and one voice, the voice she knew best, rose over the silence. It fell; the air was filled with cheers; the fife and drum struck up, with the shouting, singing, and laughing again, but now retreating; and a single figure came hurrying up the avenue.

She ran down to meet her lover and clung to him. He was very gay, and he put his arm round her with a boisterous laugh. "Well, you must call me Captain now; or Cap, if you prefer; that's what the boys call me. Yes, we've had a meeting at the town-hall, and everybody has volunteered; and they selected me for captain, and I'm going to the war, the big war, the glorious war, the holy war ordained by the pocket Providence that blesses butchery. Come along; let's tell the whole family about it. Call them from their downy beds, father, mother, Aunt Hitty, and all the folks!"

But when they mounted the veranda steps he did not wait for a larger audience; he poured the story out upon Editha alone.

"There was a lot of speaking, and then some of the fools set up a shout for me. It was all going one way, and I thought it would be a good joke to sprinkle a little cold water on them. But you can't do that with a crowd that adores you. The first thing I knew I was sprinkling hell-fire on them. 'Cry havoc, and let slip the dogs of war.' That was the style. Now that it had come to the fight, there were no two parties; there was one country, and the thing was to fight to a finish as quick as possible. I suggested volunteering then and there, and I wrote my name first of all on the roster. Then they elected me--that's all. I wish I had some ice-water."

She left him walking up and down the veranda, while she ran for the ice-pitcher and a goblet, and when she came back he was still walking up and down, shouting the story he had told her to her father and mother, who had come out more sketchily dressed than they commonly were by day. He drank goblet after goblet of the ice-water without noticing who was giving it, and kept on talking, and laughing through his talk wildly. "It's astonishing," he said, "how well the worse reason looks when you try to make it appear the better. Why, I believe I was the first convert to the war in that crowd to-night! I never thought I should like to kill a man; but now I shouldn't care; and the smokeless powder lets you see the man drop that you kill. It's all for the country! What a thing it is to have a country that can't be wrong, but if it is, is right, anyway!"

Editha had a great, vital thought, an inspiration. She set down the ice-pitcher on the veranda floor, and ran up-stairs and got the letter she had written him. When at last he noisily bade her father and mother, "Well, good-night. I forgot I woke you up; I sha'n't want any sleep myself," she followed him down the avenue to the gate. There, after the whirling words that seemed to fly away from her thoughts and refuse to serve them, she made a last effort to solemnize the moment that seemed so crazy, and pressed the letter she had written upon him.

"What's this?" he said. "Want me to mail it?"

"No, no. It's for you. I wrote it after you went this morning. Keep it--keep it--and read it sometime--" She thought, and then her inspiration came: "Read it if ever you doubt what you've done, or fear that I regret your having done it. Read it after you've started."

They strained each other in embraces that seemed as ineffective as their words, and he kissed her face with quick, hot breaths that were so unlike him, that made her feel as if she had lost her old lover and found a stranger in his place. The stranger said: "What a gorgeous flower you are, with your red hair, and your blue eyes that look black now, and your face with the color painted out by the white moonshine! Let me hold you under the chin, to see whether I love blood, you tiger-lily!" Then he laughed Gearson's laugh, and released her, scared and giddy. Within her wilfulness she had been frightened by a sense of subtler force in him, and mystically mastered as she had never been before.

She ran all the way back to the house, and mounted the steps panting. Her mother and father were talking of the great affair. Her mother said: "Wa'n't Mr. Gearson in rather of an excited state of mind? Didn't you think he acted curious?"

"Well, not for a man who'd just been elected captain and had set 'em up for the whole of Company A," her father chuckled back.

"What in the world do you mean, Mr. Balcom? Oh! There's Editha!" She offered to follow the girl indoors.

"Don't come, mother!" Editha called, vanishing.

Mrs. Balcom remained to reproach her husband. "I don't see much of anything to laugh at."

"Well, it's catching. Caught it from Gearson. I guess it won't be much of a war, and I guess Gearson don't think so either. The other fellows will back down as soon as they see we mean it. I wouldn't lose any sleep over it. I'm going back to bed, myself.

Gearson came again next afternoon, looking pale and rather sick, but quite himself, even to his languid irony. "I guess I'd better tell you, Editha, that I consecrated myself to your god of battles last night by pouring too many libations to him down my own throat. But I'm all right now. One has to carry off the excitement, somehow."

"Promise me," she commanded, "that you'll never touch it again!"

"What! Not let the cannikin clink? Not let the soldier drink? Well, I promise."

"You don't belong to yourself now; you don't even belong to me. You belong to your country, and you have a sacred charge to keep yourself strong and well for your country's sake. I have been thinking, thinking all night and all day long."

"You look as if you had been crying a little, too," he said, with his queer smile.

"That's all past. I've been thinking, and worshipping you. Don't you suppose I know all that you've been through, to come to this? I've followed you every step from your old theories and opinions."

"Well, you've had a long row to hoe."

"And I know you've done this from the highest motives--"

"Oh, there won't be much pettifogging to do till this cruel war is--"

"And you haven't simply done it for my sake. I couldn't respect you if you had."

"Well, then we'll say I haven't. A man that hasn't got his own respect intact wants the respect of all the other people he can corner. But we won't go into that. I'm in for the thing now, and we've got to face our future. My idea is that this isn't going to be a very protracted struggle; we shall just scare the enemy to death before it comes to a fight at all. But we must provide for contingencies, Editha. If anything happens to me--"

"Oh, George!" She clung to him, sobbing.

"I don't want you to feel foolishly bound to my memory. I should hate that, wherever I happened to be."

"I am yours, for time and eternity--time and eternity." She liked the words; they satisfied her famine for phrases.

"Well, say eternity; that's all right; but time's another thing; and I'm talking about time. But there is something! My mother! If anything happens--"

She winced, and he laughed. "You're not the bold soldier-girl of yesterday!" Then he sobered. "If anything happens, I want you to help my mother out. She won't like my doing this thing. She brought me up to think war a fool thing as well as a bad thing. My father was in the Civil War; all through it; lost his arm in it." She thrilled with the sense of the arm round her; what if that should be lost? He laughed as if divining her: "Oh, it doesn't run in the family, as far as I know!" Then he added gravely: "He came home with misgivings about war, and they grew on him. I guess he and mother agreed between them that I was to be brought up in his final mind about it; but that was before my time. I only knew him from my mother's report of him and his opinions; I don't know whether they were hers first; but they were hers last. This will be a blow to her. I shall have to write and tell her--"

He stopped, and she asked: "Would you like me to write, too, George?"

"I don't believe that would do. No, I'll do the writing. She'll understand a little if I say that I thought the way to minimize it was to make war on the largest possible scale at once--that I felt I must have been helping on the war somehow if I hadn't helped keep it from coming, and I knew I hadn't; when it came, I had no right to stay out of it."

Whether his sophistries satisfied him or not, they satisfied her. She clung to his breast, and whispered, with closed eyes and quivering lips: "Yes, yes, yes!"

"But if anything should happen, you might go to her and see what you could do for her. You know? It's rather far off; she can't leave her chair--"

"Oh, I'll go, if it's the ends of the earth! But nothing will happen! Nothing can! I--"

She felt her lifted with his rising, and Gearson was saying, with his arm still round her, to her father: "Well, we're off at once, Mr. Balcom. We're to be formally accepted at the capital, and then bunched up with the rest somehow, and sent into camp somewhere, and got to the front as soon as possible. We all want to be in the van, of course; we're the first company to report to the Governor. I came to tell Editha, but I hadn't got round to it."

She saw him again for a moment at the capital, in the station, just before the train started southward with his regiment. He looked well, in his uniform, and very soldierly, but somehow girlish, too, with his clean-shaven face and slim figure. The manly eyes and the strong voice satisfied her, and his preoccupation with some unexpected details of duty flattered her. Other girls were weeping and bemoaning themselves, but she felt a sort of noble distinction in the abstraction, the almost unconsciousness, with which they parted. Only at the last moment he said: "Don't forget my mother. It mayn't be such a walk-over as I supposed," and he laughed at the notion.

He waved his hand to her as the train moved off--she knew it among a score of hands that were waved to other girls from the platform of the car, for it held a letter which she knew was hers. Then he went inside the car to read it, doubtless, and she did not see him again. But she felt safe for him through the strength of what she called her love. What she called her God, always speaking the name in a deep voice and with the implication of a mutual understanding, would watch over him and keep him and bring him back to her. If with an empty sleeve, then he should have three arms instead of two, for both of hers should be his for life. She did not see, though, why she should always be thinking of the arm his father had lost.

There were not many letters from him, but they were such as she could have wished, and she put her whole strength into making hers such as she imagined he could have wished, glorifying and supporting him. She wrote to his mother glorifying him as their hero, but the brief answer she got was merely to the effect that Mrs. Gearson was not well enough to write herself, and thanking her for her letter by the hand of someone who called herself "Yrs truly, Mrs. W. J. Andrews."

Editha determined not to be hurt, but to write again quite as if the answer had been all she expected. Before it seemed as if she could have written, there came news of the first skirmish, and in the list of the killed, which was telegraphed as a trifling loss on our side, was Gearson's name. There was a frantic time of trying to make out that it might be, must be, some other Gearson; but the name and the company and the regiment and the State were too definitely given.

Then there was a lapse into depths out of which it seemed as if she never could rise again; then a lift into clouds far above all grief, black clouds, that blotted out the sun, but where she soared with him, with George--George! She had the fever that she expected of herself, but she did not die in it; she was not even delirious, and it did not last long. When she was well enough to leave her bed, her one thought was of George's mother, of his strangely worded wish that she should go to her and see what she could do for her. In the exaltation of the duty laid upon her--it buoyed her up instead of burdening her--she rapidly recovered.

Her father went with her on the long railroad journey from northern New York to western Iowa; he had business out at Davenport, and he said he could just as well go then as any other time; and he went with her to the little country town where George's mother lived in a little house on the edge of the illimitable cornfields, under trees pushed to a top of the rolling prairie. George's father had settled there after the Civil War, as so many other old soldiers had done; but they were Eastern people, and Editha fancied touches of the East in the June rose overhanging the front door, and the garden with early summer flowers stretching from the gate of the paling fence.

It was very low inside the house, and so dim, with the closed blinds, that they could scarcely see one another: Editha tall and black in her crapes which filled the air with the smell of their dyes; her father standing decorously apart with his hat on his forearm, as at funerals; a woman rested in a deep arm-chair, and the woman who had let the strangers in stood behind the chair.

The seated woman turned her head round and up, and asked the woman behind her chair: "Who did you say?"

Editha, if she had done what she expected of herself, would have gone down on her knees at the feet of the seated figure and said, "I am George's Editha," for answer.

But instead of her own voice she heard that other woman's voice, saying: "Well, I don't know as I did get the name just right. I guess I'll have to make a little more light in here," and she went and pushed two of the shutters ajar.

Then Editha's father said, in his public will-now-address-a-few-remarks tone: "My name is Balcom, ma'am--Junius H. Balcom, of Balcom's Works, New York; my daughter--"

"Oh!" the seated woman broke in, with a powerful voice, the voice that always surprised Editha from Gearson's slender frame. "Let me see you. Stand round where the light can strike on your face," and Editha dumbly obeyed. "So, you're Editha Balcom," she sighed.

"Yes," Editha said, more like a culprit than a comforter.

"What did you come for?" Mrs. Gearson asked.

Editha's face quivered and her knees shook. "I came--because--because George--" She could go no further.

"Yes," the mother said, "he told me he had asked you to come if he got killed. You didn't expect that, I suppose, when you sent him."

"I would rather have died myself than done it!" Editha said, with more truth in her deep voice than she ordinarily found in it. "I tried to leave him free--"

"Yes, that letter of yours, that came back with his other things, left him free."

Editha saw now where George's irony came from.

"It was not to be read before--unless--until-- I told him so," she faltered.

"Of course, he wouldn't read a letter of yours, under the circumstances, till he thought you wanted him to. Been sick?" the woman abruptly demanded.

"Very sick," Editha said, with self-pity.

"Daughter's life," her father interposed, "was almost despaired of, at one time."

Mrs. Gearson gave him no heed. "I suppose you would have been glad to die, such a brave person as you! I don't believe he was glad to die. He was always a timid boy, that way; he was afraid of a good many things; but if he was afraid he did what he made up his mind to. I suppose he made up his mind to go, but I knew what it cost him by what it cost me when I heard of it. I had been through one war before. When you sent him you didn't expect he would get killed."

The voice seemed to compassionate Editha, and it was time. "No," she huskily murmured.

"No, girls don't; women don't, when they give their men up to their country. They think they'll come marching back, somehow, just as gay as they went, or if it's an empty sleeve, or even an empty pantaloon, it's all the more glory, and they're so much the prouder of them, poor things!"

The tears began to run down Editha's face; she had not wept till then; but it was now such a relief to be understood that the tears came.

"No, you didn't expect him to get killed," Mrs. Gearson repeated, in a voice which was startlingly like George's again. "You just expected him to kill some one else, some of those foreigners, that weren't there because they had any say about it, but because they had to be there, poor wretches--conscripts, or whatever they call 'em. You thought it would be all right for my George, your George, to kill the sons of those miserable mothers and the husbands of those girls that you would never see the faces of." The woman lifted her powerful voice in a psalm-like note. "I thank my God he didn't live to do it! I thank my God they killed him first, and that he ain't livin' with their blood on his hands!" She dropped her eyes, which she had raised with her voice, and glared at Editha. "What you got that black on for?" She lifted herself by her powerful arms so high that her helpless body seemed to hang limp its full length. "Take it off, take it off, before I tear it from your back!"

The lady who was passing the summer near Balcom's Works was sketching Editha's beauty, which lent itself wonderfully to the effects of a colorist. It had come to that confidence which is rather apt to grow between artist and sitter, and Editha had told her everything.

"To think of your having such a tragedy in your life!" the lady said. She added: "I suppose there are people who feel that way about war. But when you consider the good this war has done--how much it has done for the country! I can't understand such people, for my part. And when you had come all the way out there to console her--got up out of a sick-bed! Well!"

"I think," Editha said, magnanimously, "she wasn't quite in her right mind; and so did papa."

"Yes," the lady said, looking at Editha's lips in nature and then at her lips in art, and giving an empirical touch to them in the picture. "But how dreadful of her! How perfectly--excuse me--how vulgar!"

A light broke upon Editha in the darkness which she felt had been without a gleam of brightness for weeks and months. The mystery that had bewildered her was solved by the word; and from that moment she rose from grovelling in shame and self-pity, and began to live again in the ideal.   1905

Narrative Form in "Editha"

As in many realistic stories, the climax comes not in external action but in internal, psychological realization. What is it that Editha comes to understand at the end of the story—and is it an accurate realization? Why is Gearson's mother so incensed by the letter Editha wrote? Recall the poem we studied by Richard Lovelace, "To Lucasta, Going to the Wars." In it, Lovelace compares his masculine sense of honor, which requires him to go to war and fight for his king, to Lucasta's honor, which is her virginity. In quoting this poem, is Editha dangling her "honor" to get Gearson to do the honorable "masculine" thing and go off to war?

Henry James (1843-1916)

Henry James' father inherited a modest fortune from his father, an Irish immigrant who had a successful business in New York. He decided that schools made passive conformists of children, so he had his children privately tutored in New York—but also in Europe, where they resided in London, Paris, and Geneva. The father's educational plan worked, for not only did Henry become a famous novelist, his brother William became a great philosopher and psychologist. Henry James continued to live in Europe as an adult, finally settling in England, though he made frequent trips back to America. He found a rich subject for fiction in the social interactions among Americans and Europeans.

Henry James was not only a great writer of fiction but one who thought deeply about the form of fiction. Early in his career, for example, he came to see that what was uppermost in writing fiction was not to simply tell a good story but to tell that story from the point of view of a particular character. It was not so much the events in a story that interested James but the impression the events of the story made upon the mind of the character through whose point of view it was told. Over the course of his career, James came to rely less and less upon exciting action in a story and more and more upon how powerfully a sensitive character's mind responded to seemingly insignificant events.

Readers in his own time and in ours have sometimes found James' fiction tediously concerned with the inner impressions of characters rather than exciting external action. The naturalist writer Frank Norris once described a James novel as "the tragedy of the broken teacup"; Mark Twain once said of another James novel, alluding to John Bunyan's stern Puritan allegory, *Pilgrim's Progress*, "I would rather be damned to John Bunyan's heaven than read that."
James also refined the fictional craft of Jane Austen (a predecessor in the art of fiction he deeply admired) by pushing her development of the third-person limited point of view. To give you an idea of how innovatively Henry James used fictional form, let's first look at "The Necklace," a much more traditional story by the French writer Guy de Maupassant, which Henry James would transform into his own short story, "Paste."

Guy de Maupassant (1850–1894)

The Necklace

The girl was one of those pretty and charming young creatures who sometimes are born, as if by a slip of fate, into a family of clerks. She had no dowry, no expectations, no way of being known, understood, loved, married by any rich and distinguished man; so she let herself be married to a little clerk of the Ministry of Public Instruction.

She dressed plainly because she could not dress well, but she was unhappy as if she had really fallen from a higher station; since with women there is neither caste nor rank, for beauty, grace and charm take the place of family and birth. Natural ingenuity, instinct for what is elegant, a supple mind are their sole hierarchy, and often make of women of the people the equals of the very greatest ladies.

Mathilde suffered ceaselessly, feeling herself born to enjoy all delicacies and all luxuries. She was distressed at the poverty of her dwelling, at the bareness of the walls, at the shabby chairs, the ugliness of the curtains.

All those things, of which another woman of her rank would never even have been conscious, tortured her and made her angry. The sight of the little Breton peasant who did her humble housework aroused in her despairing regrets and bewildering dreams. She thought of silent antechambers hung with Oriental tapestry, illumined by tall bronze candelabra, and of two great footmen in knee breeches who sleep in the big armchairs, made drowsy by the oppressive heat of the stove. She thought of long reception halls hung with ancient silk, of the dainty cabinets containing priceless curiosities and of the little coquettish perfumed reception rooms made for chatting at five o'clock with intimate friends, with men famous and sought after, whom all women envy and whose attention they all desire.

When she sat down to dinner, before the round table covered with a tablecloth in use three days, opposite her husband, who uncovered the soup tureen and declared with a delighted air, "Ah, the good soup! I don't know anything better than that," she thought of dainty dinners, of shining silverware, of tapestry that peopled the walls with ancient personages and with strange birds flying in the midst of a fairy forest; and she thought of delicious dishes served on marvellous plates and of the whispered gallantries to which you listen with a sphinxlike smile while you are eating the pink meat of a trout or the wings of a quail.

She had no gowns, no jewels, nothing. And she loved nothing but that. She felt made for that. She would have liked so much to please, to be envied, to be charming, to be sought after.

She had a friend, a former schoolmate at the convent, who was rich, and whom she did not like to go to see any more because she felt so sad when she came home.

But one evening her husband reached home with a triumphant air and holding a large envelope in his hand.

"There," said he, "there is something for you."

She tore the paper quickly and drew out a printed card which bore these words:

The Minister of Public Instruction and Madame Georges Ramponneau request the honor of M. and Madame Loisel's company at the palace of the Ministry on Monday evening, January 18th.

Instead of being delighted, as her husband had hoped, she threw the invitation on the table crossly, muttering:

"What do you wish me to do with that?"

"Why, my dear, I thought you would be glad. You never go out, and this is such a fine opportunity. I had great trouble to get it. Every one wants to go; it is very select, and they are not giving many invitations to clerks. The whole official world will be there."

She looked at him with an irritated glance and said impatiently:

"And what do you wish me to put on my back?"

He had not thought of that. He stammered:

"Why, the gown you go to the theatre in. It looks very well to me."

He stopped, distracted, seeing that his wife was weeping. Two great tears ran slowly from the corners of her eyes toward the corners of her mouth.

"What's the matter? What's the matter?" he answered.

By a violent effort she conquered her grief and replied in a calm voice, while she wiped her wet cheeks:

"Nothing. Only I have no gown, and, therefore, I can't go to this ball. Give your card to some colleague whose wife is better equipped than I am."

He was in despair. He resumed:

"Come, let us see, Mathilde. How much would it cost, a suitable gown, which you could use on other occasions--something very simple?"

She reflected several seconds, making her calculations and wondering also what sum she could ask without drawing on herself an immediate refusal and a frightened exclamation from the economical clerk.

Finally she replied hesitating:

"I don't know exactly, but I think I could manage it with four hundred francs."

He grew a little pale, because he was laying aside just that amount to buy a gun and treat himself to a little shooting next summer on the plain of Nanterre, with several friends who went to shoot larks there of a Sunday.

But he said:

"Very well. I will give you four hundred francs. And try to have a pretty gown."

The day of the ball drew near and Madame Loisel seemed sad, uneasy, anxious. Her frock was ready, however. Her husband said to her one evening:

"What is the matter? Come, you have seemed very queer these last three days."

And she answered:

"It annoys me not to have a single piece of jewelry, not a single ornament, nothing to put on. I shall look poverty-stricken. I would almost rather not go at all."

"You might wear natural flowers," said her husband. "They're very stylish at this time of year. For ten francs you can get two or three magnificent roses."

She was not convinced.

"No; there's nothing more humiliating than to look poor among other women who are rich."

"How stupid you are!" her husband cried. "Go look up your friend, Madame Forestier, and ask her to lend you some jewels. You're intimate enough with her to do that."

She uttered a cry of joy:

"True! I never thought of it."

The next day she went to her friend and told her of her distress.

Madame Forestier went to a wardrobe with a mirror, took out a large jewel box, brought it back, opened it and said to Madame Loisel:

"Choose, my dear."

She saw first some bracelets, then a pearl necklace, then a Venetian gold cross set with precious stones, of admirable workmanship. She tried on the ornaments before the mirror, hesitated and could not make up her mind to part with them, to give them back. She kept asking:

"Haven't you any more?"

"Why, yes.

Look further; I don't know what you like."

Suddenly she discovered, in a black satin box, a superb diamond necklace, and her heart throbbed with an immoderate desire. Her hands trembled as she took it. She fastened it round her throat, outside her high-necked waist, and was lost in ecstasy at her reflection in the mirror.

Then she asked, hesitating, filled with anxious doubt:

"Will you lend me this, only this?"

"Why, yes, certainly."

She threw her arms round her friend's neck, kissed her passionately, then fled with her treasure.

The night of the ball arrived. Madame Loisel was a great success. She was prettier than any other woman present, elegant, graceful, smiling and wild with joy. All the men looked at her, asked her name, sought to be introduced. All the attaches of the Cabinet wished to waltz with her. She was remarked by the minister himself.

She danced with rapture, with passion, intoxicated by pleasure, forgetting all in the triumph of her beauty, in the glory of her success, in a sort of cloud of happiness comprised of all this homage, admiration, these awakened desires and of that sense of triumph which is so sweet to woman's heart.

She left the ball about four o'clock in the morning. Her husband had been sleeping since midnight in a little deserted anteroom with three other gentlemen whose wives were enjoying the ball.

He threw over her shoulders the wraps he had brought, the modest wraps of common life, the poverty of which contrasted with the elegance of the ball dress. She felt this and wished to escape so as not to be remarked by the other women, who were enveloping themselves in costly furs.

Loisel held her back, saying: "Wait a bit. You will catch cold outside. I will call a cab."

But she did not listen to him and rapidly descended the stairs. When they reached the street they could not find a carriage and began to look for one, shouting after the cabmen passing at a distance.

They went toward the Seine in despair, shivering with cold. At last they found on the quay one of those ancient night cabs which, as though they were ashamed to show their shabbiness during the day, are never seen round Paris until after dark.

It took them to their dwelling in the Rue des Martyrs, and sadly they mounted the stairs to their flat. All was ended for her. As to him, he reflected that he must be at the ministry at ten o'clock that morning.

She removed her wraps before the glass so as to see herself once more in all her glory. But suddenly she uttered a cry. She no longer had the necklace around her neck!

"What is the matter with you?" demanded her husband, already half undressed.

She turned distractedly toward him.

"I have--I have--I've lost Madame Forestier's necklace," she cried.

He stood up, bewildered.

"What!--how? Impossible!"

They looked among the folds of her skirt, of her cloak, in her pockets, everywhere, but did not find it.

"You're sure you had it on when you left the ball?" he asked.

"Yes, I felt it in the vestibule of the minister's house."

"But if you had lost it in the street we should have heard it fall. It must be in the cab."

"Yes, probably. Did you take his number?"

"No. And you--didn't you notice it?"

"No."

They looked, thunderstruck, at each other. At last Loisel put on his clothes.

"I shall go back on foot," said he, "over the whole route, to see whether I can find it."

He went out. She sat waiting on a chair in her ball dress, without strength to go to bed, overwhelmed, without any fire, without a thought.

Her husband returned about seven o'clock. He had found nothing.

He went to police headquarters, to the newspaper offices to offer a reward; he went to the cab companies--everywhere, in fact, whither he was urged by the least spark of hope.

She waited all day, in the same condition of mad fear before this terrible calamity.

Loisel returned at night with a hollow, pale face. He had discovered nothing.

"You must write to your friend," said he, "that you have broken the clasp of her necklace and that you are having it mended. That will give us time to turn round."

She wrote at his dictation.

At the end of a week they had lost all hope. Loisel, who had aged five years, declared:

"We must consider how to replace that ornament."

The next day they took the box that had contained it and went to the jeweler whose name was found within. He consulted his books.

"It was not I, madame, who sold that necklace; I must simply have furnished the case."

Then they went from jeweler to jeweler, searching for a necklace like the other, trying to recall it, both sick with chagrin and grief.

They found, in a shop at the Palais Royal, a string of diamonds that seemed to them exactly like the one they had lost. It was worth forty thousand francs. They could have it for thirty-six.

So they begged the jeweler not to sell it for three days yet.

And they made a bargain that he should buy it back for thirty-four thousand francs, in case they should find the lost necklace before the end of February.

Loisel possessed eighteen thousand francs which his father had left him. He would borrow the rest.

He did borrow, asking a thousand francs of one, five hundred of another, five louis here, three louis there. He gave notes, took up ruinous obligations, dealt with usurers and all the race of lenders. He compromised all the rest of his life, risked signing a note without even knowing whether he could meet it; and, frightened by the trouble yet to come, by the black misery that was about to fall upon him, by the prospect of all the physical privations and moral tortures that he was to suffer, he went to get the new necklace, laying upon the jeweler's counter thirty-six thousand francs.

When Madame Loisel took back the necklace Madame Forestier said to her with a chilly manner:

"You should have returned it sooner; I might have needed it."

She did not open the case, as her friend had so much feared. If she had detected the substitution, what would she have thought, what would she have said? Would she not have taken Madame Loisel for a thief?

Thereafter Madame Loisel knew the horrible existence of the needy. She bore her part, however, with sudden heroism. That dreadful debt must be paid. She would pay it. They dismissed their servant; they changed their lodgings; they rented a garret under the roof.

She came to know what heavy housework meant and the odious cares of the kitchen. She washed the dishes, using her dainty fingers and rosy nails on greasy pots and pans. She washed the soiled linen, the shirts and the dishcloths, which she dried upon a line; she carried the slops down to the street every morning and carried up the water, stopping for breath at every landing. And dressed like a woman of the people, she went to the fruiterer, the grocer, the butcher, a basket on her arm, bargaining, meeting with impertinence, defending her miserable money, sou by sou.

Every month they had to meet some notes, renew others, obtain more time.

Her husband worked evenings, making up a tradesman's accounts, and late at night he often copied manuscript for five sous a page.

This life lasted ten years.

At the end of ten years they had paid everything, everything, with the rates of usury and the accumulations of the compound interest.

Madame Loisel looked old now. She had become the woman of impoverished households--strong and hard and rough. With frowsy hair, skirts askew and red hands, she talked loud while washing the floor with great swishes of water. But sometimes, when her husband was at the office, she sat down near the window and she thought of that gay evening of long ago, of that ball where she had been so beautiful and so admired.

What would have happened if she had not lost that necklace? Who knows? who knows? How strange and changeful is life! How small a thing is needed to make or ruin us!

But one Sunday, having gone to take a walk in the Champs Elysees to refresh herself after the labors of the week, she suddenly perceived a woman who was leading a child. It was Madame Forestier, still young, still beautiful, still charming.

Madame Loisel felt moved. Should she speak to her? Yes, certainly. And now that she had paid, she would tell her all about it. Why not?

She went up.

"Good-day, Jeanne."

The other, astonished to be familiarly addressed by this plain good-wife, did not recognize her at all and stammered:

"But--madame!--I do not know---- You must have mistaken."

"No. I am Mathilde Loisel."

Her friend uttered a cry.

"Oh, my poor Mathilde! How you are changed!"

"Yes, I have had a pretty hard life, since I last saw you, and great poverty--and that because of you!"

"Of me! How so?"

"Do you remember that diamond necklace you lent me to wear at the ministerial ball?"

"Yes. Well?"

"Well, I lost it."

"What do you mean? You brought it back."

"I brought you back another exactly like it. And it has taken us ten years to pay for it. You can understand that it was not easy for us, for us who had nothing. At last it is ended, and I am very glad."

Madame Forestier had stopped.

"You say that you bought a necklace of diamonds to replace mine?"

"Yes. You never noticed it, then! They were very similar."

And she smiled with a joy that was at once proud and ingenuous.

Madame Forestier, deeply moved, took her hands.

"Oh, my poor Mathilde! Why, my necklace was paste! It was worth at most only five hundred francs!"   1884

Narrative Form in "The Necklace"

While "The Necklace" is a wonderful story, in terms of fictional form, it is very traditionally told—by an omniscient narrator who alternates between scene and summary. The power of the story depends upon the plot—what happens—as the married couple slave to repay what they think was a lost diamond necklace, only to find, in a surprise ending, that the necklace Mathilde borrowed was merely cheap, costume jewelry. While we get some sense of the characters in the story, we do not go very fully into their minds, which, after all, seem to have little depth beyond wanting material things.

Henry James decided to do what we'd now call a "cover" on this story. He changed the plot so that a seemingly worthless necklace may possibly be very valuable, focused the story on a single character, and presented it in a way that blended "showing" and "telling," dramatic scene and narrative summary, almost completely from her third-person limited point of view. So deeply does James root us in Charlotte's point of view at the beginning of the story that he does not explain who she is, where she is, or even tell us her name. He just plunges us into her consciousness as she speaks with her cousin, whose name is also not given (because "she," of course knows her cousin's name—as well as her own).

From Henry James' "Paste"

"I've found a lot more things," her cousin said to her the day after the second funeral; "they're up in her room--but they're things I wish you'd look at."

All we know is that there has been a "second" funeral—nothing yet about the first—and that her cousin wants her to look at "things" in "her room"—presumably the room of the woman who has died.

Why is James opening this story so abruptly and elusively? Imagine that we could enter your mind and listen to your thoughts as you conversed with someone in your family. You would not "explain" to yourself the identities of the various other family members were you spoke about. In your mind, they would be familiar parents, siblings, and relatives. James treats "her" thoughts in the same way—supplying no additional information as omniscient narrator. Such a use of third-person limited point of view is extremely realistic in that it renders "her" thoughts exactly the way your thoughts would take form in a conversation with your relative. It does, however, make for a very difficult story for a reader to "pick up' as it goes along. After this opening bit of dialogue, James gives some exposition about the situation but completely from "her" point of view.

The pair of mourners, sufficiently stricken, were in the garden of the vicarage together, before luncheon, waiting to be summoned to that meal, and Arthur Prime had still in his face the intention, she was moved to call it rather than the expression, of feeling something or other. Some such appearance was in itself of course natural within a week of his stepmother's death, within three of his father's; but what was most present to the girl, herself sensitive and shrewd, was that he seemed somehow to brood without sorrow, to suffer without what she in her own case would have called pain.

From this passage, we learn that "her" cousin's name is Arthur Prime, that his father has died three weeks earlier, and that the "second" funeral was that of his stepmother who has died within the past week. We also learn that the two characters are in a vicarage (a house attached to a church where the minister—the "vicar"—lives with his family). We also learn that the main character does not think her cousin Arthur really seems to be grieving over his stepmother's death.

We then learn that the "things" Arthur wanted "her" to look at were his stepmother's costume jewelry pieces so that "she" could choose something as a remembrance of her aunt. As the main character goes up to her aunt's room, she looks at the costume jewelry and thinks about how her aunt and uncle met and married.

They met her eyes for the first time, but in a moment, before touching them, she knew them as things of the theatre, as very much too fine to have been with any verisimilitude things of the vicarage. They were too dreadfully good to be true, for her aunt had had no jewels to speak of, and these were coronets and girdles, diamonds, rubies and sapphires. Flagrant tinsel and glass, they looked strangely vulgar, but if after the first queer shock of them she found herself taking them up it was for the very proof, never yet so distinct to her, of a far-off faded story. An honest widowed cleric with a small son and a large sense of Shakespeare had, on a brave latitude of habit as well as of taste--since it implied his having in very fact dropped deep into the "pit"--conceived for an obscure actress several years older than himself an admiration of which the prompt offer of his reverend name and hortatory hand was the sufficiently candid sign. The response had perhaps in those dim years, so far as eccentricity was concerned, even bettered the proposal, and Charlotte, turning the tale over, had long since drawn from it a measure of the career renounced by the undistinguished comedienne--doubtless also tragic, or perhaps pantomimic, at a pinch--of her late uncle's dreams. This career couldn't have been eminent and must much more probably have been comfortless.

From this passage we learn that the main character's name is Charlotte, and as she looks at her aunt's jewelry she reflects on the way her aunt and uncle met and married. He had been a vicar who lost his first wife after his son Arthur was born. He was a great lover of theatre and fell in love with "an obscure actress several years older than himself." He had proposed marriage, and she had accepted, knowing she would never be a famous actress and was getting older. She "settled" for the security of being a minister's wife. As Charlotte rummages through the costume jewelry, she comes across a string of heavy pearls that she thinks might be real rather than "paste" and asks Arthur if he's sure the pearls are not real.

"This perhaps *is* worth something. Feel it." And she passed him the necklace, the weight of which she had gathered for a moment into her hand.

He measured it in the same way with his own, but remained quite detached. "Worth at most thirty shillings."

"Not more?"

"Surely not if it's paste?"

"But *is* it paste?"

He gave a small sniff of impatience. "Pearls nearly as big as filberts?"

"But they're heavy," Charlotte declared.

"No heavier than anything else." And he gave them back with an allowance for her simplicity. "Do you imagine for a moment they're real?"

She studied them a little, feeling them, turning them round. "Mightn't they possibly be?"

"Of that size--stuck away with that trash?"

"I admit it isn't likely," Charlotte presently said. "And pearls are so easily imitated."

"That's just what--to a person who knows--they're not. These have no lustre, no play."

"No--they *are* dull. They're opaque."

"Besides," he lucidly enquired, "how could she ever have come by them?"

"Mightn't they have been a present?"

Arthur stared at the question as if it were almost improper. "Because actresses are exposed--?" He pulled up, however, not saying to what, and before she could supply the deficiency had, with the sharp ejaculation of "No, they mightn't!" turned his back on her and walked away.

By suggesting that the pearls might be real, Charlotte has offended her cousin Arthur. His step-mother had been an actress, and if she had received a present of real pearls it could have been a gift in return for sexual favors from a wealthy admirer. When Charlotte leaves after the funeral, Arthur makes a point of insisting that the pearls cannot be real.

His manner made her feel she had probably been wanting in tact, and before he returned to the subject, the last thing that evening, she had satisfied herself of the ground of his resentment. They had been talking of her departure the next morning, the hour of her train and the fly that would come for her, and it was precisely these things that gave him his effective chance. "I really can't allow you to leave the house under the impression that my stepmother was at *any* time of her life the sort of person to allow herself to be approached--"

"With pearl necklaces and that sort of thing?" Arthur had made for her somehow the difficulty that she couldn't show him she understood him without seeming pert.

It at any rate only added to his own gravity. "That sort of thing, exactly."

"I didn't think when I spoke this morning--but I see what you mean."

"I mean that she was beyond reproach," said Arthur Prime.

"A hundred times yes."

"Therefore if she couldn't, out of her slender gains, ever have paid for a row of pearls--"

"She couldn't, in that atmosphere, ever properly have had one? Of course she couldn't. I've seen perfectly since our talk," Charlotte went on, "that

that string of beads isn't even as an imitation very good. The little clasp itself doesn't seem even gold. With false pearls, I suppose," the girl mused, "it naturally wouldn't be."

"The whole thing's rotten paste," her companion returned as if to have done with it. "If it were *not*, and she had kept it all these years hidden--"

"Yes?" Charlotte sounded as he paused.

"Why I shouldn't know what to think!"

"Oh I see." She had met him with a certain blankness, but adequately enough, it seemed, for him to regard the subject as dismissed; and there was no reversion to it between them before, on the morrow, when she had with difficulty made a place for them in her trunk, she carried off these florid survivals.

When Charlotte returns to the home where she works as a governess, she shows the pearls to her friend, Mrs. Guy.

"But I don't, my dear, understand."

"Understand what?"

Mrs. Guy gave a very lighted stare. "How you come to have such things."

Poor Charlotte smiled. "By inheritance."

"Family jewels?"

"They belonged to my aunt, who died some months ago. She was on the stage a few years in early life, and these are a part of her trappings."

"She left them to you?"

"No; my cousin, her stepson, who naturally has no use for them, gave them to me for remembrance of her. She was a dear kind thing, always so nice to me, and I was fond of her."

Mrs. Guy had listened with frank interest. "But it's *he* who must be a dear kind thing!"

Charlotte wondered. "You think so?"

"Is *he*," her friend went on, "also 'always so nice' to you?"

The girl, at this, face to face there with the brilliant visitor in the deserted breakfast-room, took a deeper sounding. "What is it?"

"Don't you know?"

Something came over her. "The pearls--?" But the question fainted on her lips.

"Doesn't *he* know?"

Charlotte found herself flushing. "They're *not* paste?"

"Haven't you looked at them?"

She was conscious of two kinds of embarrassment. "*You* have?"

"Very carefully."

"And they're real?"

Mrs. Guy became slightly mystifying and returned for all answer: "Come again, when you've done with the children, to my room."

Mrs. Guy borrows the pearls to wear at a party in the house that evening, and after Charlotte puts the children in her care to bed, she goes to Mrs. Guy's room and sees her wearing the pearls.

This lady's white shoulders heaved, under the pearls, with an emotion that the very red lips which formed, as if for the full effect, the happiest opposition of colour, were not slow to translate. "My dear, you should have seen the sensation--they've had a success!"

Charlotte, dumb a moment, took it all in. "It *is* as if they knew it--they're more and more alive. But so much the worse for both of us! I can't," she brought out with an effort, "be silent."

"You mean to return them?"

"If I don't I'm a thief."

Mrs. Guy gave her a long hard look: what was decidedly not of the baby in Mrs. Guy's face was a certain air of established habit in the eyes. Then, with a sharp little jerk of her head and a backward reach of her bare beautiful arms, she undid the clasp and, taking off the necklace, laid it on the table. "If you do you're a goose."

As Charlotte struggles over whether to return the potentially valuable pearl necklace to her cousin, at the risk of offending him by insulting his step-mother's honor, Mrs. Guy grows increasingly enamoured of the pearls.

"I'm dying for them. There's a special charm in them--I don't know what it is: they tell so their history."

"But what do you know of that?"

"Just what they themselves say. It's all *in* them--and it comes out. They breathe a tenderness--they have the white glow of it. My dear," hissed Mrs. Guy in supreme confidence and as she buttoned her glove--"they're things of love!"

"Oh!" our young woman vaguely exclaimed.

"They're things of passion!"

"Mercy!" she gasped, turning short off. But these words remained, though indeed their help was scarce needed, Charlotte being in private face to face with a new light, as she by this time felt she must call it, on the dear dead kind colourless lady whose career had turned so sharp a corner in the middle. The pearls had quite taken their place as a revelation. She might have received them for nothing--admit that; but she couldn't have kept them so long and so unprofitably hidden, couldn't have enjoyed them only in secret, for nothing; and she had mixed them in her reliquary with false things in order to put curiosity and detection off the scent. Over this strange fact poor Charlotte interminably mused: it became more touching, more attaching for her than she could now confide to any ear. How bad or how happy--in the sophisticated sense of Mrs. Guy and the young man at the Temple--the effaced Miss Bradshaw must have been to have had to be so mute! The little governess at Bleet put on the necklace now in secret sessions; she wore it sometimes under her dress; she came to feel verily a haunting passion for it. Yet in her penniless state she would have parted with it for money; she gave herself also to dreams of what in this direction it would do for her. The sophistry of her so often saying to herself that Arthur had after all definitely pronounced her welcome to any gain from his gift that might accrue--this trick remained innocent, as she perfectly knew it for what it was. Then there was always the possibility of his--as she could only picture it--rising to the occasion. Mightn't he have a grand magnanimous moment?--mightn't he just say "Oh I couldn't of course have afforded to let you have it if I had known; but since you HAVE got it, and have made out the truth by your own wit, I really can't screw myself down to the shabbiness of taking it back"?

After Mrs. Guy tells Charlotte that not only are the pearls real but that they are "things of passion" that her aunt received as a gift from a lover, Charlotte undergoes the kind of startling revelation that lies at the heart of realistic fiction. She imagines that her aunt hid the real pearls among her cheap costume jewelry and took them out in secret and put them on to remind herself of her former lover. Charlotte finds herself putting on the pearls in the privacy of her room. She remembers that her cousin Arthur told her she could keep them and profit by any gain she made in selling them, but she feels that it would be deeply dishonest to profit from them herself if they really are worth a great deal of money. She even hopes that if she did offer to return them, Arthur would be magnanimous enough to say she could keep them even if they were the real thing. When Bleet, the house where she works as a governess, gives her a vacation, she goes to London to meet with Arthur.

She had, as it proved, to wait a long time--to wait till, at the end of several months, the great house of Bleet had, with due deliberation, for the season, transferred itself to town; after which, however, she fairly snatched at her first freedom to knock, dressed in her best and armed with her disclosure, at the door of her doubting kinsman. It was still with doubt and not quite with the face she had hoped that he listened to her story. He had turned pale, she thought, as she produced the necklace, and he appeared above all disagreeably affected. Well, perhaps there was reason, she more than ever remembered; but what on earth was one, in close touch with the fact, to do? She had laid the pearls on his table, where, without his having at first put so much as a finger to them, they met his hard cold stare.

"I don't believe in them," he simply said at last.

"That's exactly then," she returned with some spirit, "what I wanted to hear!"

She fancied that at this his colour changed; it was indeed vivid to her afterwards--for she was to have a long recall of the scene--that she had made him quite angrily flush. "It's a beastly unpleasant imputation, you know!"--and he walked away from her as he had always walked at the vicarage.

"It's none of *my* making, I'm sure," said Charlotte Prime. "If you're afraid to believe they're real--"

"Well?"--and he turned, across the room, sharp round at her.

"Why it's not my fault."

He said nothing more, for a moment, on this; he only came back to the table. "They're what I originally said they were. They're rotten paste."

"Then I may keep them?"

"No. I want a better opinion."

"Than your own?"

"Than *your* own." He dropped on the pearls another queer stare; then, after a moment, bringing himself to touch them, did exactly what she had herself done in the presence of Mrs. Guy at Bleet--gathered them together, marched off with them to a drawer, put them in and clicked the key. "You say I'm afraid," he went on as he again met her; "but I shan't be afraid to take them to Bond Street."

"And if the people say they're real--?"

He had a pause and then his strangest manner. "They won't say it! They shan't!"

There was something in the way he brought it out that deprived poor Charlotte, as she was perfectly aware, of any manner at all. "Oh!" she simply sounded, as she had sounded for her last word to Mrs. Guy; and within a minute, without more conversation, she had taken her departure.

A fortnight later she received a communication from him, and toward the end of the season one of the entertainments in Eaton Square was graced by the presence of Mrs. Guy. Charlotte was not at dinner, but she came down afterwards, and this guest, on seeing her, abandoned a very beautiful young man on purpose to cross and speak to her. The guest displayed a lovely necklace and had apparently not lost her habit of overflowing with the pride of such ornaments.

"Do you see?" She was in high joy.

They were indeed splendid pearls--so far as poor Charlotte could feel that she knew, after what had come and gone, about such mysteries. The poor girl had a sickly smile. "They're almost as fine as Arthur's."

"Almost? Where, my dear, are your eyes? They *are* 'Arthur's'!" After which, to meet the flood of crimson that accompanied her young friend's start: "I tracked them--after your folly, and, by miraculous luck, recognised them in the Bond Street window to which he had disposed of them."

"*Disposed* of them?" Charlotte gasped. "He wrote me that I had insulted his mother and that the people had shown him he was right--had pronounced them utter paste."

Mrs. Guy gave a stare. "Ah I told you he wouldn't bear it! No. But I had, I assure you," she wound up, "to drive my bargain!"

Charlotte scarce heard or saw; she was full of her private wrong. "He wrote me," she panted, "that he had smashed them."

Mrs. Guy could only wonder and pity. "He's really morbid!" But it wasn't quite clear which of the pair she pitied; though the young person employed in Eaton Square felt really morbid too after they had separated and she found herself full of thought. She even went the length of asking herself what sort of a bargain Mrs. Guy had driven and whether the marvel of the recognition in Bond Street had been a veracious account of the matter. Hadn't she perhaps in truth dealt with Arthur directly? It came back to Charlotte almost luridly that she had had his address.1899

Narrative Form in "Paste"

In realistic fiction, as we have seen, the most exciting, climactic moment occurs not in outward action but inward realization—when the character through whose point of view the story has been told comes to a new understanding (or fails to). James Joyce called this moment, borrowing the religious term for a religious revelation, an *epiphany*. What does Charlotte come to realize at the end of this story? How has her impression of Mrs. Guy changed?

Henry James does not explain what Charlotte has come to realize. We have to figure it out from the rapid series of thoughts that pass through her mind at the end. How has her experience with the pearls, Arthur, and Mrs. Guy changed her over the course of the story? Charlotte works as a governess, teaching the children of a wealthy English family who live in a mansion called "Bleet." Insofar as this name suggests the "bleat" of a poor lamb, how can Charlotte be regarded as an innocent lamb for much of the story? Has she matured at the end and gained a grim sense of the ugliness of the real world—or remained a helpless innocent?

Henry James and Narrative Form

Henry James experimented constantly with point of view in his fiction, and his late novels and stories are so anchored in the consciousness of a single character that it is sometimes difficult to understand what that character is experiencing. Here, for example, is the opening paragraph of one of Henry James' late novels, *The Ambassadors* (1903):

from *The Ambassadors*

Strether's first question, when he reached the hotel, was about his friend; yet on his learning that Waymarsh was apparently not to arrive till evening he was not wholly disconcerted. A telegram from him bespeaking a room "only if not noisy," reply paid, was produced for the enquirer at the office, so that the understanding they should meet at Chester rather than at Liverpool remained to that extent sound. The same secret principle, however, that had prompted

> Strether not absolutely to desire Waymarsh's presence at the dock, that had led him thus to postpone for a few hours his enjoyment of it, now operated to make him feel he could still wait without disappointment. They would dine together at the worst, and, with all respect to dear old Waymarsh--if not even, for that matter, to himself--there was little fear that in the sequel they shouldn't see enough of each other. The principle I have just mentioned as operating had been, with the most newly disembarked of the two men, wholly instinctive--the fruit of a sharp sense that, delightful as it would be to find himself looking, after so much separation, into his comrade's face, his business would be a trifle bungled should he simply arrange for this countenance to present itself to the nearing steamer as the first "note," of Europe. Mixed with everything was the apprehension, already, on Strether's part, that it would, at best, throughout, prove the note of Europe in quite a sufficient degree.

In this paragraph James fuses narrative scene and narrative summary even more than he did in "Paste.' The character whose point of view the story assumes is an American named Strether, who checks in to a hotel in England and asks if his friend Waymarsh has arrived yet. When the hotel clerk tells him that Waymarsh will not arrive till that evening, Strether is, surprisingly, not very disappointed ("not wholly disconcerted"). The hotel clerk then verifies Waymarsh's later arrival by producing a telegram in which Waymarsh asks for a room that is not noisy. Strether is reassured by the telegram, for the two men had originally planned to meet at Liverpool but then decided instead to meet at Chester, a little farther south on the western coast of England. Strether reflects that while it would have been nice to have seen his friend Waymarsh when he first arrived in Europe, he's happy to be in Europe all by himself until evening. He'll see plenty of Waymarsh in the days and weeks ahead, and he even fears that the constant presence of his American friend will make it hard for him to enjoy Europe. (Kind of like traveling to Europe with an American friend who only wants to do things such as eat at McDonald's restaurants, go to Euro Disney World, etc.) Guiltily, Strether plans to enjoy the few hours he has in Chester and experience Europe, for a while, all by himself.

Once you see how James is using point of view in this innovative way, it is possible to follow him, but the style of his late novels and stories is still difficult. It was made even more intricate when James stopped writing out his fiction by hand and instead dictated his novels and stories to a secretary who took them down on a relatively new invention called the typewriter. It's interesting that James' convoluted late fiction, like Milton's dense poetry in *Paradise Lost*, was, at least partially, the result of the author dictating his words to an amanuensis.

Virtually every twentieth-century fiction writer, American and British, drew on the innovations of Henry James. Even a writer such as Ernest Hemingway, who on the surface seems so different from James in his stories of hunting, war, and bullfighting, was deeply indebted to James' fiction. Here, for example, is the opening of "Indian Camp," one of Hemingway's early short stories:

from Ernest Hemingway, "Indian Camp"

At the lake shore there was another rowboat drawn up. The two Indians stood waiting.

Nick and his father got in the stern of the boat and the Indians shoved it off and one of them got in to row. Uncle George sat in the stern of the camp rowboat. The young Indian shoved the camp boat off and got in to row Uncle George.

The two boats started off in the dark. Nick heard the oarlocks of the other boat quite a way ahead of them in the mist. The Indians rowed with quick choppy strokes. Nick lay back with his father's arm around him. It was cold on the water. The Indian who was rowing them was working very hard, but the other boat moved further ahead in the mist all the time.

"Where are we going, Dad?" Nick asked.

"Over to the Indian camp. There is an Indian lady very sick."

"Oh," said Nick.

Although the opening of "Indian Camp" may not seem as confusing as the opening of Henry James' "Paste," Hemingway is every bit as anchored in the point of view of his main character as James was in Charlotte's point of view in "Paste." A more traditional writer might have begun this story in this way:

At a lakeside cabin in the woods of northern Michigan, Doctor Henry Adams was on a fishing vacation with his brother-in-law George and his young son Nick. One night, two Indians rowed to their cabin and asked Doctor Adams to come to their reservation and help with the birth of an Indian woman's baby. The doctor, George, and Nick got into canoes drawn up at the lake shore, one canoe theirs, the other canoe brought by the Indians. The Indians swiftly paddled them across the lake to their reservation.

But Hemingway, like James, so plunges us into the story and anchors us in young Nick's point of view that he says, not "At *a* lake shore" but "At *the* lake shore," because that's how Nick would see "the" lake where he has been camping. Similarly, Nick already knows their canoe is at the shore, so he sees that there is "another" canoe there now—the one the Indians have traveled in. Nick, who has already encountered the Indians does not see, as another writer might describe them, "Two Indians stood waiting" but "*The* two Indians stood waiting." Can you see how Hemingway is drawing upon the technique of Henry James, who began "Paste" with the sentence, "'I've found a lot more things,' her cousin said to her the day after the second funeral"?

Where Hemingway differed so markedly from James was that he seldom went into the minds of his characters to let us know what they were thinking. When Nick's father tells him that they are going to help an Indian woman who is sick, all Nick says is "Oh." We have to infer what his thoughts, his fears, and his feelings are from what he sees, what he does, and what he says.

Hemingway described such inferences as the "iceberg effect." Pointing out that seven-eighths of an iceberg lies under the surface of the water, Hemingway presented only the smallest details of action and dialogue in his fiction; the reader had to infer from that minimal material what emotional depths lie under the surface of the characters—what their impressions were (as in James' fiction) of what happens in the story.

Here is the opening of "Barn Burning" (1939), a story by another twentieth-century writer who was deeply influenced by Henry James—William Faulkner.

from William Faulkner, "Barn Burning"

The store in which the Justice of the Peace's court was sitting smelled of cheese. The boy, crouched on his nail keg at the back of the crowded room, knew he smelled cheese, and more: from where he sat he could see the ranked shelves close-packed with the solid, squat, dynamic shapes of tin cans whose labels his stomach read, not from the lettering which meant nothing to his mind but from the scarlet devils and the silver curve of fish - this, the cheese which he knew he smelled and the hermetic meat which his intestines believed he smelled coming in intermittent gusts momentary and brief between the other constant one, the smell and sense just a little of fear because mostly of despair and grief, the old fierce pull of blood. He could not see the table where the Justice sat and before which his father and his father's enemy (our enemy he thought in that despair; ourn! mine and hisn both! He's my father!) stood, but he could hear them, the two of them that is, because his father had said no word yet:

Like James and Hemingway, Faulkner plunges us directly into the story from the point of view of a character, a young boy in this case, whose name at first we don't even know. We have to figure out that he and his father are in a country store in the South, where, in a makeshift courtroom, his father is being tried for a crime—burning another man's barn—by a justice of the peace. The boy, through whose eyes we see the action, seems never to have been in a store. He's obviously hungry and obsessed with the smell of cheese and the strange tin cans on the shelves. Although he cannot read, he sees on the labels of the cans pictures of little red devils (for devilled ham) and silver fish (sardines) and intuits that the cans contain meat and fish. Hungry as he is, the boy's thoughts turn fiercely to what's happening in the courtroom as the justice of the peace hears the complaint another man brings against his father for burning a barn.

In this passage, Faulkner is also drawing on another of the most innovative fictional techniques Henry James developed, which came to be called, borrowing a term from his brother William's work on psychology, *stream-of-consciousness.* Both Henry and William knew that the human mind did not process thoughts in straightforward, logical fashion but in a rambling "stream" of perceptions, ideas, memories, reflections, and anticipations. Think of how your mind "rambles" when you are making a long drive by yourself—your thoughts flit from who you're going to see, to memories of that person in the past, to associations with places you pass—all in a shifting, incoherent order.

The complexity and intensity of such a passage of stream-of-consciousness intrigued writers who came after James. Some writers, such as James Joyce and Virginia Woolf, took the technique of stream-of-consciousness to new levels of sophistication. Here, for example, is a passage from Virginia Woolf's novel, *Mrs. Dalloway* (1925), where the heroine, Clarissa Dalloway, thinks her random thoughts as she walks through London and hears Parliament's "Big Ben" toll the time:

from Virginia Woolf, *Mrs. Dalloway*

For having lived in Westminster—how many years now? over twenty,— one feels even in the midst of the traffic, or waking at night, Clarissa was positive, a particular hush, or solemnity; an indescribable pause; a suspense (but that might be her heart, affected, they said, by influenza) before Big Ben strikes. There! Out it boomed. First a warning, musical; then the hour, irrevocable. The leaden circles dissolved in the air. Such fools we are, she thought, crossing Victoria Street. For Heaven only knows why one loves it so, how one sees it so, making it up, building it round one, tumbling it, creating it every moment afresh; but the veriest frumps, the most dejected of miseries sitting on doorsteps (drink their downfall) do the same; can't be dealt with, she felt positive, by Acts of Parliament for that very reason: they love life. In people's eyes, in the swing, tramp, and trudge; in the bellow and the uproar; the carriages, motor cars, omnibuses, vans, sandwich men shuffling and swinging; brass bands; barrel organs; in the triumph and the jingle and the strange high singing of some aeroplane overhead was what she loved; life; London; this moment of June.

Another great example of stream-of-consciousness in fiction is the ending of James Joyce's *Ulysses* where the heroine, Molly Bloom, fantasizes about losing her virginity to Leopold Bloom. Although they have been married for a long time and she has cheated on him this very day, she thinks of their first lovemaking as she masturbates and, in her way, is as faithful to him as Penelope was to Odysseus, the classical epic upon which Joyce's *Ulysses* is based. This stream-of-consciousness passage goes on for many passages but here is its last section:

from James Joyce, *Ulysses*

the sun shines for you he said the day we were lying among the rhododendrons on Howth head in the grey tweed suit and his straw hat the day I got him to propose to me yes first I gave him the bit of seedcake out of my mouth and it was leap year like now yes 16 years ago my God after that long kiss I near lost my breath yes he said I was a flower of the mountain yes so we are flowers all a woman's body yes that was one true thing he said in his life and the sun shines for you today yes that was why I liked him because I saw he understood or felt what a woman is and I knew I could always get round him and I gave him all the pleasure I could leading him on till he asked me to say yes and I wouldn't answer first only looked out over the sea and the sky I was thinking of so many things he didn't know of Mulvey and Mr Stanhope and Hester and father and old captain Groves and the sailors playing all birds fly and I say stoop and washing up dishes they called it on the pier and the sentry in front of the governors house with the thing round his white helmet poor devil half roasted and the Spanish girls laughing in their shawls and their tall combs and the auctions in the morning the Greeks and the Jews and the Arabs and the devil knows who else from all the ends of Europe and Duke street and the fowl market all clucking outside Larby Sharons and the poor donkeys slipping half asleep and the vague fellows in the cloaks asleep in the shade on the steps and the big wheels of the carts of the bulls and the old castle thousands of years old yes and those handsome Moors all in white and turbans like kings asking you to sit down in their little bit of a shop and Ronda with the old windows of the posadas glancing eyes a lattice hid for her lover to kiss the iron and the wine shops half open at night and the castanets and the night we missed the boat at Algeciras the watchman going about serene with his lamp and O that awful deep down torrent O and the sea the sea crimson sometimes like fire and the glorious sunsets and the fig trees in the Alameda gardens yes and all the queer little streets and the pink and blue and yellow houses and the rose gardens and the jessamine and geraniums and cactuses and Gibraltar as a girl where I was a Flower of the mountain yes when I put the rose in my hair like the Andalusian girls used or shall I wear a red yes and how he kissed me under the Moorish wall and I thought well as well him as another and then I asked him with my eyes to ask again yes and then he asked me would I yes to say yes my mountain flower and first I put my arms around him yes and drew him down to me so he could feel my breasts all perfume yes and his heart was going like mad and yes I said yes I will Yes.

No writer developed the form of narrative more fully—and inspired other writers, such as Ernest Hemingway, William Faulkner, Virginia Woolf, and James Joyce to experiment further—than Henry James.

Chapter 12
American Naturalistic Fiction

Although Realism and Naturalism sound, based on their names, like similar styles, they were two very different movements in the history of fiction and two very different ways of handling narrative form. Realism, as we have seen, was a reaction, led by Howells and James in the latter half of the nineteenth century, against the unrealistic Gothic fiction of writers such as Poe. Naturalism, in turn, was a reaction against Realism, led by writers, such as Jack London and Stephen Crane, at the end of the nineteenth and the beginning of the twentieth century. They disliked the emphasis of Realists on everyday social life among middle-class people. They wanted more exciting action in stories set in exotic locales. They cared less about how sensitive, sophisticated characters responded to everyday events; they were interested in what *happens* to a character—not the character's *impression* of things.

Jack London (1876–1916)

Jack London grew up in abject poverty in San Francisco, selling newspapers, working in a bowling alley, doing anything to earn a few cents for his family. When he was a teenager, he went to sea then wandered the country as a hobo. When gold was discovered in the Yukon, he prospected in Alaska but came back with nothing except ideas he could turn into fiction.

During his wanderings, London read widely and learned the writer's craft. In 1903, he published a short novel, *The Call of the Wild*, about a domestic dog, abandoned in Alaska, who joins a wolf pack and manages to survive and endure in the wilderness. The book was an enormous success and established London as one of the major fiction writers of his time. During his short career, he wrote fifteen books but died at the age of forty from profligate living, drink, and drugs.

Here is a naturalistic story by Jack London based on his experience in the Alaska gold rush. In what ways does it differ from stories such as "Paste" and "Editha"?

To Build a Fire

Day had broken cold and grey, exceedingly cold and grey, when the man turned aside from the main Yukon trail and climbed the high earth-bank, where a dim and little-travelled trail led eastward through the fat spruce timberland. It was a steep bank, and he paused for breath at the top, excusing the act to himself by looking at his watch. It was nine o'clock. There was no sun nor hint of sun, though there was not a cloud in the sky. It was a clear day, and yet there seemed an intangible pall over the face of things, a subtle gloom that made the day dark, and that was due to the absence of sun. This fact did not worry the man. He was used to the lack of sun. It had been days since he had seen the sun, and he knew that a few more days must pass before that cheerful orb, due south, would just peep above the sky-line and dip immediately from view.

The man flung a look back along the way he had come. The Yukon lay a mile wide and hidden under three feet of ice. On top of this ice were as many feet of snow. It was all pure white, rolling in gentle undulations where the ice-jams of the freeze-up had formed. North and south, as far as his eye could see, it was unbroken white, save for a dark hair-line that curved and twisted from around the spruce-covered island to the south, and that curved and twisted away into the north, where it disappeared behind another spruce-covered island. This dark hair-line was the trail--the main trail--that led south five hundred miles to the Chilcoot Pass, Dyea, and salt water; and that led north seventy miles to Dawson, and still on to the north a thousand miles to Nulato, and finally to St. Michael on Bering Sea, a thousand miles and half a thousand more.

But all this--the mysterious, far-reaching hairline trail, the absence of sun from the sky, the tremendous cold, and the strangeness and weirdness of it all--made no impression on the man. It was not because he was long used to it. He was a new-comer in the land, a *chechaquo*, and this was his first winter. The trouble with him was that he was without imagination. He was quick and alert in the things of life, but only in the things, and not in the significances. Fifty degrees below zero meant eighty odd degrees of frost. Such fact impressed him as being cold and uncomfortable, and that was all. It did not lead him to meditate upon his frailty as a creature of temperature, and upon man's frailty in general, able only to live within certain narrow limits of heat and cold; and from there on it did not lead him to the conjectural field of immortality and man's place in the universe. Fifty degrees below zero stood for a bite of frost that hurt and that must be guarded against by the use of mittens, ear-flaps, warm moccasins, and thick socks. Fifty degrees below zero was to him just precisely fifty degrees below zero. That there should be anything more to it than that was a thought that never entered his head.

As he turned to go on, he spat speculatively. There was a sharp, explosive crackle that startled him. He spat again. And again, in the air, before it could fall to the snow, the spittle crackled. He knew that at fifty below spittle crackled on the snow, but this spittle had crackled in the air. Undoubtedly it was colder than fifty below--how much colder he did not know. But the temperature did not matter. He was bound for the old claim on the left fork of Henderson Creek, where the boys were already. They had come over across the divide from the Indian Creek country, while he had come the roundabout way to take a look at the possibilities of getting out logs in the spring from the islands in the Yukon. He would be in to camp by six o'clock; a bit after dark, it was true, but the boys would be there, a fire would be going, and a hot supper would be ready. As for lunch, he pressed his hand against the protruding bundle under his jacket. It was also under his shirt, wrapped up in a handkerchief and lying against the naked skin. It was the only way to keep the biscuits from freezing. He smiled agreeably to himself as he thought of those biscuits, each cut open and sopped in bacon grease, and each enclosing a generous slice of fried bacon.

He plunged in among the big spruce trees. The trail was faint. A foot of snow had fallen since the last sled had passed over, and he was glad he was without a sled, travelling light. In fact, he carried nothing but the lunch wrapped in the handkerchief. He was surprised, however, at the cold. It certainly was cold, he concluded, as he rubbed his numbed nose and cheek-bones with his mittened hand. He was a warm-whiskered man, but the hair on his face did not protect the high cheek-bones and the eager nose that thrust itself aggressively into the frosty air.

At the man's heels trotted a dog, a big native husky, the proper wolf-dog, grey-coated and without any visible or temperamental difference from its brother, the wild wolf. The animal was depressed by the tremendous cold. It knew that it was no time for travelling. Its instinct told it a truer tale than was told to the man by the man's judgment. In reality, it was not merely colder than fifty below zero; it was colder than sixty below, than seventy below. It was seventy-five below zero. Since the freezing-point is thirty-two above zero, it meant that one hundred and seven degrees of frost obtained. The dog did not know anything about thermometers. Possibly in its brain there was no sharp consciousness of a condition of very cold such as was in the man's brain. But the brute had its instinct. It experienced a vague but menacing apprehension that subdued it and made it slink along at the man's heels, and that made it question eagerly every unwonted movement of the man as if expecting him to go into camp or to seek shelter somewhere and build a fire. The dog had learned fire, and it wanted fire, or else to burrow under the snow and cuddle its warmth away from the air.

The frozen moisture of its breathing had settled on its fur in a fine powder of frost, and especially were its jowls, muzzle, and eyelashes whitened by its crystalled breath. The man's red beard and moustache were likewise frosted, but more solidly, the deposit taking the form of ice and increasing with every warm, moist breath he exhaled. Also, the man was chewing tobacco, and the muzzle of ice held his lips so rigidly that he was unable to clear his chin when he expelled the juice. The result was that a crystal beard of the colour and solidity of amber was increasing its length on his chin. If he fell down it would shatter itself, like glass, into brittle fragments. But he did not mind the appendage. It was the penalty all tobacco- chewers paid in that country, and he had been out before in two cold snaps. They had not been so cold as this, he knew, but by the spirit thermometer at Sixty Mile he knew they had been registered at fifty below and at fifty-five.

He held on through the level stretch of woods for several miles, crossed a wide flat of nigger-heads, and dropped down a bank to the frozen bed of a small stream. This was Henderson Creek, and he knew he was ten miles from the forks. He looked at his watch. It was ten o'clock. He was making four miles an hour, and he calculated that he would arrive at the forks at half-past twelve. He decided to celebrate that event by eating his lunch there.

The dog dropped in again at his heels, with a tail drooping discouragement, as the man swung along the creek-bed. The furrow of the old sled-trail was plainly visible, but a dozen inches of snow covered the marks of the last runners. In a month no man had come up or down that silent creek. The man held steadily on. He was not much given to thinking, and just then particularly he had nothing to think about save that he would eat lunch at the forks and that at six o'clock he would be in camp with the boys. There was nobody to talk to and, had there been, speech would have been impossible because of the ice-muzzle on his mouth. So he continued monotonously to chew tobacco and to increase the length of his amber beard.

Once in a while the thought reiterated itself that it was very cold and that he had never experienced such cold. As he walked along he rubbed his cheek-bones and nose with the back of his mittened hand. He did this automatically, now and again changing hands. But rub as he would, the instant he stopped his cheek-bones went numb, and the following instant the end of his nose went numb. He was sure to frost his cheeks; he knew that, and experienced a pang of regret that he had not devised a nose-strap of the sort Bud wore in cold snaps. Such a strap passed across the cheeks, as well, and saved them. But it didn't matter much, after all. What were frosted cheeks? A bit painful, that was all; they were never serious.

Empty as the man's mind was of thoughts, he was keenly observant, and he noticed the changes in the creek, the curves and bends and timber- jams, and always he sharply noted where he placed his feet. Once, coming around a bend, he shied abruptly, like a startled horse, curved away from the place where he had been walking, and retreated several paces back along the trail. The creek he knew was frozen clear to the bottom--no creek could contain water in that arctic winter--but he knew also that there were springs that bubbled out from the hillsides and ran along under the snow and on top the ice of the creek. He knew that the coldest snaps never froze these springs, and he knew likewise their danger. They were traps. They hid pools of water under the snow that might be three inches deep, or three feet. Sometimes a skin of ice half an inch thick covered them, and in turn was covered by the snow. Sometimes there were alternate layers of water and ice-skin, so that when one broke through he kept on breaking through for a while, sometimes wetting himself to the waist.

That was why he had shied in such panic. He had felt the give under his feet and heard the crackle of a snow-hidden ice-skin. And to get his feet wet in such a temperature meant trouble and danger. At the very least it meant delay, for he would be forced to stop and build a fire, and under its protection to bare his feet while he dried his socks and moccasins. He stood and studied the creek-bed and its banks, and decided that the flow of water came from the right. He reflected awhile, rubbing his nose and cheeks, then skirted to the left, stepping gingerly and testing the footing for each step. Once clear of the danger, he took a fresh chew of tobacco and swung along at his four-mile gait.

In the course of the next two hours he came upon several similar traps. Usually the snow above the hidden pools had a sunken, candied appearance that advertised the danger. Once again, however, he had a close call; and once, suspecting danger, he compelled the dog to go on in front. The dog did not want to go. It hung back until the man shoved it forward, and then it went quickly across the white, unbroken surface. Suddenly it broke through, floundered to one side, and got away to firmer footing. It had wet its forefeet and legs, and almost immediately the water that clung to it turned to ice. It made quick efforts to lick the ice off its legs, then dropped down in the snow and began to bite out the ice that had formed between the toes. This was a matter of instinct. To permit the ice to remain would mean sore feet. It did not know this. It merely obeyed the mysterious prompting that arose from the deep crypts of its being. But the man knew, having achieved a judgment on the subject, and he removed the mitten from his right hand and helped tear out the ice- particles. He did not expose his fingers more than a minute, and was astonished at the swift numbness that smote them. It certainly was cold. He pulled on the mitten hastily, and beat the hand savagely across his chest.

At twelve o'clock the day was at its brightest. Yet the sun was too far south on its winter journey to clear the horizon. The bulge of the earth intervened between it and Henderson Creek, where the man walked under a clear sky at noon and cast no shadow. At half-past twelve, to the minute, he arrived at the forks of the creek. He was pleased at the speed he had made. If he kept it up, he would certainly be with the boys by six. He unbuttoned his jacket and shirt and drew forth his lunch. The action consumed no more than a quarter of a minute, yet in that brief moment the numbness laid hold of the exposed fingers. He did not put the mitten on, but, instead, struck the fingers a dozen sharp smashes against his leg. Then he sat down on a snow-covered log to eat. The sting that followed upon the striking of his fingers against his leg ceased so quickly that he was startled, he had had no chance to take a bite of biscuit. He struck the fingers repeatedly and returned them to the mitten, baring the other hand for the purpose of eating. He tried to take a mouthful, but the ice-muzzle prevented. He had forgotten to build a fire and thaw out. He chuckled at his foolishness, and as he chuckled he noted the numbness creeping into the exposed fingers. Also, he noted that the stinging which had first come to his toes when he sat down was already passing away. He wondered whether the toes were warm or numbed. He moved them inside the moccasins and decided that they were numbed.

He pulled the mitten on hurriedly and stood up. He was a bit frightened. He stamped up and down until the stinging returned into the feet. It certainly was cold, was his thought. That man from Sulphur Creek had spoken the truth when telling how cold it sometimes got in the country. And he had laughed at him at the time! That showed one must not be too sure of things. There was no mistake about it, it was cold. He strode up and down, stamping his feet and threshing his arms, until reassured by the returning warmth. Then he got out matches and proceeded to make a fire. From the undergrowth, where high water of the previous spring had lodged a supply of seasoned twigs, he got his firewood. Working carefully from a small beginning, he soon had a roaring fire, over which he thawed the ice from his face and in the protection of which he ate his biscuits. For the moment the cold of space was outwitted. The dog took satisfaction in the fire, stretching out close enough for warmth and far enough away to escape being singed.

When the man had finished, he filled his pipe and took his comfortable time over a smoke. Then he pulled on his mittens, settled the ear-flaps of his cap firmly about his ears, and took the creek trail up the left fork. The dog was disappointed and yearned back toward the fire. This man did not know cold. Possibly all the generations of his ancestry had been ignorant of cold, of real cold, of cold one hundred and seven degrees below freezing-point. But the dog knew; all its ancestry knew, and it had inherited the knowledge. And it knew that it was not good to walk abroad in such fearful cold. It was the time to lie snug in a hole in the snow and wait for a curtain of cloud to be drawn across the face of outer space whence this cold came. On the other hand, there was keen intimacy between the dog and the man. The one was the toil-slave of the other, and the only caresses it had ever received were the caresses of the whip- lash and of harsh and menacing throat-sounds that threatened the whip-lash. So the dog made no effort to communicate its apprehension to the man. It was not concerned in the welfare of the man; it was for its own sake that it yearned back toward the fire. But the man whistled, and spoke to it with the sound of whip-lashes, and the dog swung in at the man's heels and followed after.

The man took a chew of tobacco and proceeded to start a new amber beard. Also, his moist breath quickly powdered with white his moustache, eyebrows, and lashes. There did not seem to be so many springs on the left fork of the Henderson, and for half an hour the man saw no signs of any. And then it happened. At a place where there were no signs, where the soft, unbroken snow seemed to advertise solidity beneath, the man broke through. It was not deep. He wetted himself half-way to the knees before he floundered out to the firm crust.

He was angry, and cursed his luck aloud. He had hoped to get into camp with the boys at six o'clock, and this would delay him an hour, for he would have to build a fire and dry out his foot-gear. This was imperative at that low temperature--he knew that much; and he turned aside to the bank, which he climbed. On top, tangled in the underbrush about the trunks of several small spruce trees, was a high-water deposit of dry firewood--sticks and twigs principally, but also larger portions of seasoned branches and fine, dry, last-year's grasses. He threw down several large pieces on top of the snow. This served for a foundation and prevented the young flame from drowning itself in the snow it otherwise would melt. The flame he got by touching a match to a small shred of birch-bark that he took from his pocket. This burned even more readily than paper. Placing it on the foundation, he fed the young flame with wisps of dry grass and with the tiniest dry twigs.

He worked slowly and carefully, keenly aware of his danger. Gradually, as the flame grew stronger, he increased the size of the twigs with which he fed it. He squatted in the snow, pulling the twigs out from their entanglement in the brush and feeding directly to the flame. He knew there must be no failure. When it is seventy- five below zero, a man must not fail in his first attempt to build a fire--that is, if his feet are wet. If his feet are dry, and he fails, he can run along the trail for half a mile and restore his circulation. But the circulation of wet and freezing feet cannot be restored by running when it is seventy-five below. No matter how fast he runs, the wet feet will freeze the harder.

All this the man knew. The old-timer on Sulphur Creek had told him about it the previous fall, and now he was appreciating the advice. Already all sensation had gone out of his feet. To build the fire he had been forced to remove his mittens, and the fingers had quickly gone numb. His pace of four miles an hour had kept his heart pumping blood to the surface of his body and to all the extremities. But the instant he stopped, the action of the pump eased down. The cold of space smote the unprotected tip of the planet, and he, being on that unprotected tip, received the full force of the blow. The blood of his body recoiled before it. The blood was alive, like the dog, and like the dog it wanted to hide away and cover itself up from the fearful cold. So long as he walked four miles an hour, he pumped that blood, willy-nilly, to the surface; but now it ebbed away and sank down into the recesses of his body. The extremities were the first to feel its absence. His wet feet froze the faster, and his exposed fingers numbed the faster, though they had not yet begun to freeze. Nose and cheeks were already freezing, while the skin of all his body chilled as it lost its blood.

But he was safe. Toes and nose and cheeks would be only touched by the frost, for the fire was beginning to burn with strength. He was feeding it with twigs the size of his finger. In another minute he would be able to feed it with branches the size of his wrist, and then he could remove his wet foot-gear, and, while it dried, he could keep his naked feet warm by the fire, rubbing them at first, of course, with snow. The fire was a success. He was safe. He remembered the advice of the old-timer on Sulphur Creek, and smiled. The old-timer had been very serious in laying down the law that no man must travel alone in the Klondike after fifty below. Well, here he was; he had had the accident; he was alone; and he had saved himself. Those old-timers were rather womanish, some of them, he thought. All a man had to do was to keep his head, and he was all right. Any man who was a man could travel alone. But it was surprising, the rapidity with which his cheeks and nose were freezing. And he had not thought his fingers could go lifeless in so short a time. Lifeless they were, for he could scarcely make them move together to grip a twig, and they seemed remote from his body and from him. When he touched a twig, he had to look and see whether or not he had hold of it. The wires were pretty well down between him and his finger-ends.

All of which counted for little. There was the fire, snapping and crackling and promising life with every dancing flame. He started to untie his moccasins. They were coated with ice; the thick German socks were like sheaths of iron half-way to the knees; and the moccasin strings were like rods of steel all twisted and knotted as by some conflagration. For a moment he tugged with his numbed fingers, then, realizing the folly of it, he drew his sheath-knife.

But before he could cut the strings, it happened. It was his own fault or, rather, his mistake. He should not have built the fire under the spruce tree. He should have built it in the open. But it had been easier to pull the twigs from the brush and drop them directly on the fire. Now the tree under which he had done this carried a weight of snow on its boughs. No wind had blown for weeks, and each bough was fully freighted. Each time he had pulled a twig he had communicated a slight agitation to the tree--an imperceptible agitation, so far as he was concerned, but an agitation sufficient to bring about the disaster. High up in the tree one bough capsized its load of snow. This fell on the boughs beneath, capsizing them. This process continued, spreading out and involving the whole tree. It grew like an avalanche, and it descended without warning upon the man and the fire, and the fire was blotted out! Where it had burned was a mantle of fresh and disordered snow.

The man was shocked. It was as though he had just heard his own sentence of death. For a moment he sat and stared at the spot where the fire had been. Then he grew very calm. Perhaps the old-timer on Sulphur Creek was right. If he had only had a trail-mate he would have been in no danger now. The trail-mate could have built the fire. Well, it was up to him to build the fire over again, and this second time there must be no failure. Even if he succeeded, he would most likely lose some toes. His feet must be badly frozen by now, and there would be some time before the second fire was ready.

Such were his thoughts, but he did not sit and think them. He was busy all the time they were passing through his mind, he made a new foundation for a fire, this time in the open; where no treacherous tree could blot it out. Next, he gathered dry grasses and tiny twigs from the high-water flotsam. He could not bring his fingers together to pull them out, but he was able to gather them by the handful. In this way he got many rotten twigs and bits of green moss that were undesirable, but it was the best he could do. He worked methodically, even collecting an armful of the larger branches to be used later when the fire gathered strength. And all the while the dog sat and watched him, a certain yearning wistfulness in its eyes, for it looked upon him as the fire-provider, and the fire was slow in coming.

When all was ready, the man reached in his pocket for a second piece of birch-bark. He knew the bark was there, and, though he could not feel it with his fingers, he could hear its crisp rustling as he fumbled for it. Try as he would, he could not clutch hold of it. And all the time, in his consciousness, was the knowledge that each instant his feet were freezing. This thought tended to put him in a panic, but he fought against it and kept calm. He pulled on his mittens with his teeth, and threshed his arms back and forth, beating his hands with all his might against his sides. He did this sitting down, and he stood up to do it; and all the while the dog sat in the snow, its wolf-brush of a tail curled around warmly over its forefeet, its sharp wolf-ears pricked forward intently as it watched the man. And the man as he beat and threshed with his arms and hands, felt a great surge of envy as he regarded the creature that was warm and secure in its natural covering.

After a time he was aware of the first far-away signals of sensation in his beaten fingers. The faint tingling grew stronger till it evolved into a stinging ache that was excruciating, but which the man hailed with satisfaction. He stripped the mitten from his right hand and fetched forth the birch-bark. The exposed fingers were quickly going numb again. Next he brought out his bunch of sulphur matches. But the tremendous cold had already driven the life out of his fingers. In his effort to separate one match from the others, the whole bunch fell in the snow. He tried to pick it out of the snow, but failed. The dead fingers could neither touch nor clutch. He was very careful. He drove the thought of his freezing feet; and nose, and cheeks, out of his mind, devoting his whole soul to the matches. He watched, using the sense of vision in place of that of touch, and when he saw his fingers on each side the bunch, he closed them--that is, he willed to close them, for the wires were drawn, and the fingers did not obey. He pulled the mitten on the right hand, and beat it fiercely against his knee. Then, with both mittened hands, he scooped the bunch of matches, along with much snow, into his lap. Yet he was no better off.

After some manipulation he managed to get the bunch between the heels of his mittened hands. In this fashion he carried it to his mouth. The ice crackled and snapped when by a violent effort he opened his mouth. He drew the lower jaw in, curled the upper lip out of the way, and scraped the bunch with his upper teeth in order to separate a match. He succeeded in getting one, which he dropped on his lap. He was no better off. He could not pick it up. Then he devised a way. He picked it up in his teeth and scratched it on his leg. Twenty times he scratched before he succeeded in lighting it. As it flamed he held it with his teeth to the birch-bark. But the burning brimstone went up his nostrils and into his lungs, causing him to cough spasmodically. The match fell into the snow and went out.

 The old-timer on Sulphur Creek was right, he thought in the moment of controlled despair that ensued: after fifty below, a man should travel with a partner. He beat his hands, but failed in exciting any sensation. Suddenly he bared both hands, removing the mittens with his teeth. He caught the whole bunch between the heels of his hands. His arm-muscles not being frozen enabled him to press the hand-heels tightly against the matches. Then he scratched the bunch along his leg. It flared into flame, seventy sulphur matches at once! There was no wind to blow them out. He kept his head to one side to escape the strangling fumes, and held the blazing bunch to the birch-bark. As he so held it, he became aware of sensation in his hand. His flesh was burning. He could smell it. Deep down below the surface he could feel it. The sensation developed into pain that grew acute. And still he endured it, holding the flame of the matches clumsily to the bark that would not light readily because his own burning hands were in the way, absorbing most of the flame.

 At last, when he could endure no more, he jerked his hands apart. The blazing matches fell sizzling into the snow, but the birch-bark was alight. He began laying dry grasses and the tiniest twigs on the flame. He could not pick and choose, for he had to lift the fuel between the heels of his hands. Small pieces of rotten wood and green moss clung to the twigs, and he bit them off as well as he could with his teeth. He cherished the flame carefully and awkwardly. It meant life, and it must not perish. The withdrawal of blood from the surface of his body now made him begin to shiver, and he grew more awkward. A large piece of green moss fell squarely on the little fire. He tried to poke it out with his fingers, but his shivering frame made him poke too far, and he disrupted the nucleus of the little fire, the burning grasses and tiny twigs separating and scattering. He tried to poke them together again, but in spite of the tenseness of the effort, his shivering got away with him, and the twigs were hopelessly scattered. Each twig gushed a puff of smoke and went out. The fire-provider had failed. As he looked apathetically about him, his eyes chanced on the dog, sitting across the ruins of the fire from him, in the snow, making restless, hunching movements, slightly lifting one forefoot and then the other, shifting its weight back and forth on them with wistful eagerness.

The sight of the dog put a wild idea into his head. He remembered the tale of the man, caught in a blizzard, who killed a steer and crawled inside the carcass, and so was saved. He would kill the dog and bury his hands in the warm body until the numbness went out of them. Then he could build another fire. He spoke to the dog, calling it to him; but in his voice was a strange note of fear that frightened the animal, who had never known the man to speak in such way before. Something was the matter, and its suspicious nature sensed danger,--it knew not what danger but somewhere, somehow, in its brain arose an apprehension of the man. It flattened its ears down at the sound of the man's voice, and its restless, hunching movements and the liftings and shiftings of its forefeet became more pronounced but it would not come to the man. He got on his hands and knees and crawled toward the dog. This unusual posture again excited suspicion, and the animal sidled mincingly away.

The man sat up in the snow for a moment and struggled for calmness. Then he pulled on his mittens, by means of his teeth, and got upon his feet. He glanced down at first in order to assure himself that he was really standing up, for the absence of sensation in his feet left him unrelated to the earth. His erect position in itself started to drive the webs of suspicion from the dog's mind; and when he spoke peremptorily, with the sound of whip-lashes in his voice, the dog rendered its customary allegiance and came to him. As it came within reaching distance, the man lost his control. His arms flashed out to the dog, and he experienced genuine surprise when he discovered that his hands could not clutch, that there was neither bend nor feeling in the fingers. He had forgotten for the moment that they were frozen and that they were freezing more and more. All this happened quickly, and before the animal could get away, he encircled its body with his arms. He sat down in the snow, and in this fashion held the dog, while it snarled and whined and struggled.

But it was all he could do, hold its body encircled in his arms and sit there. He realized that he could not kill the dog. There was no way to do it. With his helpless hands he could neither draw nor hold his sheath-knife nor throttle the animal. He released it, and it plunged wildly away, with tail between its legs, and still snarling. It halted forty feet away and surveyed him curiously, with ears sharply pricked forward. The man looked down at his hands in order to locate them, and found them hanging on the ends of his arms. It struck him as curious that one should have to use his eyes in order to find out where his hands were. He began threshing his arms back and forth, beating the mittened hands against his sides. He did this for five minutes, violently, and his heart pumped enough blood up to the surface to put a stop to his shivering. But no sensation was aroused in the hands. He had an impression that they hung like weights on the ends of his arms, but when he tried to run the impression down, he could not find it.

A certain fear of death, dull and oppressive, came to him. This fear quickly became poignant as he realized that it was no longer a mere matter of freezing his fingers and toes, or of losing his hands and feet, but that it was a matter of life and death with the chances against him. This threw him into a panic, and he turned and ran up the creek-bed along the old, dim trail. The dog joined in behind and kept up with him. He ran blindly, without intention, in fear such as he had never known in his life. Slowly, as he ploughed and floundered through the snow, he began to see things again--the banks of the creek, the old timber-jams, the leafless aspens, and the sky. The running made him feel better. He did not shiver. Maybe, if he ran on, his feet would thaw out; and, anyway, if he ran far enough, he would reach camp and the boys. Without doubt he would lose some fingers and toes and some of his face; but the boys would take care of him, and save the rest of him when he got there. And at the same time there was another thought in his mind that said he would never get to the camp and the boys; that it was too many miles away, that the freezing had too great a start on him, and that he would soon be stiff and dead. This thought he kept in the background and refused to consider. Sometimes it pushed itself forward and demanded to be heard, but he thrust it back and strove to think of other things.

It struck him as curious that he could run at all on feet so frozen that he could not feel them when they struck the earth and took the weight of his body. He seemed to himself to skim along above the surface and to have no connection with the earth. Somewhere he had once seen a winged Mercury, and he wondered if Mercury felt as he felt when skimming over the earth.

His theory of running until he reached camp and the boys had one flaw in it: he lacked the endurance. Several times he stumbled, and finally he tottered, crumpled up, and fell. When he tried to rise, he failed. He must sit and rest, he decided, and next time he would merely walk and keep on going. As he sat and regained his breath, he noted that he was feeling quite warm and comfortable. He was not shivering, and it even seemed that a warm glow had come to his chest and trunk. And yet, when he touched his nose or cheeks, there was no sensation. Running would not thaw them out. Nor would it thaw out his hands and feet. Then the thought came to him that the frozen portions of his body must be extending. He tried to keep this thought down, to forget it, to think of something else; he was aware of the panicky feeling that it caused, and he was afraid of the panic. But the thought asserted itself, and persisted, until it produced a vision of his body totally frozen. This was too much, and he made another wild run along the trail. Once he slowed down to a walk, but the thought of the freezing extending itself made him run again.

And all the time the dog ran with him, at his heels. When he fell down a second time, it curled its tail over its forefeet and sat in front of him facing him curiously eager and intent. The warmth and security of the animal angered him, and he cursed it till it flattened down its ears appeasingly. This time the shivering came more quickly upon the man. He was losing in his battle with the frost. It was creeping into his body from all sides. The thought of it drove him on, but he ran no more than a hundred feet, when he staggered and pitched headlong. It was his last panic. When he had recovered his breath and control, he sat up and entertained in his mind the conception of meeting death with dignity. However, the conception did not come to him in such terms. His idea of it was that he had been making a fool of himself, running around like a chicken with its head cut off--such was the simile that occurred to him. Well, he was bound to freeze anyway, and he might as well take it decently. With this new-found peace of mind came the first glimmerings of drowsiness. A good idea, he thought, to sleep off to death. It was like taking an anesthetic. Freezing was not so bad as people thought. There were lots worse ways to die.

He pictured the boys finding his body next day. Suddenly he found himself with them, coming along the trail and looking for himself. And, still with them, he came around a turn in the trail and found himself lying in the snow. He did not belong with himself any more, for even then he was out of himself, standing with the boys and looking at himself in the snow. It certainly was cold, was his thought. When he got back to the States he could tell the folks what real cold was. He drifted on from this to a vision of the old-timer on Sulphur Creek. He could see him quite clearly, warm and comfortable, and smoking a pipe.

"You were right, old hoss; you were right," the man mumbled to the old-timer of Sulphur Creek.

Then the man drowsed off into what seemed to him the most comfortable and satisfying sleep he had ever known. The dog sat facing him and waiting. The brief day drew to a close in a long, slow twilight. There were no signs of a fire to be made, and, besides, never in the dog's experience had it known a man to sit like that in the snow and make no fire. As the twilight drew on, its eager yearning for the fire mastered it, and with a great lifting and shifting of forefeet, it whined softly, then flattened its ears down in anticipation of being chidden by the man. But the man remained silent. Later, the dog whined loudly. And still later it crept close to the man and caught the scent of death. This made the animal bristle and back away. A little longer it delayed, howling under the stars that leaped and danced and shone brightly in the cold sky. Then it turned and trotted up the trail in the direction of the camp it knew, where were the other food-providers and fire-providers.   1908

Narrative Form in "To Build a Fire"

Think of all the ways the form of this story differs from realistic short stories such as "Paste" and "Editha."

Let's begin with setting. While "Paste" and "Editha" take place in the everyday social world of that era's typical middle-class reader, where characters interact with one another pretty much as we do, the setting of "To Build a Fire" is in a world utterly unfamiliar to most readers—the wilds of Alaska.

The action, too, in "To Build a Fire" is very different from the action in "Paste" and "Editha." In those realistic stories, relatively little external action occurs—Charlotte receives a necklace; Editha sends her lover off to war (but we never see the battle in which he is killed). But in the naturalistic story "To Build a Fire," the external action is gripping and exciting as we watch a man struggle to survive a conflict with the elements.

Perhaps the greatest difference between a realistic story and a naturalistic story is that Realists such as James and Howells are not so concerned with telling an outwardly exciting story as they are with tracing a character's impressions of what might be fairly ordinary events. London, however, has little interest in his character's impression of what's happening to him. In fact, in the third paragraph he says events made "no impression" on the man, then goes on to make fun of the kind of fiction James and Howells wrote, tracing the mental reflections of characters upon what happens to them. In fact, at several points in the story London says that his character "did not think."

Obviously, Naturalists had a very different sense of character from Realists. Realists liked characters, such as James' Charlotte, who were astute, sensitive, and intellectually sophisticated. How their minds dealt with events was the main interest, and the climax of a realistic story was frequently an epiphany where such a character came to a new understanding of herself or her situation.

Naturalists, however, were more interested in characters who were not especially intelligent, sensitive, or sophisticated. Their view of character was deeply influenced by what came to be called, in the latter part of the nineteenth century, "Social Darwinism"—the application of Darwin's theory of evolution to human society. Social Darwinists saw human society as a "struggle of the fittest" to adapt to their environment. That environment, in turn, shaped and determined character, so that children who grew up in slum conditions, for example, turned to crime. The naturalistic writer sometimes approached the writing of fiction the way a scientist experimented with laboratory mice: put this mouse in a new environment and see how it successfully adapts—or fails to adapt.

Naturalists, therefore, are less interested in what a character *thinks* than in what *happens* to a character, and what happens to characters is that they become *victims* of forces in their social and natural environment. The naturalistic writer seldom goes into the minds of such characters—certainly not in the extensive way realistic writers explore a character's impressions. Instead, Naturalists portray what happens to characters as they are buffeted by forces in their environment. Their characters usually cannot understand, much less control, what happens to them.

These different approaches to action and character between Realists and Naturalists led to other differences in the form of their fiction. Realists often told their stories from the point of view of the main character—such as Charlotte or Editha—using either the first-person or third-person limited point of view. In that way, the story can best emphasize the characters' impressions of what happens to them.

In naturalistic fiction, however, the writer often chooses to tell the story from an omniscient narrator's point of view. Such a narrator can occasionally let us know what a character is thinking but is much more interested in watching, like a scientist observing an experiment, how a character tries to adapt to changes in its environment. At certain points, as you may have noticed, London even goes into the point of view of the dog as another "creature," like the man, trying to survive.

The differences in form between realistic and naturalistic fiction even extend to the use of narrative scene and narrative summary. In realistic fiction, we usually get much more narrative scene as characters interact with one another in their social world. In naturalistic fiction, we tend to get more narrative summary as the omniscient narrator describes what is happening to his characters in their changing environment. As fairly unsophisticated victims of environmental forces, their dialogue would hardly sparkle with the intelligence and wit of characters in Henry James' works.

Consider these different aspects of fictional form as you read another naturalistic short story, Stephen Crane's "The Bride Comes to Yellow Sky."

Stephen Crane (1871–1900)

If Jack London's death at the age of forty seems premature, then Stephen Crane's, at twenty-nine, was even more so. The son of a Methodist minister in New Jersey, Crane went to college but dropped out when both of his parents died. He moved to New York City and wrote fiction and journalism about its horrible slums, but publishers refused his work because of its sordid subject matter.

Crane borrowed money from his brother, a successful journalist, to publish a long story, *Maggie: A Girl of the Streets* (1893), about a girl from the slums of New York who becomes a prostitute. While the book was not a success, a few influential writers, such as William Dean Howells, recognized Crane's genius and encouraged him.

In 1894, Crane wrote a story about the Civil War, even though he had never witnessed war firsthand. The novel, *The Red Badge of Courage*, became an enormous success. That success garnered Crane journalistic assignments to cover the settling of the West, which in turn, gave him material for such stories as "The Bride Comes to Yellow Sky."

Diagnosed with tuberculosis, Crane moved to England with a woman who had run a New York brothel. In England, he befriended many British and American writers, most notably Henry James. He wrote prolifically to ward off increasing debt before he died.

The Bride Comes to Yellow Sky

I

The great Pullman was whirling onward with such dignity of motion that a glance from the window seemed simply to prove that the plains of Texas were pouring eastward. Vast flats of green grass, dull-hued spaces of mesquite and cactus, little groups of frame houses, woods of light and tender trees, all were sweeping into the east, sweeping over the horizon, a precipice.

A newly married pair had boarded this coach at San Antonio. The man's face was reddened from many days in the wind and sun, and a direct result of his new black clothes was that his brick-colored hands were constantly performing in a most conscious fashion. From time to time he looked down respectfully at his attire. He sat with a hand on each knee, like a man waiting in a barber's shop. The glances he devoted to other passengers were furtive and shy.

The bride was not pretty, nor was she very young. She wore a dress of blue cashmere, with small reservations of velvet here and there and with steel buttons abounding. She continually twisted her head to regard her puff sleeves, very stiff, straight, and high. They embarrassed her. It was quite apparent that she had cooked, and that she expected to cook, dutifully. The blushes caused by the careless scrutiny of some passengers as she had entered the car were strange to see upon this plain, under-class countenance, which was drawn in placid, almost emotionless lines.

They were evidently very happy. "Ever been in a parlor-car before?" he asked, smiling with delight.

"No," she answered, "I never was. It's fine, ain't it?"

"Great! And then after a while we'll go forward to the diner and get a big layout. Finest meal in the world. Charge a dollar."

"Oh, do they?" cried the bride. "Charge a dollar? Why, that's too much -- for us -- ain't it, Jack?"

"Not this trip, anyhow," he answered bravely. "We're going to go the whole thing."

Later, he explained to her about the trains. "You see, it's a thousand miles from one end of Texas to the other, and this train runs right across it and never stops but four times." He had the pride of an owner. He pointed out to her the dazzling fittings of the coach, and in truth her eyes opened wider as she contemplated the sea-green figured velvet, the shining brass, silver, and glass, the wood that gleamed as darkly brilliant as the surface of a pool of oil. At one end a bronze figure sturdily held a support for a separated chamber, and at convenient places on the ceiling were frescoes in olive and silver.

To the minds of the pair, their surroundings reflected the glory of their marriage that morning in San Antonio. This was the environment of their new estate, and the man's face in particular beamed with an elation that made him appear ridiculous to the negro porter. This individual at times surveyed them from afar with an amused and superior grin. On other occasions he bullied them with skill in ways that did not make it exactly plain to them that they were being bullied. He subtly used all the manners of the most unconquerable kind of snobbery. He oppressed them, but of this oppression they had small knowledge, and they speedily forgot that infrequently a number of travelers covered them with stares of derisive enjoyment. Historically there was supposed to be something infinitely humorous in their situation.

"We are due in Yellow Sky at 3:42," he said, looking tenderly into her eyes.

"Oh, are we?" she said, as if she had not been aware of it. To evince surprise at her husband's statement was part of her wifely amiability. She took from a pocket a little silver watch, and as she held it before her and stared at it with a frown of attention, the new husband's face shone.

"I bought it in San Anton' from a friend of mine," he told her gleefully.

"It's seventeen minutes past twelve," she said, looking up at him with a kind of shy and clumsy coquetry. A passenger, noting this play, grew excessively sardonic, and winked at himself in one of the numerous mirrors.

At last they went to the dining-car. Two rows of negro waiters, in glowing white suits, surveyed their entrance with the interest and also the equanimity of men who had been forewarned. The pair fell to the lot of a waiter who happened to feel pleasure in steering them through their meal. He viewed them with the manner of a fatherly pilot, his countenance radiant with benevolence. The patronage, entwined with the ordinary deference, was not plain to them. And yet, as they returned to their coach, they showed in their faces a sense of escape.

He sat with a hand on each knee, like a man waiting in a barber's shop.

To the left, miles down a long purple slope, was a little ribbon of mist where moved the keening Rio Grande. The train was approaching it at an angle, and the apex was Yellow Sky. Presently it was apparent that, as the distance from Yellow Sky grew shorter, the husband became commensurately restless. His brick-red hands were more insistent in their prominence. Occasionally he was even rather absent-minded and far-away when the bride leaned forward and addressed him.

As a matter of truth, Jack Potter was beginning to find the shadow of a deed weigh upon him like a leaden slab. He, the town marshal of Yellow Sky, a man known, liked, and feared in his corner, a prominent person, had gone to San Antonio to meet a girl he believed he loved, and there, after the usual prayers, had actually induced her to marry him, without consulting Yellow Sky for any part of the transaction. He was now bringing his bride before an innocent and unsuspecting community.

Of course, people in Yellow Sky married as it pleased them, in accordance with a general custom; but such was Potter's thought of his duty to his friends, or of their idea of his duty, or of an unspoken form which does not control men in these matters, that he felt he was heinous. He had committed an extraordinary crime. Face to face with this girl in San Antonio, and spurred by his sharp impulse, he had gone headlong over all the social hedges. At San Antonio he was like a man hidden in the dark. A knife to sever any friendly duty, any form, was easy to his hand in that remote city. But the hour of Yellow Sky, the hour of daylight, was approaching.

He knew full well that his marriage was an important thing to his town. It could only be exceeded by the burning of the new hotel. His friends could not forgive him. Frequently he had reflected on the advisability of telling them by telegraph, but a new cowardice had been upon him.

He feared to do it. And now the train was hurrying him toward a scene of amazement, glee, and reproach. He glanced out of the window at the line of haze swinging slowly in towards the train.

Yellow Sky had a kind of brass band, which played painfully, to the delight of the populace. He laughed without heart as he thought of it. If the citizens could dream of his prospective arrival with his bride, they would parade the band at the station and escort them, amid cheers and laughing congratulations, to his adobe home.

He resolved that he would use all the devices of speed and plains-craft in making the journey from the station to his house. Once within that safe citadel he could issue some sort of a vocal bulletin, and then not go among the citizens until they had time to wear off a little of their enthusiasm.

The bride looked anxiously at him. "What's worrying you, Jack?"

He laughed again. "I'm not worrying, girl. I'm only thinking of Yellow Sky."

She flushed in comprehension.

A sense of mutual guilt invaded their minds and developed a finer tenderness. They looked at each other with eyes softly aglow. But Potter often laughed the same nervous laugh. The flush upon the bride's face seemed quite permanent.

The traitor to the feelings of Yellow Sky narrowly watched the speeding landscape. "We're nearly there," he said.

Presently the porter came and announced the proximity of Potter's home. He held a brush in his hand and, with all his airy superiority gone, he brushed Potter's new clothes as the latter slowly turned this way and that way. Potter fumbled out a coin and gave it to the porter, as he had seen others do. It was a heavy and muscle-bound business, as that of a man shoeing his first horse.

The porter took their bag, and as the train began to slow they moved forward to the hooded platform of the car. Presently the two engines and their long string of coaches rushed into the station of Yellow Sky.

"They have to take water here," said Potter, from a constricted throat and in mournful cadence, as one announcing death. Before the train stopped, his eye had swept the length of the platform, and he was glad and astonished to see there was none upon it but the station-agent, who, with a slightly hurried and anxious air, was walking toward the water-tanks. When the train had halted, the porter alighted first and placed in position a little temporary step.

"Come on, girl," said Potter hoarsely. As he helped her down they each laughed on a false note. He took the bag from the negro, and bade his wife cling to his arm. As they slunk rapidly away, his hang-dog glance perceived that they were unloading the two trunks, and also that the station-agent far ahead near the baggage-car had turned and was running toward him, making gestures. He laughed, and groaned as he laughed, when he noted the first effect of his marital bliss upon Yellow Sky. He gripped his wife's arm firmly to his side, and they fled. Behind them the porter stood chuckling fatuously.

II.

The California Express on the Southern Railway was due at Yellow Sky in twenty-one minutes. There were six men at the bar of the "Weary Gentleman" saloon. One was a drummer who talked a great deal and rapidly; three were Texans who did not care to talk at that time; and two were Mexican sheepherders who did not talk as a general practice in the "Weary Gentleman" saloon. The barkeeper's dog lay on the board walk that crossed in front of the door. His head was on his paws, and he glanced drowsily here and there with the constant vigilance of a dog that is kicked on occasion. Across the sandy street were some vivid green grass plots, so wonderful in appearance amid the sands that burned near them in a blazing sun that they caused a doubt in the mind. They exactly resembled the grass mats used to represent lawns on the stage. At the cooler end of the railway station a man without a coat sat in a tilted chair and smoked his pipe. The fresh-cut bank of the Rio Grande circled near the town, and there could be seen beyond it a great, plum-colored plain of mesquite.

Save for the busy drummer and his companions in the saloon, Yellow Sky was dozing. The new-comer leaned gracefully upon the bar, and recited many tales with the confidence of a bard who has come upon a new field.

" -- and at the moment that the old man fell down stairs with the bureau in his arms, the old woman was coming up with two scuttles of coal, and, of course -- "

The drummer's tale was interrupted by a young man who suddenly appeared in the open door. He cried: "Scratchy Wilson's drunk, and has turned loose with both hands." The two Mexicans at once set down their glasses and faded out of the rear entrance of the saloon.

The drummer, innocent and jocular, answered: "All right, old man. S'pose he has. Come in and have a drink, anyhow."

But the information had made such an obvious cleft in every skull in the room that the drummer was obliged to see its importance. All had become instantly solemn. "Say," said he, mystified, "what is this?" His three companions made the introductory gesture of eloquent speech, but the young man at the door forestalled them.

"It means, my friend," he answered, as he came into the saloon, "that for the next two hours this town won't be a health resort."

The barkeeper went to the door and locked and barred it. Reaching out of the window, he pulled in heavy wooden shutters and barred them. Immediately a solemn, chapel-like gloom was upon the place. The drummer was looking from one to another.

"But, say," he cried, "what is this, anyhow? You don't mean there is going to be a gun-fight?"

"Don't know whether there'll be a fight or not," answered one man grimly. "But there'll be some shootin' -- some good shootin'."

The young man who had warned them waved his hand. "Oh, there'll be a fight fast enough if anyone wants it. Anybody can get a fight out there in the street. There's a fight just waiting."

The drummer seemed to be swayed between the interest of a foreigner and a perception of personal danger.

"What did you say his name was?" he asked.

"Scratchy Wilson," they answered in chorus.

"And will he kill anybody? What are you going to do? Does this happen often? Does he rampage around like this once a week or so? Can he break in that door?"

"No, he can't break down that door," replied the barkeeper. "He's tried it three times. But when he comes you'd better lay down on the floor, stranger. He's dead sure to shoot at it, and a bullet may come through."

Thereafter the drummer kept a strict eye upon the door. The time had not yet been called for him to hug the floor, but, as a minor precaution, he sidled near to the wall. "Will he kill anybody?" he said again.

The men laughed low and scornfully at the question.

"He's out to shoot, and he's out for trouble. Don't see any good in experimentin' with him."

"But what do you do in a case like this? What do you do?"

A man responded: "Why, he and Jack Potter -- "

"But," in chorus, the other men interrupted, "Jack Potter's in San Anton'."

"Well, who is he? What's he got to do with it?"

"Oh, he's the town marshal. He goes out and fights Scratchy when he gets on one of these tears."

"Wow," said the drummer, mopping his brow. "Nice job he's got."

The voices had toned away to mere whisperings. The drummer wished to ask further questions which were born of an increasing anxiety and bewilderment; but when he attempted them, the men merely looked at him in irritation and motioned him to remain silent. A tense waiting hush was upon them. In the deep shadows of the room their eyes shone as they listened for sounds from the street. One man made three gestures at the barkeeper, and the latter, moving like a ghost, handed him a glass and a bottle. The man poured a full glass of whisky, and set down the bottle noiselessly. He gulped the whisky in a swallow, and turned again toward the door in immovable silence. The drummer saw that the barkeeper, without a sound, had taken a Winchester from beneath the bar. Later he saw this individual beckoning to him, so he tiptoed across the room.

"You better come with me back of the bar."

"No, thanks," said the drummer, perspiring. "I'd rather be where I can make a break for the back door."

Whereupon the man of bottles made a kindly but peremptory gesture. The drummer obeyed it, and finding himself seated on a box with his head below the level of the bar, balm was laid upon his soul at sight of various zinc and copper fittings that bore a resemblance to armor-plate. The barkeeper took a seat comfortably upon an adjacent box.

"You see," he whispered, "this here Scratchy Wilson is a wonder with a gun -- a perfect wonder -- and when he goes on the war trail, we hunt our holes -- naturally. He's about the last one of the old gang that used to hang out along the river here. He's a terror when he's drunk. When he's sober he's all right -- kind of simple -- wouldn't hurt a fly -- nicest fellow in town. But when he's drunk -- whoo!"

There were periods of stillness. "I wish Jack Potter was back from San Anton'," said the barkeeper. "He shot Wilson up once -- in the leg -- and he would sail in and pull out the kinks in this thing."

Presently they heard from a distance the sound of a shot, followed by three wild yowls. It instantly removed a bond from the men in the darkened saloon. There was a shuffling of feet. They looked at each other. "Here he comes," they said.

III

A man in a maroon-colored flannel shirt, which had been purchased for purposes of decoration and made, principally, by some Jewish women on the east side of New York, rounded a corner and walked into the middle of the main street of Yellow Sky. In either hand the man held a long, heavy, blue-black revolver. Often he yelled, and these cries rang through a semblance of a deserted village, shrilly flying over the roofs in a volume that seemed to have no relation to the ordinary vocal strength of a man. It was as if the surrounding stillness formed the arch of a tomb over him. These cries of ferocious challenge rang against walls of silence. And his boots had red tops with gilded imprints, of the kind beloved in winter by little sledding boys on the hillsides of New England.

The man's face flamed in a rage begot of whisky. His eyes, rolling and yet keen for ambush, hunted the still doorways and windows. He walked with the creeping movement of the midnight cat. As it occurred to him, he roared menacing information. The long revolvers in his hands were as easy as straws; they were moved with an electric swiftness. The little fingers of each hand played sometimes in a musician's way. Plain from the low collar of the shirt, the cords of his neck straightened and sank, straightened and sank, as passion moved him. The only sounds were his terrible invitations. The calm adobes preserved their demeanor at the passing of this small thing in the middle of the street.

There was no offer of fight; no offer of fight. The man called to the sky. There were no attractions. He bellowed and fumed and swayed his revolvers here and everywhere.

The dog of the barkeeper of the "Weary Gentleman" saloon had not appreciated the advance of events. He yet lay dozing in front of his master's door. At sight of the dog, the man paused and raised his revolver humorously. At sight of the man, the dog sprang up and walked diagonally away, with a sullen head, and growling. The man yelled, and the dog broke into a gallop. As it was about to enter an alley, there was a loud noise, a whistling, and something spat the ground directly before it. The dog screamed, and, wheeling in terror, galloped headlong in a new direction. Again there was a noise, a whistling, and sand was kicked viciously before it. Fear-stricken, the dog turned and flurried like an animal in a pen. The man stood laughing, his weapons at his hips.

Ultimately the man was attracted by the closed door of the "Weary Gentleman" saloon. He went to it, and hammering with a revolver, demanded drink.

The door remaining imperturbable, he picked a bit of paper from the walk and nailed it to the framework with a knife. He then turned his back contemptuously upon this popular resort, and walking to the opposite side of the street, and spinning there on his heel quickly and lithely, fired at the bit of paper. He missed it by a half inch. He swore at himself, and went away. Later, he comfortably fusilladed the windows of his most intimate friend. The man was playing with this town. It was a toy for him.

But still there was no offer of fight. The name of Jack Potter, his ancient antagonist, entered his mind, and he concluded that it would be a glad thing if he should go to Potter's house and by bombardment induce him to come out and fight. He moved in the direction of his desire, chanting Apache scalp-music.

When he arrived at it, Potter's house presented the same still front as had the other adobes. Taking up a strategic position, the man howled a challenge. But this house regarded him as might a great stone god. It gave no sign. After a decent wait, the man howled further challenges, mingling with them wonderful epithets.

Presently there came the spectacle of a man churning himself into deepest rage over the immobility of a house. He fumed at it as the winter wind attacks a prairie cabin in the North. To the distance there should have gone the sound of a tumult like the fighting of 200 Mexicans. As necessity bade him, he paused for breath or to reload his revolvers.

IV

Potter and his bride walked sheepishly and with speed. Sometimes they laughed together shamefacedly and low.

"Next corner, dear," he said finally.

They put forth the efforts of a pair walking bowed against a strong wind. Potter was about to raise a finger to point the first appearance of the new home when, as they circled the corner, they came face to face with a man in a maroon-colored shirt who was feverishly pushing cartridges into a large revolver. Upon the instant the man dropped his revolver to the ground, and, like lightning, whipped another from its holster. The second weapon was aimed at the bridegroom's chest.

There was silence. Potter's mouth seemed to be merely a grave for his tongue. He exhibited an instinct to at once loosen his arm from the woman's grip, and he dropped the bag to the sand. As for the bride, her face had gone as yellow as old cloth. She was a slave to hideous rites gazing at the apparitional snake.

The two men faced each other at a distance of three paces. He of the revolver smiled with a new and quiet ferocity.

"I ain't got a gun on me, Scratchy, ... Honest, I ain't."

"Tried to sneak up on me," he said. "Tried to sneak up on me!" His eyes grew more baleful. As Potter made a slight movement, the man thrust his revolver venomously forward. "No, don't you do it, Jack Potter. Don't you move a finger toward a gun just yet. Don't you move an eyelash. The time has come for me to settle with you, and I'm goin' to do it my own way and loaf along with no interferin'. So if you don't want a gun bent on you, just mind what I tell you."

Potter looked at his enemy. "I ain't got a gun on me, Scratchy," he said. "Honest, I ain't." He was stiffening and steadying, but yet somewhere at the back of his mind a vision of the Pullman floated, the sea-green figured velvet, the shining brass, silver, and glass, the wood that gleamed as darkly brilliant as the surface of a pool of oil -- all the glory of the marriage, the environment of the new estate. "You know I fight when it comes to fighting, Scratchy Wilson, but I ain't got a gun on me. You'll have to do all the shootin' yourself."

His enemy's face went livid. He stepped forward and lashed his weapon to and fro before Potter's chest. "Don't you tell me you ain't got no gun on you, you whelp. Don't tell me no lie like that. There ain't a man in Texas ever seen you without no gun. Don't take me for no kid." His eyes blazed with light, and his throat worked like a pump.

"I ain't takin' you for no kid," answered Potter. His heels had not moved an inch backward. "I'm takin' you for a -- -- -- fool. I tell you I ain't got a gun, and I ain't. If you're goin' to shoot me up, you better begin now. You'll never get a chance like this again."

So much enforced reasoning had told on Wilson's rage. He was calmer. "If you ain't got a gun, why ain't you got a gun?" he sneered. "Been to Sunday-school?"

"I ain't got a gun because I've just come from San Anton' with my wife. I'm married," said Potter. "And if I'd thought there was going to be any galoots like you prowling around when I brought my wife home, I'd had a gun, and don't you forget it."

"Married!" said Scratchy, not at all comprehending.

"Yes, married. I'm married," said Potter distinctly.

"Married?" said Scratchy. Seemingly for the first time he saw the drooping, drowning woman at the other man's side. "No!" he said. He was like a creature allowed a glimpse of another world. He moved a pace backward, and his arm with the revolver dropped to his side. "Is this the lady?" he asked.

"Yes, this is the lady," answered Potter.

There was another period of silence.

"Well," said Wilson at last, slowly, "I s'pose it's all off now."

"It's all off if you say so, Scratchy. You know I didn't make the trouble." Potter lifted his valise.

"Well, I 'low it's off, Jack," said Wilson. He was looking at the ground. "Married!"

He was not a student of chivalry; it was merely that in the presence of this foreign condition he was a simple child of the earlier plains. He picked up his starboard revolver, and placing both weapons in their holsters, he went away. His feet made funnel-shaped tracks in the heavy sand.   1897

Narrative Form in "The Bride Comes to Yellow Sky"

Notice how Crane moves back and forth in time in this story. When do the events in the first section take place in relation to those in the second section? Into which characters' minds does the omniscient narrator of the story enter to tell us their thoughts or let us view events from their perspective? What details in the story indicate that the "Wild West" of Scratchy Wilson is already getting "tamed" even before the arrival of the bride? The title suggests that the arrival of Potter's bride in Yellow Sky is a momentous event, but why does the bride herself seem so insignificant in terms of what she says and does? In what way is she the kind of environmental force that affects characters in Naturalism?

Credits

Chapter 1

1. Helen Keller, The Story of My Life, pp. 35-36. Copyright in the Public Domain.
2. Aesop, "The Fox and the Grapes," Harvard Classics Volume 17: Folklore and Fable, ed. Charles W. Eliot. Copyright in the Public Domain.
3. Aesop, "The Hare and the Tortoise," Harvard Classics Volume 17: Folklore and Fable, ed. Charles W. Eliot. Copyright in the Public Domain.
4. Anonymous, "The Seafarer," New Age, trans. Ezra Pound. Copyright in the Public Domain.

Chapter 2

5. Cædmon, "Creation-Hymn." Copyright in the Public Domain.
6. The Norton Anthology of Poetry, ed. Margaret Ferguson, Mary Jo Salter, and Jon Stallworthy, pp. 1. Copyright © 2005 by W. W. Norton & Company, Inc. Reprinted with permission.
7. Jacques Tahureau, "Shadows of His Lady," Grass of Parnassus, trans. Andrew Lang. Copyright in the Public Domain.
8. Anonymous, "The Ballad of Sir Patrick Spens." Copyright in the Public Domain.
9. The Norton Anthology of Poetry, ed. Margaret Ferguson, Mary Jo Salter, and Jon Stallworthy, pp. 103-104. Copyright © 2005 by W. W. Norton & Company, Inc. Reprinted with permission.
10. Anonymous, "The Three Ravens." Copyright in the Public Domain.
11. The Norton Anthology of Poetry, ed. Margaret Ferguson, Mary Jo Salter, and Jon Stallworthy, pp. 101-102. Copyright © 2005 by W. W. Norton & Company, Inc. Reprinted with permission.
12. Anonymous, "The Twa Corbies." Copyright in the Public Domain.
13. The Norton Anthology of Poetry, ed. Margaret Ferguson, Mary Jo Salter, and Jon Stallworthy, pp. 102-103. Copyright © 2005 by W. W. Norton & Company, Inc. Reprinted with permission.
14. Anonymous, "Western Wind." Copyright in the Public Domain.

Chapter 3

15. Sir Thomas Wyatt, "They Flee from Me." Copyright in the Public Domain.
16. The Norton Anthology of Poetry, ed. Margaret Ferguson, Mary Jo Salter, and Jon Stallworthy, pp. 127-128. Copyright © 2005 by W. W. Norton & Company, Inc. Reprinted with permission.
17. Sir Philip Sidney, "Sonnet 31." Copyright in the Public Domain.
18. The Norton Anthology of Poetry, ed. Margaret Ferguson, Mary Jo Salter, and Jon Stallworthy, pp. 214-215. Copyright © 2005 by W. W. Norton & Company, Inc. Reprinted with permission.
19. William Shakespeare, "Sonnet 73." Copyright in the Public Domain.
20. William Shakespeare, "Sonnet 116." Copyright in the Public Domain.
21. William Shakespeare, "Sonnet 129." Copyright in the Public Domain.
22. William Shakespeare, "Sonnet 130." Copyright in the Public Domain.
23. The Norton Anthology of Poetry, ed. Margaret Ferguson, Mary Jo Salter, and Jon Stallworthy, pp. 263-264, 266-268. Copyright © 2005 by W. W. Norton & Company, Inc. Reprinted with permission.
24. William Shakespeare, "Sonnet 72." Copyright in the Public Domain.
25. Felicia Dorothea Hemans, "The Boy Stood on the Burning Deck." Copyright in the Public Domain.
26. W. S. Gilbert, The Pirates of Penzance. Copyright in the Public Domain.
27. Christopher Marlowe, "The Passionate Shepher to His Love." Copyright in the Public Domain.
28. The Norton Anthology of Poetry, ed. Margaret Ferguson, Mary Jo Salter, and Jon Stallworthy, pp. 256. Copyright © 2005 by W. W. Norton & Company, Inc. Reprinted with permission.

29. Walter Ralegh, "The Nymph's Reply to the Shepherd," England's Helicon. Copyright in the Public Domain.
30. The Norton Anthology of English Literature, Volume 2: The Romantic Period through the Twentieth Century, ed. E. Talbot Donaldson, et al. pp. 152. Copyright © 1993 by W. W. Norton & Company, Inc. Reprinted with permission.

Chapter 4

31. Unknown, "Guy Fawkes Night Ditty."
32. Ben Johnson, "To Celia." Copyright in the Public Domain.
33. Robert Herrick, "Delight in Disorder." Copyright in the Public Domain.
34. The Norton Anthology of Poetry, ed. Margaret Ferguson, Mary Jo Salter, and Jon Stallworthy, pp. 355. Copyright © 2005 by W. W. Norton & Company, Inc. Reprinted with permission.
35. Robert Herrick, "To the Virgins, to Make Much of Time. Copyright in the Public Domain.
36. Edmund Waller, "Song." Copyright in the Public Domain.
37. The Norton Anthology of Poetry, ed. Margaret Ferguson, Mary Jo Salter, and Jon Stallworthy, pp. 393. Copyright © 2005 by W. W. Norton & Company, Inc. Reprinted with permission.
38. Richard Lovelace, "To Lucasta, Going to the Wars." Copyright in the Public Domain.
39. Sir John Suckling, "The Constant Lover." Copyright in the Public Domain.
40. John Donne, "The Canonization." Copyright in the Public Domain.
41. The Norton Anthology of Poetry, ed. Margaret Ferguson, Mary Jo Salter, and Jon Stallworthy, pp. 296-297. Copyright © 2005 by W. W. Norton & Company, Inc. Reprinted with permission.
42. John Donne, "A Valediction Forbidding Mourning." Copyright in the Public Domain.
43. The Norton Anthology of Poetry, ed. Margaret Ferguson, Mary Jo Salter, and Jon Stallworthy, pp. 306-307. Copyright © 2005 by W. W. Norton & Company, Inc. Reprinted with permission.
44. John Donne, "Holy Sonnet 10." Copyright in the Public Domain.
45. John Donne, "Holy Sonnet 14." Copyright in the Public Domain.
46. The Norton Anthology of Poetry, ed. Margaret Ferguson, Mary Jo Salter, and Jon Stallworthy, pp. 320. Copyright © 2005 by W. W. Norton & Company, Inc. Reprinted with permission.
47. Andrew Marvell, "To His Coy Mistress." Copyright in the Public Domain.
48. The Norton Anthology of Poetry, ed. Margaret Ferguson, Mary Jo Salter, and Jon Stallworthy, pp. 478-479. Copyright © 2005 by W. W. Norton & Company, Inc. Reprinted with permission.
49. John Milton, "On His Blindness." Copyright in the Public Domain.
50. The Norton Anthology of Poetry, ed. Margaret Ferguson, Mary Jo Salter, and Jon Stallworthy, pp. 478-479. Copyright © 2005 by W. W. Norton & Company, Inc. Reprinted with permission.
51. John Milton, "Books I, IV, VII, VIII, and IX," Paradise Lost. Copyright in the Public Domain.
52. The Norton Anthology of English Literature, Vol. I, ed. M. H. Abrams, et al. pp. 1038, 1097-1098. Copyright © 1968 by W. W. Norton & Company, Inc. Reprinted with permission.

Chapter 5

53. Alexander Pope, "An Essay on Criticism." Copyright in the Public Domain.
54. The Norton Anthology of Poetry, ed. Margaret Ferguson, Mary Jo Salter, and Jon Stallworthy, pp. 600. Copyright © 2005 by W. W. Norton & Company, Inc. Reprinted with permission.
55. Lady Mary Wortley Montagu, "A Receipt to Cure the Vapors." Copyright in the Public Domain.
56. The Norton Anthology of Poetry, ed. Margaret Ferguson, Mary Jo Salter, and Jon Stallworthy, pp. 642-643. Copyright © 2005 by W. W. Norton & Company, Inc. Reprinted with permission.
57. Thomas Gray, "Elegy Written in a Country Churchyard." Copyright in the Public Domain.
58. The Norton Anthology of Poetry, ed. Margaret Ferguson, Mary Jo Salter, and Jon Stallworthy, pp. 669-672. Copyright © 2005 by W. W. Norton & Company, Inc. Reprinted with permission.

59. Phyllis Wheatley, "On Being Brought from Africa to America." Copyright in the Public Domain.
60. The Norton Anthology of Poetry, ed. Margaret Ferguson, Mary Jo Salter, and Jon Stallworthy, pp. 720-721. Copyright © 2005 by W. W. Norton & Company, Inc. Reprinted with permission.
61. Daniel Defoe, Moll Flanders. Copyright in the Public Domain.
62. Henry Fielding, Tom Jones. Copyright in the Public Domain.
63. Jane Austen, Pride and Prejudice. Copyright in the Public Domain. Jonathan Edwards, Personal Narrative. Copyright in the Public Domain.
64. Jonathan Edwards, Personal Narrative. Copyright in the Public Domain.
65. Benjamin Franklin, The Autobiography of Benjamin Franklin. Copyright in the Public Domain.

Chapter 6

66. Robert Burns, "Auld Lang Syne." Copyright in the Public Domain.
67. The Norton Anthology of English Literature, Volume 2: The Romantic Period through the Twentieth Century, ed. E. Talbot Donaldson, et al. pp. 97-98. Copyright © 1993 by W. W. Norton & Company, Inc. Reprinted with permission.
68. The Norton Anthology of Poetry, ed. Margaret Ferguson, Mary Jo Salter, and Jon Stallworthy, pp. 753. Copyright © 2005 by W. W. Norton & Company, Inc. Reprinted with permission.
69. Robert Burns, "Green Grow the Rashes." Copyright in the Public Domain.
70. The Norton Anthology of English Literature, Volume 2: The Romantic Period through the Twentieth Century, ed. E. Talbot Donaldson, et al. pp. 85. Copyright © 1993 by W. W. Norton & Company, Inc. Reprinted with permission.
71. The Norton Anthology of Poetry, ed. Margaret Ferguson, Mary Jo Salter, and Jon Stallworthy, pp. 747-748. Copyright © 2005 by W. W. Norton & Company, Inc. Reprinted with permission.
72. Robert Burns, "A Red, Red Rose." Copyright in the Public Domain.
73. William Blake, "The Tyger." Copyright in the Public Domain.
74. William Blake, "London." Copyright in the Public Domain.
75. The Norton Anthology of English Literature, Volume 2: The Romantic Period through the Twentieth Century, ed. E. Talbot Donaldson, et al. pp. 744-745. Copyright © 1993 by W. W. Norton & Company, Inc. Reprinted with permission.
76. William Wordsworth, "Lines Composed a Few Miles Above Tintern Abbey," Lyrical Ballads. Copyright in the Public Domain.
77. The Norton Anthology of English Literature, Volume 2: The Romantic Period through the Twentieth Century, ed. E. Talbot Donaldson, et al. pp. 136-140. Copyright © 1993 by W. W. Norton & Company, Inc. Reprinted with permission.
78. William Wordsworth, "A Slumber Did My Spirit Seal." Copyright in the Public Domain.
79. The Norton Anthology of English Literature, Volume 2: The Romantic Period through the Twentieth Century, ed. E. Talbot Donaldson, et al. pp. 155. Copyright © 1993 by W. W. Norton & Company, Inc. Reprinted with permission.
80. William Wordsworth, "The World Is Too Much With Us." Copyright in the Public Domain.
81. Samuel Taylor Coleridge, "The Rime of the Ancient Mariner," Lyrical Ballads. Copyright in the Public Domain.
82. The Norton Anthology of English Literature, Volume 2: The Romantic Period through the Twentieth Century, ed. E. Talbot Donaldson, et al. pp. 330-346. Copyright © 1993 by W. W. Norton & Company, Inc. Reprinted with permission.
83. Percy Bysshe Shelley, "Ode to the West Wind." Copyright in the Public Domain.
84. The Norton Anthology of English Literature, Volume 2: The Romantic Period through the Twentieth Century, ed. E. Talbot Donaldson, et al. pp. 676-678. Copyright © 1993 by W. W. Norton & Company, Inc. Reprinted with permission.
85. Percy Bysshe Shelley, "Ozymandius." Copyright in the Public Domain.
86. John Keats, "On First Looking into Chapman's Homer." Copyright in the Public Domain.

87. John Keats, "La Belle Dame Sans Merci." Copyright in the Public Domain.
88. The Norton Anthology of Poetry, ed. Margaret Ferguson, Mary Jo Salter, and Jon Stallworthy, pp. 917-918. Copyright © 2005 by W. W. Norton & Company, Inc. Reprinted with permission.
89. John Keats, "To Autumn." Copyright in the Public Domain.
90. The Norton Anthology of Poetry, ed. Margaret Ferguson, Mary Jo Salter, and Jon Stallworthy, pp. 939-940. Copyright © 2005 by W. W. Norton & Company, Inc. Reprinted with permission.
91. Lord Byron, "Childe Harold's Pilgrimage." Copyright in the Public Domain.
92. Lord Byron, "She Walks in Beauty." Copyright in the Public Domain.
93. Leigh Hunt, "Jenny Kissed Me." Copyright in the Public Domain.

Chapter 7

94. Washington Irving, Rip Van Winkle. Copyright in the Public Domain.
95. Edgar Allen Poe, "The Cask of Amontillado." Copyright in the Public Domain.

Chapter 8

96. Alfred Lord Tennyson, "Ulysses." Copyright in the Public Domain.
97. The Norton Anthology of English Literature, Volume 2: The Romantic Period through the Twentieth Century, ed. E. Talbot Donaldson, et al. pp. 1067-1069. Copyright © 1993 by W. W. Norton & Company, Inc. Reprinted with permission.
98. Robert Browning, "My Last Duchess." Copyright in the Public Domain.
99. The Norton Anthology of English Literature, Volume 2: The Romantic Period through the Twentieth Century, ed. E. Talbot Donaldson, et al. pp. 1190-1192. Copyright © 1993 by W. W. Norton & Company, Inc. Reprinted with permission.
100. Matthew Arnold, "Dover Beach." Copyright in the Public Domain.
101. The Norton Anthology of English Literature, Volume 2: The Romantic Period through the Twentieth Century, ed. E. Talbot Donaldson, et al. pp. 1366-1367. Copyright © 1993 by W. W. Norton & Company, Inc. Reprinted with permission.
102. Elizabeth Barrett Browning, "How Do I Love Thee?" Copyright in the Public Domain.
103. Edward Fitzgerald, "The Rubáiyát of Omar Khayyám." Copyright in the Public Domain.
104. The Norton Anthology of Poetry, ed. Margaret Ferguson, Mary Jo Salter, and Jon Stallworthy, pp. 962. Copyright © 2005 by W. W. Norton & Company, Inc. Reprinted with permission.
105. Thomas Hardy, "Drummer Hodge." Copyright in the Public Domain.
106. The Norton Anthology of English Literature, Volume 2: The Romantic Period through the Twentieth Century, ed. E. Talbot Donaldson, et al. pp. 1696-1697. Copyright © 1993 by W. W. Norton & Company, Inc. Reprinted with permission.
107. Thomas Hardy, "The Darkling Thrush." Copyright in the Public Domain.
108. The Norton Anthology of English Literature, Volume 2: The Romantic Period through the Twentieth Century, ed. E. Talbot Donaldson, et al. pp. 1967. Copyright © 1993 by W. W. Norton & Company, Inc. Reprinted with permission.
109. Thomas Hardy, "Channel Firing." Copyright in the Public Domain.
110. The Norton Anthology of English Literature, Volume 2: The Romantic Period through the Twentieth Century, ed. E. Talbot Donaldson, et al. pp. 1703-1704. Copyright © 1993 by W. W. Norton & Company, Inc. Reprinted with permission.
111. Gerard Manly Hopkins, "The Windhover." Copyright in the Public Domain.

Credits

112. The Norton Anthology of English Literature, Volume 2: The Romantic Period through the Twentieth Century, ed. E. Talbot Donaldson, et al. pp. 1548. Copyright © 1993 by W. W. Norton & Company, Inc. Reprinted with permission.
113. Gerard Manly Hopkins, "Pied Beauty." Copyright in the Public Domain.
114. The Norton Anthology of English Literature, Volume 2: The Romantic Period through the Twentieth Century, ed. E. Talbot Donaldson, et al. pp. 1548. Copyright © 1993 by W. W. Norton & Company, Inc. Reprinted with permission.
115. Gerard Manly Hopkins, "Spring and Fall: To a Young Child." Copyright in the Public Domain.
116. Gerard Manly Hopkins, "No Worst, There is None." Copyright in the Public Domain.
117. The Norton Anthology of English Literature, Volume 2: The Romantic Period through the Twentieth Century, ed.
118. E. Talbot Donaldson, et al. pp. 1552. Copyright © 1993 by W. W. Norton & Company, Inc. Reprinted with permission.
119. E. Housman, "Loveliest of Trees, the Cherry Now." Copyright in the Public Domain.
120. E. Housman, "When I Was One-and-Twenty." Copyright in the Public Domain.
121. E. Housman, "To an Athlete Dying Young." Copyright in the Public Domain.

Chapter 9

122. The Norton Anthology of Poetry, ed. Margaret Ferguson, Mary Jo Salter, and Jon Stallworthy, pp. 1174-1175. Copyright © 2005 by W. W. Norton & Company, Inc. Reprinted with permission.
123. Frederick Douglass, "Chapters I, XI," Narrative of the Life of Frederick Douglass. Copyright in the Public Domain.
124. Mark Twain, Old Times on the Mississippi. Copyright in the Public Domain.

Chapter 10

125. Walt Whitman, "Song of Myself." Copyright in the Public Domain.
126. The Norton Anthology of American Literature, Vol. C, ed. Jeanne Campbell Reesman and Arnold Krupat, pp. 33-34, 38, 47-48, 74. Copyright © 2007 by W. W. Norton & Company, Inc. Reprinted with permission.
127. Walt Whitman, "Cavalry Crossing a Ford." Copyright in the Public Domain.
128. Walt Whitman, "The Dalliance of the Eagles." Copyright in the Public Domain.
129. Emily Dickinson, "I Felt a Funeral, in My Brain," The Poems of Emily Dickinson, ed. Ralph W. Franklin. Copyright © 1998 by Harvard University Press. Reprinted with permission.
130. Emily Dickinson, "A Bird Came Down the Walk," The Poems of Emily Dickinson, ed. Ralph W. Franklin. Copyright © 1998 by Harvard University Press. Reprinted with permission.
131. Emily Dickinson, "A Bird Came Down the Walk," The Poems of Emily Dickinson, ed. Ralph W. Franklin. Copyright © 1998 by Harvard University Press. Reprinted with permission. The Norton Anthology of Poetry, ed. Margaret Ferguson, Mary Jo Salter, and Jon Stallworthy, pp. 1117. Copyright © 2005 by W. W. Norton & Company, Inc. Reprinted with permission.
132. Emily Dickinson, "Because I Could Not Stop for Death," The Poems of Emily Dickinson, ed. Ralph W. Franklin. Copyright © 1998 by Harvard University Press. Reprinted with permission.
133. The Norton Anthology of Poetry, ed. Margaret Ferguson, Mary Jo Salter, and Jon Stallworthy, pp. 1119-1120. Copyright © 2005 by W. W. Norton & Company, Inc. Reprinted with permission.
134. Emily Dickinson, "I Heard a Fly Buzz—When I Died," The Poems of Emily Dickinson, ed. Ralph W. Franklin. Copyright © 1998 by Harvard University Press. Reprinted with permission.
135. Emily Dickinson, "I Started Early—Took My Dog," The Poems of Emily Dickinson, ed. Ralph W. Franklin. Copyright © 1998 by Harvard University Press. Reprinted with permission.

Chapter 11

136. William Dean Howells, "Editha." Copyright in the Public Domain.
137. Guy de Maupassant, "The Necklace," The Complete Works Of Guy de Maupassant: Mad, and Short Stories, trans. Albert M. C. McMaster, A. E. Henderson, and Clara Bell. Copyright in the Public Domain.
138. Henry James, Paste. Copyright in the Public Domain.
139. Henry James, The Ambassadors. Copyright in the Public Domain.
140. Ernest Hemingway, "Indian Camp," In Our Time. Copyright © 1925 by Simon & Schuster, Inc.
141. William Faulkner, "Barn Burning." Copyright © 1939 by W. W. Norton & Company, Inc.
142. Virginia Woolf, Mrs. Dalloway. Copyright © 1925 by Houghton Mifflin Harcourt.
143. James Joyce, Ulysses. Copyright in the Public Domain.

Chapter 12

144. Jack London, "To Build a Fire." Copyright in the Public Domain.
145. Stephen Crane, "The Bride Comes to Yellow Sky." Copyright in the Public Domain.

CPSIA information can be obtained
at www.ICGtesting.com
Printed in the USA
LVHW01s2355230818
587918LV00015B/163/P

9 781631 899362